Paul
The Man and the Myth

Studies on Personalities of the New Testament

D. Moody Smith, Series Editor

Paul
The Man and the Myth

Calvin J. Roetzel

University of South Carolina Press

© 1998 University of South Carolina

Published in Columbia, South Carolina, by the
University of South Carolina Press

Manufactured in the United States of America

02 01 00 99 98   5 4 3 2 1

Library of Congress Cataloging-in-Publication Data

Roetzel, Calvin J.
        Paul : the man and the myth / Calvin J. Roetzel.
        p. cm.—(Studies on personalities of the New Testament)
        Includes bibliographical references and index.
        ISBN 1-57003-264-5
        1. Paul, the Apostle, Saint.   2. Apostles—Biography.   3. Christian
saints—Biography.   I. Title.   II. Series.
        BS2506.R595   1998
        225.9'2—ddc21
        [B]   98-25446

In Memory of
Thelma and Werth Kendall

Contents

Acknowledgments

I gratefully acknowledge my debt to many who assisted in countless ways with the preparation of this manuscript. Generous grants from Macalester College enabled me to work on this book while spending a year at Linacre College, Oxford, and a semester at the Institut für antikes Judentum und hellenistische Religionsgeschichte at the university in Tübingen. I am especially grateful to Rev. Robert Morgan at Oxford and Professors Martin Hengel and Hermann Lichtenberger for their innumerable courtesies and material assistance in the research for this book. Dean Peter Stuhlmacher offered his warm hospitality and encouragement. The always helpful library staff of the Theologicum at the university in Tübingen made my work much easier. Over countless lunches in the Mensa in Tübingen, David Aune was a stimulating and helpful conversation partner helping me think through various problems associated with this work. Carl Holladay heard parts of this work delivered in oral form and offered invaluable suggestions. Jouette Bassler, Mark Reasoner, and Philip Sellew read parts of the manuscript and improved both the content and arrangement of the book. D. Moody Smith, Jr., has read the manuscript in its entirety and offered invaluable advice. Paul Achtemeier read the manuscript in its entirety and offered invaluable suggestions. My debt to my colleagues in the Pauline Theology Group of the Society of Biblical Literature is encyclopedic. The vigorous and sustained discussion that lasted for the better part of a decade affected my thinking about Paul in dramatic fashion and enormously complicated my reading and understanding of Paul. Members of the Trial Balloon Society in the Twin Cities also provided patient, gracious, and constructive criticism of parts of this work presented to them. On almost every page of the work my debt to the wider scholarly community will be obvious to all. I must also mention my office assistant, Barbara Wells-Howe, who in season and out has always provided valuable help with the completion of this work. Finally, the managing editor of the University of South Carolina Press, Ms. Margaret V. Hill, was diligent, patient, and skillful in her efforts to improve this manuscript, and Barry Blose, the acquisitions editor, was diligent, supportive, and helpful in multiple ways. Linda Webster brought great skill and experience to the index preparation. I am enormously grateful. I in no way wish to trade on the good name of this great community of assistance, and I freely acknowledge that any mistakes, misjudgments, erroneous conclusions, and failures of logic are my own.

Finally, I wish to honor with this book the memory of Thelma and Werth Kendall, my mother-in-law and father-in-law. My debt to them is incalculable. Without their moral support, encouragement, and generosity of spirit I would never have entered graduate school and, consequently, would never have been able to explore that distant century of Paul's birth and to reflect on his life as I have been able to do here.

Abbreviations

ABD	*Anchor Bible Dictionary*
ANRW	*Aufsteig und Niedergang der römischen Welt*
BZ	*Biblische Zeitschrift*
CBQ	*Catholic Biblical Quarterly*
CQ	*Classical Quarterly*
ER	*Encyclopedia of Religion*
ETR	*Études Théologiques et Religieuses*
EvT	*Evangelische Theologie*
HTR	*Harvard Theological Review*
IDB	*Interpreter's Dictionary of the Bible*
IESS	*International Encyclopedia of Social Sciences*
INT	*Interpretation*
JAAR	*Journal of the American Academy of Religion*
JAC	*Jahrbuch für Antike und Christentum*
JAS	*Journal of Asian Studies*
JBL	*Journal of Biblical Literature*
JR	*Journal of Religion*
JTS	*Journal of Theological Studies*
LCL	Loeb Classical Library
NT	*Novum Testamentum*
NTS	*New Testament Studies*
RAC	*Reallexikon für Antike und Christentum*
RGG	*Die Religion in Geschichte und Gegenwart*
RSR	*Religious Studies Review*
TDNT	*Theological Dictionary of the New Testament*

TLZ	*Theologische Literaturzeitung*
TR	*Theologische Rundschau*
TRE	*Theologische Realenzyklopädie*
TSK	*Theologische Studien unk Kritiken*
VT	*Vetus Testament*
WW	*Word and World*
ZKG	*Zeitschrift für Kirchengeschichte*
ZNW	*Zeitschrift für neutestamentliche Wissenschaft und die Kunde der älteren Kirche*
ZThK	*Zeitschrift für Theologie und Kirche*

Paul
The Man and the Myth

Introduction

Whenever we look at a painting, read a novel, hear a story, experience a poem, or evaluate a news account we must use our imagination, experience, or knowledge to fill the yawning gaps. We may fill these gaps by drawing on our own human experience or our knowledge of the context, or even with musings on a world only imagined. Although we know more about the eastern Mediterranean world of the first century than ever before, that time is still very foreign to us and there is much we do not know. We are left to reconstruct a portrait of Paul with only scraps of what was once a large and imposing canvas—a small collection of letters and a historical narrative written a generation after his death. This reconstruction focuses on important parts of the image that usually fall in the shadows, parts dealing with Paul's sexual asceticism, his preoccupation with holiness—holy Spirit, holy community, and holy ethos—the evolution of his theology, and his emergence as a legendary figure. Although I have tried to follow the strict rules of historical investigation, of necessity much guesswork is involved in any exploration of Paul's life. In 2 Cor. 12:4, for example, Paul spoke of hearing "unutterable words which a human is not able to speak." What Paul could not tell us, others have dared to speak.[1] Paul prayed repeatedly for the removal of a "thorn in [his] flesh." Paul left this metaphor unexplained, but others, many others, have offered inspired guesses that the "thorn" was anything from epilepsy to migraine headaches. Whereas Paul nowhere names a single miracle that he performed, other writers, such as Luke in Acts, have dared to describe these in vivid detail. All of these efforts are attempts to deal with the gaps in the text, understood in the broadest sense to include not just Paul's written words but also the culture, social world, and political realities surrounding them. All such reconstructions are acts of historical imagination, and the reader will have to decide if the reconstruction presented here is credible.

Why should we or anyone else be interested in filling the gaps? Why not simply take the story as it is? Why run the risk of falsification through an appeal to historical imagination? First, we do so because there is no alternative. Because no text is self-interpreting we simply cannot take the story just as it is. Like the sympathetic observer who imagines an entire table where Rembrandt painted only a corner or a tree where e.e. cummings poetically replicates only a falling leaf, the reader of New Testament texts must be able to construct a coherent whole from mere fragments. Second, such an effort is an appropriate response to a text by a scholar seeking better to understand the world of the text. By filling the gaps, the scholar may attempt to capture some of the richness and power of the text, understood in the broad sense as including paintings, personalities, and physical remains. (Paul himself referes to people as text in 2 Cor. 3:2, in which he describes the inhabitants of Corinth as "a letter," and in light of this there is justification for this broad understanding.) Third, we fill gaps to obtain a better sense of the character and power of the personalities we encounter in the text. Fourth, we join the ancients in the exercise of mythically resurrecting a past that at one level is gone forever but at another can be entered anew through imagination. Although we conjure the past, the task is far from easy, and we must not be content with facile solutions. There are more gaps than text, more questions than answers, more imponderables than certainties.

In my portrait of Paul, I have also questioned the historicity of some attempts to fill in the gaps of Paul's life. For instance, the historical evidence leaves me unconvinced that Paul was a Roman citizen, a view advanced first by Luke in Acts and shared by many Pauline scholars. I am also unconvinced that Paul spent his formative years in Jerusalem studying under the great rabbi Gamaliel II, from whom Luke suggests he learned Pharisaism. I also am somewhat uncertain about what Paul meant in Phil. 3:5 when he referred to himself as *kata nomon pharisaios* which is usually translated "as to the law, a Pharisee" (NRSV), but I am more certain that he was strongly inclined to a Pharisaism that influenced him in various ways throughout his life.

Most important for this investigation, I have come to see Paul as a marginal Jew who faced enormous tensions between different cultural and religious commitments that sometimes pulled in contrary directions. The emphasis here is on the continuities between Paul and his native Judaism and between Paul and his native Hellenism throughout his life. It is sometimes suggested that Paul inhabited the Hellenistic world but was not influenced by it in any substantial way, but I am drawn to the opposite position—the belief that Paul did not just *use* hellenistic language, anthropology, and worldviews as mute, value-neutral entities but that he was influenced by them at a deep level. Some also refer to the apostle Paul as the "former Jew" or "the former Pharisee," but increasingly I am convinced that Paul never left his native Judaism though he did significantly redefine it in light of Christ. He was born a Jew, lived as a Jew, and died as a Jew, albeit a hellenized Diaspora Jew. Those realities did not always fit comfortably together, and as a result Paul often found himself on the margins of his faith. For example, his Jewishness placed him on the margins of Hellenistic popular religion. His life "in Christ" placed him at odds with many synagogues. His conviction that the gospel he preached included Gentiles without any precondition of law observance or circumcision caused him to be marginalized by other Jewish apostles of Christ. His strict Jewish monotheism that would brook no rivals placed him and his converts on the fringes of Hellenistic popular religion. The reconstruction here is mindful of those tensions that we judge not to be radical discontinuities. Not until after his death was Paul's marginal status overcome, but that resolution was at the expense of his Jewishness and the deep tensions within his gospel between the now and the not-yet, between power and weakness, and between the world above and the world below.

Because of his marginal status, Paul was a person whose religious commitments generated enormous conflict throughout his life as an apostle. This book traces the tensions that pulled Paul in different directions and that generated conflict between him and the cultural and religious traditions that shaped his identity. The position taken here is that we best learn how Paul's own thinking emerged by examining the points of friction generated by his marginal status, for these points can reveal the locus of thought about issues worth fighting for. Even while remaining acutely aware of Paul's theological genius we have tried not to lose sight of the human Paul—the language he spoke, the education he received, the work he did as a tentmaker, the sleepless nights he spent in agony over the churches, and his acute consciousness of the loci of power, whether that of governments, sex, the spirit, demons, or sin. And we have tried to balance those considerations with his theological achievement.

The opening chapter places us in the Hellenistic-Jewish world of Paul's youth. Paul was a child of a thoroughly hellenized urban setting that engaged the Diaspora Jewish community in a vital reciprocity. Either in Tarsus or in some other similarly hellenized urban setting Paul learned his first language, Greek. It is important to realize that language does not merely express ideas, it shapes ideas. As Wittgenstein so aptly stated, "A whole mythology is deposited in our language."[2] The position taken here is that as a Greek speaker Paul could not avoid being deeply influenced by Hellenistic philosophy and religion. In that urban setting he received his early formal and informal education. An important feature of that education was the study of the Septuagint, and in the course of that study he would have gained an understanding of Jewish Scriptures, traditions, institutions, and festivals. He probably grew up in a Judaism that was strongly Pharisaic and apocalyptic. Paul's first encounter with Christ through his followers brought active resistance on Paul's part and led him to persecute the early followers so fiercely that the memory of these deeds haunted him for decades. But during that persecution a personal encounter with Christ persuaded Paul that his persecution of these messianists was an egregious offense. Like the prophets of old, he felt called to be an advocate of Christ and his followers instead of an opponent. This about-face set Paul on a path that had profound implications for the gentile mission and the future of this messianist movement.

Paul's apostleship that was so central to this later period was fiercely contested by competitors and defended by his own pen and his co-workers. On what basis could a latecomer such as Paul defend his claim to be an apostle? To base that claim on an epiphany of Christ did not persuade those who wanted something as concrete as a historical connection with the Jesus of the flesh. And if Paul could claim apostolic authority, could not others, many others do the same? Examining Paul's vigorous defense of his status as an apostle, which is discussed in chapter 2 of the present study, may give us a better appreciation of an important feature of Paul's identity as a man in Christ. In the end the issue could not be resolved on ideological grounds alone, or even on the basis of political adeptness, but rather it was decided on pragmatic grounds, namely, the demonstration of the marks of an apostle.

One of the chief weapons in Paul's arsenal for the defense of his apostolic authority and gospel was the letter. His choice of the letter was a means of communication and a way to deal in absentia with his scattered congregations. Other literary forms were available—the apocalypse, the historical novel, and possibly also the gospel—but history has fully justified his invention and use of the apostolic letter. Paul's success in his defense was due at least in part to the power of the literary form he used as well as to the persuasiveness of his arguments, for as discussed in chapter 3, the age in which Paul was writing was quintessentially the age of the letter.

In those letters we see Paul the theologian as he interacts with his churches, a role that will be discussed in chapter 4. In the face of challenges from both the right and the left Paul was forced to work to reinterpret, in light of Christ's death, resurrection, and imminent return, the venerable Jewish traditions so important to him. The thesis driving this investigation is that Paul did not begin his apostolic ministry with a developed theology in mind, and that he often did not know what he thought about a given subject until he faced a context that required its discussion, and the composition of a written statement. If this thesis is viable then Paul's theology must be viewed as an emergent theology and not a systematic theology, as an interactive theology rather than just a proclaimed theology, and as a product of a dialogue rather than a monologue. By taking two items, one that was key to Paul's self-understanding as a Jew (election) and one that was important to his experience in Christ (participation in Christ), and tracing the way Paul treats them in 1 Thessalonians, 1 Corinthians, and Romans, whose relative chronology is not in doubt, we hope to catch Paul in the act of theologizing, and to be able to trace the emergence of his theology. (In treating Romans I have also given an excursus on Galatians and 2 Corinthians as earlier works in which Paul had faced some of the same issues he faced in Romans. Therefore, they can be viewed as part of a process leading up to the composition of Romans.)

Election is especially crucial to this consideration for it came increasingly to the fore as Paul was forced to defend his inclusion of Gentiles among the elect people of God and as he sought to shape the identity of the gentile church. We move from 1 Thessalonians, in which Paul shows no sign that he was aware of the theological difficulty of the inclusion of Gentiles; to Galatians, where Paul argues heatedly for the inclusion of Gentiles without requiring law observance as a condition of inclusion; to Romans, where Paul must answer the charge that the Galatian version of the gentile gospel suggests that God had reneged on historic promises made to Israel. He must also respond to the charge that his law-free gospel encourages immorality. In attempting to appreciate the role that context played in shaping Paul's thought, and in emphasizing the theological particularity of each of the letters, I have tried to disturb the synthesis so often imposed on the Pauline letters and to gain a better appreciation of how Paul came to the position he took in Rom. 9–11 and 6:1–7:6.

In taking this approach to Paul's theologizing I obviously have had to omit much that is important. I also resisted the temptation to organize Paul's theology topically—for example God, Christ, Holy Spirit, righteousness, resurrection, and so on. I believe that such an arrangement of Paul's theology obscures the development of his thought and the dynamic and interactive nature of his theologizing and gives the reader a false sense of the whole. The approach taken here argues against stitching together a theology of Paul with scraps taken willy-nilly from first one letter and then another without regard to either context or chronology. Instead we learn what Paul meant by even such frequently used words as *God, cross, spirit*, and *flesh* by observing the way he used the words in a specific setting and not by abstracting a universally applicable meaning from them.

While chapter four deals with Paul's theologizing, chapter five deals with his "anthropologizing," or with *one important aspect* of his anthropology that is reflected in a sexual asceticism informed by eschatology. When I first came to believe that there was a secure historical basis for asserting that Paul was celibate (1 Cor. 7), I was surprised by how little attention had been given to his explicit preference for celibacy, and I was impressed by the subtlety and imaginative appeal of celibacy in a world that self-consciously supported marriage and the family as core values. In Jewish and later Christian experience celibacy offered a means of reclaiming a lost world or even a lost innocence and provided a way of forging an identity outside of assigned gender roles. It was also offered a way of defying the cultural and political emphases on marriage and the family that closed off or limited other possibilities. Within Paul's apocalypticism, celibacy offered a mythic encounter with a reality that tran-

scended this world and with a symbol that enabled one to cross gender boundaries safe from the liabilities of sex.

Although it is likely that Paul was executed in Rome around 60 CE, the
story does not end there. While Paul had used his pen and visits to the
churches by his co-workers with consummate skill to defend and advance his
position and pseudepigraphic letters were written under the umbrella of Paul's
authority after his death to deal with various ideological threats, the letter form
did not readily lend itself to speculation on the personality of Paul. Before the
end of the first century a canonical historical novel like Acts already was
portraying Paul as a legendary figure who could shake a biting snake from his
hand into a fire without being affected in any way, who could predict the
future with total reliability, and who was honored as a god. Paul emerges as
an even more impressive mythic figure in the Apocryphal Acts of the second
century. We have looked at these legendary accounts to see what of Paul
survived. We noticed that it was not the Paul who preached justification by
faith who was remembered but Paul the ascetic, Paul the miracle worker, and
Paul the martyr. As fanciful and entertaining as these stories were, they enjoyed a tie, however loose it was, to history. They actively engaged the letters
and expanded on features of Paul's personality appearing there. And, they
also served valuable functions in their new contexts. They gave women the
liberty to transgress rigid social boundaries; they articulated core values about
a just outcome of history; they witnessed to the presence of a power not of
this world and gave that power a benevolent face; they encouraged and enno-
bled an underclass; and they affirmed a future in which class and oppression
were not the primary realities of the day. They provided an example of defi-
ance and courage when those were called for, and they provided an escape
from brutal realities. In thus giving encouragement and comfort they mediated
the power to which they witnessed. The struggles of the day largely dictated
where the emphasis would be in recounting the life of Paul. Other emphases
that doubtlessly occur in the letters would come to the fore at another time.
While there is an emphasis on the heroic, courageous, dauntless, confident,
powerful, godlike Paul, we find in these accounts no interest in the sickly,
weak, unimposing, inadequate Paul of the letters. We find almost no interest
whatsoever in the Jewish Paul or in Paul the consummate theologian. We miss
Paul the great, creative, ingenious, scriptural exegete, and we find little interest
in the enormous tensions that run through many of Paul's letters between
inclusion and exclusion, between strength and weakness, between Jew and
non-Jew, between spirit and flesh, and between the universal and the particular. Yet with all of their omissions the Apocryphal Acts nevertheless called
upon Paul to speak to their day.

A final caveat is in order. This book does not pretend to offer a comprehensive view of Paul; rather it aims to take roads less traveled into Paul and

thereby to open up another way to view this important historical figure. I seek to place Paul in his world as a Semite, and, while acknowledging that he spoke harshly of other Jews who challenged his gospel, I point out that he nowhere repudiated his native religion. And had he repudiated one expression of Judaism, would that mean he repudiated all Judaisms? For there was no one Judaism of the day that provided a standard by which all Jewishness could be measured, nor was there even a set of precepts universally agreed to. The Judaism Paul espoused which showed some affinity with a Greek philosophical monotheism, admittedly was different in *degree* from the Judaisms we know of the period—those of the Pharisees, Sadducees, Essenes, and Alexandrian Jews—but the evidence will not support the view that it was different in *kind*.

CHAPTER ONE

The Early Paul

The complex and conflicted personality of Paul has led to speculation about his character—his thoughts, beliefs, acts, doubts, convictions, and even his appearance. Throughout history a kaleidoscope of images of the apostle Paul has continually offered fresh combinations. The Deutero-Paulines speak of Paul as chief among the apostles, as first among the saints, and as the church's great pastor and theological warrior.

A second century document gives us our earliest description of Paul's physical appearance. Having heard of the imminent visit of Paul to Iconium, Onesiphorus gathers his wife, Lectra, and their two children, Simmias and Zeno, to camp by the royal road to Lystra to catch a glimpse of the traveling apostle. Armed with Titus's description, they wait, scanning the faces of all passing by, hoping that Paul, when he comes, will accept an invitation to their house. Finally, excitement ripples through their small circle. Then Onesiphorus "saw Paul coming, a man small of stature, with a bald head and crooked legs, in a good state of body, with eyebrows meeting and nose somewhat hooked, full of friendliness; for now he appeared like a man, and now he had the face of an angel."[1]

In contrast to this second century literary sketch stands Rembrandt's seventeenth century painting of Paul as a wiry, deeply reflective, introspective, Caucasian intellectual, fully at home in the piety and spirit of the Enlightenment and with a quill in his hand. And equally sympathetic is the Reformation sketch of Paul as a guilt-ridden victim of a burdensome law who found in salvation by grace a fitting substitute for redemption through works of the law. Burdened by his own failure to fulfill God's requirements, Martin Luther was angered that even the gospel exacted justice, and he was discomfited by Paul's statement in Rom. 1:18: "the wrath of God is being revealed from heaven against all ungodliness and wickedness." (Unless otherwise noted I cite from the New Revised Standard Version.) Despairing of ever fulfilling God's just demand, his eyes lit on Rom. 1:17, and he was astonished at what he saw: "the just shall live by faith" (KJV). This exciting discovery unlocked the meaning of all Scripture for him, from Psalms to Revelation, and forever set Western civilization on a different track. Luther saw Paul as the one who taught that it was through faith in Christ rather than works of the law that one was set in a proper relationship with God. While elements of all of these portraits and many others may remain in the popular imagination, all descriptions of Paul have hardly been as flattering as these.

Paul's own letters contain starkly negative sketches of the apostle as a weak, uncharismatic, dishonest, self-serving, unimposing interloper in the apostolic circle (2 Cor. 10:1–2, 10). Late third or early fourth century documents sympathetic to Peter present Paul as a Greek who converted to Judaism after falling in love with the daughter of the high priest. Spurned by his love, he responded in kind by rejecting Judaism in a huff—its law, its Sabbath, and its rite of circumcision.[2] Elsewhere he is cast as a messenger of Satan who peddled a false gospel.[3]

Much later, in 1912 in his *Androcles and the Lion,* George Bernard Shaw offered a similarly unflattering portrait. As "the eternal enemy of Woman" Paul appears as a friend of repression and superstition, as a dogmatic antithesis of Jesus: "He is more Jewish than the Jews, more Roman than the Romans, proud both ways, full of startling confessions and self-revelations that would not surprise us if they were slipped into the pages of Nietzsche."[4]

In 1986 Hyam Maccoby's *The Mythmaker, Paul and the Invention of Christianity* presents Paul as a Gentile who was frustrated in his attempt to become a Jew. He set out to invent a new religion, and the religion he founded incorporated all of the animus that a rejected Paul felt toward Judaism. From Gnosticism Paul borrowed a world-weariness that promised salvation without requiring him to assume any responsibility for making the world a better place and also a bitter anti-Semitism.[5] From the Judaism he knew he appropriated a view of salvation history but twisted it to accommodate Jesus as the messianic savior figure and the church as the recipient of God's promises to Abraham. Thus for Maccoby Paul was a tormented, confused, vindictive Gentile who lied about his Pharisaism and left a legacy of anti-Semitism.

Recently Elizabeth A. Castelli has drawn on Derrida to offer a sketch of Paul as an apostle who rationalized his superordinate status as natural and true (i.e., divine) and called on his addressees to imitate him. Then he used this power position to repress difference and enforce unity on the church. To some following Castelli, Paul might appear as a bully who is intolerant of any truth save his own.[6]

While this profusion of images could be multiplied a thousand times over if one were to survey the whole history of Pauline interpretation, and while no modern discussion can or should ignore that discourse, our aim here is more modest—to attempt an overview of Paul's life in light of his historical context and the New Testament and apocryphal writings either by him or about him. Our interest is in the man of and behind the text, the only author of New Testament texts that we can identify with certainty. Of primary importance in our study are the seven undisputed letters of Paul (1 Thess., 1 Cor., 2 Cor., Gal., Phil., Philem., and Rom.); of lesser but still valued significance for this study is Acts. Wherever disagreements occur in these two bodies of material, we shall give credence more readily to Paul's own words.

For over half a century scholars have recognized that the "Luke" who gave us Acts was more author than historian. If we had only Acts for information about Paul we would either be missing valuable information or we would have information that at some points seriously distorts our view of Paul. We would not know, for example, that Paul was a letter writer.[7] We would not know that the nine speeches that Acts places on Paul's lips reveal little of the theology of the undisputed letters and none of the literary style or rhetorical character of their argumentation.[8] We would not know of the importance of the cross for Paul. We would have no inkling of the apocalypticism that suffuses Paul's gospel and some of his letters nor of Paul's emphasis on the imminence of Jesus' *parousia;* we would be virtually ignorant of Paul's view of women; and we would have no clue as to the role the righteousness of God played in Paul's theology.

On the other hand, it is Acts, not the letters, that tells us that Paul was a Roman citizen, that he was from Tarsus, that he studied under Gamaliel in Jerusalem, that he spoke Hebrew, that he was arrested in Jerusalem and, appealing to his right as a Roman citizen, was taken to Rome for trial, or that he was totally innocent of any crime against the Roman state or against the religion of Israel. We also would not know that his life and mission are datable by their association with the proconsulship of Gallio in Corinth in 50–51, or that as a persecutor of the church he placed followers of "the Way" in jail, traveling far and wide to apprehend members of the sect and bring them to Jerusalem for trial.

Both bodies of material agree that Paul was once a persecutor of the church, though the exact nature of that persecution is unclear in the letters. Both agree that he was a Pharisee. Both agree that he was a traveling missionary, although the emphasis on Paul's apostleship is somewhat muted in Acts. Both seem to agree that Paul defended his gospel before an "apostolic council" in Jerusalem and gained endorsement for his mission to the Gentiles though they disagree about the specifics of that agreement and the authority of the Twelve in Jerusalem to preside over the Christian church everywhere.

Our investigation relies more heavily on information from Paul's letters than on Acts for reconstructing his life. We shall judge the historicity of Acts on a case by case basis. Where Acts material does not reflect Lucan theology and where it does not contradict Paul's letters we shall be predisposed to accept it as reliable. Where, however, it reflects a Lucan *Tendenz* and is at odds with either implicit or explicit historical information in Paul we shall use it with extreme caution.[9] One Important item found in Acts is Luke's report that Paul was born in Tarsus (Acts 22:3), a reference that appears to have no ideological value for Luke and, therefore, seems quite plausible if not historically probable.

PAUL'S BIRTHPLACE

Biography is inevitably tied to geography in complex and interesting ways. The Hellenistic urban setting of Paul's youth had a profound impact on his anthropology, his worldview, his openness to Gentiles, and his religious consciousness. Paul himself nowhere tells us where he was reared. Because of his references to repeated visits to Damascus, some feel his home was there.[10] Luke, however, reports that Paul was born in Tarsus, a coastal town in the province of Cilicia (Acts 22:3), and since that tradition betrays no theological bias and finds indirect support in the Hellenistic outlook and style of the undisputed Pauline letters, there is no reason to reject it. While Paul nowhere tells us he went home after his apostolic call, a natural thing to do, he does speak of a mission to Cilicia somewhat later (Gal. 1:21).

If Paul was born in Tarsus, did he live there long enough to be influenced by its powerful, alluring Hellenistic environment? Acts suggests he did not: "I am a Jew, born in Tarsus in Cilicia, *but brought up (anatethrammenos)* in this city [Jerusalem] at the feet of Gamaliel" (Acts 22:3, NRSV, emphasis added). A generation ago van Unnik argued for the historicity of this reference, suggesting that Paul was taken to Jerusalem in earliest childhood and spent his youth in that city. Then as a young man he studied under Gamaliel and became a Pharisee. Van Unnik states unequivocally that in a biography of Paul all emphasis ought to fall on the fact that he grew up "in the center of Judaism, where the Torah prevailed in the home and in the street . . . and that he imbibed that atmosphere. He grew up *not as a typical Jew of the Diaspora cut off from all that* . . . but as a man for whom there was only one possibility, one ideal and one delight, namely the fulfillment of the law and will of the Lord"[11] (emphasis added). Moreover, van Unnik believes that the tongue in which Paul first learned to express himself was Aramaic, not Greek, and that it was in Aramaic that he conversed both on the street and in school.[12]

Like van Unnik, Martin Hengel thinks Paul was more profoundly influenced by Jerusalem than by Tarsus. Nevertheless, in light of scholarly research of the past three decades Hengel knows that Greek, not Aramaic, was Paul's first language and that Paul was, as Adolf Deissmann noted, "a Septuagint Jew."[13] "In my view," Hengel notes, "both Paul's excellent command of his Greek mother tongue and his sovereign treatment of the Greek Bible suggest that Tarsus cannot be pushed completely into the background, even if it must take second place to Jerusalem in Paul's growth."[14]

Haenchen has shown that van Unnik's view will not stand close scrutiny. Had Jerusalem been the locus of years of study under Gamaliel, zealous Pharisaic activity, and vicious persecution of the church, Paul's statement in Gal. 1:22 that he was "unknown by sight to the churches in Judea" would make little sense.[15] Moreover, the Lucan emphasis on the symbolic importance of Jerusalem as the beginning and end of his gospel story and as the epicenter of the Christian mission also casts doubt on van Unnik's belief that Paul resided there from childhood, studied there under Gamaliel, and therein waged his vicious and violent persecution of the church.[16] Van Unnik's theory also requires the assumption that the obvious influence of Hellenism on Paul came *after* his "conversion," and such a belief strains credulity.[17] Finally, there is no evidence in the letters that Paul knew or spoke Aramaic. These weighty objections make it unlikely that Paul studied under Gamaliel in Jerusalem or that he lived there from early childhood well into his adult years.[18]

If Paul grew up in Tarsus rather than Jerusalem (Acts 22:3), the Hellenistic idiom of his letters must be viewed in a wholly different light. Although Jerusalem was no stranger to Hellenistic influence it is difficult to explain Paul's preference for the Septuagint, his familiarity with Stoicism, his facility in the use of idioms and rhetorical strategies, his close acquaintance with Hellenistic literary styles, and even his anthropology on the basis of an extended residence there.[19] If Tarsus offers a more plausible explanation for Paul's Hellenistic outlook, what kind of a city was Tarsus?

TARSUS—"NO MEAN CITY"

Both material and literary artifacts attest to the importance of Tarsus in the ancient world.[20] Beginning a thousand years before the Iron Age, Tarsus was continuously occupied until it was destroyed by the Assyrian ruler Sennacherib in 696 BCE.[21] Its strategic location as a port city encouraged trade, invited a diverse population, and promoted a vibrant cosmopolitan culture. From the ninth century BCE on Tarsus was a port of call for Greek sailing vessels[22] and a vital trade partner of Egypt. Coins minted in Tarsus reveal a rich political and mythic legacy that embraced both East and West.[23]

Straddling the crossroads between north and south, east and west, Tarsus was ideally positioned for cultural interaction and commerce. Located a few miles from the Mediterranean on the river Cydnus with a small lake to the south, Tarsus offered a harbor safe from pirates and storms and ideally situated for trade.[24] With the road to the north running through a narrow mountain pass, the Cilician Gates, and connecting Tarsus to Syria and the top of the

Fertile Crescent, Tarsus offered a place where Greek and Semitic cultures could meet and enjoy a vital reciprocity. Its strategic importance caused Strabo to rank Tarsus with Athens and Alexandria as one of the three most important cities of the Mediterranean world (*Geography,* 13).

Long before Alexander the Great marched through this region in 334 BCE, Tarsus came under a Hellenic spell. Greek mercenary soldiers, traders, and immigrants seeking to escape desperate conditions in their homeland came with their language, philosophy, customs, and culture. Legends of Tarsus's Greek origins sprang up like mushrooms. In an oration, Dio Chrysostom recognized the civic pride of the Tarsians, albeit in a distinctly condescending manner:

> I wonder what on earth is your purpose, and what your expectation or desire, in seeking to have such persons as myself discourse for you. . . . is it because you expect . . . some patriotic hymn in praise of your city, all about Perseus and Heracles and the Lord of the Trident and the oracles that you have received, and how you are Hellenes, yes, Argives or even better, and how you have as founders . . . Titans?[25]

Even Dio Chrysostom's ridicule of his audience for naming Heracles as the founder of their city and the Titans as their primordial ancestors associates the Tarsians with the dominant Hellenistic culture. But coins suggest that Tarsians bowed to the Orient as well as to the Occident. A Tarsian coin minted between 379 and 374 BCE displays a Greek goddess on one side and a Greek warrior on the other and is inscribed in Aramaic.[26] That exciting combination continued well into the second century, when under the Seleucid ruler Antiochus, Tarsus exchanged its time honored name for "Antioch [after Antiochus] on the Cydnus."[27]

The Hellenistic presence did much to establish Tarsus as an important center for the study of philosophy. While Dio Chrysostom reported that the dominant influence in Tarsus was oriental, Strabo was impressed by the Tarsian passion for learning: "The people at Tarsus have devoted themselves so eagerly, not only to philosophy, but also to the whole round of education in general, that they have surpassed Athens, Alexandria, or any other place that can be named where there have been schools and lectures or philosophers. . . . Further, the city of Tarsus has all kinds of schools of rhetoric."[28] Stoics whom Strabo numbered among the natives of Tarsus were Antipater, Archedemus, Nestor, and the two Athenodoruses. Two other philosophers, Plutiades and Diogenes, were joined by the grammarians Artemidorus and Diodorus. The "best tragic poet among those enumerated in the 'Pleias' was Dionysides."[29] While Ramsay's description of this center of learning in Tarsus as the "University of Tarsus" is anachronistic, for there was no "university" in Tarsus in the English or European sense, Strabo's estimation of Tarsus as an important intellectual center is historical. The powerful Cynic and Stoic presence in the city did have an impact on Paul. Whether that influence was direct or indirect is not as important as the fact that it provided an atmosphere that Paul breathed and that influenced his own outlook.

The political ascendancy of Tarsus received a powerful boost with the refounding of the city under Antiochus IV (175–64 BCE) and the granting of permission to mint its own coins.[30] Although the city was presented as a "gift" to a mysterious Antiochis (perhaps a sister, a niece, or a daughter of the sister with the same name), the "gift" in no way compromised Tarsus's autonomous status or abridged its constitution.[31] Antiochis's "ownership" probably meant only that she received a portion of the tribute that normally would have been paid to Antiochus.

While we know little about the political fortune of Tarsus in the one hundred year hiatus between the death of Antiochus Epiphanes (164 BCE) and the arrival of the Roman commander, Pompey, (a century later) Tarsus continued to enjoy self-determination with freedom to pursue a vigorous trade policy. Clearly, the mix of east and west, the cosmopolitan atmosphere, and the friendly encounter with Hellenism continued into the Roman period and thus shaped Paul's thinking. Here Paul learned Greek as his first language, received his education, and was influenced by Hellenistic rhetoric and Stoic philosophy. Here he also learned a Jewish religion that was profoundly affected by this rich cultural environment. This great cultural heritage that joined Hellenistic and Jewish influences ideally equipped Paul to translate a gospel that was fundamentally Jewish for the Hellenistic world.

ROMAN IMPACT ON TARSUS

Although we cannot be certain of the date when the Roman rule of Cilicia began, Roman control was in place by 67 BCE under Pompey. And even under Roman rule Tarsus remained an "oriental city proudly maintaining its ancient name and its ancient god but Hellenized in all important respects."[32] Under Roman control, the language of government, commerce, and culture remained Greek, and the prowess of the philosophical and rhetorical schools continued uninterruptedly in Tarsus.

As the capital of Cilicia, a large and very important eastern province, Tarsus enjoyed a favored relationship with Rome. It was such an important transportation hub between East and West that when pirates threatened the flow of grain and goods, Pompey moved decisively to rid the Mediterranean of pirates and promptly annexed Cilicia, making it a Roman province. Long before Pompey's pirate purge in 67 BCE, ships had regularly sought refuge in the strategic harbor of Tarsus both from pirates and from storms.

Just as Egypt was a gift of the Nile, Tarsus was a gift of the Cydnus which flowed through Tarsus into a lake five miles below the town and thence into the Mediterranean two miles further south. Dredged and banked the Cydnus became a major shipping channel up to the lake, ideally situated for commerce and refuge. Ringed on the east, west, and north by warehouses, businesses, and dwellings, the harbor welcomed rulers, enterprising intellectuals, and common laborers, Jew and Greek, Roman and Persian. Pompey, Mark Antony, Julius Caesar, Cassius, and even Cleopatra allegedly moored there. Cicero, the great rhetorician, was governor there in 51 BCE.

Though Tarsus lay in the path of great historical events, fortune usually smiled on the town. When the Civil War erupted in 49 BCE, Tarsus sided with the Roman military that would replace the republic with the empire. Julius Caesar stopped there briefly in 47 on his march north. As a sign of their enthusiastic support for Julius Caesar, the father of the empire, Tarsus renamed itself Juliopolis for a brief period. After the murder of Julius Caesar in 44 Tarsus sided with Augustus against the Usurpers. And though they had no choice but to yield to Cassius, who allied with Brutus, made war against Augustus and Antony, the city gave an enthusiastic welcome to Mark Antony in 42 after the defeat of the senatorial forces in Philippi. There Mark Antony was joined by the Egyptian queen Cleopatra, who sailed her elegant bark up the Cydnus into the heart of Tarsus for their fabled rendezvous.

The rewards of Tarsus's loyalty were considerable. Antony made Tarsus a free city, a *libera civitas*, which entitled the city to govern itself by its own laws, to mint its own coins and to be exempt from export and import duties. When after his victory at Actium in 31 BCE Augustus became the undisputed ruler of the entire Roman Empire, he reaffirmed the privileges bestowed on Tarsus by Antony. Just before the beginning of the Common Era Tarsus also had the good fortune to be governed by Athenodorus, a Stoic philosopher who served as young Augustus's teacher before Augustus returned to Rome to claim the office of his assassinated uncle, Julius Caesar. Athenodorus, whom Augustus invested with imperial authority, sought through rational discourse to curb the corruption and rapaciousness of Antony's evil (κακός) appointee, Boethos, and his cohort. When that failed he used his delegated authority to exile Boethos and his supporters, to reform the constitution, and to establish a just rule.[33] Certainly Paul's parents and perhaps Paul himself would have been familiar with the government of Athenodorus.

We see, therefore, that if Paul grew up in Tarsus he was the recipient of a rich cosmopolitan legacy. The social and cultural environment, the intellectual and artistic circles, the city's commercial ties to Alexandria and Athens, the political influence it exerted historically, and its vibrant Hellenistic culture all stood to influence significantly the local Jewish community, a community to which Paul would have belonged.

THE JEWISH PRESENCE

When or under what conditions Paul's ancestors came to live in Tarsus is uncertain. In his commentary on Phil. 23 Jerome writes that the Romans relocated Paul and his parents in Tarsus from Gischala in Galilee, but that viewpoint meets variously with everything from complete credulity to absolute skepticism.[34] Given the scope of the Jewish Diaspora in the Mediterranean world, in process for centuries before Paul's day, and given the Jewish presence in most cities of the Mediterranean, a forced repatriation of Jews from Galilee to Cilicia need not be assumed to account for a considerable Jewish presence in Tarsus. Paul's autobiographical remarks about his proficiency in and zeal for "the traditions of the ancestors" (Gal. 1:14) suggest this presence. Nils Dahl correctly locates much of Paul's hellenization in a Jewish community involved with and influenced by the dominant Hellenistic culture. Clear evidence of Paul's deep roots in a Jewish tradition engaged in a lively conversation with the Hellenistic milieu is seen in his rich Hellenistic vocabulary, his use of the Stoic diatribe and Hellenistic rhetoric, his use of the Hellenistic letter form, and his skillful modulation of contradictory claims made by his Jewish tradition and the Hellenistic view of the world.

The formative influence of this Hellenistic environment on Paul is most evident in his use of the Septuagint.[35] While known in Jerusalem it hardly enjoyed the unrivaled preeminence there that it possessed in Alexandria and Tarsus.[36] In Alexandria festivals celebrated its genesis and abiding truth. Commentaries from Artapanus, Aristobulus, Pseudo-Aristeas, and most importantly Philo sprang up linking its text and truth to changing circumstance. More than a mere text requiring interpretation, it itself was the interpretation.[37] The Septuagint went beyond expressing the view and ethos of the Jewish community in Tarsus to actually shaping that community's religious understanding, its identity, its view of reality, and its interaction with its "pagan" context.[38] As philosophers of language have shown, language, myths, metaphors, cultic acts, and symbols are not merely outward expressions of the community's inner self but rather affect and express the community's sense of self. They collaborate to shape the community's identity and to give its members a language to express their understanding of the world. The process is circular. Language mediates the community's impressions of the world, and at the same time the community's worldview affects its use of language. Theological or religious ideas do not merely exist as independent entities expressed by functional language. Instead, the essence of these ideas is itself shaped by language.[39] Thus the Septuagint offers us a window onto the Jewish community in Tarsus and insight into Paul.[40]

The Septuagint's stories of Israel and its nuanced translations of the Law and the Prophets provided a protocol for fruitful interaction between the Jewish community and the dominant Hellenistic culture. In that Diaspora context daily interaction with representatives of the majority culture was inevitable. Intermarriage with Gentiles was not uncommon; Jewish merchants traded with Gentiles to survive; Jewish day laborers hired themselves out to Gentiles; and Jewish employers hired Gentiles as well. Jews attended the same theater and games as Gentiles and often shared places in the gymnasia with them. Even though some in the community resisted these accommodations, in Alexandria and perhaps in Tarsus they were a minority. While there were tensions between accommodation and resistance to Hellenistic influence in most Diaspora communities, the majority of Jews seemed open to the Hellenistic culture. This openness to the Gentiles was certainly reinforced by parts of the Septuagint that Paul especially favored. The Septuagintal emphasis on *oikoumene* in Isaiah, for example, self-consciously expands the boundary of God's people to include Gentiles.[41] We see this emphasis especially in the Septaugint of Isa. 23:14–24:1, where instead of condemning the "pagan" Tyre to "play the harlot with *all the kingdoms of the world upon the face of the ground*" as the Hebrew Scriptures (MT emphasis added) express it, the Septuagint offers Tyre a positive role to play in the coming redemption. The condemnation of Tyre for its historic association with the Canaanite fertility cult so pronounced in the Hebrew is totally absent from the Greek text. Surprisingly, the LXX reverses the condemnation in the MT and recognizes Tyre as the gateway through which the eschatological offerings will flow to Jerusalem: "The God of Tyre shall make a visitation and she will turn again to the old ways and shall be a port of merchandise for all the kingdoms of the world (*pasais tais basileiais tes oikoumenes*) and her merchandise and *her hire shall be holy unto the Lord*" (emphasis added).

In this passage we see how the foreigner whom the MT condemns to a future of shameful and humiliating prostitution makes a holy offering to God.[42] Such a pluralistic vision affects the translation and reading of texts and the protocol that the texts offer for interact in a pluralistic setting. So, even while the Septuagint (LXX) vigorously reaffirmed the centrality of the Jewish tradition, it left open the possibility of a fruitful encounter with Gentile neighbors who also were seen as world citizens.

This is not to say that the relationship of Jew and gentile was free of tension or ambiguity. Even before Philo wrote of the factionalism in the Jewish community in Alexandria, the LXX of Isaiah responded to conflict between different members of a Diaspora community. Seeing themselves as an island in a sea of *anomia* (lawlessness) the LXX translators changed the Hebrew text of Isa. 24:16 to warn those who were too lax in their observance of *nomos* (law). Where the Hebrew text reads: "Woe is *me*! For the *treacherous deal treacherously*; woe is *me* for the *treacherous deal treacherously*" (emphasis added), the Septuagint has "Woe to *those setting aside. Those setting aside the Law*" (emphasis added). The changes transformed a text that was fundamentally apocalyptic into a text condemning those who had become careless about the requirements of *nomos*.

Over four decades ago Seeligmann observed similar changes that the LXX made to the Hebrew text of Isa. 8:12–16. The changes totally ignored the way the Masoretic Text warned against political expediency in the face of a looming Assyrian threat and exchanged these warnings for an indictment of Jews who fail to teach the law and who hinder strict Torah observance.[43] In numerous texts the translators condemn conduct outside the traditions of Israel as *anomia*, and this is done even while their translation endorses Hellenistic values. Consequently, we see in Diaspora Judaism a profound ambiguity about Hellenistic culture; on the one hand it appropriated or even embraced the language, the rhetoric, and even the worldview of the dominant culture, and yet on another level it resisted or even repressed that influence.

Even where there are attempts to gloss over that influence, it is obvious that Diaspora Judaism was affected at very deep levels. Identity and the appropriate level of interaction could hardly be maintained by a simple recall and recitation of tradition. The community had to find a means of preserving a sense of continuity with the ancestral traditions while living in a context fraught with moral ambiguity.

This conflict between inclusion and exclusion so typical of Alexandrian and probably Tarsian Judaism would account for the complex and often conflicted expressions we see in the Pauline letters.[44] In Rom. 9–11 Paul argues for the validity of his gospel to the Gentiles even while passionately insisting that this inclusion in no way implies a rejection of Israel on God's part or that Israel has stumbled so as to fall (Rom. 11:1, 11). The tension between Paul's *kerygma* for the *oikoumene* (Rom. 10:18) and his affirmation of divine loyalty to Israel is so powerful that his letter almost throbs in our hands.

Nils Dahl has noted how the radical monotheism of Paul that removed traditional distinctions between Jews and Gentiles owed much to a "Greek philosophical monotheism, which was universalistic and more or less cosmopolitan."[45] At the same time Paul includes himself among God's covenant people, Israel (2 Cor. 11:22–23). Location in this magnetic field between boundedness and boundlessness threatened to pull Paul's argument apart. Realizing that the resolution of these contrary tendencies is a *human* impossibility, Paul found a mediation in the mystery of the Godhead itself as he exclaimed in wonderment: "O the depth of the riches, and wisdom and knowledge of God" (11:33–36).

Although tension between Jew and Greek was an important part of life in Judaea in the first century, Diaspora Jews were inevitably more isolated, more aware of their minority status, and more acutely conscious of their vulnerability (or were aware of all this in a different way). Consequently, Paul's knowledge of and response to the tension between insiders and outsiders, between his own native religion and the popular religions of the day, are best understood within a context such as Tarsus offered.

The ambiguity that suffused the Diaspora setting, so obvious in the Septuagint, appears also in an abundant body of apologetic literature known to the Jewish community in Alexandria. While we have no evidence that Paul personally was familiar with that material, his Jewish community in Tarsus had sufficient opportunity for interaction with Alexandrian Jews, and influence by their ideas cannot be ruled out. In sum, Paul's outlook, his strategies of communication, his own sense of self, and his understanding of his mission were deeply influenced by his early years in a Diaspora Jewish community.

WAS PAUL A ROMAN CITIZEN?

While an understanding of the social and cultural setting of Paul's youth is of great significance, the burning, outstanding question about Paul's past concerns Luke's reference to him as a Roman citizen. As Acts presents him, Paul was arrested and charged with creating a civil disturbance when he was in Jerusalem delivering the offering from the Gentiles for the poor. To this outrage, Paul objects to the Roman centurion, "Is it legal for you to flog a *Roman citizen* who is uncondemned?" (Acts 22:25; emphasis added). The centurion then warns the tribune, "What are you about to do? This man is a *Roman citizen*" (Acts 22:26; emphasis added). Then the tribune asks Paul directly, "Tell me, are you a *Roman citizen*?" (Acts 22:27). And Paul replies, "I was born a citizen" (Acts 22:28). Thus Paul makes his own citizenship the key element in his appeal and his transfer to Rome to defend himself before Caesar.

As plausible as it may sound, the historicity of this Lucan account is hotly disputed. C. Bradford Welles states unequivocally that "Paul's" claim to be a Roman citizen (Acts 22:25–29) "can be accepted as literally true."[46] He is joined by A. N. Sherwin-White, who also accepts Luke's reference to Paul's citizenship at face value and notes that Rome did grant citizenship to some indigents for distinguished service.[47] He adds, however, that Paul's claim to dual citizenship in Tarsus *and* Rome would have been impossible for imperial Rome had reversed that policy before Paul's time.[48] And, in the absence of compelling evidence to the contrary, Hengel accepts the attribution of Roman citizenship to Paul in Acts as historical. Noting that Luke has Paul receiving his citizenship by birth, Hengel believes it was possible if not probable that Paul's forbears were enslaved during the Roman invasion of Palestine by Pompey in 63 BCE and then upon their release were involuntarily granted citizenship status.[49] While this position agrees with the older view of Ramsay that Rome granted citizenship to Paul's ancestors for forced resettlement at manumission it leans heavily on a Jerome tradition that Eduard Meyer thought was "quite absurde" (*ganz absurde*).[50]

Other scholars, however, vigorously dispute the historical accuracy of Paul's citizenship. W. W. Tarn resolutely argued that Paul was neither a citizen of Rome nor a citizen of Tarsus.[51] E. R. Goodenough found it incredible that Paul either inherited Roman citizenship from his father or that this tentmaker would have come from "one of the greatest families in the East" by virtue of Roman citizenship.[52] And Victor Tcherikover doubted that solid evidence exists to support the claim of citizenship for Jews as a group in any city of the Hellenistic world in the first century.[53] Other scholars such as Stegeman, Conzelmann, Haenchen, and Koester, are also skeptical that Paul was a Roman citizen.

Scholars list four major arguments against Roman citizenship for Paul:

(1) The granting of citizenship to Jews in the East was rare, and on those infrequent occasions when it was granted it usually went to wealthy and influential people who had performed distinguished service to Rome.[54] To be sure, we do know of Jews who aspired to and were granted citizenship. Philo tells us of his nephew Tiberias Julius Alexander, who became a citizen of Alexandria and a Roman equestrian and rose to a position of power and influence.[55] But he was singled out by Josephus for deserting the traditions of the fathers.[56] The physical evidence supports the view that only a few Jews who were wealthy, powerful, and profoundly attracted to Hellenistic and Roman culture became citizens. In a survey of the epigraphical evidence Stegeman finds only 552 residents of Asia Minor who were citizens. We know of no citizens in Pergamum in the time of Augustus, and interestingly only 3 of 103 names from Ephesus contain the name of Julius, a probable indicator of citizenship. All of the evidence suggests that citizenship status was rarely granted in the eastern provinces.[57]

(2) If Paul's piety reflects that of his parents, the piety of his home would argue against Roman citizenship.[58] A condition of citizenship was participation in the civic cult, offering of obeisance to the gods of the city, sharing in the festivals of the polis, which were by definition religious, and offering homage to the Roman gods and allegiance to the imperial cult. Paul's own deep religious commitments as a pious Jew would certainly have conflicted with those obligations. Paul himself tells us with some pride of his blamelessness before the law (Phil. 3:6), that he advanced in Judaism "beyond many among my people of the same age, for I was far more zealous for the traditions

of my ancestors" (Gal. 1:14), and that the same zeal led him to persecute the church (Phil. 3:6). A Jew of such intense devotion to the ancestral traditions would have found it impossible to share in the religion of the Graeco-Roman world or to participate in its educational institution, the gymnasium.[59] There is no sign in the letters that Paul was a student of the Greek classics or that he had been exposed to the exercise regimen, including exercise in the nude, associated with a gymnasium education.

(3) Certain omissions in the letters argue against citizenship. If Paul were a Roman citizen his endurance of oppression so severe that he despaired of life itself (2 Cor. 1:8, f9) is difficult to understand when an appeal to his Roman citizenship offered a ready escape. The omission of any mention of his Roman citizenship in his reference to his new heavenly citizenship is also puzzling (Phil. 3:20). It would also have been useful for him to have noted the ironic contrast between his citizen status and his condition as the "off scouring of the world" (my trans.) in 1 Cor. 4:13, but again he was silent. But, more importantly, Paul's failure to refer to his citizenship in his letter to the church at Rome is perplexing.[60] While an *argumentio ex silentio* when taken alone is hardly convincing, when added to the other evidence noted previously it weighs against Roman citizenship.

(4) Paul's citizenship clearly served Luke's theological interests. By insisting on Paul's faithfulness to Judaism as a loyal Pharisee until the day of his death *and* his Roman citizenship Luke was able to argue for Paul's respectability and innocence at a time when the Christian movement had come under suspicion for its unwillingness to participate in the imperial cult, its refusal to serve in the military, its pacifistic lifestyle, and its secret meetings. By lifting up Paul as a respected and loyal citizen Luke could show that the movement he represented was innocent of treason or subversive activity.

Conzelmann, Koester, Dibelius, Haenchen, and Stegeman all have noted how Luke's emphasis on Paul's citizenship serves this apologetic interest.[61] Stegeman thinks that Luke expands Paul's reference in Rom. 15:25 and the following verses to his journey to Jerusalem, his planned departure for Rome, and ultimately his mission to Spain to include the final scenario in Jerusalem leading to Paul's arrest, appeal as a citizen, and transfer to Rome for trial.[62]

While we cannot know with certainty whether or not Paul was a Roman citizen, the evidence weighs against it. Even if the Acts account is not historical, there is an element of truth in it nevertheless. Since the time of Julius Caesar, the right of Jews to practice their ancestral religion had been protected. Ethnic Jews were given the right to govern themselves by their laws, to impose their own discipline, and to enjoy some autonomy as long as they remained loyal to Rome. They were not granted citizenship in the cities, but they were given the right to create their own administrative and judicial organization, which was called a *politeuma*.[63] Lentz quite correctly notes that these colonies (*politeumata*) "became the focus of civic, religious, and ethnic identity."[64] Mary Smallwood has shown that to be a citizen (πολιτης), did not necessarily imply that one was a Roman citizen but rather indicated that one was a member of a *politeuma*.[65] Thus Jews with membership in a *politeuma* held something of an intermediate status between citizens and resident aliens (metics), enjoyed exemption from some taxes, for example, the poll tax (*laographia*), and received certain privileges of limited self-governance. Paul's recognition of his addressees in Philippi as members of the *politeuma* in heaven (Phil. 3:20) may support this viewpoint, but it could also just as easily be intended as compensation for the lack of citizen status in this world.

Applebaum offers support for Smallwood's position. He observes that at least in Seleucia on the Tigris River there were separate *politeumata* of Greeks, Syrians, and Jews, and apparently they enjoyed equal rights.[66] Evidently, Jewish colonies throughout the eastern provinces were somewhat autonomous and were free to preside over their internal affairs, to exercise community discipline, to make arrests, to dispatch embassies to the emperor and to remit the half shekel tax to Jerusalem. Thus Jews occupied an intermediate status somewhere between indigent metics and citizens. While instances of anti-Semitism did occur, such occurrences were sporadic and localized, for Roman emperors from Julius Caesar through Augustus to Vespasian and Titus guaranteed Jewish communities throughout the empire the right to practice their ancestral religion without hindrance or molestation.[67]

If Paul was not a citizen, then it is probable that he was a member of a Diaspora Jewish *politeuma* or association in Tarsus. The unlikelihood that Paul was a Roman citizen has implications for a decision about Paul's class or status, as we shall note later. While Roman citizenship would be prima facie evidence that Paul was advantaged and came from the upper class, his membership in a *politeuma* by itself would not. Because Paul was a handworker, Deissmann argued a long time ago that he came from the middle or lower class.[68] W. M. Ramsay, on the other hand, placed Paul among the upper classes of society, largely on the strength of his citizenship status.[69] If Paul were not a citizen then the view that he came from the upper class loses some credibility. The possibility that Paul did not belong to the upper class has relevance for our understanding of his education.

PAUL'S EDUCATION

We know much more about the outcome of Paul's schooling than about the type of school he attended. From his education he gained an intimate knowledge of the Septuagint and became skilled in methods of its interpretation. He was immersed in the traditions of Israel and became especially sympathetic to the Pharisaic understanding of Torah, its breadth, its focus, its interpretation, and its belief in the one God of Israel in whose hands the outcome of history was vested. But it is also clear that his schooling was open to Hellenistic concerns. In the course of that schooling he learned basic literary skills, the art of letter writing, the strategy of rhetoric or argumentation, and the basis of a religion that was itself influenced by Hellenistic anthropology, Stoic methods of argumentation, and even a Stoic understanding of natural law. It was this instruction that brought two worlds together even as it held them in tension.

But did this educational achievement exempt Paul from manual work? And, if so, was the apostle's tent making or leatherwork a voluntary act of self-denial, of status renunciation for the sake of the gospel? Hock thinks Paul came from the "élite";[70] Charles Dodd noted in comments on 1 Cor. 4:12 that "A man born to manual labor does not speak self-consciously of 'labouring with my own hands.'" Some scholars who are persuaded that Paul was a Roman citizen may presume that he came from a privileged or upper class, and others who accept Luke's statement that Paul studied under Gamaliel assume that he learned a trade as part of his Pharisaic training. Dibelius spoke for many when he said, "Paul . . . must not be regarded as having the social status of a manual worker; the Jew who intended to devote himself to the service of the Law learnt a trade for the sake of his independence."[71] It may be, however, that our view of Paul as an intellectual is greatly influenced by the enormously privileged position of today's university professors, who typically are separated from manual laborers. If it indeed is doubtful that Paul was a Roman citizen or studied under Gamaliel and if, as Hock so compellingly argues, Paul learned his trade of leatherworking from his father, then much of the historical support for Paul's upper class origin disappears, and the claim that he was from the "socially élite" is without merit.[72] If Paul's father was a manual laborer and trained Paul in his skill as an artisan then it appears that Paul was a child of a manual laborer and was reared in a tradition of manual labor.[73] He obviously was precocious and learned much from those around him. His letters themselves suggest he also enjoyed a formal but not a gymnasium education. It is sheer speculation to argue that Paul came from the upper classes but voluntarily subordinated himself to better embody the cross. It is equally adventurous to suggest, as does Jerome Murphy-O'Connor, that after being disinherited by his native Judaism and deprived of institutional support, Paul was forced to learn a trade in order to survive (Phil. 3:8). While Murphy-O'Connor cites Acts 18:3 to support this view, that passage notes only that Aquila and Priscilla were "of the same trade."[74] It seems more likely that Paul learned his trade from his father and from the beginning worked with his hands to support himself. Unlike the Sophists and popular philosophers Paul showed no inclination to beg or to accept money for his teaching.

Moreover, he surely felt that being a burden to others would compromise not only his independence but also his gospel.

PAUL THE PHARISEE

In Phil. 3:4–6 Paul offers the reader a rare glimpse into his past. In response to Jewish Christian missionaries preaching a gospel that included initiation by circumcision and obviously seeking to discredit Paul's gospel of grace outside the law, Paul erupts: "If anyone else has reason to be confident in the flesh, I have more: circumcised on the eighth day, a member of the people of Israel, of the tribe of Benjamin, a Hebrew born of Hebrews; *as to the law a Pharisee* (κατὰ νόμον φαρισαῖος); as to zeal, a persecutor of the church; as to righteousness under the law, blameless." Luke also has Paul claim his religious affiliation before a mixed company of Pharisees and Sadducees: "Brothers, I am a Pharisee, a son of Pharisees" (23:6). Before Agrippa he repeats the claim: "I have belonged to the strictest sect of our religion and lived as a Pharisee" (26:4). And responding to his Jewish accusers in Jerusalem he claims to have been "brought up in this city at the feet of Gamaliel, educated strictly according to our ancestral law." (22:3) But only in Phil. 3:5 do we find Paul himself claiming an association with Pharisaism. One wonders why Paul's reference to his advancement in Judaism "beyond many of my own age among my people" and his extreme zeal "for the traditions of my fathers" (my trans. Gal. 1:14) makes no mention of his Pharisaism.

And would it have been possible for Paul to be a strict Pharisee in the Diaspora?[75] The evidence for the existence of Pharisees in the Diaspora is very weak, but caution is needed. There was more variety in first century Pharisaism than we usually allow, and Pharisaic influence was hardly confined to Palestine. Might Paul's interest in Pharisaism have been inspired by his parents? Did they order their lives by and nurture their souls on Pharisaic traditions? Or, was the lineage of Paul's Pharisaism less direct, filtered through Jewish teachers in Tarsus who were partial to Pharisaism and its liberal interpretation of Scriptures? Did Paul's statement that he was "according to the law a Pharisee" mean something like: "I am sympathetic to and inclined toward the Pharisaic point of view"? We cannot know with absolute certainty the answer to any of these questions, but we can know that Paul, the Diaspora Jew, shared a broad range of convictions, an evaluation of what was scriptural, and an approach to texts that were Pharisaic. We now turn to some of those issues.

Pharisaism in Paul's Time

Two very important studies by Jacob Neusner and Ellis Rivkin dealing with all of the major sources (rabbinic, Josephus, and the New Testament) come to diametrically opposed conclusions about Pharisaism in Paul's day.[76] Neusner is especially critical of Jewish and Christian scholars who sift materials from the Mishnah (ca. 200 CE), Talmud (fifth and sixth centuries), and Midrashim (Middle Ages) for sayings, laws, and stories allegedly coming from the pre-70 period and who then paste them together without regard to context or intent to form a pastiche of first century Pharisaism. While such a harmonization would be deplored if used on Christian texts, it was widely and uncritically practiced on rabbinic texts by Christian and Jewish scholars alike. Using a rigorous historical-critical method Neusner's study of these materials brought him to a set of conclusions quite at variance with earlier synthetic studies.

Neusner found the genesis of the Pharisees in the Hasmonean period (ca. 150 BCE) in a lay response to the Syrian appointment of Jonathan as *strategos and* high priest. Priests withdrew from the temple and formed the Qumran community to protest this pollution of the temple; pious laity protested this cultic violation by applying cultic law to everyday life. They sought to apply temple law to "the field and the kitchen, the bed and the street."[77] This radical understanding of the command to be a "kingdom of priests" (Exod. 19:6) challenged the unrivaled power of the temple priesthood. Pharisaic scribes, or interpreters of Torah, emerged who were politically active and influential until Herod the Great drove them from the political arena, a trend that the Romans continued. In Neusner's view, during the early decades of the first century when they were deprived of political power, the Pharisees turned to a more pietistic and quietistic lifestyle concerned primarily with ritualistic matters.

While the gospel polemics against the Pharisees as "vipers," "hypocrites," "blind guides," "whitewashed tombs," and murderers of the prophets are vicious caricatures (e.g., Matt. 3:7; 12:34: 23:16, 23, 24, 27, 31, 33) Neusner believes nevertheless that these accounts reveal Pharisaic concerns that parallel early traditions from the Mishnah and Tosefta. For example, both rabbinic materials and the Gospels say the Pharisees were intensely concerned with laws of purity prescribing ritualistic bathing for cleansing from impurity incurred in a business transaction, from physical contact with a corpse, and from bodily discharges such as running sores, seminal emissions, or menstrual flows. Marking the boundary between the clean and unclean, these purity laws defined the community by excluding the ritually impure—tax gatherers, the sick, the emotionally disturbed, or the physically handicapped (note, e.g., Mark 2:16). Laws for fasting (Mark 2:18), food consumption, tithing (Luke 11:42), and Sabbath observance (Mark 2:23–28) all collaborated to define the community, to order life within it, and to protest an unholy Roman rule and any priestly collaboration with it. In an apt summary of Neusner's position, Saldarini says, "These laws set out an agenda of holiness for the land and people which was a fitting response for a powerless people dominated by the Romans because these laws pertain to the parts of domestic life—food, sex, and marriage—which can be controlled by people out of power in their own society. Food and reproduction within the household, rather than the public cult at the Temple and the governance of society, are within the grasp of a subject people."[78]

Ellis Rivkin has vigorously challenged Neusner's view, arguing that the Pharisees, far from being quietistic or apolitical, were political revolutionaries. As a scholarly class they served as the chief interpreters of both oral and written law, and, as the dominant party of the day, they tried to impose their understanding of law "in all realms: cultus, property, judicial procedures, festivals, etc."[79] Because of its popularity with the masses, this scholarly class was able to dictate policy to its rivals, the Sadducees. Not quietistic at all, these Pharisees aggressively imposed their will on the social and political life of the Jews; they founded the synagogue, promulgated new law, advocated a twofold law, one written and one oral, and defended their belief in the resurrection, judgment, and life after death.

Critics have seen weakness in the works of both scholars. Neusner has been charged with a historical reductionism, and his view that the Pharisees were quietistic and apolitical in the first century has met widespread skepticism. But, there is no gainsaying, Neusner brought a historical rigor to the study of Mishnah, Tosefta, and Talmud that was needed. Critics have faulted Rivkin for his uncritical reading of rabbinic materials, gospel texts, and the writings of Josephus. His attempt to force all of the evidence from widely different periods and conditions into agreement with Josephus creates a synthesis that is historically false.

In spite of the many weaknesses of Rivkin's methodology and conclusions, one of his emphases has special merit—namely, his insistence on the involvement of the Pharisees in the political arena. Josephus's emphasis on the popularity of the Pharisees with the masses and their political power agrees in some ways with the portrait painted by the gospel writers (*War* 2.8.2–14 [119–66] and *Ant.* 18.1.2–6 [11–25]).[80] From Josephus we learn that the Sadducees were the privileged, governing class while the Pharisees, though influential with the masses, occupied less powerful positions.

Saldarini especially has disputed the claim of Morton Smith and Jacob Neusner that Josephus exaggerated the power of the Pharisees to legitimize their rule in Roman eyes two decades and more after the war. He shows instead that Josephus' treatment of the Pharisees in *Antiquities* correlates in significant measure with that in the *War*. Both depict the Pharisees positively and negatively, and both admit Pharisaic involvement in political activity. Saldarini acknowledges that during the first century they exerted less political influence than in earlier periods (e.g., during the rule of Alexandra), and that was because "they had no royal patron like Alexandra and there was no central Jewish authority, like Herod, with whom to come into conflict."[81]

While the Gospels paint the opponents of Jesus in starkly unflattering colors to display the Lord to advantage, much of historical value can be learned from them if used with caution. In Mark we do have evidence of political activity by the Pharisees. Their collaboration with the Herodians to destroy Jesus (3:6) suggests that some occupy positions of power. Later they join the Herodians to entrap Jesus with a question about taxes paid to the Roman occupiers (12:13–17). Such references certainly support Saldarini's view that Pharisees were active politically.[82] Actually, in the first century there was no separation of politics and piety. Even quietistic behavior was a political statement against an overwhelming political adversary.[83]

Josephus's summary of the core beliefs of Pharisaic religion partially agrees with some of those of the Gospels: ". . . the Pharisees, who are considered the most accurate interpreters of the laws, and hold the position of the leading sect, attribute everything to Fate and to God; they hold that to act rightly or otherwise rests, indeed, for the most part with man, but that in each action Fate co-operates. Every soul, they maintain, is imperishable, but the soul of the good alone passes into another body, while the souls of the wicked suffer eternal punishment" (*War* 2:162–63). A central lineament of this summary is its emphasis on the resurrection and the future judgment. That trait also noted by the Gospels and Acts (Mark 12:13–27; Matt. 22:23–33; Luke 20:27–40; Acts 23:6–8) was apparently "the very core of Pharisaic teaching" and clashed with the proclamation of the messianists that the resurrection of Jesus had already inaugurated the end of this world.[84]

Spiritualization of Text and Tradition

Although this Pharisaic piety was text based, the Pharisees recognized that texts were hardly self-interpreting but required diligent study to decipher their laws. Their canon of Scripture extended far beyond the Pentateuch to include the Prophets and Writings. Whether at this stage they included oral traditions is uncertain. From the range of his citations we know that Paul shared this broad definition as well.[85] And like the interpretation of the Pharisees Paul's theologizing was also text based.

The Pharisaic spiritualization of the priestly code offered a fresh interpretation of the rules of purity and an extension of the rubrics of the cult into the ordinary life of the laity.[86] Yet the Pharisees were hardly alone in the spiritualization of the cult. The Stoics, Diaspora Jews like Philo, and even the martyrological traditions all spiritualized features of the cult, and Paul would have been influenced by them all.

Although Philo was no Pharisee, he accepted nevertheless the temple and its cult as a vital part of the Hebrew religion and extended its reach through allegorization and spiritualization. Unlike the Stoics, who repudiated the sacrificial cult,[87] Philo clung to it tenaciously. He tells us of only one visit to Jerusalem in his lifetime, yet his imagination was alive with ways to continually experience the cult. He viewed both the whole cosmos and the individual soul as temples (spec. leg., I, 66). While affirming the importance of the literal sacrifice, he emphasized the importance of inner readiness to make an offering. The self-offering of the worshiper, he argued, was the best sacrifice (spec. leg., I, 272). The rising of the leaven was barred from the sacrifice, Philo believed, because "none approaching the altar should be uplifted or puffed up by arrogance" (spec. leg., I, 293). The offering of the firstfruits reminds one that becasue these belong to God they can hardly be treated as "personal property," and this offereing also teaches one not to take "all things for gain" (On the Virtues, 95). Of the more than 150 references Philo makes to the sacrifice ($\theta \upsilon \sigma \acute{\iota} \alpha$), a very high percentage spiritualizes the sacrifice, emphasizing the importance of inner preparation necessary to legitimate the sacrifice.

Philo, of course, was hardly alone in this spiritualizing tendency. Jewish martyrological traditions regarded martyrdom as a "perfect sacrifice" or as an "act of expiation" (e.g., 4 Macc. 17:21–22).[88] Qumran texts praised blameless behavior (1 QS 9:5) and the suffering of the community in exile (1 QS 8:3)[89] as sacrificial acts.[90] And the Hellenistic church also found in Jesus' death the supreme sacrifice.[91] Because Paul was a Diaspora Jew sympathetic to the point of view reflected in Philo, his theologizing was a tangle of all of these influences.[92]

Paul's Spiritualization of Text and Tradition

That Paul's understanding of the death of Jesus as an atoning sacrifice was rooted in early gospel tradition he nowhere disputes. In Rom. 3:23–25 Paul speaks of Jesus' death "put forward" as a *hilasterion,* a "sacrifice of atonement," whose blood through faith effects forgiveness of sins. Paul uses this familiar, basic tradition to support the universal embrace of his gospel for Greeks and non-Greeks, Jews and Gentiles. While the vicarious significance of a righteous martyr's death in Jewish martyrological traditions (4 Macc. 17:21–22) may have helped shape the tradition of Jesus' death as sacrifice in the Jewish Christian church, a lingering Pharisaic tendency in Paul to spiritualize the sacrificial cult might have reinforced this messianic understanding of Jesus' death. Its importance for Paul is well illustrated by the archetypal significance it carried for his own behavior ("I die daily"), for his refutation of the charge that his gospel was antinomian (Rom. 6:3), and for his understanding of the vicarious nature of Jesus' death (Rom. 5:6, 8; 14:15; 2 Cor. 5:14, 15, 21; Gal. 1:4; 2:20; 1 Thess. 5:10).[93]

As the heading for the ethical instruction (paraenesis) to follow, one can imagine Rom. 12:1 on the lips of a Paul whose sympathies lay with the Pharisees: "I beseech you, brothers and sisters, through the mercies of God, to present your bodies as a living sacrifice (θυσίαν), holy (ἁγίαν) and well pleasing (εὐάρεστον) to God, which is your reasonable service (or worship, λογικὴν λατρείαν)." The expression "reasonable service" (λογικὴν λατρείαν) doubtless reveals a Hellenistic Jewish provenance,[94] but the admonition to "present your bodies as a living sacrifice (θυσίαν ζῶσαν), holy and acceptable to God," with its emphasis on physicality and holiness, flies in the face of Hellenistic world rejection.[95] Whatever its provenance the sacrificial metaphor here responds to the charge against his law-free gospel that it wittingly or unwittingly encouraged immorality (6:1–7:6).[96]

The priestly allusions in Rom. 15:15–16 are obviously self-referential. Paul admits to having spoken boldly "because of the grace given me by God to be a minister (λειτουργὸν) to the Gentiles in *making a sacrifice as a priest* for the gospel of God (ἱερουργοῦντα τὸ εὐαγγέλιον) in order that the *sacrifice of the Gentiles* may be acceptable, made holy (ἡγιασμένη) by the Holy Spirit" (emphasis added). The description of his apostolic ministry as a priestly, sacrificial act[97] through which the Gentiles are offered up, holy and wellpleasing to God, is a richly metaphorical statement whose background is left unexplored by commentators. Unlike Rom. 12:1 there is no trace of Hellenistic influence here. Posing as a priest, Paul offers the fruits of his apostolic ministry, that is the Gentiles, as a sacrifice, a powerful apocalyptic metaphor echoing Isa. 2:2–4. Just as the Pharisees transposed the command to be a kingdom of priests into a new key, Paul now gathers together the results of his mission to urge on his addressees a believing obedience (see Rom. 15:18) holy and wellpleasing to God as a sacrificial act. Although Paul spiritualizes the cultic language as would any Pharisee, his aim to "win *obedience* from the gentiles" (15:18–19; emphasis added) as an apostle of Christ gives this apocalyptic pronouncement a twist that put him at odds with his Pharisaic peers. By making sacrifice and obedience synonymous and associating them with his priestly ministry, Paul emphasizes the consecration of the Gentiles being brought to completion in the last days.[98] In this context, therefore, we see cultic imagery that still appears to carry vestiges of Paul's earlier Pharisaism even while he places his apostolic mission in an eschatological perspective. We see then from these examples how Paul's spiritualization of the language of the cult reflects his Pharisaic sympathies.[99]

JEWISH VERSIONS OF HOLINESS IN PAUL

To modern (or postmodern) folk for whom the idea of the holy is an act of separation that alienates and estranges, the biblical notion of the Hebrew word *qadosh* may appear as an affectation or an utterly false construction of superstitious minds. To more traditional biblical critics the role that the holy played in Paul's communities may appear as something of an embarrassment, at odds with his theological emphasis on grace.[100] But to priestly circles in ancient Israel, to Qumran covenanters, to Pharisees, to Diaspora Jews, and even to Paul himself, religious piety and the idea of the holy were inseparable.

God as the Source of Holiness

The river of holiness ran wide and deep throughout the traditions of Israel, and all holiness was rooted in and oriented toward the God of Israel, the Holy One, who consecrated. This Holy One, Israel took pains to point out, was totally other, differing from the creature and the creation and from other gods.[101] This meant that God was God and not human; being *totally* other did not mean that God was unknowable but rather that God was unlike the gods of neighboring peoples. The distance between Elohim and Molech, for example, was so chasmic that any who prostituted themselves to Molech were placed under a penalty of death (Lev. 20:5). God's name, integral to the very Godhead itself, was so holy that any profanation of the name was an egregious sin (Lev. 22:2, 32). And any unclean or unholy person who transgressed against the holy space of the Holy One was to be "cut off" from God's presence (Lev. 22:3). This same presumption of the holiness of God also ran through priestly separatist movements like the Qumran community.

The traditional language of the Holiness Code resounded throughout the Qumran scrolls with holiness motifs. The Most High who was so "from before e[ternity]" (1 QH 13:1) was seen as the quintessential "Fountain of *Holiness*" (1 QS 10:12). God's spirit was a "*holy* Spirit" (1 QH 3:34; 1 QS 8:16; 1 QH 9:32; 12:12; 16:2, 3, 7, 12; 17:26); his name was a "[*h*]*oly* Nam[e]" (1 QpH 2:4; CD 20:34; 1 QM 11:3); and his dwelling was a "*holy* abode" (1QH 3:4; 12:2). Times were "*holy* Sabbaths" (CD 3:14) and "days of *holiness*" (1 QS 10:5); reflection was "*holy* thought" (1 QS 11:19); the city was "*holy*" (CD 20:22); laws were "precepts of his *holiness*" (CD 20:30); and the company of heaven was "*holy*" (1 QM 7:6; 10:11; 12:1, 4). And most importantly, the elect community was a "*holy* Congregation" (1 QS 5:20), "the House of *holiness*" (1 QS 8:5–6), "the Purification of the men of *holiness*" (1 QS 8:17), "the men of perfect *holiness*" (1 QS 8:20), and "the *holy* Community" (9:2). The Qumran community believed that God "granted them a share in the lot of the *Holy* Ones [saints or angels] and . . . united their assembly, the Council of the Community, with the Sons of Heaven" (1 QS 11:8; emphasis added in all of the preceding).

This same pattern appears with some consistency in Diaspora Jewish communities. Philo, for example, referred to the holiness of God (Sacr. abe., 101; Som., I, 254; Praem. Poen., 123), of the divine name (Vit. Mos., II, 208), of the cult (Leg. Gai., 278; Leg. All., III, 125), of the Holy of Holies (Mut. Nom., 192), and of the priestly drama (Som., I, 82; II, 34). He also believed the Scriptures were holy (Spec. Leg., III, 119), as were the Sabbath (Spec. Leg., II, 194), the Mosaic Law and divine wisdom (Sacr., 101; Fug., 196; Praem. Poen., 124). As God's people, Israel was seen as holy (Praem. Poen., 123), and by implication the community's behavior must reflect that holy status. As one would expect, Philo's thought also differed in some important ways from the priestly traditions in the way he found in natural law a venue for the holy. What was true for Philo and Qumran was evidently the case also for other forms of Jewish piety of the day.

The Ethical Imperative of Holiness

Although in a near primal sense Yahweh was seen as the source of and model for the holiness emphasized in the many Judaisms of Paul's day, that holiness served important ethical and ordering functions as well. No Jew of Paul's day would have been unaware of the command of the priestly code: "You shall be holy; for I the Lord your God am holy" (Lev. 19:2; 20:7–8, 26; 21:6, 8), a command that obligated Israel to separate itself through cult and behavior from the profane world. This command encouraged no vague mystical identification with the Holy One though it certainly possessed mystical elements. It was a call to observe concrete statutes and ordinances (20:8–27) that attached special opprobrium to sexual acts such as incest, temple prostitution, sodomy, homosexuality, and sexual intercourse with a woman "in her impurity" (Lev. 18:6–20:21), that protected the sanctity of the holy place and the cult (Lev. 12–26), that condemned occult wizards and mediums (20:27), that prescribed love for and just dealings with one's neighbors (Lev. 19:11–18; 25:13–17), and that offered rubrics concerning festivals and sacrifices for the priesthood (Lev. 21:1–25:12). The people must respect and not desecrate sacred space, must revere and not profane the holy name, must worship the Holy One alone and not go "awhoring" after other gods, and must abide by the priestly code that stood "like signs . . . at every turn [and] inspired meditation on the oneness, purity and completeness of God"[102] and imposed order upon social and cultural chaos. And as Zimmerli has noted, the exhortation to an *Imitatio Dei* ("be holy as I am holy") hardly appeared as an arrogant act of human pretension. Only Yahweh, the Jewish community was convinced, had the power to separate Israel from all other peoples, and even the human distinction made between the holy and the profane had its genesis in God. Thus human holiness seen as only a shadow of the holiness of the Holy One,[103] was viewed as a *theo*logical act.

At Qumran, likewise, the ethical concern with holiness was linked to reverence for the Holy One and was intensified by a feverish apocalypticism. By its fervent commitment to law observance the priestly community readied itself for God's imminent visitation, when the temple would be cleansed of its pollution and restored to holiness.

Like any intellectual who had drunk deeply from the Hellenistic fountain, Philo sacralized important aspects of that tradition, attributing holy status to reason, natural law, cosmic order, and the individual soul which he called God's temple (Som., I, 149). Philo's social situation was much more complex than that of either Qumran or the community of the Levitical code. Because Philo lived within a powerful Hellenistic culture, the whole process of boundary setting, boundary maintenance, and the establishment of a protocol for interaction with the dominant culture was much more difficult. And yet the evidence suggests that his struggle against alienation was successful. The Jewish community was threatened by two forms of alienation—its members could be separated from the majority culture by retreat into the minority community, or they could become separated from the minority culture through absorption into the majority culture.[104] Philo's view of the holy reflects the delicate balance he was able to maintain, which was achieved through a skillful law interpretation reflecting deep ethical convictions.

Holiness and Order

The human imperative linked to God's holiness is a truism, but the way holiness served as a bulwark against chaos is often overlooked. In this respect the heavenly epiphany described in Isa. 6 is archetypal. In the vision Isaiah was transported into the heavenly temple, was confronted by the "glory" of God and surrounded by the antiphonal singing of the heavenly choir, "holy, holy, holy," and felt a dread so profound that he was overwhelmed not only by his own uncleanness but also by that of his people. Purged by fire from the heavenly altar, he heard and heeded the call to serve as a divine messenger to a deaf and hard-hearted people (Isa. 6:3–13). Isaiah's reflection on the "Holy One of Israel" (Isa. 12:6; 17:1; 29:19), however, was set in a context of terrifying political and social instability. The vision came "In the year that king Uzziah died" (6:1), a death that unleashed a chain of events that threatened to engulf Judah in chaos. The holy, or more appropriately, the Holy One, in Isaiah's view offered the only avenue to order and peace in that dark moment.

Hosea, a contemporary of Isaiah, was a prophet to Israel under even more desperate conditions. An awesome Assyrian threat, as well as competition from an aggressive, popular, compelling Canaanite religion, posed a formidable challenge. Hosea reports the conflict in Yahweh's heart between anger that wants to reject and love that will not let Israel go. The sign that love won out came in Elohim's plaintive cry: "How can I give you up, O Ephraim? How can I hand you over, O Israel? . . . I will not execute my fierce anger; I will not again destroy Ephraim; for I am God [El] and no mortal, the *Holy One* in your midst, and I will not come in wrath" (11:8–9, emphasis added). Here a barricade was erected against a "godforsakenness" synonymous with annihilation and death.

As striking as are these references, it is the Holiness Code itself (Lev. 17–26) that most strongly emphasizes Yahweh's holiness. The word *qadosh* appears over eighty times in these ten chapters, and this holiness language informed both the understanding of God and the ethical imperative of the priestly writing.[105] As scholars have long noted, the final redaction of the Holiness Code, though rooted in ancient traditions, is a response to the historical catastrophe associated with the Babylonian invasion. The Holiness Code makes no effort to interpret the meaning of holiness, but it does offer a window on the unspeakable horror the people faced as they were devastated by the sword, pestilence, starvation, destruction of holy places, and deportation (Lev. 26:25–33). Memories linger there that are almost too painful for words: corpses stacked like cordwood in the cities; hunger so desperate that people resorted to cannibalism, devouring their sons and daughters (Lev. 26:29–30); once beautiful, ordered cities reduced to rubble (Lev. 16:31). The editors of the code understood this devastation as punishment for sin and superimposed another memory on the haunting recollections. Into a litany of punishments for iniquity the priestly writers inserted the statement: "then will I remember my covenant with Jacob, I will remember also my covenant with Isaac and also my covenant with Abraham, and I will remember the land" (Lev. 26:42). Their conclusion of the code is dramatic: "Yet for all that, when they are in the land of their enemies, I will not spurn them, or abhor them so as to destroy them utterly and break my covenant with them; *for I am the Lord their God* . . ." (Lev. 26:44, emphasis added). This God they addressed as the Holy One who required holiness (Lev. 20:26). That covenant with the Holy One governed the way Israel ordered its world in upheaval, its code in times of *anomia,* and, as we see here, its historical memory when that memory seemed discredited. This relationship with the Holy One and the imperative linked with it to "be holy, for I the Lord your God am holy" (NRSV, Lev. 19:2) separated Israel from those worshiping other gods and from Israelites compromising their covenant religion. In practical terms total isolation was never possible, and interaction with other peoples was inevitable. But, when assimilation threatened, representatives of the priestly tradition expressed a burning preoccupation with holiness (*qadosh*) that reinforced the distinction between holy and unholy, pure and impure, and sacred and profane.

After the pact was recalled, its imperative was articulated. That pact with the Holy One carried obligations to separate oneself through cult and behavior from the profane world. Lev. 20:26 aptly summarizes that recurring theme: "You shall be holy to me; for I the Lord am holy, and I have *separated you from other peoples* to be mine" (emphasis added; see also 21:8, 23b). This segregation, hardly simplistic and never total, left room for the "stranger in your midst" or the "alien" and was impossible to enforce totally, even when the people were not under the heel of a foreign oppressor. And when the people were under the conqueror's boot experiencing deprivation, humiliation, despair, and death, they were not powerless. The distinctions they drew between themselves and their oppressors offered protection. Through an emphasis on holiness they reinforced an identity that brought a system of the absurd into question.

Paul and Holiness

The source of Paul's emphasis on holiness was his Jewish religion, yet this tradition too was revalued in light of his messianism. Like the Pharisaism he was partial to, the Diaspora Judaism that nurtured him in his youth, and the apocalyptic Judaism that marked him for life, Paul viewed God as the source of holiness (Rom. 1:7; 1 Cor. 1:2). Now present in Spirit, this God was the author of the consecration (ἁγιάσαι) of believers and their advocate in the final judgment, keeping their souls, spirits, and bodies "blameless" (ἀμέμπτως) at Jesus' *parousia* (1 Thess. 5:23). God's eschatological presence and power were *Holy* Spirit (1 Cor. 6:19; 3:17; 12:3; 2 Cor. 13:13; Rom. 5:5; 8:27; 9:1; 14:17; 15:13, 16, 19; 1 Thess. 1:5; 4:8), making believers *holy* at baptism (1 Cor. 1:2; 6:11), inspiring believers (1 Cor. 6:19), interceding with their spirit "with sighs too deep for words" (Rom. 8:26), and bearing fruit in them (e.g., Gal. 5:22) for holiness.[106]

Paul followed a well-marked trail in his association of deity and identity. His mode of address presumed a community of "holy ones" that in some sense knew what it was and what it was for. Note that in the salutations of Philippians, 1 and 2 Corinthians, and Romans Paul addressed the church as "holy ones," or "saints" (ἅγιοι). In 1 Thessalonians he grouped "the elect" (1:4) or those who are "in God" (1:1) with the "saints" who will soon join at the *parousia* (3:13). He praised Philemon for refreshing "the hearts of the holy ones" (my trans., 7). And, in a sweeping gesture, he referred in 1 Corinthians to all *ekklesiai* without exception as "the churches of the saints," or "assemblies of the holy ones" (my trans., 1 Cor. 14:33).

In 1 Corinthians Paul exploited the logic of the connection between holy God and holy people to urge all to be of a common mind for the sake of the common good. The logic of the temple metaphor was rooted in his Pharisaic legacy: God is holy. God dwells in the temple. Therefore, the temple is holy. By comparison, the church or assembly is the temple, and since the temple is holy, the assembly is holy. This logic led Paul to ask rhetorically: "You know, don't you, that you all are God's temple and that God's Spirit dwells among you all? If anyone destroys God's temple, God will destroy that one. For God's temple is holy, and you are that temple" (my trans., 1 Cor. 3:16–17) Although the Qumran community employed the temple metaphor in the same self-referential way, Paul's manipulation of the metaphor as an egalitarian referent was distinctive. He made the plural "you all" refer to all of his addressees as holy rather than to a priestly, conventicle community as was the case among the priests at Qumran *and* Jerusalem. Moreover, the metaphor in Paul's hands has a sharp polemical thrust threatening the factious with eschatological destruction. Such a solemn warning would have shocked those who had not made the connection between their holy status as charismatics and the accompanying corporate responsibility. Paul did not use the holiness emphasis that figures so prominently in this letter to divide insiders from outsiders. Rather, through the holiness language Paul admonished the Corinthians to "be what they are," the elect of God (1:24), "called to be saints," "made holy in Christ Jesus" (my trans., 1:2). While Paul was aware of the "outsiders" (14:20–25) as potential converts, no threat from them darkened the horizon of the Corinthians. Much of the instruction on holiness in 1 Corinthians, therefore, aimed to help the addressees better understand who they were, to recall them to features of their identity in danger of being lost or so fatefully compromised that the future of the church was clouded.[107]

Reflecting his Jewish tradition Paul extended the chain of holiness from holy God and holy people to holy acts. God's imperative to believers, he noted, is "to *be holy* ones" (my trans., Rom. 1:6–7; 1 Cor. 1:2), through Christ who brings sanctification:[108] "He [God] is the source of your (pl.) life in Christ Jesus, who became for us wisdom from God, and righteousness and sanctification (ἁγιασμὸς)" (1 Cor. 1:30).[109]

Paul's instructions on the life of holiness, however, were situational and specific. For example, Romans reveals Paul's sensitivity to the charge that his law-free gospel of grace encouraged immorality. In response he linked the life in Christ to the life of holiness. He contrasted the people's former life when they were "slaves of impurity (ἀκαθαρσία) and lawlessness (ἀνομια) on top of lawlessness" with their life in Christ when they are to be "slaves to righteousness for holiness (ἁγιασμόν)" (my trans., 6:19). He juxtaposed the slavery to sin with slavery to God in whose service they are to produce fruit "for holiness (ἁγιασμόν)" (my trans., 6:22). Holiness for Paul, as for the priestly tradition, had a definitive ethical dimension that was no mere private virtue but was part and parcel of the church's identity (cf. 1 Cor. 5:1–8) as "holy ones."

A further illustration of this point is seen in 1 Thess. 3:11–13; 4:1–8, where Paul invoked divine authority for this emphasis on holiness. While Paul nowhere cited the Holy Scriptures in 1 Thessalonians, his exhortation to holiness was more than a distant echo of the Levitical command to "be holy as I am holy." In 3:11–13 he offered a theological rationale for the paraenesis of 4:1–8. Giving his exhortation to holiness a christological as well as an eschatological basis, he prayed that the "Lord Jesus" would generate holiness in his addressees: "may he so strengthen your hearts in holiness (ἁγιωσύνη) that you may be blameless (ἀμέμπτους) before our God and Father at the coming of our Lord Jesus with all his holy ones (ἁγίων)" (my trans., 3:13). Paul then defined this holiness by contrasting it with the behavior of the out-siders: "For this is the will of God, your holiness (ὁ ἁγιασμὸς) that you abstain from immorality (πορνείας)" (4:3). Then follow two paraenetic con-trasts: "that each of you know how to take a wife [or vessel] for himself in holiness and honor (ἁγιασμῷ καὶ τιμῇ) *not* in passionate desire (πάθει ἐπιθυμίας) like the *ethne* who do *not* know God" (my trans., 4:4–5; emphasis added).[110] In 4:7 comes his second contrast: "For God did *not* call us to impu-rity (ἀκαθαρσίᾳ) *but* in holiness (my trans., ἁγιασμῷ)" (emphasis added). He thus marked off the believers from the Gentiles, holiness from passion and desire, and purity from uncleanness, and this holiness he saw as one of the distinctive marks of the elect (1:4). On the positive side Paul associated these "holy ones" with the angelic host or God's "holy ones" (3:13) that in the end will join the Lord Jesus. This imaginative link to that other world was espe-cially apposite for a community whose experience of death had appeared to sever irrevocably the intimate ties to the believing community, and it offered consolation to those pushed toward hopelessness by the deaths of believers who had believed they would survive to see Jesus' victorious return. Paul's stress on the union of the saints with the deceased believers and holy angels (3:13) offered an antidote to despair, but it did more. It provided an ultimate source of meaning, consolation and guidance in the face of persecution and rejection (1:6; 2:14 if genuine; 5:14–15).

Limited space prohibits a fuller discussion of this neglected feature of Paul's theological grammar, but in chapter 5 we shall explore the way Paul linked holiness and celibacy in a manner reminiscent of Qumran.[111] We have already noted how Paul spiritualized the sacrifice to make it deal with ethical concerns of everyday life, thus placing the Roman Christians in the inner sanctum of holiness (12:1–2). Our discussion risks leaving the erroneous im-pression that Paul was more fastidious about the laws of purity than in fact he was. He did agree in principle with the Corinthians, for example, that eating meat offered to other gods was morally permissible since those gods do not really exist, but in deference to and genuine concern for the less sophisticated sister or brother, he thought it better to avoid altogether the meat offered to "idols" (1 Cor. 8:1–13). He ate with Gentiles and publicly condemned Peter's hypocrisy, so he says, for first joining Gentiles at their table and then drawing back under threat of criticism from "those from James" (Gal. 2:11–14).[112] To those "outside the law" Paul stated: "I became as one outside the law (though I am not free from God's law but am under Christ's law) so that I might win those outside the law" (1 Cor. 9:21). He stated his conviction in Rom. 14:14 that "in the Lord Jesus that nothing is unclean in itself" and in 14:20 that "Everything is indeed clean."

We see, therefore, that Paul's casual attitude toward the laws of purity, his free association with non-Jews, his commitment to Messiah Jesus, and his conviction that God's final struggle was already under way to reclaim the world differed from Pharisaic tradition. But, in other ways Paul continued to be influenced by Pharisaism. While nothing requires a Pharisaic origin for his view of holiness, Pharisaism apparently influenced Paul's understanding of holiness for the rest of his life. His view of the resurrection of God's righteous at the end of history, his emphasis on human freedom and responsibility, his tendency to spiritualize priestly tradition, and the role he gives to holiness in everyday life all suggest a Pharisaic home ground. So, even if Paul's messianism led him to compromise and reinterpret his Pharisaic sympathies, to suggest that Paul emphatically and decisively rejected all aspects of Pharisaism is too extreme. In light of the fact that many of Paul's instincts, inclinations, and basic presuppositions remained Pharisaic, it would be more correct to say that Paul reevaluated those traditions in light of the eschatological significance of Jesus' cross and resurrection than to say that he rejected Pharisaism outright.[113] While his conviction that the advent of the last days had been inaugurated in Messiah Jesus did lead to a revaluation of his Jewish heritage, that fresh appraisal sparked no effort by Paul to purge his thought of every vestige of Pharisaic influence, for even if Paul were not literally a Pharisee, he shared the religious world of Pharisaism in some very important ways, and many of those views remained to shape his messianism.

Certainly in Paul's letters one sees vestiges of a Jewish apocalypticism, and the precise lineage of that mythology also is unclear. It may have drawn some inspiration and substance from Pharisaism, some from the Essenes, some from other Jewish groups who found apocalyptic symbols useful and comforting, but there is simply no way to tell. We do know that apocalyptic communities flourished from the time of Daniel (168–65 BCE) until well into the second century. Qumran we know best, but certainly other communities combined to leave behind a varied apocalyptic legacy. While it is impossible to locate the precise source of Paul's apocalypticism, it was undeniably Jewish. It bequeathed to him a rich vocabulary and a paradigm that easily accommodated the messianism he came to embrace. In chapter 4 we shall note Paul's energetic and creative intellectual appropriation of that apocalyptic mythology. A linkage between apocalyptic expectation and holiness was common, and it should not be surprising that this linkage also occurs in Paul.

PERSECUTOR OF THE CHURCH

In Acts 9:1 Paul appears as a bitter enemy of the church fulminating "threats and murder against the disciples of the Lord" (RSV). As a young man he stood by as an approving official at whose feet the mob laid its garments before stoning the saintly Stephen (Acts 7:58). Although complicit in this grisly deed through his passivity, he would soon actively and brutally repress followers of "the Way" by breaking into houses to drag men and *women* off to prison without due process (Acts 8:3; emphasis added). In the end, Luke has Paul summarize this ghastly chapter of his life as follows:

> I not only shut up many of the saints in prison, by authority from
> the chief priests, but when they were put to death I cast my vote
> against them. And I punished them often in all the synagogues
> and tried to make them blaspheme; and in raging fury against
> them, I persecuted them even to foreign cities. (RSV, 26:10–11)

This picture sketched by Luke simply cannot be reconciled with Paul's own account or with the historical situation of Paul's time. Paul remarks in Gal. 1:13: "You have heard, no doubt, of my earlier life in Judaism. I was violently persecuting the church of God and was trying to destroy it." This autobiographical statement recalls a dark chapter in Paul's life. With painful regret, he confesses his unworthiness of the Christophany he received "Last of all": "For I am the least of the apostles, unfit to be called an apostle, because I persecuted the church of God" (1 Cor. 15:9). He recalls his achievements as a Pharisee when he was "as to zeal, a persecutor of the church" (Phil. 3:6). From a distance of over two decades he looks back on his persecution of the church and contrasts that vicious episode with the church's recent astonishment at the change that Christ had effected in him: "The one who formerly was persecuting us is now proclaiming the faith he once tried to destroy" (Gal. 1:23). Except for the persecution itself, Paul's remarks in the letters have little in common with the Lucan account in Acts.

In spite of these dual accounts, we know distressingly little about Paul's persecution of the church. Its causes, its nature, its victims, or even its location are largely hidden from us. In spite of its fuller narrative account, Acts is of little help to us since its use of Paul's persecution as a foil against which to display his missionary activity to advantage betrays a profound Lucan bias. Yet, the letters also are inadequate, for they leave aching voids in our knowledge of this episode in Paul's life. Given these gaps it is no wonder that scholars offer no consensus on the nature of and motivations for Paul's persecution of the church.

According to Bultmann Paul persecuted Hellenistic Christianity "because he could not help seeing it as an attack on the law."[114] Arland Hultgren thinks Paul's crusade sought to silence the confession of the church in Judaea of Jesus as Messiah "as a form of national apostasy"[115] Hengel believes that Paul persecuted Hellenistic Jewish Christians because of their opposition to the temple and rejection of Torah, and their active proclamation as Messiah of "an accused deceiver who had led people astray."[116] Douglas Hare argues the persecution was driven by social and political forces manifested in the elevation of Christ over Torah, temple, and Holy City, the "central symbols of Jewish solidarity."[117] Jack Sanders holds that missionizing by messianist deviants prompted a brutal response from the Jewish majority.[118] Paula Fredriksen is convinced that the proclamation of Jesus as Messiah was so politically dangerous that the fear of savage Roman reprisals causing irreparable harm moved Jews like Paul to attempt to silence messianists in his "home" synagogue in Damascus.[119]

Because the issue is so complex and our information so scanty it is impossible to offer a fully satisfying explanation. It is easier to say what the persecution was not than what it was. For example, the cause was neither solely theological nor solely political. In this setting theological and political issues were so intertwined that they could not be untangled. Social and political issues were informed by a theological rationale, and theological convictions had a social and a political dimension. To confess Jesus as Messiah in that setting was inevitably both a theological and a political statement. To be sure, a Roman reprisal might be driven by political considerations alone, but from the Jewish side the motives for the persecution were probably mixed. Paul himself states that the churches in Judaea report that he once tried to destroy "the faith" (Gal. 1:23), which suggests that theological issues were at stake. But, as Jack Sanders notes, in response to severe "economic, political and military pressure," Paul and other like-minded Jews "struck out at the deviant Christians in order to preserve [their] boundaries, [their] self-identity as a culture; for these Christians were eroding those boundaries just at the time when gentiles were threatening to destroy them."[120] Both may be correct, for social and theological concerns almost always intersect.

Paul's persecution of messianists did not include capital punishment. The description in Acts that Paul engaged in murderous persecution of followers of "the Way," pursuing men and women under the authority of the high priest and council (22:5) to return them bound to Jerusalem for punishment, and then voted for the death penalty (Acts 22:4) is unhistorical. Luke's exaggeration of Paul's brutality only highlights the more his apostolic ministry. The reasons for this judgment are compelling. Neither the high priest nor the Sanhedrin had the authority to administer capital punishment in Paul's lifetime.[121] Hultgren correctly notes that "Paul does not understand persecution as a procedure which ends in the death of the victim."[122] Paul, he says, persecuted the church "to the utmost" (καθ᾽ ὑπερβολὴν), not "violently" as the RSV and NRSV have it. *Kath' hyperbolen* then refers not to the intensity of the persecution but to the intensity of Paul's zeal (as in Phil. 3:6).[123] The synagogue could prescribe flogging ("forty lashes less one"), and in rare instances mob action might lead to a stoning (2 Cor. 11:25), but capital punishment was the sole preserve of the Roman occupying power.

Paul harassed only Jewish believers, not Gentiles. Attacks on Gentiles by a Jewish zealot or attempts to haul them before a panel of synagogue officials would have invited savage reprisals from the civil authorities. Gentile messianists could be and were persecuted by other Gentiles (1 Thess. 1:6; 3:3, 8) and Jewish messianists by Jews (if 1 Thess. 2:14–16 is authentic), but the Romans recognized the danger of intraethnic rivalries and responded to them swiftly and decisively.

Paul did not confine his persecution of the church to its Hellenistic Jewish wing because he believed the church was offering salvation outside the law. This popular view follows from the identification of Stephen in Acts as a Hellenist and may leave the impression that Paul's presence at his stoning suggests he targeted Hellenistic Jewish followers of Jesus (6:1–15) in Judaea. But, as Hill has shown, the identification of the Hellenists as a separate group is a creation of Luke.[124] There is no evidence that Hellenistic Jewish messianists repudiated Torah. Rather they would have seen the belief in Jesus as Messiah as being fully compatible with Torah. As Hultgren correctly observes, according to the Stephen of Acts, "It is not he, but his opponents, who have been untrue to the law."[125] If that is so, then we must assume that all Jews devoted to Jesus were potential targets of episodic and localized persecution led by figures like Paul.

Paul's persecution of messianists was not for admitting Gentile males into the church without requiring circumcision, for he would have known that the synagogue welcomed gentile "god-fearers" without demanding circumcision as a condition for attending the assembly. (Note the Ethiopian eunuch who comes up to Jerusalem to worship before being circumcised or baptized! [Acts 8:27].) God-fearers were embraced by the synagogue, and many remained active in the congregation, surrendering their worship of idols, giving their children Jewish names, receiving instruction in Torah, observing Jewish Sabbaths and holy days, and even serving as generous patrons *without converting and receiving circumcision.*[126] In Fredriksen's words, "Gentiles within Paul's own synagogue could attend services without receiving circumcision; why then should Paul and his community persecute an internal subgroup for following exactly the same practice?"[127]

If a male wanted to become a Jewish convert then circumcision would have been required, but if messianist Gentiles had no desire to become proselytes to Judaism, there would have been no absolute requirement of circumcision and no persecution for retaining a god-fearer status even as a messianist. There were efforts in churches in Galatia and Philippi, however, to make circumcision of males a *condition* of *belonging* to the eschatological people of God. That requirement was driven by the conviction that conversion to Judaism was a prerequisite for participation in the Messianic Age, and by questions about the adequacy of the gospel, but was quite different. The pressure in Galatia and Philippi was exerted by other messianists whereas the persecution by Paul occured before his apostolic call.

Paul's persecution of messianists was not because they had spoken out against the temple. While the temple was the most important religious symbol of Paul's day, it was not immune to criticism. Jesus' criticism of the temple cult contributed in part to his execution. The condemnation of the temple cult by the Teacher of Righteousness at Qumran led to his brutal assassination. But would Paul, who was partial to a Pharisaism with a history of bitter conflict with Sadducees who were temple functionaries, accept a commission as an enforcer to protect the sanctity of the temple? That is difficult to imagine.[128] Early messianist criticism of the temple establishment may have met a violent priestly response, and that would explain some of the persecution, but it would not explain the involvement of Paul.

Then, what can we say about the cause and nature of the persecution? One cannot rule out entirely Fredriksen's view that the fear of Roman retaliation played a role in Paul's repression of messianists. Everyone in occupied territories knew that Roman reprisals for dangerous or apparent seditious activity could be severe and indiscriminate, recoiling on the heads of the innocent as well as those of the guilty. Military action could inflict both immense physical suffering and also profound economic hardship. So, pressure on compatriots to avoid provocative behavior was severe.

But, there were religious issues involved as well. Hultgren may be correct that Paul's persecution was of the *church and its leaders* because of a "faith" that sounded dangerous in an explosive environment.[129] It is hardly clear, however, that Paul opposed this messianist movement because it was a "national apostasy."[130] But, if Hultgren is correct, the slander, insults, afflictions, and physical abuse that Paul suffered may reflect the persecution he also administered. Paul speaks of five times receiving "forty lashes less one." He recalls "countless beatings" and "imprisonments" (2 Cor. 11:23–24). Lashings and imprisonments were punishments meted out by legitimate juridical processes in the synagogue, and it is conceivable that in unusual circumstances Paul might have hauled Jewish messianist leaders or influential Jewish members of churches before the synagogue judges or may have encouraged synagogues to move against the messianists in their midst to discipline them.[131] He might also have provoked ugly confrontations with small house assemblies, ridiculing their faith and attacking them for proclaiming a gospel that was politically dangerous and that might provoke a Roman intervention that threatened the very existence of the people of Israel. Thus his persecution of the church would have been both religious and political, both physical and verbal, but in no case did it involve torture unto death.

SUMMARY

From the preceding discussion we have learned that Paul grew up in a strongly hellenized environment, probably Tarsus, and he was greatly influenced by that environment. His language, method of argumentation, Scriptures, anthropology, and literary style all reflect the Hellenistic influence of a vibrant, cosmopolitan setting. Paul's urban upbringing influenced him throughout his life and even informed his mission to the Gentiles. He was also schooled in Jewish traditions and the content and interpretation of the Septuagint, and he came from a devout home. It is doubtful that he was a citizen of either Rome or Tarsus, but it is likely that he was a member of a Jewish *politeuma* or association that ran its own affairs, made and enforced its own civil law, and celebrated festivals together—acts that reinforced a strong sense of Jewish identity.

As a member of the working class he learned a skill from his father that he practiced for most of his adult life. Later he used this skill to support his mission and to distinguish himself from Sophists and Jewish Christian missionaries who preached or taught for profit. While it is unlikely that Paul studied under the great Pharisee Gamaliel in Jerusalem, his early preference for and zeal for the Pharisaic traditions are clear. While Paul nowhere appeals to his status as a Pharisee after his apostolic call, his letters show traces of his Pharisaic legacy—for example, his view of what was scriptural, his belief in the resurrection and future judgment, his linkage of divine predestination and human responsibility, his spiritualization of the Levitical code and sacrificial cult, his copious use of holiness language and metaphor, and conceivably his apocalyptic worldview. In light of his experience of Messiah Jesus, he radically revalued much of that Pharisaic legacy concerning the laws of purity, Torah, and the role of the Gentiles in the Messianic Age. These departures placed Paul at odds with most of his Pharisaic peers. As one partial to Pharisaism before his call to be an apostle, Paul was a vigorous opponent of messianists and actively persecuted them for a complex mix of reasons. And it was in the midst of this fanatical persecution that an epiphany of Christ changed Paul's direction and the course of human history forever.

CHAPTER TWO

The Apostle to the Gentiles

The move from persecutor of the church to apostle of Christ was for Paul so dramatic that many over the centuries have spoken of it as a conversion. In their view Paul was converted on the road to Damascus from Pharisaism to Christianity (Acts 9:1–9; 22:6–11; 26:12–18) and abandoned his Judaism for a Christian gospel that offered salvation by grace rather than by law observance. In this view, Paul divided his life into two parts—one before his conversion, when he was so frustrated by his inability to observe every detail of the law that he suffered under an unbearable burden of guilt, and the other after his conversion, when he gained release from this bondage to sin and the law. The Jewish phase is depicted as joyless, the Christian phase as joyful. In the Jewish phase Paul was under bondage to the law and sin; in the Christian phase he was liberated from the powers of sin and death by Christ. In the Jewish phase Paul was under the stern taskmaster God; in the Christian phase he was in the service of the God of grace. In support of this periodization scholars have noted such passages as Phil. 3:8, where Paul refers to his considerable achievements under the law as "dung," and Rom. 3:21, where he refers to righteousness "apart from Law." They contrasted Rom. 7 as an autobiographical description of Paul's former life under the law—"I was once alive apart from the law, but when the commandment came, sin revived and I died" (7:9)—with Rom. 8 with its praise of life in the spirit and in the "love of Christ" (8:35, 37). This conversion of the wretched Paul from the body of death (7:24) to a life in Christ as his apostle emphasized the discontinuity between Judaism and Christianity in the sharpest possible terms, and the portrait of Judaism that was painted was the total opposite of Paul's new religion.

Increasingly, however, scholars have come to question this description as a grotesque caricature of Judaism and a parody of what Paul himself says about his continuing life as a Jew. They point out that nowhere does Paul suggest that he found it impossible to observe the law; Phil. 3:6 suggests to the contrary that he was "under the law blameless." They note that there is not a single line in Paul referring to an intolerable burden of guilt that he suffered under the law. Furthermore, they call attention to the Qumran texts where law and grace were hardly the polar opposites that Pauline exegetes have claimed. Moreover, they point out that Paul's allusion to his considerable achievements in law observance as "dung" (Phil. 3:8) was less a repudiation of his Jewish observance than a revaluation of it in light of Christ. They observe that the revaluation sounds quite different when viewed as a polemic against competing rival Jewish Christian missionaries. At points in his letters, they observe, Paul expresses a warm appreciation of his Jewish heritage (e.g., Rom. 9:4–5) and continues to the end of his correspondence to affirm his Jewishness (Rom. 11:1). In his appeal to the prophets and to Abraham, they note, Paul not only believed that this new life in Christ had its genesis in Israel but that it would embrace Israel at the end of history (Rom. 11:26–36). At the very least, they note, the complete rupture between Judaism and Christianity once attributed to Paul is historically false. While tensions existed between Paul and his Jewish peers, to say that Paul rejected Judaism in favor of Christianity is going too far.

Strictly speaking, Paul's own reference to his radical turn from persecutor of the church to apostle of Christ appears in Gal. 1:15–16 as a "call" rather than a conversion. Paul's own account of his call resonates to statements made by Jeremiah and Isaiah: "When it pleased God who separated me from my mother's womb and *called me* by his grace to reveal his son in me so that I might proclaim him among the gentiles" (Gal. 1:14–15; emphasis added). The servant song of Isa. 49 opens with the words "The Lord called me from the womb" (ἐκ κοιλίας μητρός μου ἐκάλεσεν τὸ ὄνομά μου, LXX, v. 1), and closes with the commission to the Gentiles (49:6): "I will give you as a light to the gentiles" (ἐθνῶν, LXX). Jer. 1:4–5 also refers to being chosen before he was born for a mission to the Gentiles:

> Now the word of the Lord came to me saying, "Before I formed you in the womb I knew you, and before you were born I consecrated you; I appointed you a prophet to the gentiles." (my trans.)

A generation ago, Munck persuasively argued that Paul's reference here to separation from his mother's womb and his commission to "proclaim him [God's son] to the gentiles" was deliberately used by Paul, "giving him a place in the history of salvation in line with those Old Testament figures."[1] If viewed in this way, neither Acts (9:1–19; 22:4–16; 26:9–19) nor Paul's own autobiographical remarks (Gal. 1:11–17) reports a change of religion as our word *conversion* suggests but rather a divine mission similar to that of the prophets.[2]

If this argument is sound, it is misleading to speak of Paul as a convert or apostate from Judaism. His language, his Scriptures, his holy symbols, and his institutions were and remained Jewish, and his personal reflections suggest a continuing attachment. Certainly there were tensions between Paul and his Jewish peers, but those were tensions that inevitably came from being a liminal or marginal figure. They were intra-, not extramural. In sum, Paul was born a Jew, lived as a Jew, and in all likelihood died as a Jew. When he became an apostle of Christ, as his letters tell us, he continued to see himself as a Jew and to think of his apocalyptic gospel in Jewish terms. After his Christophany he did make a radical turn from persecuting the church to being its advocate as an apostle of Christ. It is to that aspect of his life that we now turn.

THE GENESIS OF THE USE OF *APOSTLE* IN THE EARLY CHURCH

The origin and meaning of the term *apostle* as Paul came to use it are difficult to discern. A century ago Erich Haupt groaned that the question of the genesis of the apostolate "is one of the most intricate and difficult problems of New Testament Scholarship."[3] And more recently Walther Schmithals agreed, noting that the discussion can be carried forward only with either new sources or new ideas, neither of which "are however . . . to be expected."[4] But, whether the Greek term *apostolos* came from the Hebrew *schaliach* (Rengstorf),[5] or from secular Greek,[6] or from popular Hellenistic religion[7] or from the Hellenistic church (Schneemelcher),[8] or from Syriac Gnosticism (Schmithals),[9] or from a blend of Judaism and Syrian Gnosticism (Betz),[10] in the final analysis the challenges to Paul's apostleship and gospel may have done as much to shape his understanding of this gift (charism) as did the background of the term. The damaging criticisms of scholars of each of the previously mentioned theories leave the genesis of the term *apostle* "shrouded in mystery"[11] and leave open the possibility that the term *apostle* may have had multiple sources. Paul's letters offer us the earliest record of its use in the church yet Paul nowhere claims to have been the *first* Apostle to the Gentiles so clearly the term was already in use in the church at the time of Paul's call.[12] Paul admits to standing at the end of a line of persons—some of whom were apostles—receiving epiphanies of the resurrected Lord: "Last of all," he says, "as to one untimely born, he appeared also to me" (1 Cor. 15:8). Thus, there was a gentile mission before Paul, and there were apostles of Christ active in it.

Although Paul seemed aware of his status as an apostle from the beginning, (1 Thess. 2. 7), his understanding of that office developed over time. When facing vigorous challenges, typically he alluded to his apostleship in the epistolary prescript, telegraphing to the readers his right to the title (Gal.

1:1; 1 Cor. 1:1; 2 Cor. 1:1; Rom. 1:1). In the autobiographical section of his first letter (1 Thess. 2:1–20), Paul recalled painful opposition from unidentified outsiders in Thessalonica (2:2–3, 5–6). The sharp, unflattering contrasts Paul drew in 2:3–6 of his philosophical rival help define his own apostolic image: "For our appeal," Paul says, "does *not* (οὐκ) spring from *deceit* (πλάνη), *neither* (οὐδὲ) out of *impure motives* (ἀκαθαρσίας), *neither* (οὐδὲ) from *trickery* (δολῳ), but just as we have been approved by God to be entrusted with the gospel, thus we speak, *not* to *please mortals* (ἀνθρώποις ἀρέσκοντες), but to please God who tests our hearts. As you know and as God is our witness, we *neither* (οὔτε) came with *flattering words* (λόγῳ κολακείας), as you know, *nor* (οὔτε) with a *pretext for greed* (προφάσει πλεονεξίας), as God is witness, *neither* (οὔτε) seeking *human glory* (ἀνθρώπων δόξαν), *nor* (οὔτε) [praise] *from you or from others*" (my trans., emphasis added). By further contrast Paul notes that "as apostles of Christ" (2:7) they could have made demands that they chose not to make, and he invoked metaphors of unselfish giving—the nursing mother giving of her very self (2:7) and the loving father urging and encouraging his children (2:11–12). He recalled his example and that of his colleagues: how they toiled night and day to spare others the burden of their upkeep (2:9) and how, as God knows, they behaved in a "holy and righteous and blameless" (RSV) manner toward the believers in Thessalonica (2:10). So, although there were challenges from teaching philosophers and there was the danger that a failure of nerve would cause believers to backslide, Paul's apostleship faced no frontal challenge in Thessalonica from rival missionaries, and thus there was no need to think through its essential character. Nevertheless, there do appear here in embryonic form signs of an apostolic ministry. Later, however, in the face of opposition in the Galatian and Corinthian churches Paul would self-consciously reflect on the validity and traits of his apostolic claim. As we consider Paul's view of his apostleship, then, a consideration of the context becomes crucial.

PAUL'S DEFENSE OF HIS APOSTLESHIP IN GALATIANS

In Galatians Paul faced a fierce challenge to his gospel and apostleship (mounted by Judaizing believers). While Paul recognized Judaizing opponents elsewhere (Phil. 3:2, 18–19; 2 Cor. 10–13), the fury of his response in Galatia is unparalleled.[13] He pronounced a double curse on those who "pervert the gospel of Christ" (1:7–9). He threatened those troubling him who bore on his body the "marks of Jesus" (στίγματα τοῦ Ἰησοῦ, 6:17), implying that those who "trouble" him also abuse Jesus. In his outrage, he substituted a cry of astonishment at their desertion of the one who called them for the usual epistolary thanksgiving (1:6–9). He branded his challengers as agitators (5:12) out to "pervert the gospel of Christ" (1:7). Summoning up an ugly pun, he warned gentile converts who somehow had concluded that circumcision was required for inclusion in the covenant people that those accepting circumcision cut themselves off from Christ (5:4), and he used language bordering on the vulgar when he expressed the wish that "those who unsettle you would castrate themselves!" (5:12). This tooth and nail fight demanded that Paul defend his apostleship here if he were to remain credible elsewhere.

But what brought on this angry retort? It seems that someone, either rival missionaries or local Judaizers, could not square Gen. 17:11, 14 with Paul's law-free gospel. The requirement of circumcision in Gen. 17:11, 14 is unambiguous and is to serve as a mark of membership in the covenant people of God: "God said to Abraham, . . . 'You shall circumcise the flesh of your foreskins, and it shall be a sign of the covenant between me and you.'" The practice of circumcision by the parent church in Jerusalem, contrasted absolutely with Paul's practice. Because of their direct, historical ties with Jesus—the Jerusalem "pillar" apostles, Peter and James, the Lord's brother—could claim authority for their practice of circumcision that eluded Paul completely. By contrast, Paul's claim to be an apostle was weak and his gospel suspect. He was no disciple. He had not known Jesus "according to the flesh." His gospel, therefore, came not directly from Jesus but from other sources (human?). He had once been a persecutor of the church, seeking to eradicate it. His gospel had previously been challenged in Philippi. And, in the view of some his commission and gospel appeared to be totally dependent on human, not divine, sources.[14] So a great deal was riding on Paul's defense of his apostleship and his gospel. From that defense we gain some insight into what Paul thought were the essential marks of an apostle of Christ.

MARKS OF AN APOSTLE (IN GALATIANS)

Apostle through a Revelation of Jesus Christ

Paul could hardly expect his addressees to accept him as an apostle simply because he asserted his claim or even because he threatened rival missionaries with curses. While Paul's logic may seem to us to be absolutely impeccable and thoroughly persuasive, first century believers who had come to appreciate the logic of a rival gospel would have hardly been persuaded by a simple or even forceful declaration from Paul. For him to be credible, some evidence for his apostleship and gospel was required. Paul began his persuasion with three negative and three positive references to his apostolic call. Already in the salutation (1:1) he telegraphed his concern over questions about the source of his apostleship: "Paul an apostle—*neither from humans nor through humans but through Jesus Christ* and God the father who raised him from the dead" (my trans., emphasis added). In 1:11–12 Paul returned to this emphasis:

> For I want you to know, brothers and sisters, that the gospel that was proclaimed by me *is not of human origin; for I did not receive it from a human source, nor was I taught it, but I received it through a revelation of Jesus Christ* (emphasis added).

And in 1:15–16 in a style reminiscent of the Hebrew prophets he repeated this theme for emphasis:

> But when God, who had set me apart from my mother's womb and called me by his grace, was pleased to reveal his Son to me, so that I might proclaim him among the Gentiles, *I did not confer with flesh and blood* (my trans., emphasis added).

Paul's recollection of his visits to Jerusalem and conference with the pillars (2:1–14) underscores his independence of human authority. In 1:15, 16 especially, he claimed like Jeremiah of old to have been chosen from birth and now through a divine epiphany to have received his commission. This succinct summary of a much fuller narrative includes two essential elements—(1) the call or revelation itself and (2) a reference to the commission. Paul is to "proclaim him among the Gentiles" (1:16).[15] Although Paul was influenced by the church and his thinking was informed by its traditions, he traced (his apostleship and gospel) directly to God acting through Christ. This repeated stress on his call and commission by the exalted Christ subverted the exclusive claims of those with a direct connection to the historical Jesus. And while Paul gives himself to the congregation, and is influenced by its traditions, he traces the authority for his call and commission directly to Christ. Added to this threefold denial of dependence on the Jerusalem pillars, other missionaries, or even church tradition for his apostolic commission was Paul's report of a Christophany that offered divine proof of his legitimacy.[16]

Later in some circles believers were extremely skeptical of this attempt to base an apostolic claim on *apocalypsis* (revelation). In the third century the Pseudo-Clementine Homilies reveal an earlier tradition profoundly critical of the claim by Paul to be called by a revelation of Christ to be an apostle. There Peter challenges Paul's claim:

> We know . . . that many idolaters, adulterers and other sinners have seen visions and had true dreams, and also that some have had visions that were wrought by demons." (H XVII.13, 16:1)[17]

Later Peter is allowed to ask:

> Can any one be made competent to teach through a vision? And
> if your opinion is, "That is possible," why then did our teacher
> spend a whole year with us who are awake? . . . But if you were
> visited by him for the space of an hour and were instructed by him
> and thereby have become an apostle, then proclaim his words,
> expound what he has taught, be a friend to his apostles and do not
> contend with me, who am his confidant; for you have in hostility
> *withstood* me, who am a firm rock, the foundation stone of the
> church. If you were not an enemy, then you would not slander me
> and revile my preaching in order that I may not be believed when
> I proclaim what I have heard in my own person from the Lord.
> (H XVII. 13; 19:1–5)[18]

Judging from 2 Cor. 12 Paul would have been aware that visions are hardly
unambiguous. There the tables were turned, and his Jewish Christian missionary opponents claimed visions that authenticated their gospel and apostleship
and invalidated Paul's. Paul's response shows his recognition that visions
alone hardly prove the truth or reliability of a message. Perhaps that was why
Paul added other proofs in Galatians of the authenticity of his gospel and the
integrity of his apostleship.

Apostle as Founder of Churches

Paul seeks the approval of his gospel and apostleship through his recall
of the shared experience of the founding of the church and the shared experience of the gospel. Of course, religious experience, like visions, is not self-
interpreting and can be as ambiguous as visions themselves. For that reason
Gal. 4:12–20 has puzzled many commentators. There Paul recalls their common experience—how after falling ill and being ministered to by the Galatians, he founded the church in Galatia from his sick bed. Some think Paul's
hard logic here gives way to a soft emotionalism.[19] Others, like Schlier, put a
more pleasing face on the argument, calling it "an argument from the heart."[20]
Against those who think Paul gives up on rational argument for an emotional
appeal, Betz places Paul's discussion within the friendship *topos* of the Hellenistic world.[21]

In 4:19–20 the *topos* expands to include Paul's self-designation as a
mother laboring to give birth to Christ in his addressees.[22] He addresses his
readers with an endearing diminutive, "my little children," that clashes with
the harsh, threatening polemic suffusing the letter. With the words "for whom

I am *again* in birth pangs," (my trans.) he speaks of once more being in labor "until Christ is formed in you" to those to whom he gave birth in the first place (emphasis added). In her work on Jesus as mother in the Middle Ages, Caroline Bynum has shown that men and women experience the same symbols in distinctly different ways.[23] She has noted how the analogies men drew between their own maternity and Jesus as mother not only inverted their gender but also symbolized the surrender of their privileged position to identify with the disadvantaged. This renunciation of authority, privilege, and power to identify with the feminine was a radical act of inversion.

Admittedly, there are vast differences between Europe in the Middle Ages and the eastern Mediterranean of the first century. First century pluralism is markedly different from the almost exclusively Christian Europe of the Middle Ages. Moreover, Bynum had available writings from women dealing with many of the same issues men addressed, whereas from the first century we have few writings from the hands of women that we can identify with certainty. Paul's own liminal status differed markedly from the status of monks and nuns in a culture replete with monasticism. Yet, there are enough similarities to justify an experiment with Bynum's model. First century men like the males of the Middle Ages were socially advantaged by their gender. Authority, the right to correct others, and power were normally vested in males. Furthermore, human experience may be gendered as Bynum argues. If that is the case, Paul's identification of himself as the mother of the Galatian church might represent a significant social as well as biological inversion dealing with the founding and nurture of the church.

Doubtless there is tension between Paul's references to himself as mother of the church and other images more consistent with traditional definitions of maleness in his society. In 1 Cor. 4:21, for example, he threatens a recalcitrant and factious church that he may have to come "with a rod" (1 Cor. 4:21). In Gal. 1:8–19 and 1 Cor. 16:22 he pronounces curses on those who preach "another gospel" and those whose loveless behavior threatens the survival of the church. In 1 Corinthians while in absentia he orders the church to hand a man "over to Satan" (5:5) who was "living with his father's wife" (5:1) and to ratify an apostolic curse on the one doing such a thing. In Gal. 6:17 Paul threatens those who trouble him whose scars make him a surrogate of Christ. The apostle as an emissary of Christ shares his authority and is not, as Schmithals argues, fundamentally a member and emissary of the congregation.[24] This execution of judgment by the apostle was based on the assumption that as a special emissary of Christ he shared in his eschatological power.[25] By likening himself to the pregnant woman giving birth, he surrenders, for the moment, however, that superordinate status. He voluntarily vacates the elevated position that his gender, his culture and his apostolic commission have bestowed upon him to become the mother of his "little children" (4:19).

This humbling act was a part of an understanding of apostleship one sees elsewhere in Gal. In 2:19 and 5:14 Paul shared in Christ's humiliation by entering metaphorically into the experience of the cross. And this imagery softens the harsh, authoritarian metaphors of his apostleship and modifies traditional models of male authority.

Paul also invokes maternal imagery in other letters to emphasize the nurturing nature of his apostleship. In an extended autobiographical section of 1 Thessalonians he applied the metaphor of nurse to himself and his apostolic co-workers: "we were gentle [babes] among you, like a nurse tenderly caring for her own children. So deeply do we care for you that we are determined to share with you not only the gospel of God but also our own selves" (2:7, 8).[26] Whether Paul means that the nurse cares for the children as if they were her own or that the mother tends the children as would a nurse is unclear and of no great moment. The nurse metaphor, like that of the mother, is highly evocative. The nurse was revered and honored for her care. She often nursed her charges from her own breast. When the child was to be weaned, she chewed the solid food first placed in the infant's mouth. She bathed, cleaned, and dressed the child; she came to the child when it cried out at night; she rocked it in her arms; sang lullabies to it; told it stories; taught it poems, songs, and even a second language. Nurses were often greatly revered, and families pledged in monuments erected to their honor that they would keep their memory alive.[27] This metaphor, therefore, which called up images of loyalty, tenderness, devotion, and attention to vital and sometimes messy tasks was so common and so feminine that, Gaventa is correct, its application to grown men is "a jarring image."[28] It did more, however, than shock; it opened up new levels of thinking about apostleship, and softened the authoritarian edge normally associated with an apostle as a powerful, eschatological figure. While Paul can give the image of father nurturing significance (e.g., 1 Cor. 4:21), it was women who gave birth to, nursed, and reared children. Paul's becoming female in that metaphorical world, therefore, was more than a mere act of individual self-denial; it was also a qualification of the world's constructions of status, power, and authority. As we shall see subsequently, such reconfigurations were not always welcomed.

The Suffering Apostle (in 2 Corinthians)

Before the news arrived of the assault on Paul's gospel and apostleship, he had already expressed his worry to the Corinthians about competitors who might challenge his apostleship. "If I am not an apostle to others," he says confidently, "at least I am to you." Little did he realize that even that recognition would come under question. In 1 Cor. 9:3 and the following verses he offers a defense "to those who would examine me" (9:3). And in 9:2 he appealed to the special relationship between him and the readers who are "the seal of my apostleship in the Lord." In 1 Cor. 15:3–11 Paul aims not to cite witnesses whose testimony supports belief in the resurrection but to offer a narrative supportive of his inclusion among the apostles: "Last of all, as to one untimely born, he appeared also to me" (15:8). Already then, when 1 Corinthians was written some were questioning the legitimacy of Paul's apostleship. While that challenge in 1 Corinthians is vague, in 2 Corinthians a frontal assault became quite specific and, therefore, threatening. In the face of that challenge Paul offered a heated two-pronged response, featuring an attack on his critics and a delineation of the marks of a true apostle. The view of apostleship articulated here is hardly intended to be comprehensive, but rather in each case the agenda is set by the opposition that Paul then tries to subvert.

Suffering as the mark of an apostle is a persistent emphasis in Paul's letters. From the beginning, Paul linked suffering with the proclamation of the gospel. In 1 Thess. 2:1 he noted that during their ministry in Philippi they "had already suffered and been shamefully mistreated." In Thessalonica Paul's preaching elicited "great opposition" (2:2), and his suffering provided a model for their converts who "in spite of persecution received the word with joy" (1:6), thus becoming an example to believers in Macedonia and Achaia (1:7). Though not a prerequisite for life in Christ, suffering was nevertheless a part of the world believers inhabited (3:3). Paul recalls warning believers beforehand that suffering was simply a necessary, even destined, part of belief (3:3–14). Believers, Paul says, participate in a "fellowship of his sufferings" (Phil. 3:10) that is no mere huddle against the icy blasts but is a mystical participation in the death of Christ (Rom. 6:3). This persecution, Paul admits, left some shaken (1 Thess. 3:3), but it also validated the frame of reference of this sect, distinguishing it from the world and confirming its status as the "children of light" opposed to the "children of darkness" (1 Thess. 5:5). In Rom. 5:3 Paul notes how this suffering produces "endurance," "character," and "hope."

While all believers must suffer, an apostle was in a class by himself or herself. It was not just that suffering was a condition of life in Christ, which of course it was, it was that the apostolic ministry involved the apostle in a ministry of suffering for others. The apostle, for Paul, was a mediator of the suffering of Christ and also of God's comfort and consolation.[29] God, according to Paul, is the one "who consoles us in all our affliction, so that we may be able to console those who are in any affliction with the consolation with which we ourselves are consoled" (2 Cor. 1:4). Ironically, Pual portrays the apostle here as a superordinate of suffering who participates in Christ's suffering and becomes a model of suffering for new converts.

As an emissary of Christ Paul expects to share in his suffering. He views the scars left on his body as the "*stigmata* of Jesus" (Gal. 6:17). From a prison, perhaps in Ephesus, where the death penalty hangs ominously over him, Paul explains his suffering as an opportunity to witness as Christ's apostle: "I want you to know, brothers and sisters, that what has happened to me has actually helped to spread the gospel" (Phil. 1:12). In addition, that suffering has a mythic quality that places him in Christ's presence: "I want to know Christ and the power of his resurrection and the sharing of his sufferings by becoming like him in his death" (Phil. 3:11).

Similarly, 1 Corinthians associates suffering with the apostolic task, and as in Galatians its appeal to apostolic suffering is sharply polemical. If the Corinthian premise that they already enjoyed eschatological bliss and knowledge were correct, apostles would be irrelevant. In response Paul strikes out at the religious enthusiasts with biting sarcasm: "Already you are full; already you are rich; without us you would rule" (4:8, my trans.). Having done so, he then draws a stark contrast between his life as an apostle and their charismatic fullness:

> For I think that God has exhibited us apostles as last of all, as people under a death sentence, for we have become a spectacle to the world, and angels and human beings. We are fools for Christ, but you are wise in Christ. We are weak, but you are strong. You are held in honor, we in dishonor. Until the present hour we are hungry and thirsty. We go half-naked, and we are battered and homeless, and we are weary from hard work. When cursed, we bless. When persecuted, we endure. When slandered, we speak gently. We have become like the refuse of the world, the dregs of all things, until the present moment. (4:9–13, my trans.)

Paul here juxtaposed a *theologia crucis* against a *theologia gloriae,* and made the *theologia crucis* central to the life and gospel of the apostle.

With the exception of Galatians, nowhere was the challenge to Paul's apostleship more intense than in 2 Corinthians, and nowhere else was suffering more prominently displayed as a mark of an apostle. Jewish Christian apostles from the outside entered the Corinthian congregation and openly attacked the legitimacy of Paul's apostleship.[30] They may have known the earthly Jesus or may have gained access to the Jesus according to the flesh through others who knew him,[31] but since their teaching was not preoccupied with law it seems unlikely that they came from the Jerusalem church. They were Jews appealing to their status as Hebrews, Israelites, and sons of Abraham (11:22–23), and they were messianists serving as apostles with powerful spiritual gifts (11:13–15; 10:5; 12:11).[32] They claimed to be ministers of

Christ and servants of righteousness (11:23); they possessed compelling rhetorical skills, skills that shared a Hellenistic *Tendenz;* and unlike Paul they were physically imposing. Their superior rhetorical skill, appearance, and ability to work miracles were presented as proofs of spirit possession and grounds for their claim of sufficiency (ἱκανο'ς, 2:16).[33] Through this spirit possession they professed a superior wisdom (1:12). They claimed access to divine epiphanies through visions (12:1–5), and like Moses, whose appearance was altered during his encounter with Yahweh on Sinai, they expected the physique of the spirit possessed apostle of Christ to radiate the glory of the redeemer. Their skill in spontaneous oratory was proof to many of their spirit possession, and these individuals then willingly offered their written testimonials of the success and divine character of the missionary work and gospel of these missionaries elsewhere (3:1). On the basis of their stellar reputation as charismatics these apostles, like most philosophers, felt entitled to monetary support for their teaching so long as such support was neither excessive nor compromising.[34] It would be wrong to assume that they were driven by unmitigated greed and that their gospel was a fraud. Of course, it was possible to mask selfishness with a screen of selflessness. But, as apostles, ministers of Christ, and servants of righteousness who strongly emphasized their charismatic gifts and the heavenly character of their experience, they were as likely as Paul to be driven by a desire "to proclaim the spiritual power given to them and thereby confirm their relationship to Christ and justify their apostolic existence."[35] To be sure, Paul calls them "false apostles, deceitful workers, disguising themselves as apostles of Christ" and even ministers of Satan (2 Cor. 11:13–14), and they may have heaped similar invective on Paul. But such name-calling came in the heat of an angry exchange and surely represents neither their own understanding of themselves nor the perception of many believers persuaded by the power and authority of their gospel.

These apostles, however, were hardly ready to proclaim their gospel and let it stand on its own feet; they felt impelled to attack Paul's gospel and his apostolic status, both of which sharply differed from their own. They belittled Paul's credentials and accused him of duplicity and cowardice: duplicity because while refusing gifts of money directly, he solicited money for the Jerusalem offering, from which they suspected he was skimming off gifts to line his own pockets (11:11; 12:16, 17–18); and cowardice because after a painful shouting match on a quick visit to Corinth, he beat a hasty retreat (2:1) and from a safe distance in Ephesus shot off a letter studded with biting sarcasm and blistering critique of his opponents. The opponents in turn mocked Paul's "brave" defense as he, smarting from their ridicule, reported: "For they say, 'His letters are weighty and strong, but his bodily presence is weak, and his speech is of no account' " (10:10). They charged that Paul, in contrast to their own experience, lacked proofs or signs of a genuine apostle (12:12, σημεῖα τοῦ ἀποστόλου). If he were a true pneumatic his speech would be more powerful, but as it was they said, "his speech is of no account" (10:10). Moreover, Paul's physical appearance, some claimed, betrayed a lack of spirit, thus earning their contempt: "his bodily presence is weak' " (10:10).

In this atmosphere charged with acrimony and suspicion, Paul defended his apostleship as the opposite of theirs.[36] Much was riding on the persuasiveness of his defense. If Paul were discredited here, his mission to the West would have been jeopardized, and his mission in Greece, Macedonia, and western Asia Minor might have failed completely. With the exception of Galatians, only here must Paul directly confront his adversaries, and he does so with a severe critique. He sarcastically refers to the rival missionaries as "super apostles" (11:5; 12:11) and calls them "false apostles" (11:13) and minions of Satan (11:13–15). He expresses the flash points in the dispute with strong contrasts introduced with a negation (e.g., *ou* or *mē* [not]) followed by an adversative "but" (*alla*).[37] He calls his condescending critics money grubbing "hucksters" (2:17), braggarts who boast in appearances (5:12). He implies that his antagonists, unlike himself, preach themselves (4:5) and that they live for themselves as well (5:15). In short, Paul lumps them with religious or philosophical quacks who go about swindling the gullible.

Most painful of all, Paul found the Corinthians all too ready to submit to the agenda of his critics. A poignant expression of that disappointment appears in 11:4: "For if someone comes and proclaims another Jesus than the one we have proclaimed, or if you receive a different spirit from the one you received, or a different gospel from the one you accepted, you submit to it readily enough."[38] Two parts of the letter (2:14–7:4, minus the interpolation 6:14–7:1, and 10:1–13:10) contain Paul's defense of the legitimacy of his apostleship. And in the first part, in an effort to convince his converts of the truth of his claim, Paul challenges both the rivals' pretensions to adequacy and their frame of reference for reading human experience.

Scholars have long recognized the critical role boasting played in this heated exchange. As early as 1914 Hans Windisch saw the contribution popular Hellenistic philosophy made to this exchange,[39] and his work has profoundly influenced exegetes up to the present day.[40] While Sophists and some popular philosophers self-consciously boasted about the truth or superiority of their teaching, in the first century no less than in our own time, such boasting was considered as distasteful and offensive as it was commonplace among the crude and arrogant. Plutarch (b. 46 CE) notes that "no other talk is so odious or offensive" (De se ipsum, 547 D). Because of its "powerful base of operations" in "self-love" (546 B), this "hunger for praise" often cannot wait for the praise of others but must "feed unnaturally" on itself (540 A). And braggarts thus "arrogate to themselves what it is for others to bestow" (539

D). Plutarch recognizes, however, circumstances in which boasting is justified and inoffensive.

Following Pericles, Plutarch notes the appropriateness of self-praise when "you are defending your good name or answering a charge" (De se ipsum, 540 C). Likewise, in the face of adversity "using self-glorification to pass from a humbled and piteous state to an attitude of triumph and pride, strikes us not as offensive or bold, but as great and indomitable" (541 B). Tempering self-praise with admission of fault also removes envy, according to Plutarch: "Many also blunt the edge of envy by occasionally inserting into their own praise a confession even of poverty and indigence or actually of low birth" (544 B). The admission of weakness, or a slip or mistake, also was seen as tactful or gracious (544 A). Given the opprobrium associated with bald faced, unprovoked self-praise, it seems unlikely that the boasting of the rival apostles focused entirely on themselves. Given their religious experience, their visions, and their experiences of the spirit, their boasting was most likely rendered inoffensive by offering praise to God for their charismata. Such an attribution would have fit naturally in the Hellenistic setting and also could claim rootage in their native Judaism.

Judaism shared the Hellenistic revulsion for boasting. Philo locates its source in the love of pleasure that makes its practitioner into a "buffoon," a "coward," and a "braggart" (ἀλαζὼν) (Sacr. Abel, 32). Moreover, there was broad scriptural warrant against boasting that not only protested against the haughtiness of the ungodly but also condemned the boasting of individual Israelites. The psalmist cries out against the arrogance of Israel's oppressor: "Why do you boast, O mighty one, of mischief done against the godly?" (52:1). And for the psalmist the contempt of the mighty for the lowly people of God raises the theodicy question with special poignancy: "how long shall the wicked boast?" (94:3). This same condemnation also blankets the braggart in Israel. Especially guilty is the creature of the creator who simply takes the future for granted: "Do not boast about tomorrow, for you do not know what a day may bring" (Prov. 27:1). The Deuteronomist is also keenly aware of the arrogance that may come with success (8:17), and Jeremiah is sensitive to the temptation of the powerful, the educated, and the wealthy to boast (9:23). In contrast to this odious boasting that is based on a sense of personal power and superiority or on privileged status and wealth that one may falsely believe guarantees the future, there is another form of boasting that is quite acceptable, the boasting that relies on Yahweh. Acutely conscious of human weakness and mortality, of vulnerability to the thousand and one perils that may lie ahead, the pious who rely on God's strength and promise may authentically boast. Perhaps it is Jeremiah who most finely draws the line between true and false boasting:

> Thus says the Lord: Do not let the wise boast in their wisdom, do
> not let the mighty boast in their might, do not let the wealthy boast
> in their wealth; but let those who boast boast in this, that they
> understand and know me, that I am the Lord; I act with steadfast
> love, justice, and righteousness in the earth, for in these things I
> delight, says the Lord. (9:23–24)

Since the rivals were Jews, as was Paul, and since they, if Georgi is correct, were also Hellenists, as was Paul, it is likely that they, like Paul, were influenced by both the tradition of Hellenistic popular philosophy and Jewish usage. Paul's response to their propaganda, however, is quite unusual.[41] Given their attacks on him and the unflattering comparison they drew between themselves and him, he might have met their boasting with boasting of his own without feeling that he was creating any uneasiness on the hearer's part. For, as noted previously, in one's own defense boasting was fully justified in the popular imagination. Paul's boasting, however, takes a surprising turn when he assumes the role of a fool. Windisch first suggested that Paul had witnessed the dramatic presentation of a fool's speech (Narrenrede) and had not only learned from but imitated it by himself becoming the mime playing the role of the fool. He distinguished himself from the mime, however, in that he took the role with utmost seriousness, acting the role of the apostle himself.[42] This adaptation of what might have been a literary form was then suffused with sarcasm and irony, with pointed antitheses, and with bitter polemic. To the demand for proofs of apostleship from the addressees (13:3), Paul offers his evidence (δοκιμή), boasting like a fool of the horrors he has endured— numbing toil, imprisonments, floggings, stonings, shipwrecks, being adrift at sea, perilous travels, hunger, thirst, cold, nakedness, and anxiety about the churches (11:21b–29; 4:7–10; 6:4–10). In addition he was afflicted with a "thorn in the flesh," a "messenger of Satan" (12:7), that stubbornly persisted in spite of repeated prayerful petitions for its removal. He cannot nor does he try to conceal his weakness; on the contrary he boasts in his weaknesses, for his role as an apostle was based on the conviction that "power [i.e., God's power] is made perfect in weakness" (2 Cor. 12:8). As he himself says: "So (οὖν), I will boast all the more gladly in my weaknesses, so that (ἵνα) the power of Christ may dwell in me" (2 Cor. 12:9).

In the fool's speech Paul parodies the pretentious self-glorification of the "super apostles" (11:12–12:10).[43] He mimes their proud assertions with a lengthy enumeration of his sufferings (11:23–29). He mimics their claim of superior wisdom derived from their visions with a vision of his own whose substance, unlike that of their visions, is unutterable (12:1–7). He mocks their powerful rhetoric with a simple appeal to his suffering (11:17). Yet, in the final analysis, Paul's repeated apologies show (11:21, 23; 12:1) that he recognizes that his boasting is a self-contradiction, even an act of silliness. Nevertheless, he offers this list of sufferings not just as a framework for but as a mark of his apostleship and a symbolic participation in the suffering and death of Christ.

In what is likely a later letter to the Corinthians, Paul contrasts his desperation with the Corinthian sense of self-sufficiency.[44] Speaking autobiographically, he recalls suffering so intense in Asia Minor that he despaired of life itself: "Why, we felt that we had received the sentence of death; but that was to make us *rely not on ourselves* but [unlike the rivals] on God who raises the dead" (1:9, emphasis added). While it is unlikely that the rival apostles actually preached a gospel of self-sufficiency, their boasting led Paul to assume that they were confident of their sufficiency. By contrast Paul admits his own inadequacy and credits God instead: "*not* that we are sufficient (ἱκανοί) of ourselves, *but* our sufficiency (ἱκανότης) is from God" (3:5, emphasis added). Except for Rom. 15:23, Paul only refers to *hikanos* or its derivatives in the Corinthian correspondence, and he similarly condemns those who commend themselves (10:12, 18; 3:1); he repeatedly contrasts his own commendation with the self-praise of his rivals (4:2; 5:12; 6:4; also 10:12, 18; 3:1) and proposes an antidote to such a self-referential attitude that is somewhat surprising. He suggests that brutal experience reveals one's mortality and in *extremis* one may learn to rely on God, who raised Jesus from the dead. He realized that, compared to the robust spirituality of the rivals that radiated vitality and power, his mortal weakness, suffering, vulnerability, and even ineptness might appear to some to give off an odor of decay. But, if Furnish is correct that 2:14–17 introduces a discussion of apostleship that runs to 5:21, then Paul's metaphor of sweet and acrid aromas in 2:15–16 offers an alternative reading of his experience:[45] "We are the aroma of Christ to God among those who are being saved and among those who are perishing; to the one a fragrance from death to death, to the other a fragrance from life to life." Through the use of this metaphor Paul invites those swayed by the rival apostles to think of human frailty and impotence in quite a different way—not as the source of the acrid stench of death but as the origin of the "sweet aroma of [the resurrected] Christ (χριστοῦ εὐωδία)" (2:15). And it also summoned "those who are perishing" (2:15) to recognize in these odors an epiphany of the life and resurrection of Christ. The odors of life and death commingle, and the resulting ambiguity allows some to deny death through grandiose pretensions of life, glory, success, and power and some to see in death an epiphany of the life to be shared by those in Christ. Apostolic suffering thus, according to Paul, not only validated his apostolic status, it also served as a primary text in which discerning eyes could see evidence of God's work, that is, the message of the resurrection.

This was the basic difference between Paul and his rivals. All people suffer hardship, disappointment, loss, and real physical and psychological pain. To be human is to suffer. However, as Georgi observed, Paul saw in his weakness and suffering "the primary sphere for the manifestation of divine power," whereas the rivals believed that "signs, wonders, and mighty works" (12:12) were the main focus of God's activity.[46] Surely, neither the idea of the apostle nor its characteristics originated with Paul, but the designation of suffering and weakness as marks of an apostle appears to be distinctly Pauline. In line with early church tradition Paul held apostleship to be a charismatic gift (1 Cor. 12:28), and the signs of that apostleship he accepts without question. In 2 Cor. 12:12, he reminds those enamored with his rival charismatic apostles that while he was among them "The signs of a true apostle were performed among you with utmost patience, signs (σημείοις) and wonders (τέρασιν) and mighty works (δυνάμεσιν)." Paul may here be citing a slogan of the opponents but nevertheless a slogan with traditional elements as is indicated by its virtual repetition in Rom. 15:18–19. Windisch held that this slogan from rivals delineated proofs of the legitimacy of both the preaching and office of one claiming to be an apostle. First framed in Jerusalem by the inner circle of apostles, it spread to include the mission to the Gentiles as well.[47] Thus when Paul refers to his apostolic mission to the Gentiles "by word and deed, by the power of signs (σημείων) and wonders (τεράτων)" in such a nonpolemical letter as Rom. 15:18, he willingly takes his place in an early tradition.[48]

Apostle as Miracle Worker

Paul's reference to himself as an apostolic miracle worker may offend the modern reader so accustomed to the portrait of the apostle as a theological and intellectual giant. But such a self-understanding would have been totally consistent with the apocalyptic world Paul inhabited. In 1 Cor. 12:10, 28, 29 Paul lists healers and miracle workers among the charismatically gifted, that is, those empowered by the gift of God's spirit whose outpouring he associates with the arrival of the new age. While Paul did not here associate healing and miracle working specifically with apostleship, neither did he specifically disassociate them. With the arrival of the end of the old age, and God's final and decisive action to reclaim the world from the control of demonic powers and personalities, an apostle of Christ could be expected to share in that struggle. Since popular myths attributed both illness and demon possession to Satan (2 Cor. 12:7), an apostle of Christ empowered by God's spirit and functioning as an agent of this new age was believed to share in God's assault on Satan's rule. To the popular imagination these magical arts offered some protection in a hostile, capricious environment infested with frightful figures, and the rival apostles obviously held the experience of the miraculous as synonymous with salvation itself. Moreover, as Betz noted, they understood the miraculous as liberation from the excruciating pain and limitations of flesh and human weakness.[49] In this setting, healings and exorcisms could be viewed as a result of having gained access to divine power or God's spirit, or, if one shared an apocalyptic outlook, miracles could be understood as a part of the violent struggle between God and the demonic powers to gain control over creation. Healings and exorcisms could be seen as a sign of the advent of God's rule and as a prolepsis of the arriving apocalyptic denouement when the whole creation "will be set free from its bondage to decay and will obtain the freedom of the glory of the children of God" (Rom. 8:21). Certainly, Paul's view of the miraculous was tinged with apocalypticism. The resurrection of the Messiah Jesus who was crucified by the rulers of this world age (1 Cor. 2:6–8) signaled the beginning of God's final assault on these evil powers (Rom. 6:23; 1 Cor. 15:26, 55). Their subjugation, Paul believed, was imminent. Paul's status as an apostolic miracle worker is best viewed in light of this powerful mythological understanding.

While Paul accepts miracle working as an expression of the spirit, he nowhere limits its performance to the apostles nor does he stress its importance for authenticating one's apostolic status, though he does note that it is a mark of apostleship. He appears quite unwilling in 2 Corinthians to engage in a competitive comparison of his miracle working abilities with those of the rival apostles. Instead, it is in the ironic discussion of his suffering and weakness that Paul makes a deliberately foolish contrast with the signs of apostleship of his rivals. Elsewhere, as Furnish has observed, Paul subordinates his miracle working powers to the "primary and distinguishing task of the apostle," namely, the proclamation of the gospel.[50] So, although Paul owns his place in the circle of miracle workers, his miracle working status is clearly subordinated to other features of his apostleship. Here also, conflict with opponents critical of Paul's claim to be an apostle shaped his own understanding and the development of his view of what it meant to be an apostle of Christ. If we allow ourselves to set aside our respect for the canonical position Paul occupies and view him in light of the controversy that swirls around him, it is easy to see why Paul's claim to be an apostle was heatedly contested in the early church. To those who respected the historical continuity between the Jerusalem circle and the historical Jesus, and who trusted the veracity of their gospel and apostleship, Paul's claim to be an apostle must have seemed fantastic if not fanciful, as the texts themselves indicate. Paul's definition of apostleship that relied on no human authority but on divine revelation did not win acceptance easily and was ridiculed well into the third century. Although this divine origin gave Paul's status as an apostle a distinctly charismatic quality.

Paul's argument for weakness and suffering as marks of apostleship was unusual. That argument did two things: it firmly rooted apostleship in the human experience, and it simultaneously linked it with the suffering and dying Christ. Thus Paul's apostleship was given a firm connection with this world. In accepting the performance of miracles as a sign of his apostleship Paul shares a broadly based early tradition that saw in miracles an authentication of the status of a holy man or an apostle of God. While we are left to guess about precisely the kind of miracles *he* performed, we know he listed healing among the charismatic gifts. In the Corinthian struggle in particular, Paul admits his status as a miracle worker and a recipient of visions, but in contrast to his opponents he assigns them a lesser value than suffering and weakness. Nowhere does he elevate them to validate his apostleship, although he nowhere denies their validity as signs of apostleship and the approaching end. Throughout his letters he subordinated miracle working to the proclamation of the gospel.

Apostle to the Gentiles

In Romans in particular Paul explicitly speaks of himself as the Apostle to the Gentiles (1:1–1:5). As we shall note in a later chapter, this apostleship was informed and energized by an apocalyptic mind-set aptly noted by Schoeps: "We should misunderstand the apostle's letters as a whole, and the governing consciousness from which they sprang, if we failed to recognize that Paul only lives, writes, and preaches in the unshakeable conviction that his generation represents the last generation of [humankind]."[51] Schoeps's remarks have special relevance for Paul's view of himself as "the apostle to the gentiles" (Rom. 11:13). Paul's understanding of that mission hardly came out of thin air. It was a part of a deep conviction that God was finally putting things right. So much of his theological language was rooted in that conviction—language dealing with justification, judgment, wrath, the new creation, and the outpouring of the spirit. So much of his activity was driven by the belief that he lived in the last generation of this world age and that he along with his addressees would participate in that final eschatological moment: "Then we who are alive, who are left, will be caught up" (1 Thess. 4:17). So much of the energy of his mission came from the belief that he was playing a powerful role as herald of the good news that all must hear before the end.

Paul's coupling of emphases on the approaching end and the mission to the Gentiles, though hardly unique, was certainly central to his self-understanding. Of course, belief that the final divine "visitation" was imminent came from a Jewish lineage and greatly influenced the behavior and outlook of apocalyptic communities like Qumran. And long before Qumran, prophets spoke of the inclusion of Gentiles in the last days, an inclusion that Paul's Scriptures, the Septuagint, gave additional emphasis.[52] Isaiah's forecast that in the "days to come" Gentiles would stream up to the temple "that he may teach us his ways and that we may walk in his paths" (2:2–4) was surely known to Paul, and the prediction that Gentiles would bring their gifts (60:11) in that final eschatological grand procession probably stands behind Paul's collection from the Gentile churches for the "poor among the saints" in Jerusalem.

Yet the location of the genesis of Paul's mission to the Gentiles solely in biblical tradition is simplistic. Given Paul's upbringing in the Diaspora, his Diaspora Scriptures, and his Hellenistic language, education, and community, some openness to the gentile majority in that world must be assumed. A generation ago, Nils Dahl's exegesis of Rom. 3:29–30 showed that Paul's radical monotheism that forbade any distinction between Jew and Gentile owes something to a Hellenistic philosophical monotheism with strong cosmopolitan or universalistic tendencies.[53] This universalizing tendency, however, when combined with the apocalypticism of Paul's Jewish heritage produced a hybrid that also generated explosive tensions between inclusion and exclusion, between boundlessness or universalization and boundedness or particularity.[54] By Turner's model, Paul would have been a liminal figure between two worlds—one dying and one being born—and also on the boundary between two communities—one Jewish and the other gentile. And the tensions between these worlds were so great that the logic of Paul's gentile mission defied human understanding, as we see in Rom. 11:25–36, and its mystery was hidden in the mystery of the Godhead itself.

Preaching as the Mark of an Apostle

That preaching was the principal feature of Paul's apostolic activity seems clear.[55] What the content of that preaching was, however, is less obvious. The letters themselves assume the gospel was preached everywhere among the churches, but nowhere in the letters does Paul summarize the content of one of those sermons preached to gentile unbelievers. Almost a generation later, Luke sought to remedy this omission with a sketch of a Pauline sermon on the Areopagus in Athens (Acts 17:16–31). This truncated sermon that can be read in a couple of minutes recognizes the religiousness of the Athenians that was reflected in the inscription "To an unknown god" and then goes on to confess the creator God, "Lord of heaven and earth," who made every people from one man. According to this sermon, all people are God's offspring. God is willing to overlook their ignorance, but in light of the approaching "fixed" judgment "by a man whom he has appointed" they are expected to repent (17:31). The impending judgment seems assured by God's "raising this man from the dead" (17:31).

This sermon surely does not represent Paul's preaching. The main body of the sermon reflects a Stoic interest in cosmopolitanism, and only at the end of the speech do we have an allusion, not a reference, to Jesus, his resurrection, and the final judgment. There is nothing in the sermon about bondage to sin, death, principalities, and powers or the deliverance effected through Jesus' death on the cross. There is no reference to the faithfulness of Christ or the acceptance of the salvation coming through Jesus that inaugurates the Messianic Age. Dibelius correctly noted that "the theology of the Areopagus speech is absolutely foreign to Paul's own theology,"[56] and Haenchen suggested that it is obviously a creation of Luke's fertile imagination.[57]

The sermon's strong emphasis on cosmopolitanism and knowledge of God shows that it is a Hellenistic speech through and through with a weak Christian ending. For a better accounting of Paul's preaching we must turn to the letters themselves.

Of continuing importance for consideration of Paul's preaching is Dodd's work, *The Apostolic Preaching and its Developments.*[58] It is obviously difficult to summarize Paul's preaching with certainty. The challenges rival missionaries threw in Paul's face forced him to develop his thinking about his gospel. The letters show that Paul sometimes did not know what he thought about a given issue until he was faced challenges that forced him to develop positions, to clarify thinking, and sometimes to change emphases in light of new circumstances. Given this development and the elasticity it implies, how dare we attempt a reconstruction?[59] We may dare if we admit in the beginning that our construction is tentative and that it relies on minimal clues scattered throughout the letters. Such a cautious approach was used years ago by Dodd to offer some sense of the content of Paul's preaching. We go beyond Dodd, however, in attending to the context of that preaching and the impact it may have had on Paul's gospel.

Paul's letters nowhere confirm the Acts scenario that Paul turned to the Gentiles only after the failure of his mission *in each case* to the Jews. Galatians tells us instead that the Jerusalem agreement divided responsibilities for the mission between Peter and Paul, with Peter going "to the circumcised" and "me to the Gentiles" (Gal. 2:8). Although Paul nowhere suggests that he turned to Gentiles only after Jews rejected his gospel, the climactic chapters of Romans (9–11) sketch a scenario that runs like this: Christian proclamation of Messiah Jesus, Jewish rejection, gentile mission, Jewish jealousy, the salvation of Israel. Although Paul's missionary strategy did not take him initially to the synagogue in each community where he encountered rejection that caused him to turn to the Gentiles, his gentile mission did in some instances bring conflict with the synagogue and led to the five instances of synagogue punishment by lashing (2 Cor. 11:24). His gentile mission also accounts for the charges against his law-free gospel that it encouraged lawlessness or libertinism (Rom. 6:1, 15; 7:1). While some of Paul's predominantly gentile audience may have been god-fearers who attended the synagogue, and a minority may have been Jews, most came from pagan settings with a history of "idol" worship. Paul was aware of their sin and its terrible consequences (Rom. 1:18–32), their "pagan" religion (Rom. 1:23; 1 Thess. 1:9), their bondage to the principalities and powers, and their enslavement to the ruling powers of death and sin (Rom. 6:12, 20; 1 Cor. 15:26), and he recognized not just their desperate plight but also their powerlessness to save themselves. He also was alert to their sense of estrangement and alienation (2 Cor. 5:19) and their victimization by Satan and the powers of evil. He knew of the general malaise many urbanites felt and was cognizant that many believed their lives were in the clutches of powers they could not pretend to understand. A growing cynicism about the fairness or effectiveness of political institutions had left many with the sense that they were mere playthings in the grip of capricious, careless, blind, amoral forces. While Paul of course would not have known the later writings of Pliny, he would have been aware of the dark pessimism Pliny articulated: "We are so much at the mercy of chance that Chance herself, by whom God is proved uncertain, takes the place of God."[60] It was this situation, which Paul would have probably acknowledged in his preaching, that would have served as a condition ripe for his gospel of deliverance. Although E. P. Sanders thinks Paul argued from solution to plight in the letters, in the missionary situation Paul's preaching probably moved in the opposite direction, from the desperate plight of his predominantly gentile audience to his gospel of salvation in Christ.[61]

While the redemption he proclaimed was centered in Christ, it was rooted in the sacred story of God's dealings with Israel. The gospel was, he claimed, promised by the prophets of Israel (Rom. 1:1–2), and from Israel came the covenant, the promises, the ancestors, and the Messiah (Rom. 9:4–5). Throughout his life Paul jealously guarded his own ties to Israel (2 Cor. 11:22), even bestowing on gentile Christians now adopted as children of God the titles "the Israel of God" (Gal. 6:16) and "the circumcised" (Phil. 3:3). Almost certainly Paul's sermons would have contained the story of Jesus, in whom God was beginning the final assault on the evil powers holding them captive, inaugurating a campaign to establish lordship over creation. The sermon would also have included the promise or warning that history's climactic moment, when the present world age would be replaced completely by God's rule, was imminent. By a close reading of traditional elements in Paul's letters one may offer the following reconstruction of his preaching:

1. A recognition of the bondage, helplessness, hopelessness, and despair of his audience (1 Thess. 1:9; Gal. 1:4; Rom. 8:38; 6:20–23). Now, at last God is bringing redemption through Jesus.
2. He was preexistent and "emptied himself, taking the form of a slave" (Phil. 2:6–7).
3. He was born of the "seed of David" (Rom. 1:3).
4. He died "for our sins in accordance with the scriptures" (1 Cor. 15:3) "to deliver us from the present evil age" (Gal. 1:4).
5. He was buried (1 Cor. 15:4).
6. He was raised according to the Scriptures as the firstfruits of those who have fallen asleep (1 Thess. 1:10; 1 Cor. 15:4; Rom. 1:4; 8:34).
7. He was exalted and is at the right hand of God (Rom. 8:34; Phil. 2:9).
8. And he will return again to gather God's elect and judge the world (1 Thess. 1:10; Rom. 2:16; 14:10).
9. To participate in Christ and share in his salvific act, one must repent of sins (Rom. 10:9), renounce gods once worshiped (1 Thess. 1:9), accept and confess Jesus as God's Messiah, and believe that after Jesus' crucifixion God raised him from the dead. The passage from one realm to the new age was marked ritualistically by baptism (1 Cor. 12:13; Gal. 3:27), and through baptism one mythically participated in Christ's death, which stood at the center of the cosmic drama under way (Rom. 6:4), and was assured that "you *will* be saved" (Rom. 10:8–9; emphasis added).

Through this Jesus, Paul believed, God liberates those shackled by sin, death, and the principalities and powers, and, on those believing, bestows the spirit and its gifts as a sign of the arriving end of the age.

Although Paul claimed that his gospel had no human origin (Gal. 1:11–18), unless he intended to flatly contradict himself, he hardly meant that the gospel he preached drew on no church tradition. Rather this statement in Galatians rises from a polemic against those who question his right to claim apostleship. That Paul's apostolic claim does not oppose a reliance on tradition is obvious in 1 Cor. 11:23–25, where he cites a eucharistic tradition of the church that he claimed to have "received from the Lord." The Lord, according to Paul, speaks through tradition as well as revelation. Moreover, his reference to "my gospel" in Rom. 2:16 can hardly be disentangled from the gospel held in common with his addressees in Rome. Therefore, the gospel story that Paul recites hardly originated with him even though he did give it his own distinctive stamp.

Such a reconstruction of Paul's preaching, of course, is something of a pastiche put together with fragments from different letters and in that sense is open to criticism. Yet such a reconstruction is defensible even though it goes beyond Dodd and Hays in its positing of a context in which such a construction took place. It agrees with both Dodd and Hays on the narrative character of Paul's *kerygma* that is embedded in the letters. Hays correctly notes that the purpose of the letters was less to retell the story than to interpret it for a given context, allude to it, assume it, evoke it, and even appeal to it.[62] New occasions required fresh applications, not just a simple repetition of the story. The story, therefore, was ever fluid as it both shaped and mirrored the inner world of the teller, whether Paul's or that of the community. Moreover, given the threat that the past would become archaic, this community found ready to hand both Jewish and Graeco-Roman precedents for the continual repossession and reexperiencing of a storied past through a ritualistic narration of divine events.[63] That past remained alive not just through Christian belief in a set of facts, or even an unquestioning acceptance of Paul's preaching as God's truth, but through the repetition of the sacred story and mythic participation in the story through the cult.[64] The story and cult thus were central not just to Paul's preaching to win converts but also to the continuing life and identity of the church.

The tie of the story of Jesus to the story of Israel may reflect Paul's fear that the gentile church would lose its moorings and become an isolated sect. Paul appears to be aware of the danger that the gospel about Jesus as a new, dynamic story would disengage from the broader narrative of Israel. Except for 1 Thessalonians, in all of his letters, Paul uses allusions, Scripture citations, allegory, and metaphor to reach back to the oldest myths of the garden, to the stories of Abraham, Sarah, Moses, and the prophetic books to forge a connection with Israel's story. This may have been in part because of charges that Paul's gospel was an outrageous novelty and partly also because of his fear of a schism between the gentile and Jewish Christian wings of the church. In any case, Paul's efforts indicate his desire to retain an association between the new cult of the end time and the time honored stories of Israel.

The story also had an apocalyptic dimension that stretched out toward the future. That future was hardly a static point in time but assumed a dynamic character impinging on the present. Like a spaceship appearing motionless in space but in reality speeding in the direction of the viewer, so also the *parousia* of Jesus and the judgment of God moved in the direction of Paul's addressees. In a following chapter we shall note this important feature in Paul's thinking and how he adapted it to address his setting.

In sum, Paul's sense of his status as an apostle of the risen Christ was absolutely central to his self-understanding. That awareness imbued his mission with a sense of cosmic significance and gave it such a profound urgency that his message spread like a prairie grass fire across Asia Minor into Thrace, Macedonia, and Achaia and reached out toward Spain, the western edge of the known world. As an emissary of Christ Paul claimed the power to pronounce judgment and announce salvation to outsiders. His identification with his Lord was so absolute that the lines sometimes seemed to blur between his pronouncements and those of Christ (e.g., 1 Cor. 16:22), and he derived great strength from and even felt pride in the scars left on his body that resembled those inflicted on Christ at his crucifixion (Gal. 6:17). With his pen and his rhetoric he ultimately won the struggle with his rivals on the right and the left—the Jerusalem apostles on the right, who sought to require law observance for membership in the church, and the later Marcionites on the left, who sought to create a Christian church sundered from its Jewish roots. Paul's acceptance as an apostle did not come easily. He was never completely accepted by the followers of the Lord, if the testimony of the letters is preferred over Acts, and he defended his right to be called an apostle precisely because it was questioned so often. Yet in the long run, the defense he crafted in his letters succeeded so well that within a generation others stood in his shadow, writing letters in his name, claiming him as their authority for a later period and insuring his place in history.

CHAPTER THREE

The Letter Writer

As an apostle of Christ, Paul wrote letters, seven of which have been preserved. No other seven letters have had such an impact on human history. Working as an indispensable feature of Paul's apostolic mission, the letters serve not only as a source of Pauline theology and an influential part of the canon, they also provide valuable windows onto Paul's personality, his moods, character, and identity as an apostle of Christ.[1] Of equal importance, they reveal the earliest stage of the church's development and its growing sense of itself as an eschatological community. In the last two decades scholars have paid increasing attention to the letter—its form and context—and the comparison of the Pauline letters with the Hellenistic papyrus letters and the letters of philosophers and rhetoricians has produced a keener appreciation of the nuances of the Pauline apostolic letter. Letters excite interest because they tell us something of the personality of the writer. In a private letter, we expect to encounter an unvarnished humanness—pettiness and jealousy, love and hate, mortality and intimations of immortality.

Most letters from the modern period are so private that sensitive readers may be a bit embarrassed to look at what their eyes were never meant to see. But while ancient letters could also have a private dimension, they most often were broadly public. While we do encounter Paul's own passion, anger, disappointment, and loss as well as his anticipation, joy, thankfulness, and devotion in his letters, his epistles were hardly strictly private communications. While they often are deeply personal, their apostolic character lends them a significance that far transcends Paul the individual. Although profoundly theological they are hardly dogmatic treatises, for they do, as Deissmann suggested, deal with real life and are in that sense "real letters."[2] As such, they offer us valuable information about Paul's life and personality.

THE LEGACY OF LETTER WRITING

Almost as soon as people learned to write, they wrote messages—inscriptions to the gods, inventories on clay tablets for the recipients of goods, magical spells on ostraca (scraps of broken pottery) warding off evil spirits, and orders for commanders in the field. At least as early as the third millennium BCE the letter came into existence as a diplomatic tool. Kings wrote to other kings, to bureaucrats at large, and to military commanders. In 1935–38 an excavation at Mari in the south of Syria on the Euphrates yielded up some five thousand letters written in the first quarter of the second millennium BCE. In late fall 1887, a Bedouin woman discovered a number of tablets while digging, unaware of the site's significance, in the ruins of the royal city of Amenophis (alias Akhenaten) about 180 miles south of Cairo. The Bedouin woman uncovered and sold some three hundred letters written between 1377 and 1360 BCE by mostly Palestinian lords imploring the king to defend them against armed aggressors. One plea of several in that collection is especially poignant:

> To the King, my lord, my pantheon, my Sun-god, say: Thus Milkilu, thy servant, the dirt [under] thy feet. At the feet of the king, my lord, my pantheon, my Sun-god, seven times, seven times I fall. Let the king, my lord, know the deed which Yanhamu did to me after I left the presence of the king, my lord. Now he seeks two thousand [shekels] of silver from my hand, saying to me: "Give me thy wife and thy children, or I will smite!" Let the king know this deed, and let my lord send to me chariots, and let him take me to himself lest I perish![3]

We hear no royal response to these desperate entreaties.

Between 1932 and 1938 in the Lachish excavation in Palestine, Hebrew letters on ostraca were uncovered that were written to "my lord Yaosh," the commander of Lachish, during the last chaotic, desperate days of the Babylonian invasion of Judaea by Nebuchadrezzar (586 BCE):

> May Yahweh cause my lord to hear this very day tidings of good! And now according to everything that my lord hath written, so hath thy servant done; I have written on the door according to all that my lord hath written to me. . . . And let [my lord] know that we are watching for the [smoke] signals of Lachish, according to all the indications which my lord hath given, for we cannot see Azekah.[4]

With the Persian ascendancy after 537 BCE came an efficient, rapid delivery system, a change that encouraged diplomatic correspondence. Between the late sixth and fourth centuries BCE, the Persians developed an organized network throughout their vast empire for the speedy delivery of diplomatic and military correspondence on horseback. Alexander later adopted and adapted the system of the Persians whom he vanquished. And the vast, sprawling empire left by Alexander the Great in 323 BCE was well served by the same system. Riders on horseback formed a relay system, meeting at conveniently placed stations a day's ride apart to pass on their correspondence to the next rider. It was the Romans, however, who perfected the Persian and Hellenistic system. Seeing the value of the system in the east, Augustus adopted and used it for his own diplomatic and military purposes.[5] With better roads, distance markers, and the location of relay stations and inns at very precise intervals, the system became much more efficient in Roman usage.[6] Provided with fresh horses at the relay stations, riders were able to average fifty miles a day.

While this postal system served diplomatic and military purposes quite efficiently, no such delivery network was available for private correspondence.[7] And, while the wealthy could afford couriers, either slaves or trusted employees, to deliver letters, the great majority of the population had to content itself with less reliable means. They turned to a traveling businessman, a friend on a journey, a total stranger, or even a camel or donkey driver willing to promise delivery for a fee. Such ad hoc arrangements were often unreliable, and the cost of delivery worked a hardship on the sender. We do not know what percentage of the letters was stolen and read, was undeliverable, or was simply discarded. We are aware that senders were often anxious that the letter or packet would never arrive. One person writes: "I sent the breadbasket to you by means of Taurinos, the camel driver; regarding which, please send word to me that you received it."[8] But surely the writer knew that the reply, even if sent, also risked being lost and that he might never know if the basket arrived. Other letter writers wrote out and sent a duplicate letter by an alternate means hoping that the success rate of delivery would be at least fifty percent. Given the cost of writing material and the fee for a carrier, the uncertainty of delivery, and the high rate of illiteracy, it is just a bit short of miraculous that we have so much correspondence from these lower ranks of society. And it is totally understandable that Paul turned to co-workers like Timothy and Titus (2 Cor. 2:4) to carry and interpret his letters (1 Cor. 1:11). (See also 1 Cor. 1:11 [Chloe's people], 1 Thess. 3:1–5 [Timothy], and Rom. 16:1–2 [Phoebe] for examples of people who carried oral and possibly written messages from Paul.)

In spite of these vagaries, in the Hellenistic period the letter became an increasingly popular form of communication of separated parties. Although letters had been used by Plato, Aristotle, and other philosophers before the time of Alexander to encourage, advise, and promote philosophy among their disciples, it was the Hellenistic period that produced an expanding private correspondence. Diplomacy, trade, and travel fostered letter writing in the far flung empire of Alexander, and letter writing became even more prominent as an instrument of public policy in the Roman period. The imperial court used letters for propagandistic purposes, as a useful tool for spreading rumors, and to transmit closely guarded political and economic information.[9] No doubt the increasing use of the letter by the imperial court contributed to its popularity in private circles. Under this Hellenistic and Roman influence, handbooks on letter writing appeared. A class of letter writing professionals sprang up serving government bureaucracies, wealthy households, and, when the situation required it, the illiterate. Under the influence of rhetoric, the letter itself became in many circles an artistic form aiming to achieve a high level of aesthetic expression. The popularity of the letter among the rich and powerful obviously permeated the whole society. As a result literally thousands of papyrus letters from the late Hellenistic and Roman periods have survived. From the pen of the wealthy Roman Cicero alone 931 letters survive. From the privileged Pliny we have another 358 letters.[10] But to place the emphasis there is mistaken. For thousands more letters from men and women, soldiers and civilians, parents and children, merchants and farmers survive that deal with everyday human matters—a parent on edge about a sick child, a father worried about the safety of a son on a voyage at sea, an official anxiously waiting for a grain shipment for a starving population. These remains state unmistakably that the late Hellenistic and Roman period was the period of the letter. It should hardly surprise us that Paul the apostle, therefore, used this instrument to instruct, encourage, rebuke, nurture, and console his churches.

But what kind of letter writer was Paul? Already at the turn of the century Adolf Deissmann sought to answer that question. He saw a yawning gulf between the fine, public epistles straining for artistic expression and the private "real letters" of ordinary people preoccupied with everyday concerns. In Deissmann's own words, "The epistle differs from a letter as the dialogue from a conversation, as the historical drama does from history, as the carefully turned funeral oration does from the halting words of consolation spoken by a father to his motherless child—as art differs from nature. The letter is a piece of life, the epistle is a product of literary art."[11] Siding with the History of Religions School (*religionsgeschichtliche Schule*) against those so fixed on Paul's Jewish background that they missed the influence of the Hellenistic world entirely, Deissmann placed Paul squarely in the tradition of writers of "real" letters: "The letters of Paul," he said, "are not literary; they are real letters not epistles; they were written by Paul not for the public and posterity, but for the person to whom they are addressed."[12]

The spell that Deissmann cast over the study of the Pauline letter has been broken of late. A number of important studies of the past two decades have shown that Paul was influenced at some level by first century rhetoric and that, therefore, his letters are hardly the unsophisticated, simple, earthy products that Deissmann made them out to be.[13] Deissmann's fascination with the everydayness of "real letters" as opposed to the artiness and artificiality of the epistles, few would deny, reveals a romantic fascination more at home in the nineteenth than in this century. While Paul certainly did reach out to the poor, the uneducated, and the lower classes (1 Cor. 1:26–29), as did the early Christian movement in general, it is going too far to cast him as a social revolutionary who became their spokesman, defender, and liberator. Moreover, the juxtaposition of private and public letters is somewhat artificial and arbitrary, for at least in the case of Paul we have "real letters" that are intensely public in their concern with corporate life.[14] All except Philemon are addressed to communities, *ekklesiai,* and even in Philemon Paul was mindful of the "church in your house" (2); all were to be read before the "brothers and sisters" (1 Thess. 5:27); all expressed not merely Paul's own private thoughts or quest for identity but the language of the past, a vision of the future, and the vocabulary of a shared and emerging identity as the eschatological elect.

Contrary to Deissmann, Klaus Berger argued that ancient philosophical letters, not the papyrus letters of Egypt, offer the most likely background for the Pauline letters.[15] Berger thought that the papyrus letters of Egypt that Deissmann and White used as their comparison group offer a base too narrow to be helpful. They not only lack the strong theological interest of the Pauline letters, but a careful comparison also shows that they offer few analogues to the Pauline letters. Most of Paul's letters are rather long for letters; the papyrus letters were usually short and to the point. They contained particular letter forms that Paul did not use. For example, letters of recommendation found among them find no exact counterpart in Paul's correspondence. While Berger questions the basic assumption of White that "certain Greek letter types rest on specific structural models" he does find analogous materials in the letters of philosophers to their students and even to cities.[16] Because of their authoritative nature and strong ideological character these letters differ markedly from the papyrus letters dominated by a pragmatic concern with concrete realities.[17] The Cynic epistles, for example, that argue for the universality of wisdom (and stupidity),[18] that admonish students to avoid pleasure that is at the root of injustice and to avoid self-indulgence,[19] that laud asceticism,[20] and that offer a philosophical justification for begging[21] elevate the ideology of the author and interact little with the recipient of the letter. This elevation of the author's authority and ideology appears to support an older view of Paul the theologian par excellence whose theology appears to be little affected by the problems he faced.[22] We see, therefore, that the apostle's authority and his gospel become, for Berger, the most important formative elements in the Pauline letters.

Although Berger's thesis is attractive, under analysis it suffers. A careful study of election, which one might assume was basic to Paul's theological outlook, shows how his interaction with differing epistolary situations contributed to the development of his theology. Moreover, there are significant differences between the Cynic letters Berger appeals to and the Pauline letters. First, they are almost all pseudepigraphic; many of them come centuries after the author to whom they are ascribed. They little resemble the form of the Pauline letter we know. The salutation is ordinarily little more than a couple of words,[23] and a formulaic letter closing is often missing altogether. These "letters" are more like treatises in epistolary form than real letters, and unlike the Pauline letters these letters reveal little interaction between the writer and the addressee. They are more like monologues than like the real conversations on which we eavesdrop in the Pauline letters. While the ideological character of the letters of philosophers and the theological character of the Pauline letters bear a faint resemblance, they are poles apart in other areas.

While Stowers, like Berger, is harshly critical of Deissmann and at least implicitly censorious of John White's work, he nevertheless recognizes the weaknesses of Berger's work. He offers a compromise position that places the Pauline letters somewhere between a papyrus letter from the "lowest levels of culture and education" and the works of those of the "highest levels of rhetorical training."[24] In that judgment Stowers is certainly correct, but one must issue a caveat. Those levels intermingled to a significant degree. The Egyptian scribe from a remote, provincial town of the delta who was writing for an illiterate peasant employed a letter form that certainly shared some elements with Cicero if not with the philosophers. With the commercial and cultural exchanges between different peoples of the eastern Mediterranean, total isolation of classes or peoples was the exception rather than the rule, and ideas and practices of the dominant Hellenistic culture respected no boundaries. This is not to minimize the different levels of sophistication, complexity and subtlety between the two types of letters but rather to caution against a dramatic separation. Moreover, Paul's letters, as we shall see subsequently, have affinities with letters from both ends of the spectrum.

Even though the influence of the Hellenistic and Roman practice and theory of letter writing was important, it would be a mistake to ignore the effect of the Jewish tradition on Paul's letter form and content. Biblical imitations of Hebrew and Aramaic letters coupled with the physical evidence of such letters, while exceedingly valuable, do not exist in sufficient numbers to give us a complete picture of their form, content and function in the first millennium BCE. Only forty-eight Hebrew letters are currently known and only seventy Aramaic examples are extant.[25] Yet, they do possess certain features that mingle in Paul's letters with traits that can only come from a Hellenistic foreground. For example, the peace wish that appears in all of Paul's letters is one of the most stable elements of the letter form. With minor variation it runs, "Grace to you and peace (χάρις ὑμῖν καὶ εἰρήνη) from God our Father and the Lord Jesus Christ" (Rom. 1:7; 1 Cor. 1:3; 2 Cor. 1:2; Phil. 1:2; Philem. 3; Gal. 1:3; and 1 Thess. 1:1). While rare in the Hellenistic letter, such a prayerful wish for the welfare of the recipient(s) had a long history in the Hebrew and Aramaic letters. As early as the sixth century BCE, the Lachish ostraca contain the peace wish or prayer in the letter opening: "Thy servant Hoshaiah hath sent to inform my lord Yaosh: May Yahweh cause my lord to hear tidings of peace [well-being, *slm*]!"[26] Over seven hundred years later, this same address and greeting formula appears everywhere in the letters from the Bar Kokhba circles[27] and in the greeting in Aramaic letters as well.[28] Sometimes included in the salutation of these ancient letters were the names of the author and the addressee: for example, Hoshaiah to Yaosh. Later such a practice was standard: "Baruch, the son of Neriah, to the brethren carried into captivity: mercy and peace!" (*2 Baruch* 78:2). Although Paul combined and altered these rather stereotyped letter forms in some interesting and highly creative ways, this combination of Semitic and Hellenistic features in the letter opening probably had its genesis in the Diaspora Jewish community. Whatever its origin, Paul owned the combination as an essential feature of his correspondence with the churches.

Because of the intrinsic importance of the letter in the Hellenistic and Roman world, Paul's career as a letter writer was no trivial matter. Although fortunately, thousands of papyrus letters from the ancient world have survived, the reception of a letter by the less privileged was a major event. Since the literacy rate was a small fraction of the whole population, and since the expense of writing materials was considerable and the prospects for letter delivery uncertain, for the average person the arrival of a letter was momentous. Like Italian immigrants in America who read letters from "home" in the public square, who rejoiced together over good news and grieved over bad, and who delighted in the contact letters brought with friends and relatives left behind, most letter recipients in the ancient world also shared the mood of the writer and read or circulated the letter in a broader circle (e.g., see 1 Thess. 5:27).[29] It is no wonder, then, that not only the underclass but also the privileged treasured these precious letters. The importance of letters qua letters was at least one important factor accounting for the preservation of the Pauline letters we possess. While their theological profundity and relevance doubtless were major factors in the letters' preservation, copying, and ultimate canonization, it is a mistake to ignore the impact of the medium itself on the early church.

We have seen in the preceding that the venerable and pervasive letter writing tradition that informed Paul's practice was rich and varied. We shall see subsequently how skillfully Paul used the letter to articulate deep passion and subtle, complex ideas of importance to the church. In his ingenious use of the letter Paul, in fact, created the "apostolic letter tradition" that was to play a major role in the shaping of the identity of the early church and its sense of mission.[30] That point leads us to think about the purposes of the letter itself.

THE FUNCTION OF THE LETTER

On one point most scholars agree: the letter aims to substitute presence for absence.[31] The one irrefutable fact that stands behind letters is distance. It may be geographical, social, psychological, or religious, but distance it is, nevertheless. And the letters aim to bridge that gulf with words one step removed from face to face conversation. Memory itself offered a way of spanning the gap: "Even though I have been separated from you for a long time, I suffer this in body only. For I can never *forget you* or the impeccable way we were reared together from childhood up" (Demetrius, *On Style* 231–32, emphasis added).[32] Paul also regularly asks his addressees to join him in recalling their previous experience together: "You know that it was because of a physical infirmity that I first announced the gospel to you; though my condition put you to the test, you did not scorn or despise me, but welcomed me as an angel of God, as Christ Jesus" (Gal. 4:13–14). With some frequency in 1 Thessalonians Paul rehearses experiences shared with his addressees: "You yourselves know, brothers and sisters, that our coming to you was not in vain" (2:1); "as you know, we had courage in our God to declare to you the gospel of God in the face of great opposition" (2:2, RSV); "For we never used either words of flattery, as you know, or a cloak for greed" (2:5, RSV); "you remember our labor and toil, brothers and sisters" (2:9, my trans.); "for you know how, like a father with his children, we exhorted each one of you and encouraged you" (2:11, RSV); "You yourselves know that this [affliction] is to be our lot" (3:3, RSV); "we told you beforehand that we were to suffer affliction . . . and as you know" (3:4, RSV). Memory thus places them in Paul's presence, and the epistolary recitation of that memory places Paul in their presence. That previous shared experience gives the letter its hold on them and opens them up to the presence the letter brings. Even in letters like Romans in which Paul can make no appeal to their physical life together, he nevertheless can assume a shared experience of the gospel: "For I am longing to see you so that I may share with you some spiritual gift to strengthen you—or rather so that we may be mutually encouraged by each other's faith, both yours and mine" (1:11–12). To talk about presence in this way is to emphasize the role the corporate imagination played in bridging the gap between Paul and his addressees.

A graphic instance of such an imaginative exercise occurs in 1 Cor. 5:1–5, where Paul asks his readers (or hearers) to join with him in the cultic exclusion of an egregious sexual offender. When they are assembled Paul asks them to conjure his presence ("and my spirit is present") "with the power of our Lord Jesus" and to "deliver this man to Satan for the destruction of the flesh" (5:4–5, RSV). He admits his physical absence to emphasize presence at another level ("I am present in spirit") then turns to the subjunctive—"and as if [physically] present"—to speak of his judgment as virtual reality (5:3, RSV). Obviously this presence requires the cooperation and even the imaginative collaboration of the community in Corinth, and implicit in this joint action is a recognition of Paul's authority as an apostle. While it is true, as Funk has shown, that Paul's letters and his emissaries were surrogates for the apostolic presence, it is helpful also to attend to the role memory and imagination played in that sense of presence.[33]

While this presence was often supportive and complimentary (e.g., Phil. 1:3–8; 1 Thess. 1:2; 1 Cor. 1:4–6; Rom.1:8–9), the anticipated "apostolic *parousia*" was not always so benign. On the strength of a rather robust sense of authority vested in him by Christ, Paul sometimes warns his addressees of his anticipated *parousia*. In 1 Cor. 4:18–21, for example, Paul threatens the "arrogant" to come "with a rod." Anxiety and belligerency coalesce in 2 Cor. 12:14–13:13—anxiety that both he and the Corinthians may be disappointed in the other when he comes and belligerency evident in his warning that if sinners remain unreconstructed on his next visit he "will not be lenient" (13:2). But such a menacing tone occurs only in letters redundant with shrill exchanges. Elsewhere, in Romans for example, Paul looks forward to a pleasant and mutually affirming encounter (1:11–12), and encouraged by Timothy's report of the faith of the Thessalonian believers, Paul prays that he may soon visit them and supply whatever is needful in their faith (1 Thess. 3:7, 8, 10; cf. Phil. 2:19–24). He speaks autobiographically of his time with the Thessalonians when he behaved "like a nurse tenderly caring for her own children" (1 Thess. 2:7). Whatever the tone, however, Funk correctly saw the apostolic *parousia* as a demonstration of Paul's authority.[34] Yet the anticipation of his *parousia* differs from the letter and the emissary. These expressions of presence are realized in the *hic et nunc*, while Paul's hope to visit his addressees, the so-called apostolic *parousia,* can only anticipate a future meeting.

Clearly, Paul's letters aim to exhort and advise. The two concrete realities that summoned the letter—that is, (1) the embryonic nature of the new religion of converts and (2) the frequent attacks on the legitimacy of Paul's apostleship and gospel—required the exhortation we see in all of Paul's letters. It is no wonder, then, that Paul's letters both instruct the converts and defend his gospel and apostleship. The instruction itself served a host of purposes. It prepared the community to present itself "blameless" at the *parousia* of the Lord Jesus (1 Thess. 5:23; 1 Cor. 1:8; Phil. 2:15); it reminded these young converts of matters they were prone to forget; and it dealt with issues that inevitably arose in this new movement when the *parousia* was delayed. While the letters made no effort to retell the gospel story, they did interpret it, and they assumed familiarity with and participation in it.[35] As such they subverted the symbolic world of the pagans previously inhabited by the converts and constructed another world with its own peculiar ethos, a world consistent with Paul's view of the "new creation" (Gal. 6:15). While Paul was influenced by both Jewish and Hellenistic forms for and types of letters, the context summoning his letters also operated to shape their form and content and to give them a high level of specificity and concreteness.

Stanley Stowers isolates several types of letters from the Mediterranean world that he believes may have informed Paul's letter writing.[36] He finds evidence for letters of friendship, familial letters, praising and blaming letters, and letters of exhortation and advice. This latter category he subdivides further into paraenetic letters, letters of advice, protreptic letters urging conversion to a particular way of life or point of view, letters of admonition, letters of rebuke, letters of reproach, letters of consolation, and letters of mediation. Each type of letter he believes contains a central if not single emphasis. While Stowers grants that Paul's letters rarely run true to type, he does believe with Malherbe that 1 Thessalonians is a paraenetic letter and Romans is a protreptic letter aiming to bring the addressees to endorse his version of the gospel.[37] But even in these two letters Stowers's view is too simplistic, for there is much in 1 Thessalonians that is not paraenesis, and Romans is so complex and appears to legitimately serve so many purposes that it frustrates all efforts to reduce it to a single type. It is more accurate to say that most if not all of Paul's letters combine many of the emphases that Greco-Roman letters may treat singly. However, all letter types were not equally influential. Letters of exhortation and advice, praise and blame were so prominent in the Hellenistic and Roman letters that one must suspect these emphases were deeply rooted in the common ethos. It is hardly surprising, therefore, that they should play a role in every one of Paul's letters.[38] For instance, in typical Hellenistic fashion, Paul appealed to his own example to exhort, encourage, admonish, and urge on the Corinthians a theology that valued suffering, lowliness, rejection, deprivation, and loss instead of glory, success, and power (1 Cor, 4:8–16). Moreover, note how he closed his letter to the Thessalonians with a list of exhortations (5:12–21) and how he took up the pen to scribble a final exhortation and warning in Galatians (6:11–17). And the list could go on. Exhortation we may assume, was one of the main functions of Paul's letters as a whole and not restricted to paraenetic sections alone.

Paul also writes to console. While he writes no letters of consolation as such, he clearly does offer comfort and encouragement to the persecuted, the discouraged, the ostracized, and the downtrodden. Although there is no disputing the claim of Stowers that "Consolation was very important in the Greco-Roman world"[39] and that an important task of the philosopher was to give consolation, the Jewish tradition even more strongly influenced Paul's emphasis on consolation in the letters. In 2 Cor. 1:3–7 we see, for example, how the Septuagintal traditions informed Paul's religious thought. Like his Scriptures, the Septuagint, Paul extolled God as the source of all consolation (2 Cor. 1:3; Isa. 40:1–11; 57:18; see also Josephus, *Test. Jos.* 1:6; 2:6; 4 *Esr.* 12:8; 10:24). Like his native Judaism, Paul emphasized the duty of those consoled to console one another even as they had been consoled (2 Cor. 1:4–7; Josephus, *Ant.* 15:61; *War* 1:627; 4 *Esr.* 10:2). That consolation should be prized in both Jewish and pagan settings, and that the dual emphases should reinforce each other in the Hellenistic Judaism of the Diaspora, should come as no surprise. While distress is indigenous to the human condition and the inclination to empathize or sympathize (συμπαθέω) with those in distress is quite common, Paul gives his emphasis on consolation an apocalyptic and Christological focus that separates it from its Hellenistic setting. In 1 Thessalonians, for example, Paul grounds the consolation he offers to the bereaved and discouraged in standard apocalyptic mythology (4:13–18). For Paul it was precisely that mythology that distinguished believers from those "who have no hope" (4:13). And while he does refer to the dead as those who "have fallen asleep" (κοιμωμένων), the consolation he offers does not depend on the euphemism, sleep, to rob death of its sting.[40] Rather, the consolation rests on Paul's belief that "Jesus died and rose again, even so, through Jesus, God will bring with him those who have fallen asleep" (4:14, RSV). Sensitive to the concern of his addressees about the fate of believers who have died, Paul cites a "word of the Lord, that we who are alive, who are left until the coming of the Lord, will by no means precede those who have fallen asleep" (4:15, RSV). Paul wraps his warrant for consolation in a recitation of the final apocalyptic scenario with the archangel's call, the sounding of a trumpet, the descent of Jesus to meet the rising dead, and the final glorious reunion of the living and dead with Jesus (4:16–18).While Paul's emphasis on consolation owes much to its Jewish and Hellenistic forbearers, its christological grounding came either from Paul's own theological reflection or the gospel of the early church.

The letter also functions as a medium for responding to his critics. Certainly in Galatians, 1 and 2 Corinthians, Philippians, and Romans, Paul responds to criticism of his gospel and apostleship. Stimulated by the argument of G. A. Kennedy that the rule of ancient rhetoric influenced Paul's response to his critics and his defense of his gospel and claim to be an apostle, in the past two decades critics have increasingly turned to rhetorical criticism to divine the subtleties of Paul's strategy of persuasion and defense.[41] Since the letter was a substitute for live speech, it seemed entirely appropriate to apply the rules governing strategies of oral persuasion or rhetoric to the letter itself. Moreover, given the influence of rhetorical theory on public discourse in the Graeco-Roman world, it seems reasonable that rhetorical practices would have influenced letter writing.[42] Hans Dieter Betz, for example, argues that Galatians is best viewed as an "apologetic letter" in which Paul writes as if he were a defendant making a courtroom speech to refute his accusers before the Galatian churches serving as the jury.[43] It was Betz's work, more than Kennedy's, that encouraged numerous scholars to read other Pauline letters through the rhetorical lens.[44] Surely this new approach has been stimulating and provocative, but it is also problematic. A comparison of rhetorical critical analyses of the Pauline letters will reveal, for instance, sharp disagreements in how well his letters fit this template. As a case in point, Galatians cannot be forced naturally into the forensic model that Betz imposes on it. Aune has argued, instead, that Galatians did not conform to a single rhetorical type but was a mix of both forensic and deliberative rhetoric.[45] Paul surely was not trained in any one rhetorical school, but to the degree that he used rhetorical strategies at all he was, as Aune shows, eclectic and inventive, using various rhetorical strategies and combining them with different literary styles.[46]

In the application of rhetorical theory to specific texts there has been little agreement. In Jewett's rhetorical analysis of 1 Thessalonians, for example, he assigns 1:1–5 to the *exordium* or introduction of Paul's "speech," whereas Kennedy assigns 1:2–10 to this category.[47] Scholars are equally divided about ways to divide 1 Corinthians. Mitchell's use of rhetorical analysis persuades her that the letter displays all of the units of a single "speech," and Pesch is convinced that 1 Corinthians contains four letters or "speeches," each embodying essential rhetorical features.[48] Other scholars disagree on the type of rhetoric 1 Corinthians typifies. Wuellner argues that it is demonstrative rhetoric, and Kennedy believes that it is deliberative.[49] How is one to understand these extreme disagreements? Jerome Murphy-O'Connor thinks they are caused by three things: (1) attempts to force the Pauline letters into a rhetorical mold that illfits the particular letters; (2) the lack of any "controls to reduce the danger of misinterpretations of both Paul and the rhetorical theorists"; and (3) the false assumption that Paul felt bound to follow the principles of rhetoric in highly situational letters (e.g., 1 Cor.).[50] Stowers correctly notes that though rhetoric carries important implications for understanding Paul's letters, a rhetorical analysis of Paul's letters "only partially works. This is because the letter writing tradition was essentially independent of rhetoric."[51] Moreover, as we have already noted, the exhortation or paraenesis that is so prominent in many Pauline letters is of little importance to rhetoricians.

While clearly Paul vigorously defends his apostolic claim and the gospel he preaches against a wide range of critics, one must studiously avoid forcing that defense into a rhetorical framework that may pinch in a number of places. The modern interpreter must understand both the limits and possibilities of rhetorical analysis. Both in his use of the letter form and in his rhetorical strategy Paul enjoyed enormous freedom to appropriate, change, distort, adapt, and combine to defend himself. His obvious use of that freedom works against efforts to frame Paul's argument by a rigid set of rules laid down in books of rhetoric. Attention to his skillful and adaptive use of that freedom can better help us appreciate the detail and subtlety of his argument. Finally, both literary and rhetorical analysis are exceedingly valuable in helping us better understand one of the purposes of Paul's writing—namely, the defense of his apostleship and gospel.

THE FORM OF THE LETTER

While the letter writing tradition was, as Stowers argued, essentially "independent of rhetoric," it was not entirely divorced from it.[52] There is good reason, however, to examine the form of the letter for clues to Paul's purposes. Because the natural or even unconscious use of the epistolary conventions of his day was so predictable, their modification offers important clues to Paul's intentions. This is especially the case with stereotypical parts of the letter such as the salutation, thanksgiving, and closing. Since the body of the letter is as varied as the human experience, in both shape and form it is less predictable and more difficult to interpret.

The Salutation

The salutation typically included the name of the person sending the letter, the intended recipient—for example, "Irenaeus to Apollinarius"—a greeting, and often good wishes: "Philoxenos to Apollos his brother greeting (χαίρειν) and good health (ἐρρῶσθαι)."[53] While these features normally appear, the salutation could and often did include additional information.[54] As Paul's ministry unfolded and opposition developed, the salutation could include items that telegraphed to the reader Paul's defense that was to follow. While Paul's debt to this form is apparent, when his letter writing informed by his Christian mission and gospel, a metamorphosis occurred.

In Galatians especially where Judaizers openly and vigorously challenged Paul's apostolic status and gospel, he expanded the reference to himself, the sender, to emphasize the divine genesis and validity of his call. The Galatians doubtless knew that Paul had no historical connection with the earthly Jesus. That missing link, some believed, excluded him from the inner circle of apostles at Jerusalem. Without these direct historical links, Paul's apostleship appeared to them to be baseless and his gospel, at best, derived from a human source. His sensitivity to this charge erupts in the first line of the letter. In the expansion of the reference to himself as the sender of the letter Paul signaled his intention to defend his apostleship with vigor: "Paul, an *apostle, not from men, neither through man* **but** through Jesus Christ **and** God the father who raised him from the dead" (1:1, emphasis added, my trans.). Later he repeated for emphasis that his gospel was "not from a human source," adding that he was not "taught it" but instead had received it "through a revelation of Jesus Christ" (1:11–12). Even if one cannot agree with Hans Dieter Betz that Galatians as a whole is apologetic rhetoric, there is little question about the apologetic character of the first two chapters and no doubt that the salutation offers a window onto that wider epistolary world.

The quite different challenges facing Paul in Corinth are previewed there also in the amplification of his role as the sender. In 1 Cor. 1:1 also Paul displayed some edginess regarding challenges to his apostleship. Different from the questions posed in Galatians, they nonetheless demonstrate the vulnerability of Paul's apostolic claim. For if Paul can maintain his apostleship through a revelation from Christ, cannot the challengers as well claim divine access and truth through their mystical identification with the risen Lord? His identification of himself, the sender, as *paulos* is entirely traditional; his appended note with its theological assertion that he was "called to be an apostle of Christ Jesus by the will of God" (1:1) has no parallel in the papyrus letters. Paul's claim to be called by God through Jesus Christ reflects not only a profound religious conviction but also reflects his nervousness over the sharp questions raised about the authenticity of or even the need for his apostleship. While the charismatic experience of the members of the church at Corinth gave them a sense of divine immediacy and personal salvation here and now, the location of Paul's apostleship in the call of God through Jesus Christ provided the authority he needed to correct and redirect their religious enthusiasm.

Except for the reference to being called [by God] Paul's parenthetical description of himself in 2 Corinthians is identical to that of 1 Corinthians, yet the conditions prompting it were entirely different. The challenge was external rather than internal. It came from other Christian apostles rather than charismatically inspired members of the congregation. And the challenge was deliberately designed to attack Paul's vulnerable points—his physical weakness, his unimpressive speech, and his suspect apostolic credentials. Because of the composite nature of 2 Corinthians, 1:1 can hardly be read as a salutation belonging to 2 Cor. 10:1–13:13. If it actually came after the writing of 10–13, as seems probable, then this piece of the salutation would reinforce the legitimacy of Paul's apostolic claim that by this time may have been recognized. Nevertheless, in this opening the sting from the scorn of his critics still lingers.

In Romans the extended reference to Paul himself likewise appears to have an apologetic character: "Paul, a slave of Christ Jesus, called to be an apostle, set aside [by God] for the gospel of God" (1:1, my trans.). Such an elaborate, richly theological statement sounds like an attempt to anticipate and refute anti-Pauline propaganda from the east. By locating himself like Moses and Abraham in the biblical tradition as a slave of God, and by anchoring his apostleship in God and by underscoring its missionary purpose, Paul offers an antidote to news of his notoriety as a maverick who was preaching a gospel that was an outrageous novelty. Perhaps that is the reason Paul uses traditional materials in 1:2–4 to describe his gospel before repeating for emphasis that his gospel has a divine source. Following the reference to "Jesus Christ our Lord" Paul quite self-consciously adds "through whom we have received grace and apostleship for the obedience of faith unto all the gentiles" (1:5, my trans.). Whereas in Paul's other letters, the addressee immediately comes into view, in Romans that appearance is delayed to 1:6–7.[55] Jerome Murphy-O'Connor thinks that these attacks on Paul came because of his break with the church at Antioch and those who had commissioned him there as an apostle to the gentiles, which caused him to lose his base of support and become increasingly vulnerable.[56] But it is hard to understand how he would have been protected from the challenge of his critics in Galatia or 2 Corinthians by a continued relationship with the church at Antioch.

The salutation of Paul's letters confirms their corporate nature.[57] Everywhere in his letters Paul addresses the *ekklēsia* or, synonymously, the saints. And Murphy-O'Connor is correct that the salutation gives the secular term *ekklēsia* (assembly) its theological nuance.[58] For example, in 1 Thessalonians Paul addresses "the assembly (*ekklēsia*) of the Thessalonians in God the father and the Lord Jesus Christ" (1:1, my trans.), and in 1 and 2 Corinthians he greets "the assemblies of God" (*ekklēsia tou theou*) (1 Cor. 1:2; 2 Cor. 1:1). And while he connects no such parenthetical phrase to the greeting of the *ekklēsiais* in Galatia and makes no reference to them as the "saints," I cannot agree with Murphy-O'Connor that these omissions deny these assemblies any religious significance.[59] Paul is obviously angry that they seek to supplement his gospel with circumcision, but he does not rule out their status as "the Israel of God" (Gal. 6:16), a highly charged religious description. In Philippians and Romans Paul addresses respectively "the saints" (1:1) and "all God's beloved in Rome, who are called to be saints" (1:7), expressions that are in the same language field with "the *ekklēsia* of God." All of these terms underscore the special status of the addressees as God's elect or chosen. When one asks "Who do these people think they are?" it becomes obvious that Paul's naming of his addressees as "saints" and "*ekklēsia* of God" reinforces their identity as God's elect.

The Thanksgiving

The contours of the second main part of the letter were first described by Paul Schubert in his epochal work, *The Form and Function of the Pauline Thanksgivings*.[60] The thanksgiving, we now know, often appeared in Hellenistic letters in which the writer thanks the gods for health, a safe journey, deliverance from danger, or good fortune. This pattern influenced even 2 Maccabees, which gives thanks for "having been saved by God out of grave dangers" and thanks God "for taking our side against the king" (1:11). Schubert observed that the thanksgiving followed the salutation, telegraphed the purpose of the letter, and in some cases provided an outline of the major concerns of the letter. He noted that a thanksgiving or blessing appears in all of Paul's letters except Galatians, and given the bad blood that had developed between Paul and the churches there, the substitution of a cry of astonishment for the normal thanksgiving is totally understandable (1:6). The acrimony was provoked by Judaizers who found Paul's gospel deficient and his apostleship suspect and preached instead a gospel that included circumcision.

Schubert noted how the thanksgiving served to bring the situation of the addressees to light and outline the major issues that the letter addresses.[61] The thanksgiving of 1 Corinthians, for example, introduces *charismata* and *gnosis* (1:5, 7), topics to which Paul will return and that he will discuss at greater length later in the letter (1:18–4:21; 12–14). And with consummate skill, in Romans Paul offers a preview of his gospel for "Greek and barbarian," prepares for his coming visit, and lays the foundation for his later reference to his Spanish mission (15:28). Schubert's thesis has profoundly influenced scholars such as John White, Nils Dahl, and William Doty, who led the North American study of the structure of the letter that in turn inspired the study of rhetorical patterns in Paul's letters.[62]

While Schubert's thesis was groundbreaking, its application was hardly as straightforward as one might expect. As noted previously, there is no thanksgiving in Galatians. 2 Corinthians contains a blessing instead of a thanksgiving (1:3–7), and 1 Thessalonians contains portions of three different thanksgivings (1:2–10; 2:13; 3:9–10). And it is difficult to locate with certainty the end of the thanksgiving in Romans. Does it end in midsentence with 1:9 as Fitzmyer suggests,[63] or does it run to 1:15 (i.e., 1:8–15) as Dunn believes,[64] or might it not also include the theme of the letter appearing in 1:16–17?[65] Even Schubert himself admits that no climactic statement occurs in Romans to mark the ending of the thanksgiving.[66] And finally, if Philippians is a composite of two letters, as Sellew has recently argued (or three letters, as many others hold), then the thanksgiving in 1:3–11 can only usefully serve as a guide through one portion of the canonical letter. Thus, though a careful reading of the thanksgiving can offer valuable clues to Paul's epistolary purposes, it is no foolproof indicator of the topics Paul aims to treat. While Paul does express his gratitude for such things as the faith, love, and hope of the congregation (1 Thess. 1:3) in the thanksgiving, the thanksgiving is more than an expression of gratitude for things of one sort or another. It also offers clues to Paul's paraenetic interests prior to their adumbration in the letter, sometimes includes references to his apocalyptic expectations (e.g., 1 Thess. 1:9–10) and eschatological hope that will be discussed later, and often contains autobiographical remarks that may encourage a persecuted church or challenge a rival group of apostles.[67] We see, therefore, that even allowing for enormous variety in the Pauline thanksgivings, they nevertheless offer valuable clues to the purpose of the letter and its outline and are the gateway to the body of the letter.

The Body of the Letter

As one would expect, the body of the letter is the least stereotypical of any of the letter parts, and, therefore, its form is the most difficult to define critically. Often introduced with a request (Παρακαλῶ, "I beseech you," 1 Cor. 1:10) or a disclosure formula (Γινώσκειν δὲ ὑμᾶς Βούλομαι, "I want you to know," Phil. 1:12), the body of the letter opens out onto a landscape broad enough to span the whole range of human experience and theological reflection.[68] Because of its comprehensive scope and almost infinite variety, the body of the letter is ill defined[69] but not entirely formless. The older tendency to divide Paul's letters into theological and paraenetic parts has been thoroughly discredited by the recognition that paraenesis and theology are so intricately intertwined in the Pauline letters that such a division is entirely artificial. And, while Doty is correct that "in the body sections of the longer letters, at least, Paul had more inclination to strike out on his own and to be least bound by epistolary structures," he does favor certain formal elements. Often, but not always, Paul opens the body of the letter with an autobiographical statement. In 1 Thess. 1:2–2:16 autobiography extends the thanksgiving with a strong paraenetic emphasis.[70] In Gal. 1:10–2:21 autobiographical references to his relationship with the Jerusalem church have a shrill apologetic character.[71] In Phil. 1:12–30 his autobiographical remarks encourage his readers by showing how his imprisonment served to advance the gospel. In 1 Cor. 1:10–17 an autobiographical note reveals how he has learned of their factious behavior and paves the way for his exhortation. The autobiographical report of grave hardships in Asia Minor, dark reminiscences about the troubled relationship between himself and his addressees, and the hoped for resolution in 2 Cor. 1:8–2:13 all provide a window onto the past and future of that relationship. In all of these cases, Paul's autobiographical remarks open the body of the letter and impinge rather sharply on the literary world of his readers.

Paraenesis is also a formal element in the letter that scholars have long recognized in the letter. And Paul's paraenesis is intricately interwoven with the perceived identity of his converts. We cannot always be certain about who Paul's converts thought they were, but Paul is more certain. They are the elect of God (1 Thess. 1:4), the saints (1 Cor. 1:2), the called (1 Cor. 1:2), God's *ekklēsia,* or assembly (2 Cor. 1:1), the circumcision (Phil. 3:3), the Israel of God (Gal. 6:16), God's adopted children (Gal. 4:5), and so on. As God's people they are to live a life worthy of that status. The aim of the paraenesis is to help these elect to present themselves blameless "before our God and Father, at the coming of our Lord Jesus with all his saints" (1 Thess. 3:13).

Because Paul recognizes that these "saints" are to live in a manner befitting their eschatological calling, the paraenesis is an important feature of his theological interests and no mere appendage to them. From the Greek παρα-ινέω meaning to exhort, urge, advise, or recommend, paraenesis is sprinkled throughout the letters from thanksgiving to letter closing. With the use of material appropriated from a variety of traditions—from Hellenistic Judaism, from the Septuagint, and possibly from Hellenistic popular moral philosophy—Paul aimed not to develop a new ethical system but to offer guidance and encouragement for those "walking" in the way of Christ.[72] While recognizing Paul's debt to his sources, it is also important to note how skillfully he adapted general "moral saws to specific and concrete account."[73] Some letters, such as 1 Thessalonians, are predominantly, though not exclusively, paraenesis,[74] and others, like Galatians, mix apologetic and ethical instruction. Normally offered by superordinates—that is a parent, a teacher, or an apostle—or a good friend, paraenesis varies greatly. It may include random, unrelated injunctions strung together like beads on a string with little to hold them together but a catchword or a similar grammatical construction (e.g., Rom. 12:9–13). It may also contain lists of virtues and vices of non-Christian origin yet taken over and used for community guidance (Gal. 5:19–23). Or it may offer extended exhortations that aim to reinforce conduct already recognized as required by God (1 Thess. 4:13–18; 5:1–11). With its extended discussion of problems revealed to Paul by Chloe's people or by the letter to Paul from the Corinthian church, 1 Corinthians contains a significant amount of paraenetic material of this latter type. Also, the descriptions of conduct in the autobiographical material in some letters provide models whose imperative for imitation have a clear paraenetic function (1 Thess. 1:6). These self-referential remarks, inasmuch as they are rooted in Jesus' death, link converts with Christ himself by following Paul's own example (1 Cor. 11:1; cf. 1 Thess. 1:6). As haphazard as these injunctions may sometimes sound, and as divorced as they may appear from a Christian ethos, they nevertheless serve Paul's epistolary purposes by offering encouragement to the discouraged, direction to those uncertain of their way, and reminders to those prone to forget what the modus vivendi really is for those in Christ. Moreover, Paul's careful choice of materials and the stress he places on certain elements give these traditional materials a sharp contextual relevance.[75] The energy driving the ethos of the church was, in Paul's view, the new life in Christ or, put another way, the life in the spirit (Rom. 6:1–7:6 and 8:1–4).

While the body of the letter contains these elements, it also includes apologetic material as diverse as the challenges to Paul's apostleship and gospel and as varied as the problems peculiar to each congregation. Nevertheless, Paul often signals the reader that the body of the letter is drawing to a close and that the letter closing is about to begin through the disclosure of travel plans. Robert Funk first saw how different facets of Paul's apostolic presence—the letter, an emissary to represent him, or his own anticipated visit—combine near the close of the letter to emphasize the purpose of the letter and to urge the recipients to follow the course of action he prescribes.[76] In the words of Funk, "All of these are media by which Paul makes his apostolic authority effective in the churches."[77] The three expressions of presence scattered about in the papyrus letters Paul gathers and uses for the most part in one discrete section marking the end of the body of the letter (Rom. 15:14–33; 1 Cor. 16:1–9, 10–ll; 2 Cor. 12:14–13:10; Phil. 2:19–24; 25–30).[78] These in turn serve as the threshold for the letter closing.

The Letter Closing

Just as "hellos" and "good-byes" smooth the way to meeting and parting, so also certain conventions in first century letters ritualize the entry into and exit from an epistolary conversation. The endings of Paul's letters were likewise shaped by the epistolary conventions of his day, both Jewish and Hellenistic. And Paul deftly adapted those habits of encounter and parting to serve his own purposes. Recently it has become clear that the ending of the letter, no less than the opening, contains important clues to Paul's intentions and efforts to edify the community and that the ending, like the beginning, is fairly stereotypical. For example, the conclusion typically contains the following elements:

1. Concluding paraenesis
2. Peace wish that may include a prayer request (1 Thess. 5:25)

  3. Greetings from Paul and his co-workers and admonition to greet one
     another with a holy kiss
  4. Final grace and benediction

We will consider each of these parts in turn.

Paul's ethical instruction urges his addressees to behave in a manner that will allow them to present themselves pure and blameless at the *parousia* of the Lord Jesus. Typically, the letter closing, like the letter opening, emphasizes an ethos consistent with this view of the new life in Christ and aspects of that ethos that have a sharp relevance for his hearers. 1 Thess. 5:16–18 immediately comes to mind, where Paul's exhortation to persevere has special significance for those blinded by their grief over the death of beloved believers, and his admonition to "do good" applies especially to those who freeload on other believers. Faced with this situation, Paul creates a general paraenetic exhortation to address it. He crafts a parallel construction strongly emphasizing tenacity in the face of discouragement and underscoring the need for perseverance in a piety genuinely indicative of the new life in Christ:

> always (πάντοτε) do good to one another and to everyone.
> Always (πάντοτε) rejoice,
> unceasingly (ἀδεαλείπτως) pray,
> in all circumstances (ἐν παντὶ) give thanks.
> For this is the will of God in Christ Jesus for you. (5:15–16)

We see, therefore, that traditional paraenesis for Paul is hardly a "bag of answers to meet recurring problems and questions common to the members of different early Christian communities."[79]

Likewise, the same protocol paves the way to the ending of 1 Corinthians. Beginning with the disclosure of his intention to visit and perhaps spend the winter before continuing on his way (16:5–7), then promising a *parousia* of Timothy (16:10–11) or even of Apollos when opportunity permits (16:12), Paul pens his final paraenetic cluster that signals the imminent end of the conversation. Nothing in that cluster betrays a Christian provenance. The four imperatives and one cohortative would be at home in any philosophical or popular religious context, and superficially what they offer seems especially bourgeois:

> Be alert (Γρηγορεῖτε), stand firm (στήνκε) in the faith, be courageous (ἀνερίζεσθε), be strong (κραταιοῦσθε), let everything be done in love (ἀγάπη).

But a close reading shows how Paul modified these ordinary injunctions to give them practical issue for the Corinthians. He chose this string of imperatives, probably adding the prepositional phrase "in the faith," and gave "love" the ultimate and commanding position in the catena. This emphasis betrays the epistolary context and is the heart of the purpose of the letter itself. Already in 13:1–13 Paul had either appropriated or created the ode to love (ἀγάπη) to shatter the charismatic hierarchy constructed and used by the Corinthians with great destructive consequence. There Paul used love as an eschatological gift that revalued every other charism, and sought to heal divisions in the church triggered by religious puffery (5:2). Later he concluded the letter with a curse on those lacking any love for the Lord (16:22). This context makes Paul's emendation of the popular paraenesis especially pertinent, and in the end it defines the essence of the eschatological status claimed by the Corinthians. We see, therefore, how these final paraenetic clusters often incorporate prime concerns of the author Paul. (See also 2 Cor. 13:11.)

The peace wish that follows signals the reader that Paul has now passed the point of no return and that the letter very shortly is coming to a close. While this peace wish functions like ἔρρωσο (farewell or good-bye) of the Hellenistic papyrus letters,[80] it more closely resembles the peace wish (*shalom*) at the end of the Semitic letter. That peace reaches beyond inner serenity to embrace the whole general welfare of the recipient. Another similarity to the peace wish in many Semitic letters is that Paul's concluding peace wish echoes that of the letter opening, "Grace to you and peace," which with some variation appears in all of Paul's letters. Although this wish was stereotypical, Paul also bent it to serve his epistolary interests.

The best example of his appropriation of the peace wish to push the agenda of his letter is 1 Thessalonians. There Paul enumerates one last time the major concerns of the letter—the stress on holiness, the emphasis on preparing for the imminent consummation, and the reaffirmation of the faithfulness of God to the elect or the called:

> May the God of peace himself sanctify you completely and may your spirit and soul and body be preserved blameless at the *parousia* of our Lord Jesus Christ. The one calling you is faithful, and he will do it.

Here Paul offers not just a prayerful wish for the whole general welfare or peace of his addressees, but instead he so defines that peace as to involve them in the act of sanctification and uses the expanded peace wish to reassure the discouraged that God is able to preserve them now and hereafter. He thus reaffirms the future they have come to doubt and involves them in active preparation for it.

While 1 Thessalonians contains the most elaborate peace wish of Paul's letters, its features appear also in other letters. Still pained by the factious behavior of the Corinthians, he encourages them to "live in peace; and the God of love and peace will be with you" (2 Cor. 13:11, NRSV). Likewise, the final peace wish in Galatians Paul pronounces on those who affirm the "new creation" in which there is no distinction of circumcised and uncircumcised: "As for those who will follow this rule—peace be upon them, and mercy, and upon the Israel of God" (6:16, NRSV). The way Paul the apostolic superordinate assures his addressees of divine peace to some extent reflects the client-lord structure of the political and social order. That is, the apostle as a superordinate or an emissary of Christ appointed directly bestows peace on his client converts. Though this is a relationship of unequals in one sense, it is mistaken to focus on this relationship of superordinate to subordinate to the exclusion of contrary emphases that subvert that hierarchical assumption. In this part of the conclusion the vital reciprocity that informed the relationship of Paul and his converts resurfaces. In the letter opening Paul had assured his readers of their place in his prayers: "We thank God always for you all, making mention of you in our prayers" (1:2–3). Now, he requests a place in their prayers: "Brothers and sisters, pray for us" (1 Thess. 5:25). Thus the letter unfolds within this prayerful embrace.

As Paul prepares to close the epistolary conversation irrevocably, he gathers those with him to reach across the painful distance separating them. He bids them farewell with a greeting that often includes his co-workers. Coupled with this final greeting is the command to greet one another with a holy kiss (only in 1 Thess. 5:26; 1 Cor. 16:20; 2 Cor. 13:12; Rom. 16:16). There is no internal evidence whatsoever that this kiss initiated the eucharistic celebration or love feast.[81] Though conventional, this habit was no mere gratuitous gesture. Certainly in Corinth this custom had special relevance for a divisive situation. In other cases (e.g., 1 Thess.) it at least implicitly reaffirmed the group solidarity of those in Christ. But, in any case, once the letter crossed this threshold, the door was nearly closed on the epistolary conversation.

Only in three letters (1 Thess. 5:27; 1 Cor. 16:22; Gal. 6:17) does a final apostolic adjuration stand before the final benediction after this greeting. The curse pronounced in 1 Cor. 16:22 springs from Paul's apostolic status with the authority inhering in the direct association with Christ that implied: "If anyone does not love the Lord, let him or her be damned (ἀνάθεμα, my trans.)." The harshness of this anathema, however, is somewhat softened by Paul's assurance of his own love for "all of you in Christ Jesus" (16:24), a final remark unique to Paul. Nevertheless, curses pronounced in the name of God sound harsh if not repugnant and dangerous in the modern world. Yet they must be viewed in their context. With the prophets of old who were called to speak or act out God's word, the distinction between the prophet's word and God's word was often blurred. As an apostle of Christ, Paul spoke and acted with the authority of the one who commissioned him, and these final, menacing moves impinged rather sharply on the conditions provoking the letters.

In Gal. 6:17, to note another example, Paul warns those who trouble him that he bears on his body the "marks of Jesus (στίγματα τοῦ Ἰησοῦ)." Could it be that Paul is drawing an unfavorable comparison between the scars left on his body gathered in the service of Christ with the marks of circumcision to which they point with pride? Does he so closely draw the connection with Christ whose suffering his scars replicate that he equates the troubles inflicted on him by his opponents with injury done to Christ? We cannot know that for certain, but the warning he utters is meant to restate the basic argument of the letter against circumcision. (Note that the strong adjuration "in the Lord" to read 1 Thessalonians to that congregation [5:27] probably also stands there for emphasis.)

This brings us to the final grace—a stable but not uniform element in the letters. Because it is so stereotypical, scholars have paid scant attention to it. Yet, because it departs so significantly from the conventions of the day it is worth noting. Let us take note of these final lines:

The grace of our Lord Jesus Christ be with you. (1 Thess. 5:28)

The grace of the Lord Jesus be with you. (1 Cor. 16:23)

The grace of the Lord Jesus Christ, the love of God, and the communion of the Holy Spirit be with all of you. (2 Cor. 13:13)

The grace of the Lord Jesus Christ be with your spirit. (Phil. 4:23)

The grace of the Lord Jesus Christ be with your spirit. (Philem. 25)

May the grace of our Lord Jesus Christ be with your spirit, brothers and sisters. Amen. (Gal. 6:18)

The grace of our Lord Jesus Christ be with you. (Rom. 16:20)

When compared to the Hellenistic letter, the ending of Paul's letter is startlingly different. Where the papyrus letters normally have a simple "goodbye" or "farewell" or "be strong" (ἔρρωσο) and perhaps the date of the letter, the conclusion of Paul's letters sounds more like a prayerful petition or benediction. As an apostle of Messiah Jesus, and in the authority bestowed by his commission, Paul pronounces a benediction of God's grace revealed in his Lord, Messiah Jesus. Thus he frames the epistolary conversation with a greeting and benediction informed by the congregation's relationship to Jesus Christ—a practice that probably had its genesis with Paul. If the client-lord relationship defines social and political relationships of the time, as seems increasingly likely, the benediction affirms the lordship of Jesus, the Messiah of the church, and reinforces the community's identity as the people of God.

In summary, although Paul's letters were highly situational and even occasional pieces, it is no wonder that within a generation a whole series of pseudepigraphic letters sprang up in his name. Nor is it surprising that his letters were collected even though they were "hard to understand" (2 Pet. 3:16) and continued to shape the thinking of the church. For these letters provide us with the best window we have onto this powerful apostolic figure, his personality and mission, and the way he theologized about the gospel and its relevance for a host of problems facing an emerging church. The letter perhaps more than a retelling of the gospel story proved to be an ideal vehicle for persuading doubters of the truth of his gospel, and it offered the most direct way of responding to rivals who thought his claim to apostleship spurious and his gospel outrageous. Moreover, the letter offered a way to be present with small house groups of converts to nurture, console, correct, cajole, exhort, remind, and instruct them in their life in Christ. In his ability to adopt and adapt the conventional form to serve his purposes Paul was ingenious, and that ingenuity as well as the content he gave the form accounts for the continuing significance the letters had for the church. So, recognition of his importance as a letter writer is crucial to understanding Paul the man and the gentile churches he founded.

CHAPTER FOUR

The Theologizer

INTRODUCTION

The modern reader's desire to find or create closure in a narrative, whether fictional or historical, influences the reading of ancient texts like the Pauline letters. Since Romans was Paul's last letter and since it does include some of Paul's most profound or some would say unsurpassed theological insight, that tendency would appear to be not only natural but correct. Yet the risk of such a reading of Paul is obvious. For once Romans is established as the goal and quintessential expression of Paul's theology, then every other letter of Paul can be read as a preliminary or provisional statement of a Pauline theology that receives its most adequate expression in Romans. This letter then becomes the canon of Paul's mature theology.[1] But surely when Paul was in the thick of things he would hardly have viewed his literary activity in the same way. When he wrote Romans he could see difficulty ahead in Jerusalem, but his mind raced westward to Rome and beyond to Spain. He clearly did not know that Romans would be his last letter, and it is even possible that it was not. Judging from the flurry of literary activity in the two or three years before Romans was written, it is hardly wild speculation to suspect that after his arraignment in Jerusalem and his imprisonment in Rome he wrote other letters.

The aim here is not to plot a progressively rising trajectory in Paul's theology so much as it is to get some idea of the way Paul's thinking emerged through conversations with his readers. Regarded in this way his theologizing is an interactive process, dynamic and flexible. We have chosen to deal with Paul's view of God's election of his converts and their identity as Jesus' people in 1 Thessalonians, 1 Corinthians, and Romans (with excursuses on Galatians and 2 Corinthians, works that cannot be precisely dated). These three are chosen because there is almost absolute certainty about their chronological order, and knowing that order makes it much easier to see how Paul's theologizing emerged. This approach will necessarily leave out much that is important in order to make a rather simple point that is widely acknowledged in theory but denied in practice, namely, that it is inappropriate to speak of Paul's theology as a fixed entity or as a systematic achievement. To put it directly, Paul composed letters, not a systematic theology.[2] And, while he hardly came to the epistolary context theologically empty, he responded to each context in a certain ad hoc manner. The letters thus offer a window onto Paul's interpretation of the gospel for a variety of contexts—situations in which persecution undermined confidence in Paul's gospel and hope for the future (1 Thess.), situations in which religious enthusiasm generated factions that threatened the very existence of the church (1 Cor.), situations in which competing apostles ridiculed Paul and sought to discredit his gospel (2 Cor.), situations in which rumors of Paul's notoriety threatened to undermine support for his mission (Rom.). By following Paul's reaction to these challenges we may gain a better appreciation of the development of Paul's theology.[3] As we shall see, Paul scarcely had in mind a developed theology from the beginning, and in some cases he appears not to have known what he thought about a given issue until he worked it through as he composed a letter. Steven Kraftchick aptly notes that "Sometimes Paul discovered where he wanted to go during the act of composition rather than prior to it."[4] As Paul wrote he thought through problems and improvised theological solutions. That improvisation often contained theological breakthroughs and radical theological departures. Thus the letters were more than a simple retelling of the gospel story; they interpreted and reinterpreted the gospel story for settings as diverse as life itself.[5] A close reading of 1 Thessalonians, 1 Corinthians, and Romans we hope will reveal the *theologizing* of Paul. I use the verb form, theologizing, advisedly rather than the phrase "the theology of Paul," for we hope to show that throughout his apostolic ministry Paul's theology was emerging. To gain some appreciation for the way Paul's theology emerged, we shall resist the temptation to construct a synthesis of Paul's theology by stitching together a patchwork from the seven undisputed letters, for such a synthesis obscures the complexity, plurality, and development of Paul's early messianist thinking.[6] The primary aim of this chapter is to disturb the previous synthesis in order to better appreciate the vitality and dynamism of his theologizing.[7]

PAUL'S THEOLOGICAL PRESUPPOSITIONS

Although Paul gave his letters an ad hoc character he did not approach his task theologically naked. He *was* driven by deep theological convictions that he presupposed but nowhere justified. They were implicit in the institutions he knew and encoded in the story of Israel. Like the grammar and syntax of the language he spoke they were simply taken for granted. Doubtless some of these convictions were foundational. For example, Paul's view of God as the God of Israel, creator and redeemer, sovereign and free, judging and gracious, came entirely from his Jewish heritage and played a crucial role in marking off Israel from other peoples. His understanding of God as the one who makes and keeps promises, who is faithful to a covenant relationship, and who watches over and preserves the elect was part of his Hebraic legacy. His conviction that God was active in history and would bring it to a glorious and positive conclusion in which the suffering chosen ones would be vindicated was a vital element of the tradition of Israel. Yet, although these presuppositions were basic for Paul, when faced with new realities he did more than simply recite these standard formulas. He improvised responses that in many cases opened up a whole new way of thinking about the gospel he preached and revised the presuppositions he harbored.

Paul's thinking was also shaped to a considerable degree by early traditions about Christ. Although Paul declared in Gal. 1:11–12 that his gospel had no "human origin" but came "through a revelation of Jesus Christ," that statement is best read as a defense against the charge that his gospel was deficient and that his dependence on the Jerusalem apostles for his gospel and authority severely compromised his claim to apostleship. Elsewhere Paul freely acknowledges his dependence on the church traditions of the death and resurrection of Christ (1 Cor. 15:3–7), of baptism into Christ (Rom. 6:4–5; Gal. 3:28), of the eucharistic meal (1 Cor. 11:23–25), and of the breathtaking hymn about Jesus' descent, obedience, death, ascent, and cosmic rule (Phil. 2:6–11). Fragments of traditional Christian prayers also appear in his use of words such as *abba* ("father," Gal. 4:6; Rom. 8:15), *amen* (Gal. 6:18; 1 Cor. 14:16; 1 Cor. 1:20), and *maranatha* (Aramaic for "our Lord, come," 1 Cor. 16:22). And since there is no evidence that Paul ever met or knew the historical Jesus, his knowledge of Jesus also, it must be presumed, came almost entirely from the early church.

While the apostle believed Jesus was the hinge of time, the inaugurator of the new age, and the key to the meaning of history, Scripture, and life, he offers little about the historical Jesus in his letters. If we had to rely on Paul for our knowledge about Jesus we would not know that he spoke in parables or that he had sisters; we would not know the name of his mother, or the name of his betrayer; we would not know about the baptism of John, about Jesus' association with tax collectors and sinners, or about his home in Galilee. We would know only a handful of his sayings, and we would not know of his conflict with Jewish leaders. Yet to fault Paul for these omissions is unfair, for we must assume that when Paul preached he told the story of Jesus, and when he wrote occasional letters to the churches there was no need to retell the story; he had to apply and interpret it for each new situation. In attempting to glean this historical information it does seem valid to attempt a reconstruction from the various letters of what Paul knew about Jesus.

The reconstruction, however, is complicated by the fact that Paul never knew the historical Jesus. He neither saw him in the flesh nor heard him speak. He came to know Jesus only as the risen Lord, and it was this exalted Lord who provided the focus for Paul's remarks about Jesus. And yet, it is clear that the Jesus "after the flesh" was important to Paul. He accepted without question the creedal statement that Jesus came from the seed of David (Rom. 1:3). He recognized that Jesus was born under the law (Gal. 4:4). He referred to Jesus' brothers (pl.; 1 Cor. 9:5) and was acquainted with Jesus' brother, James (Gal. 1:19; 2:9, 12; 1 Cor. 15:7). He recited with appreciation an early messianist hymn that Jesus was preexistent, was obedient and faithful, and sacrificed himself for others (Phil. 2:5–8; Rom. 3:22–23; Gal. 1:4; 1 Cor. 1:17). But the death of Jesus was most important to Paul's thinking about the historical Jesus, and his thinking about that death radiated out in innovative ways. Paul's conviction that God intervened to raise the dead Jesus, to establish him as Lord, and to appoint him as deliverer from the wrath to come was basic (1 Thess. 1:10). The suffering Jesus endured prior to his death invited imitation by both Paul and the persecuted church (Gal. 6:17; 1 Thess. 3:3–4; 2:14–16; 1:6), served as a model for ethical behavior (Rom. 6:1–4), subverted the charismatic hierarchy constructed by the Corinthians (1 Cor. 2:1–13), was the cornerstone of Paul's argument for including Gentiles in God's people of the end time (Gal. 3:10–14), and had salvific significance as a sacrifice for sin (Rom. 3:25–26).

Associated with Paul's estimate of the importance of Jesus were his skimpy references to the sayings of Jesus. A survey of the letters will reveal sayings on divorce (1 Cor. 7:10–11; see Matt. 5:32; 19:9; Mark 10:11; Luke 16:18), on eschewing revenge to bless persecutors (Rom. 12:14; 14:10, 13; Matt. 7:1) and revilers (1 Cor. 4:12; Luke 6:28), on being at peace with other believers (1 Thess. 5:13; Mark 9:50), on nothing being unclean in and of itself (Rom. 14:14; Mark 7:14, 19), on faith that can move mountains (1 Cor. 13:2; Matt. 17:20), on support for missionaries (1 Cor. 9:14; Luke 10:7), and on loving the neighbor (Rom. 13:8–10; Matt. 22:39–40). His references to the day of the Lord coming like a thief in the night (1 Thess. 5:2; Luke 12:39–40), to the Christian's obligation to pay taxes (Rom. 13:7; Matt. 22:15–22), and to the need to refrain from judging (Rom. 14:13; Matt. 7:1) echo if they do not repeat Jesus' words. While this list is short it is important, for it shows that the teachings of Jesus were important to Paul, and he appealed to them to authorize his argument and instruction.[8] All of these traditions then, whether from his ancestral Jewish or his messianist legacy, played a role in Paul's thinking, but in order to see what they meant to Paul one must examine their uses in the individual letters. Theological activity was hardly all one way, with Paul serving as the active agent and the churches as passive receptacles. The letters were not lectures or theological treatises; they were one side of a conversation. Paul's theologizing was interactive, and it was through this interactive process that the identity of his churches was being shaped and his theology was emerging.[9]

When Paul wrote 1 Thessalonians over a decade after his apostolic call, his thinking and convictions about Christ had developed in important ways. While some features of Paul's Christology were rooted in that early period, others bore a later signature. In 1:10 he drew on tradition to identify Jesus as Son of God whom God "raised from the dead." In 1:6 he lifted up another traditional emphasis that referred to the suffering Christ as a model for Paul's own suffering and that of his persecuted converts. And in 5:10 Paul spoke of the vicarious death of Christ "for us." Paul, however, also shaped the traditions that shaped him. Even rich legacies like the term God carry a wealth of implied meanings and nuances teased out by Paul's usage that are specific to a given context. For example, although Paul uses the word God ninety-nine times in 1 Corinthians, he gives the word a special meaning as he struggles to modify pretentious Corinthian claims to superior wisdom. His reference to the divine choice of an underclass, to his own call by this God, and to the cross as the doing of the "God of wisdom" (1:18–2:16) effectively subverted the Corinthian religious hyperbole and put another way of thinking in its place. When viewed through the cross with all of its associations of horror, godforsakenness, criminality, failure, and shame, the phrase "wisdom of God" collected a new set of meanings that inverted traditional valuations of the wise and foolish. In situations such as this where a specific context elicited fresh thinking by Paul, one catches Paul in the act of theologizing. So we begin this study not by trying to create a template for organizing and interpreting the letters, nor by treating a list of topics out of context, but rather by attempting to observe how the traditions operate within Paul's letters and thereby how they shape the reality and experience of both his addressees and himself. In his collision with differing interpretations of tradition Paul produces fresh theological applications.[10] Our basic premise is that one learns what Paul means by such terms as *God*, *Christ*, *the cross*, *righteousness*, and so forth, by observing how he uses them in their contexts. To test this way of thinking, we turn now to the letters themselves.[11]

CLUES TO PAUL'S THEOLOGICAL ACTIVITY IN THE LETTERS

Thessalonians

When we first observe Paul in conversation with the Thessalonian church in the early 50s, he already saw himself as an apostle of Christ (2:6). He had been in Arabia and Damascus for some years, had spent a fortnight in Jerusalem in conversation with Peter and James the brother of Jesus, had traveled (as a missionary?) throughout Syria and his home province of Cilicia, and had returned to Jerusalem for a second visit (Gal. 1:15–2:1).[12] It is likely that Paul had written earlier letters, but 1 Thessalonians is the earliest we have from his hand.

Paul himself describes the context for the writing of 1 Thessalonians. Before he wrote this letter his mission had carried him and his co-workers Silvanus and Timothy across the Hellespont into Thrace and Macedonia with a stop at Philippi. In Philippi he preached, founded a church, was imprisoned and released, and then made his way to Thessalonica (2:2). Working "night and day" (1:5) to supplement the support sent from the church in Philippi, he preached his gospel free of charge in Thessalonica (2:9). Even though he met fierce opposition (2:2) he enjoyed enough success to form a cell of believers. His ministry cut short by local antagonism, he headed south with Timothy and Silvanus.[13] His sudden departure would inevitably raise questions about his sincerity and motives. Was Paul like wandering philosophers who deceived their supporters or who under the guise of flattery lined their own pockets (2:3, 5)? The sudden death of some believers raised questions about his gospel. Was his prediction of the imminent return of the Messiah untrustworthy (4:13–18)? Were the old familiar ways tried and true, better after all? (4:1–8). Were the church leaders worthy of their respect? (4:12–13).

By the time Paul and his traveling companions reached Achaia, approximately two hundred miles to the south, the apostle was in so much anguish about the church that he dispatched Timothy to "strengthen and encourage" his converts in Thessalonica (3:1). Over a month later Timothy rejoined Paul in Corinth, offered his report on the status of the church, and possibly delivered a letter from the Thessalonians to Paul. Paul's concern about the vulnerability of this small circle was well founded. The church was being actively persecuted (1:6–7; 3:3, 4; if genuine 2:14–16). The premature death of some believers had produced a crisis of faith for survivors (4:13–18); the idleness of some, possibly religious enthusiasts, brought hardship on others (4:9–12; 5:14, 19–22); and although great affection for Paul remained (3:6) suspicions had arisen that he was out to fleece the congregation. In response to the report of Timothy and a possible letter from the Thessalonians, Paul then wrote a letter to address these concerns.[14]

Positive Reinforcement of Identity

Paul reinforced the Thessalonian identity with a strategy that was both positive and negative. To these addressees estranged from former sources of meaning, he offered inclusion, comfort, and encouragement. He created a cluster of family metaphors to give his converts a home. He called on traditional language that bestowed on them the highest status. He called them the

chosen of God, the elect (1:4); he noted that they were destined for salvation
(5:9); he stated that they were called by God and given a high rank as God's
chosen (2:12; 4:7; 5:24). Elsewhere he used traditional language—"church"
or "assembly," "saints," "brothers [and sisters]," and God as "father" (implicitly making believers "children") (1:1; 3:13; 3:11; 2:14)—to refer to the
special status of this small cell of believers. Since Paul's familial metaphors
and "in Christ" references might have functioned to reinforce and maintain
the world inhabited by these new converts we must give them at least a cursory
glance.

The Family of God

Paul knew following Timothy's return with news of the church in Thessalonica, if he did not know previously, that persecution and rejection had turned
this circle of believers into outcasts in need of a home. While Paul's warm
language can hardly mask the loneliness, the confusion, the hopelessness, and
the desperation of converts in Thessalonica, it could construct a substitute
family to nurture its members (5:14). Paul begins the salutation of the letter:
"To the church (ἐκκλησία or assembly) of the Thessalonians *in God the
father*" (1:1, emphasis added). Jesus appears as God's son (1:10) and the
messianists as the "beloved" of God the father (1:3–4). Repeatedly Paul addresses the community as "brothers" (ἀδελφοί, 2:1, 14; 3:7; 4:1, 6, 10; 5:14,
27) which I, following the NRSV, take to be inclusive of sisters as well. I
readily recognize that male language was the norm of Paul's time and that it
functioned either intentionally or unintentionally as an apparatus of power.
The culture privileged the oldest adult son as heir to the father's estate, and
Paul's use of the term brothers (ἀδελφοί) to refer to his siblings in Christ and
his reference to converts as "sons" share this male bias. Yet the issue is complex, for he uses the term sons to refer to both female and male heirs of God's
promise (Gal. 3:28–29). In other instances where Paul notes with appreciation
the leadership given to the church by women, this male language loses its
sexual connotation. Among these "sons" or "brothers" would have been a
number of female leaders on whom he lavishes praise. He refers, for example,
to Junia, a female apostle, to Phoebe, a female deacon of the church at Cench-
reae (Rom. 16:1, 3, 7), and to female prophets in the church (1 Cor. 11:5).
Then there was Prisca and Aquila, a husband-wife missionary team, who were
his co-workers in Christ (Rom. 16:3).

In addition to using these terms in a gender-neutral sense, Paul also combined gender-based metaphors in interesting ways. Note, for instance, his autobiographical references to his apostolic ministry: In 1 Thess. 2:7 he
reminded his readers, "we were gentle among you, like a nurse tenderly caring

for her own children." He joined the feminine metaphor with a masculine one in 2:11: "As you know, we dealt with each one of you like a father with his children, urging and encouraging you and pleading that you lead a life worthy of God, who calls you into his own kingdom and glory."[14] In this blurring of the sexual connotation of words like brothers and sons Paul subverted the very sexual distinctions that traditional symbolic kinship systems installed and defended, but he did more. He made the family constitutive of election and welcoming to both Gentile men and women.[15]

In his study of Philemon Norman Petersen argued that the kinship cluster of metaphors informs and redirects traditional master-slave metaphors.[16] Paul's command that Philemon receive back "my child," the slave Onesimus (10), as a "brother" (16) underscores Petersen's point. When Paul described both Philemon, the slaveholder, and Onesimus, the slave, as his sons in the gospel, he made them metaphorically freedmen in Christ, and that freedom in Christ fundamentally changed the relationship between them. While the primacy of the kinship metaphor is evident in this case, it is going too far to say that for Paul the kinship metaphors are more important than the concept of the covenant.[17] There is no need to choose one over the other; for Paul the family is constitutive of the elect, and the elect are constituted by God as a family. The metaphors interact, and each enriches the other. What is surprising here is Paul's inclusion of Gentiles qua Gentiles in the family of God, or among the elect, without any reference to Jewish boundary markers— circumcision, the observance of the laws of purity, festivals, and Sabbath observance. Perhaps Paul had not thought through the implications of the inclusions of heathen in the family of God. At least in the epistolary tradition the challenge that would force Paul to think through this issue would not come until later. Moreover, there is no evidence of a Jewish presence in the Thessalonian church, and without that presence Paul was free to concentrate on constructing a symbolic world that would offer a home for those whose conversion to Christ had made them social deviants.

Participation in Christ

Scholars have long recognized Paul's theological brilliance, but less often have they considered the importance of his religious experience. An early exception to this tendency was Adolf Deissmann, a German scholar who saw the influence of Hellenistic popular religion on Paul. Reacting against a stifling dogmatism, he argued that Paul's christocentrism was not a "product of a number of convictions and elevated doctrines about Christ" but instead was a "'fellowship' with Christ, [a] Christ-intimacy."[18] In his view, Christ was neither a figure of the past whom Paul came to know through meditating on his life and words, nor even "a 'historical' personage, but a reality and power of the present, an 'energy,' whose life giving powers are daily expressing themselves in him, and to whom . . . he felt a personal-cult dependence." Deissmann believed that Paul's Christ mysticism transmuted all of Christ's history and all early Christian tradition about Jesus "into a present reality."[19] This mysticism, he argued, was not mediated through reason but came instead through fellowship with either God or Christ.[20]

While Deissmann's emphasis on Paul's religious experience was needed, he mistakenly sought to erase from Paul's mind any sense of history.[21] And though he was aware of Johannes Weiss's study showing the diversity of meanings that were included in Paul's "in Christ" language, he largely ignored the role context played in Paul's usage. Moreover, Deissmann incorrectly downplayed the rational dimension of Paul's letters. Yet even if his work was in some ways a ground level mistake, it was a mistake that nevertheless opened up wholly new ways of viewing Paul and has influenced scholarly opinion to the present day.[22]

Albert Schweitzer's debt to Deissmann was obvious even when he disagreed with him. He argued, for example, that Paul's Christ mysticism was rooted in Christian apocalypticism rather than in Hellenistic popular religion as Deissmann had believed.[23] Paul's mysticism, according to Schweitzer, was "no patchwork of Hellenistic ideas" but rather was a product of his Christian eschatology.[24] He held that eschatology best explains Paul's emphasis on dying and rising with Christ and the influence that union had on the believer's everyday life.[25] Lately, Schweitzer has found a champion in E. P. Sanders, who states emphatically that "Schweitzer was completely correct in emphasizing that the 'mystical' and the eschatological conception are intimately related."[26]

Certainly Schweitzer correctly saw an eschatological dimension in Paul's mysticism and in his belief that those who participate in Christ now can anticipate vindication in the coming judgment, yet the sharp line he drew between Jewish eschatological thought and Hellenistic religion was false. Now we know that no first century Judaism was sealed off from Hellenistic influence and that what Schweitzer dismissed as a "patchwork of Hellenistic ideas" in Deissmann was more like a subtle and complex mosaic. Now we know that Schweitzer's divorce of Christian eschatology from Hellenistic religion was historically false.

If the persecution and premature death of believers brought Paul's construction of the future into question, then reminders, fresh exhortations, and further teaching were necessary. Note, for instance, his repetition of "you know" (οἴδατε, 1 Thess. 1:5; 2:1, 2, 5, 11; 3:3b–4; 4:1, 2) and reminders—for example, "as we have already told you beforehand and solemnly warned you" (4:6, 10, 11; 5:1). There is an interesting bit of redundancy here. Paul first of all grants that the community has knowledge, and then he tells it what it knows. Peter Berger has shown that such reminders, far from being superfluous, are essential for all communities that continually risk forgetting who they are.[27] The corporate identity of this gentile church of new converts was absolutely dependent upon reminders mediated by the cult, by letters from Paul, by personal contact, and by symbolic acts.

1 Thessalonians reveals a number of ways Paul used participationist language to remind his addressees of who they were. Because of the ineffable nature of God as well as the sacred name, Yahweh, mystical union with the deity itself would have been viewed by the Jewish Paul as a sacrilege. So Paul's address to "the church of the Thessalonians in God the Father and [in] the Lord Jesus Christ (1 Thess. 1:1, RSV) refers not to an organic union with God but to those in the assembly of God and the Lord Jesus Christ. Paul referred to no mystical union of the individual with God but rather to a corporate union of believers that huddled together to keep their faith alive and encourage each other in the face of persecution.[28]

Earlier we noticed that the unexpected death of believers produced a crisis in the Thessalonian church. We are not told whether this small circle expected to survive until the imminent return of Christ (2:19; 3:13; 4:15; 5:23). But Paul's emphasis on "waiting for the son of heaven" (1:10) and on hope (1:3; 4:13; 5:8) was necessary only because the reverse was true. Some were grieving like the heathen "who have no hope" (4:13). Such bad grief implicitly raised questions about the credibility of Paul's predictions of the *parousia* of Christ (2:19; 3:13; 5:23, and elsewhere only in 1 Cor. 15:23). Such doubts suggest that in his preaching of the imminent end of the age Paul may not have adequately dealt with such contingencies as the death of believers before the *parousia*. Given his belief in the imminent end of the age why should he have done so?[29] Lüdemann observes that Paul always uses the introductory phrase "we would not have you ignorant" to introduce *new* information (Rom. 1:13; 11:25; 1 Cor. 10:1; 12:1; 2 Cor. 1:8).[30] If that is the case, then Paul's use of the expression "we do not want you to be uninformed" in 4:13 would suggest that Paul's teaching in 4:13–18 about the resurrection of the dead may be new information. So if on the basis of Paul's gospel they expected all believers to be alive for the glorious return of Christ, the death of some of the faithful might have raised questions about the salvation of the remainder, as well as about the faith of the deceased. To hold such a view, however, one must presume that the writing of 1 Thessalonians was so early that Paul was previously unaware of the death of any believers. If 1 Thessalonians was written almost twenty years after the crucifixion and resurrection of Jesus it is difficult to imagine that Paul would have been unaware of deaths of believers and the crisis that these deaths produced. Even though we have no definitive solution to this dilemma, the letter is clear that the death of some believers, for whatever reason, brought consternation to the rest.

While Paul's response to this crisis was multiple, one particular aspect of his reply was ingenious. In 4:13–18 he appropriated a block of Jewish apocalyptic material and extensively edited it to fit the Thessalonian situation.[31] In its native milieu the references to the Lord's descent from heaven, God's trumpet, the archangel's call, and the resurrection of the just to join the Lord in the clouds (4:16–17) would have described God's arrival for the final judgment and the vindication of the just.[32] Here Paul introduced the Jewish apocalyptic material with the declaration that *just as* Jesus died and was raised, *so also* can believers look forward to the resurrection of deceased Christians (4:14). Paul's redactional activity, however, is most obvious in his alteration of 4:16–17. There he took the term *Lord*, which in the Jewish apocalypse means "God," to mean "Christ" who "will descend from heaven." This Lord Christ, he declares, will reunite the "dead in Christ" with the living (4:16).[33] The phrase the "dead in Christ" is a Pauline addition and refers not just to deceased Christians but to the continued fellowship that believers have with the Lord after death. In other words, Paul implies the dead believers will not miss out on participation in Christ in the future and that, rather than being disadvantaged by their death, they will be advantaged: "the dead in Christ will rise first" (4:16) and will be joined by living believers in the fellowship of Christ. With this redaction, Paul bridged the great divide and drew the boundaries of the community broadly enough to include both the living elect and the departed saints (ἁγίων, only here in 1 Thess.). By giving the dead in Christ preferential status at history's climactic moment he made them a people of destiny and transformed their tragic death into a good death. Then he gave this theological insight further practical issue: "encourage one another with these words" (4:18). Thus in his selection of a standard Jewish apocalyptic tradition and tailoring it to fit the situation in Thessalonica, we see Paul theologizing in a way unparalleled in his other letters.[34]

Elsewhere in 1 Thessalonians Paul extended this participationist language to include a number of applications. In 3:6 he encouraged his readers "to stand fast in the Lord" (3:6). He exhorted, preached, and encouraged "in the Lord Jesus" (4:1). He found in persecution a common tie that bound converts to the suffering Lord (1:6). He used the phrase "in the Lord" synonymously with participation in Christ (1:3).[35] Moreover, he gave this participation in Christ a moral dimension. In an ironic twist, he exhorted these Gentiles not to behave "with lustful passion, like the Gentiles who do not know God" (4:5). Did he think that life in Christ erased their gentile status, or did their knowledge of God differentiate them from the gentile sinners (Gal. 2:15)? Whatever he thought, the paraenesis that he offered in 4:1–6 with its strong prohibitions against promiscuity has a distinctly Jewish nuance. And this strict sexual code was clearly driven by Paul's conviction that those who will be saved at the imminent end must keep themselves in a state of holy readiness to stand before God and the Lord Jesus at the grand assize (3:13).[36]

Negative Contrasts That Define a People

Jonathan Z. Smith has aptly noted how the construction and naming of the "other" offer valuable clues to a people's self-understanding.[37] He has noted, for example, that the ancient Sumerians defined themselves in contrast to the Amorites "who do not know barley [and beer]," "who do not know city life," who consume "uncooked meat," and who do not bury their dead.[38] We know as well that the Hebrews differentiated themselves from the Canaanites whom they called sexually obsessive and perverse, and from the Moabites, whom they viewed as unspeakably brutal in warfare and descendants of an incestuous relationship of Lot with his daughters (The Hebrew word Moab means for the father.) Greeks saw all non-Greek speakers as barbarians whose speech sounded like "bar, bar, bar." This fairly common human tendency also appears in Paul, who drew at least four contrasts between insiders and outsiders.

(1) The church is a community of love and peace (4:9–12; 5:13). By contrast, those who actively persecute the church are cruel (1:6; 3:3; 2:14–15).[39] Coercion was widely used to maintain the solidarity of various groups—the family, ethnic groups, the city, and the Roman Empire. While the socialization of believers in the messianist movement was probably gradual, their singular devotion to the God of Israel and their refusal to participate in the imperial cult or worship the local deities[40] could have brought savage reprisals from families, friends, civic leaders, and even Roman officials.[41] The more precarious the group the more severe were the reprisals for abandoning an identity assigned by a family, clan, or social grouping. The persecution visited on the church in Thessalonica presumably was an attempt to impose social control. But such persecution is often counterproductive, for it can in fact solidify the resolve of the deviant group and reinforce its sense of identity. Therefore, in his insistence on the role persecution played in shaping the identity of the Thessalonian church Karl Donfried is correct, but he goes beyond the evidence in identifying those "who have fallen asleep" (4:15) with those martyred in the persecution.[42]

(2) The converts trust and serve God. The "others," Paul says, worship "idols" (1:9). The Hellenistic context framing the church was rife with the worship of local and broadly popular deities. While Paul offers no identification of these gods or "idols," archaeologists and historians have provided us with information about their cults. Participation in the worship of Isis and

Serapis, Dionysus and Cabirus, and the god of the city and in the imperial cult was doubtless common in Thessalonica.[43] As a resident of the area one was free to participate in all of the cults. By contrast to these broadly tolerant cults, the worship of the God of Israel was exclusively monotheistic; it would brook no rival, and its narrow exclusivism sometimes prompted ridicule and contempt. Paul presumed that the worship of and devotion to the one God required the rejection of all other gods. Baptism into Christ thus meant that converts could no longer gather with family and friends to observe local religious festivals. They no longer could recite the prayers or hymns habitually raised up to beloved gods. And in many cases, they no longer could enjoy the security provided by the support of the Roman pater familias. It is mistaken to think the resocialization of converts from these popular religions was sudden and dramatic, or that the rupture was total, but doubtless the gospel Paul preached did create enormous tensions with its polytheistic setting and with the major social groups of the society, and a high level of ambiguity remained that was papered over with stout statements about difference.

(3) Paul contrasted the holiness of the church with the immorality, lust, and drunkenness of outsiders (4:3–5; 5:7). In 4:5–7 he differentiated believers who act in "holiness" and "honor" from the immoral heathen "who do not know God" (4:5). Unable to control themselves, they give themselves up to impurity (4:7) and passion of lust and wrong their victims in these matters.[44]

(4) And finally, he set the children of light in opposition to the children of darkness (5:4–5). The outsiders, unlike the insiders, Paul believed, have no hope (4:13), and they will experience wrath or divine condemnation at the future, cosmic judgment (5:9). They sleep while believers are alert. They are, metaphorically speaking, drunk while believers are sober (5:7–8). In his contrast of insiders and outsiders, Paul sensed how important religious allegiances were for the identity of his converts. It was not that he was operating at such a pragmatic level, but that his theological constructions had profound, practical issue for everyday life. While difference was established by these four points, the community remained open to surprises from the "pagan" community. Categories of otherness such as race were nowhere used and should be avoided in any description of either the people of Israel or of Paul's converts.[45]

Summary

In the preceding discussion we have seen how Paul shaped Jewish and messianist traditions to reinforce the group identity of this church suffering persecution, in danger of disillusionment, tempted by immorality, and prone to idleness or disorder. He bent traditional materials to remind, exhort, teach, and warn those in danger of forgetting who they were. To those disowned, harassed, and persecuted, Paul used both covenantal and familial language to construct an identity that offered encouragement and consolation. He drew sharp contrasts between the members of the church and the cruel, immoral, pagan children of darkness that would have solidified their sense of identity. While his Thessalonian converts were predominantly if not exclusively Gentiles, Paul's silence about the implications of the inclusion of Gentiles in a sect that was fundamentally Jewish is striking. Whether he was aware of the implications we cannot say, we merely know that it was only later that he would be forced to think through these issues and defend his gospel that offered Gentiles membership in the eschatological people of God without any precondition.

1 Corinthians

Paul's ministry in Corinth, a large, cosmopolitan port city, and the surrounding countryside (2 Cor. 1:1) stretched on for eighteen months[46] and brought together a motley collection drawn largely but not exclusively from the underclass (1 Cor. 1:14). Aided by Timothy, Titus, and Silvanus, fellow missionaries, and Aquila and Prisca, Jewish Christian refugees from Rome, Paul won converts throughout the area. The gospel he preached in Corinth announced that the salvation promised by the Hebrew prophets had become manifest in the death and resurrection of Jesus and the outpouring of the spirit (Joel 2:28). Initiation into the fellowship of God's elect was by baptism, and the eucharist kept the memory alive and offered continued participation in Christ (11:25–26). Paul demonstrated the gifts of the spirit of the last days by speaking in tongues (1 Cor. 14:18), performing signs and wonders (2 Cor. 12:12), and remaining celibate in the face of the "impending distress" (1 Cor. 7:7, 26). Paul's conviction that salvation was now present (2 Cor. 6:2) and his own example profoundly influenced his converts.

Eventually Paul's ministry excited opposition. He was haled before Gallio, the Roman proconsul in Corinth in 52–53, and left Corinth either voluntarily or involuntarily soon after.[47] His journey to Ephesus may have taken him on a circuitous route through Galatia, though the existence of such a detour is little more than an inspired guess. Acts credibly reports that his ministry in Ephesus stretched on for three years (20:31) and that it was from this period that he may have written as many as nine letters, not all of which are available to us.[48] Although a full historical accounting of Paul's activity in this period is impossible, a tentative outline might include the following items:

1. Ministry in and around Corinth (eighteen months, 51–52).

2. Eventual settlement and ministry in Ephesus (three years, 52–55), after a possible visit to Galatia (Acts 18:18, 22–23)

   a. Composes Galatians (53).

   b. Composes first letter to Corinthians (1 Cor. 5:9), a fragment of which may appear in 2 Cor. 6:14–7:1. Otherwise, no trace of letter remains (53).

   c. Receives letter (1 Cor. 7:1) and delegation of Chloe's people with an oral report (1 Cor. 1:11; 16:17) (54).

   d. Composes second letter to Corinthians (1 Cor.) responding to Corinthian communications (54).

   e. Sends Timothy by land to Corinth (1 Cor. 4:17; 16:10) with instructions (54). Timothy returns to report failure of mission (early spring 55).

   f. Paul makes short, painful visit to Corinth (2 Cor. 2:1–2). Returns to Ephesus humiliated (2 Cor. 12:21) (late spring 55).

   g. Paul writes "tearful letter" (letter no. 3) "out of much affliction and anguish of heart" (2 Cor. 2:3–4, 9; 7:8–12). Hand delivered by Titus with instructions to travel to Macedonia for a rendezvous with Paul after delivering the letter (2 Cor. 8:16–24). (Possibly 2 Cor. 10–13) (late summer 55).

   h. Paul imprisoned soon after (55). Writes Philippians and Philemon (fall 55–spring 56).

   i. Paul is released; travels overland to meet Titus in Macedonia (summer 56).

   j. In Macedonia, Paul meets Titus who brings encouraging news about the change of attitude in Corinth toward Paul. Paul composes the fourth letter and dispatches Titus with it (2 Cor. 1:1–6:13; 7:2–9:15) (56).

   k. Paul visits the Corinthian churches, gathers the offering for the "poor among the saints" in Jerusalem (56).

   l. Paul composes Romans (late 56 or early 57).

   m. Paul and his delegation leave Corinth for Jerusalem (spring 57).[49]

When Paul wrote 1 Corinthians the church was troubled. Intense rivalry, jealousy, partisanship, quarreling, immorality, contention, and divisiveness threatened to splinter the church (1:11; 3:3; 6:1–6; 11:18–19). Most scholars agree that the root cause was a multifaceted religious enthusiasm.[50] Some so valued ecstatic speech as the spirit inspired language of angels (13:1) that they looked condescendingly on the less gifted. Some apparently made *glossolalia* a *prerequisite* for rather than an *expression* of life in the Kingdom.[51] Some claimed to possess a superior wisdom (1:20–31; 3:18–23);[52] and Paul's biting sarcasm suggests others were as self-assured as the rich and kings (4:8–10), believing they were beyond the need of instruction from either apostles or Scriptures (4:1–7). Others mouthed slogans such as "all things are lawful for me" (6:12) and "an idol has no real existence" (8:4), and these shibboleths opened the door to sexual license and the eating of meat offered to idols.

Doubtless, the Corinthians saw things very differently than did Paul. Evidently, they really believed Paul's declaration that "the day of salvation" was present (2 Cor. 6:2). Their ecstatic speech not only shared the rapturous language of angels, it also imitated Paul's ecstasy. Their celibacy they viewed as an expression of their transported life (7:1 and following verses) and a faithful participation in Paul's example. They too laid claim to a wisdom not of this world (1 Cor. 2:6–12), and like Paul they felt they were rich in divine gifts (1 Cor. 4:8). Gender distinctions meant nothing to them if indeed in Christ, as the baptismal rite suggested, "there is neither male and female" (Gal. 3:26–28, my trans.). And if idols have no real existence then the meat offered to them is in no way affected, and eating it carries no consequence (1 Cor. 8). Moreover, if a man were living with his stepmother "in the name of the Lord Jesus," who was to say that sexual improprieties occurred (1 Cor. 5:1–5)? Paul's diplomatic responses to the Corinthian religiosity suggest that he was acutely aware of the delicacy of his position, and the resolution of the points in dispute stood to influence the Corinthian understanding of who they were and Paul's theologizing as well.

The Elect as the Family of God

In many ways the family metaphors of 1 Corinthians resemble those of 1 Thessalonians. The term *adelphoi* occurs naturally and often in 1 Corinthians (thirty-seven times versus nineteen times in 1 Thessalonians). The salutation in 1 Corinthians offers the standard grace and peace "from God *the Father* (πατήρ) and the Lord Jesus Christ" (1:3; cf. 1 Thess. 1:1). A formula in 8:6 contrasts the "many gods and many lords" with "one God, *the Father*, from whom are all things and for whom we exist." And 15:24 looks to the end when Jesus will hand "over the kingdom to God *the Father*, after he has destroyed every authority and power" (emphasis added). As in 1 Thessalonians Paul refers to his spiritual siblings as "my beloved brothers and sisters" (15:58), and he appeals to his converts as "my beloved children" (4:14). Although 1 Corinthians mimics the use of Thessalonian familial metaphors at many points, it differs as well.

In both letters Paul applies masculine and feminine metaphors to himself, but unlike 1 Thessalonians, in which the references to himself as nurse and father blossom with tenderness and encouragement (2:7, 11–12), the tone of the same metaphors in 1 Corinthians is harsh and demeaning . As their disciplinarian father "through the gospel" (4:15) he warns those who have grown "arrogant" in his absence and who behave as if he were not returning that, if necessary, he will come to them with a switch (4:21). While Paul says he writes to admonish, not to shame (4:14), his threat to thrash them when he comes appears intended to frighten and shame the "arrogant."

In 3:1–4 Paul applies the metaphor of a nursemaid or mother to himself. He reminds the "brothers and sisters" that he fed them with milk, that is he nursed them, because they could not chew solid food. While at one level the nursing metaphor is an endearing image, at another level the metaphor offers a stinging rebuke to those who pretend to be wise or mature but are in fact spiritual infants. Why did Paul give these kinship metaphors such a sharp edge in Corinthians? Was it because he believed the family was dysfunctional? Or was it because his own authority as "father" was threatened? Or was he simply reflecting a cultural belief that this is what fathers do? While we may never know precisely, there may have been elements of all three in Paul's response. To Paul the Corinthians, after all, appear as snarling and loveless, jealous and mean spirited. They take each other to courts of law to settle disputes (6:1–6), and they heedlessly gorge themselves at the love feasts while the slaves who come later go hungry (11:21–22). In spite of his negative view of this family, Paul did not disown it. Its members remain his "beloved children" (4:14) and his "beloved brothers and sisters" (15:58).

Unlike in 1 Thessalonians, Paul here brings election motifs and family metaphors together to good effect. For example, on the heels of the thanksgiving Paul orders (βλέπετε, impv.) his siblings in Christ to reflect on their calling or election:

> Consider your own call (κλῆσις), brothers and sisters: not many of you were wise by human standards, not many were powerful, not many were of noble birth. But God *elected* (ἐξελέξατο) the foolish things of the world to shame the wise, and God *elected* (ἐξελέξατο) the weak things of the world to shame the strong, and God *elected* (ἐξελέξατο) the baseborn and despised, even the things that are not, to bring to nought the things that are. (1:26–28, my translation, emphases added)

Here Paul talks about the way God's election subverts the world's social and political hierarchy. Hierarchical structures were the primary social reality of Paul's day. No one would need to explain to the Corinthians that their lives were ruled by powers that were difficult to understand. Paul's gospel of the righteousness of God, that is God's intervention on behalf of the weak, would have had quite a different resonance in that context than it does today.

One can see how such a message might have been attractive to the Corinthians. Most of them occupied extraordinarily weak positions in the society. S. Scott Bartchy estimates that one-third of the total population of Corinth was in slavery, one-third was freedwomen and freedmen, and one-third was free.[53] Life for those on the lower rungs of that social order was excruciatingly difficult, and they were virtually powerless to alter their circumstance for the better. To be able through a mystagogue (whether Paul, Apollos, Peter, or Christ) to escape their lot and to share in the puissance of a *cosmic Lord* carried great power for attracting and energizing many of the weak, uneducated underclass. The problem was that these people compensated for their disadvantaged position in the social hierarchy by simply constructing another hierarchy that inverted the world, placing them in the power position. In 1:18–2:5 Paul uses three examples to relativize this fabrication of a new pyramid of power, and a key element in his subversion was the example of their own election. But when Paul says that "God chose what is low and despised in the world, things that are not, to reduce to nothing things that are" (2:28), it would seem that he had played into their hands. Paul's remarks seemed to endorse their own inversion of traditional hierarchies.

Later in the letter, however, Paul returns to this concern once again. Beginning in 12:1 with the introduction of his discussion of spiritual gifts, Paul addresses his "brothers and sisters" (12:1). In what was to be the final paragraph of the composition, Paul constructs a hierarchy of gifts that was diametrically opposed to that of the Corinthians. In 12:27–31, in a paragraph dripping with sarcasm, he appropriates traditional election language to show how "God *appointed* (ἔθετο) in the church first apostles, second prophets, third teachers, then miracle workers, then healers, helpers, administrators, and [lastly] speakers in various kinds of tongues" (12:28, emphasis added).

In a sudden lurch of the text in a new direction in 12:31b we may actually be watching Paul as he theologizes. A sudden flash of insight appears to come just as Paul has placed the final piece of his model in place. For just when he had completed the construction of his hierarchical model that was to subvert the model of the Corinthians that placed ecstatic speakers at the top, he drew back. Suddenly, he appears to have seen the contradiction and silliness implicit in his invention of a hierarchy to destroy a hierarchy. Instantaneously he abandoned his model just when he had come to the point of drawing an unfavorable comparison between it and that of the Corinthians. It is as if mentally he dashed his own model to bits and began anew:

> I will show you a still more excellent way. If I speak with the tongues of mortals and of angels, but do not have love, I am a noisy gong or a clanging cymbal. And if I have prophetic powers, and understand all mysteries and all knowledge, and if I have all

faith, so as to remove mountains, but do not have love, I am nothing. (12:30b–13:2)

The preceding statement is consistent with Paul's eschatological gospel that inverts the world's order. In Christ, Paul suggests, God constructs quite a different order. It goes beyond the one he had constructed earlier that privileges the uneducated, the powerless, the ill born, the weak, the despised, and even the nobodies in order to shame the wise, powerful, nobly born, strong, honored, and fortunate (1:26–31). The crucial item in his advanced construction is love as the quintessential eschatological charism.[54]

Thus love transcends and relativizes all charismatic gifts and makes a mash of the hierarchies the Corinthians constructed from them. Paul thus moves the discussion to a new level, a level that shows how love creates an order that encourages the exercise of gifts but undermines the claim to superiority by the spirit driven *glossolalia*. Instead Paul emphasizes the gifts that build up the body of Christ rather than providing excitement for the individual (12:12–26; 14:3, 5, 12, 17, 26). We can see in such remarks how Paul's election language redirects an elitist Corinthian religiosity by constructing a theology of the elect community that is concerned with the nurture of the community of Christ. Identity is here largely corporate and located in the believers' positive reinforcement of each other. That represented a significant challenge in a community riven by petty rivalries and factious behavior.

Participation in Christ

Paul features the mythic participation in Christ rather prominently in 1 Corinthians and explicitly ties this emphasis to the context. Setting the agenda of the letter already in the thanksgiving (1:4–9), Paul recognizes the grace of God given to his addressees "in Christ Jesus" who in every way "have been enriched *in him*" (1:4, emphasis added), and most importantly he recognizes the call "into the fellowship (*koinōnian*) of his Son, Jesus Christ our Lord" (1:9). Modern Christians take the Greek word *koinōnian* to refer to the convivial camaraderie of the like minded, but Paul's usage in 10:16 suggests that participation in a sphere of power is closer to his understanding.

In taking this view I follow Käsemann's discussion of Paul's radical separation of participation in the "pagan" feasts from participation in the Lord's supper (10:14–21). Upon those accustomed to drinking from many fountains in a religiously pluralistic environment, Paul seeks to impose a Jewish limitation. Participation in the Lord's meal was totally incompatible, he argued, with sharing the table of "demons." As he succinctly summarizes the issue:

The cup of blessing which we bless, is it not a participation (κοιν-ωνία) in the blood of Christ? The bread which we break, is it not a participation (κοινωνία) in the body of Christ? *For there is one loaf; we, the many, are one body. For we all partake of the one loaf.* (Emphasis is a Pauline gloss on the eucharistic tradition; 1 Cor. 10:16–17; my trans.)

Käsemann argues that Paul here took a eucharistic tradition influenced by the Hellenistic tradition and reversed the order of the elements to give the one body (bread) a paraenetic or ethical application. Although Paul shared the Hellenistic view that human identity was shaped by cultic acts through which one entered a shared world of meaning, he also strictly adhered to a Jewish monotheism that excluded participation in "pagan" feasts. And because eating the bread that symbolized the flesh of Christ and drinking the wine that symbolized the blood of Christ placed the participant in Christ's sphere of dominion, participation in the "pagan" feasts was not only religiously incompatible, it was physically dangerous. Paul later makes a point that sounds quite magical to the modern ear. Some who have participated in the Eucharist in an unworthy manner have brought judgment upon themselves, and as a result some have fallen ill and others have died (11:27–32).[55] According to Paul, to participate in the Eucharist is to participate in the body of Christ, and to participate in the body of Christ is to be mindful of the body, and that necessarily excludes both privatistic religiosity and individualistic liberties that harm the body.

The transfer into the "body" through baptism (12:13) brings with it both positive and negative obligations for those in Christ. We see the emphasis on building up the body of Christ in 14:1–39 and on the abstention from sexual immorality in 6:12–20. In the latter passage especially, heavy participation language informs the prohibition of sexual immorality or visits to "pagan" temple prostitutes. Paul opens that discussion with the citation of a Corinthian slogan: "All things are lawful for me" (6:12). The slogan reflects the religious enthusiasm and confidence of those empowered by Christ. No opprobrium attached itself to prostitution in the Hellenistic culture. Although the Hebrew prophets roundly condemned temple prostitution and fornication, Rahab, a Canaanite prostitute, occupied a special place in Israel's story for her protection of Joshua's spies (Joshua 2:1), and Judah, the great patriarch of Israel, is made to say of Tamar, who posed as a prostitute and became pregnant by him, "She is more righteous than I" (Gen. 38:26). Paul's argument against this practice is based not on a prohibition against fornication but, interestingly, on the sacredness of the bond with Christ (6:15). Harkening back to Gen. 2:24, which speaks of the one flesh union of man and woman, Paul argues curiously that those who have become "united to the Lord" cannot also be united with a prostitute. But Paul's analogy raises a host of problems. Surely Paul knew that Gen. 2:24 is not talking about union with a prostitute. If one should take the plainest reading as the intended meaning of Gen. 2:24, that is, that a man and wife become one flesh, does Paul mean to imply that that union also excludes a union with the Lord? Does Paul's argument imply more than he intends? All this is possible. His main point is that participation in Christ excludes the customary visits to prostitutes by these new gentile converts.

On the positive side Paul here for the first time refers to the church as the body of Christ (12:12–27), a common metaphor of the Hellenistic world that was often applied to the *polis* to emphasize the interdependence of its members. Paul appears to recognize the aptness of understanding the *polis* as an organism and appropriates that metaphor to instruct a community in danger of fragmenting. To be in the people of God, the *ekklesia*, or assembly, was, he noted, also to be in the body of Christ. Thus to be in the church was in some sense to participate in the body of Christ. Paul invokes a traditional formula to describe the transition from nonparticipant to participant in the body of Christ: "For in the one Spirit we were all baptized into one body—Jews or Greeks, slaves or free—and we were all made to drink of one Spirit" (12:13). The implications of that formulation were radical in a highly individualistic setting that had exacerbated tensions to the breaking point. The church as the sphere of the Lord's power has no charismatic hierarchy, no charismatic underclass, no one whose gifts are unimportant for the welfare of the whole, and no one who is an autonomous, private believer. What Paul seeks is more than tolerance of difference; he desires an appreciation of the ways the pluriformity of gifts is necessary for the health of the body. In the conclusion of the paragraph, Paul comes to his main point: But God has so arranged the body, giving the greater honor to the inferior members, "that there may be no dissension within the body" (12:24–25). Paul thus employs participationist language to win his readers to a differing valuation of their own gifts and to be surprised and nurtured by the differences facing them in the gifts of others.

Summary

In 1 Corinthians as in 1 Thessalonians, Paul bends traditional language to focus on a rather specific set of problems. These new occasions required an altered response. Boasting, pretentious claims to wisdom, a realized eschatology that emphasized identification with the risen Lord, factious behavior, jealousy, loveless acts, and a narrow individualism elicited from Paul emphases on the elect family of God, the body, and the ethical implications of participation in Christ. While Paul did allude to the death of Christ in 1 Thessalonians, in 1 Corinthians the cross is introduced to qualify the theology of glory of the converts, and the charismatic hierarchy of the Corinthians is deconstructed to make way for the construction of a community of love, a "body of Christ." Once again, therefore, we see Paul the theologizer at work. His fertile mind constructed models that he himself destroyed for yet other possibilities, and his imagination sought correction and redirection rather than repudiation of the Corinthian religiosity. From the first he granted their spirituality (1:4–9), and from the beginning he sought to qualify the religious rhetoric before him.

Excursus: 2 Corinthians

While 2 Corinthians is more an anthology of letters than a single letter, it is very difficult to know precisely how many fragments of different letters the redactor included in this collection, exactly where they begin and end, and exactly when they were written. Bornkamm held that vestiges of five or possibly six different letters appear in 2 Corinthians.[56] Schmithals claims to find fragments of six authentic Pauline letters in 2 Corinthians.[57] Betz holds that 2 Corinthians contains parts of six letters.[58] Another complicated partition has been suggested by Weiss (four letters).[59] If there is beauty in simplicity, then Hausrath's theory was indeed a thing of beauty. Only twenty-eight pages long, this study noted the seam between 9:15 and 10:1 as a sign that two letters had been joined and argued persuasively that the controversy in chapters 10–13 came before the events of 1–9.[60] Thus the references to the "tearful letter" or "severe letter" in 2:3–4, 9; 7:8, 12 allude in fact to chapters 10–13.[61] This thesis has had a profound impact on both German and English scholarship to the present day. Even so, scholars such as C. K. Barrett, Hans Windisch, F. F. Bruce, and Victor Furnish still accept Semler's thesis that the letter fragment in 1–9 came before the fragment in 10–13. Furnish holds a minority position that no trace of the "tearful letter" that Paul mentioned in 2 Cor. 2:3–4, 9 and 7:8, 12 appears in 2 Corinthians.[62] While some partition theories are more credible than others, none has gained general acceptance by scholars.

In spite of the lack of consensus on the makeup of 2 Corinthians, there is broad agreement on a number of issues. That chapters 10–13 came from a different letter is almost universally granted. That 6:14–7:1 is an interpolation is also accepted by most scholars, though Pauline authorship is doubted by many. Scholars widely disagree, however, about whether chapters 8 and 9 are fragments of separate letters though no one questions their Pauline provenance or the fact that they came near the end of Paul's literary relationship with the Corinthian churches. We maintain that even if chapters 8 and 9 were separate letters as Betz holds,[63] that they, along with 1:1–6:13; 7:2–16, were written by Paul in short order after he received word that the storm clouds over Corinth had parted. Since they come from this final phase of Paul's Corinthian correspondence it is appropriate that we consider them together as we turn to Paul's theological activity.

Between the writing of 1 and 2 Corinthians a crisis intervened, forcing Paul to fight for his apostolic life. His own integrity had come into question as well as the veracity of his gospel. The invasion was by Jewish Christian itinerant missionaries who came offering a gospel totally different from that of Paul. Dieter Georgi has taught us how Paul's slashing attack on his rivals reveals their identity, message and modus operandi.[64] They claimed to be apostles of Christ endowed with a treasure of charismatic gifts (10:5; 12:11). They boasted of their status as Hebrews, Israelites, descendants of Abraham, and "servants of Christ" (10:5; 12:11; 11:22–23). They came with written testimonials of their marvelous deeds performed elsewhere (3:1). They bragged about their superior wisdom (1:12). They claimed that their radiant physical bearing, their eloquent speech, and their visions offered proof of the presence of the glorified Lord within them (11:6; 3:7–18; 12:1–10). They preached a different Jesus, a different gospel, and a different spirit (11:4), and they presented an adequacy that inspired confidence and loyalty (3:5).[65]

As Paul himself acknowledged, he suffered from the comparison. His physique and bearing were unimpressive, and he was an *idiotēs* in speech (11:6). He made little of his visions and mighty works, and he accepted no money for his ministry. Nevertheless, he vigorously defended himself against accusations of deviousness (11:7–11), and he categorically rejected charges of deceit leveled against him, that is, refusing to take pay for his ministry and the divine gifts he proffered while at the same time cleverly gathering a collection from which he stood to profit (12:16–17). The implication was that he was fraudulently skimming off some of the offering to line his own pockets. Moreover, his "painful" visit to try to correct the conditions that Timothy had warned him about was a total disaster. He left in humiliation and shame with most of the congregation against him. He was stung by the charge of cowardice after he beat a hasty retreat from a fight with his rivals. They taunted him thusly: "His letters are weighty and strong, but his bodily presence is weak, and his speech is of no account" (10:10).[66] Paul appears in 10–13 to be losing the struggle. The charge against him that he was a charlatan was exacting a toll. The super apostles appear there to have won over a sizable faction to their gospel.

At this point, all would appear to be lost. Paul surely realized the stakes were enormous. If these rival Jewish Christian missionaries should be victorious, the future of Paul's gospel in Greece and its prospects for the western mission would have been bleak indeed. It is no exaggeration to say that the danger was very real, and it was possible that his whole mission could collapse. Paul was desperate. He attacked his critics with caustic irony, biting sarcasm, and a theological critique that undercut their theological hubris. He

made poignant appeals to his own experience—his suffering, his lack of elo-
quence, his deficiency in visions, his "thorn in the flesh,"—and he used a
fool's speech to subvert the pretensions and polished oratory of the super
apostles. But he did more than use his pen; he used his associate Titus to good
effect. Instead of sending Timothy Paul dispatched Titus as a diplomat to
patch things up, and he thus was able to stem the tide running strongly against
him. After a tortuous wait, Titus brought news to Macedonia that Paul's pen
had done its work and that the Corinthians were now ready to gather their
resources for the offering that Paul had preached for the "poor among the
saints" in Jerusalem. This good news provided the catalyst for Paul's final
epistle to the Corinthians, which was to be delivered by Titus and trusted
"brothers" ahead of his own arrival. It is to that communication that we now
turn.

The Offering Linking Corinth and Jerusalem

Paul uses few household metaphors in 2 Corinthians. Only three times
does he refer to his addressees as *adelphoi* (1:8; 8:1; 13:11), which is startling
when one recalls 1 Thessalonians, a book less than half as long, with eighteen
uses. Only once does he refer to them as "beloved" (ἀγαπητοί, 12:19),
though he does frequently speak of his love for them (2:4; 6:6; 8:7), God's
love (13:11, 13), and the love of Christ (5:14). He asks them to demonstrate
their love for an offender (2:8) and to give proof of their love for the poor
among the saints in Jerusalem (8:8, 24). And here as elsewhere God appears
as the "Father of our Lord Jesus Christ" (1:3; 11:31) and the "Father of mercies" (1:3). He refers to his readers as "the church of God" and "all the
saints" throughout Achaia (1:1). He names his auditors as partners in suffering
and consolation (1:7) and as co-workers (1:24), and he looks forward to standing with them in the presence of Jesus at the last judgment. These references
come spontaneously without much reflection or attempts to use them to address the dire threat being posed to his apostleship. Only in his discussion of
the offender and the offering for the "poor among the saints" in Jerusalem
does Paul ask them for a show of affection. Unlike the situation when 1 Corinthians was written, the unity of the church is no longer the issue; now it is the
loyalty of the church to him and his gospel that concerns him. Consequently,
Paul spends a great deal of time interpreting and defending himself. One topic
that has important implications for the Corinthians' sense of who they are and
for the future of the gentile church especially is the offering. Let us now turn
to that topic.

Nils Dahl first found importance in the richness of Paul's offering vocabulary in chapters 8 and 9.[67] He noted how Paul employed a variety of meta-

phors, synonyms, metonyms, and descriptive language to involve his readers in this enterprise. Paul referred to the offering as a "partnership" (κοινωνία, 8:4, 9:13), a service or ministry (διακονία, 8:4; 9:12, 13), a priestly service (λειτουργία, 9:12), a grace or favor (χαρίς, 8:6, 7, 19), a proof of love (ἐνδει-ξιν τῆς ἀγάπης, 8:23), seed (σπόρος, 9:6, 10), a good work (ἔργον ἀγαθόν, 9:8), a harvest of righteousness (γένημα, 9:10), and so on. In 8:4 Paul links several of these terms, magnifying their impact and complicating the task of the translator: He notes how the Macedonian churches begged "us earnestly for the privilege [*charis*] of sharing [*koinōnian*] in this ministry [*diakonia*] to the saints."[68] This fresh combination may be an excellent barometer of the theological importance that Paul gave the offering that he had promoted so vigorously in Galatia, Macedonia and now in Corinth. But why was Paul urging the churches to make an offering for the "poor among the saints" *in Jerusalem*?

The first and most obvious answer is that he had promised to promote such an offering. In Gal. 2:5–10 Paul offers a succinct summary of the negotiations leading up to the Jerusalem agreement between Paul, Barnabas, and Titus, representatives of the gentile mission, and Peter, James, and John, representatives of the Jewish Christian mission. Paul summarizes the agreement thusly:

> that we should go to the Gentiles and they to the circumcised. They asked only one thing, that we remember the poor, which was actually what I was eager to do (Gal. 2:9b–10).

Second, he promoted the offering to serve humanitarian ends. Paul himself called it a proof of love and a ministry or a "relief work" (*diakonia*).[69] Yet one is entitled to ask what made Jerusalem different. Was it the depth of the need? Or were there other factors? Holmberg has argued, for example, that the pillars imposed the offering as a symbol of their authority and power.[70] Given the direct historical ties of the "pillars" with the historical Jesus, and the role the Jerusalem church had played in the first two decades of the church's life, it would be surprising if disputes about authority did not play some role in the offering. Yet there were sound reasons for the offering that went beyond its symbolic recognition of the preeminence of the teachings of the Jerusalem apostles.

Third, and perhaps most important, Paul promoted the offering for the poor among the saints in Jerusalem as a feature of a grand eschatological scenario. Even though Paul does not specifically refer to Jerusalem in 2 Corinthians there could be no doubt about its intended recipients. He had previously named the Jerusalem church as the recipient of the offering (1 Cor. 16:3), and both earlier and later Paul named the "poor" as the beneficiaries (Gal. 2:9–10;

Rom. 15:26). Throughout chapters 8 and 9 Paul emphasizes the need of the recipients (8:14; 9:12). So although no explicit mention of "the poor" appears in 2 Corinthians, it is implied. It is hard to exaggerate the symbolic importance of Paul's use of the term *the poor*. From the Maccabean revolt until the end of the Roman-Jewish war (70 CE) the term *the poor* (*'ebyonim*) came to signify God's chosen, eschatological people. The term carried connotations of piety that come from the dependence of the destitute on Yahweh for deliverance. The Qumran community especially used the term often to identify themselves as the pious, persecuted, oppressed, humble people of God (1QpHab XII 3.6.10; XIV 7; 1 QM XI 9:13; XIII, 14; 1 QH V 13, 14, 16, 22), and in this very context Paul speaks poetically of the Lord Jesus who "though he was rich, yet for your sakes he became poor, so that by his poverty you might become rich" (8:9).

For centuries before the time of Paul, Jerusalem had stood at the geographical center of Israel's eschatological hope and the deliverance of the distressed. Isa. 14:32, in particular, brings these threads together:

> The Lord has founded Zion, and the needy [or poor] among the
> people will find refuge in her.

Written just as the Babylonian Empire was taking shape and raising its angry head, Zephaniah sketches a powerful eschatological vision of a people free of intimidation and fear. Once-hostile nations are converted and bring to Yahweh an offering from as far away as Ethiopia (3:10). The judgment on the peoples of the world leaves Judah in a bucolic setting, pasturing its flocks, free of intimidation and fear: "no one shall make them afraid" (3:13). Exulting in this time of peace and plenty, Jerusalem spontaneously breaks into singing:

> Sing aloud, O daughter Zion; shout, O Israel! Rejoice and exult
> with all your heart, O daughter Jerusalem! (3:14)

We see, therefore, that long before Paul's day Jerusalem stood as the mythic center of the redemption of Israel, and the eschatological era of peace would be inaugurated by gifts from the gentile converts. The offering to the "poor among the saints" in Jerusalem, as Munck noted, symbolized the arrival of the last days, and its presentation by Gentiles was designed to overcome the "stubborn" resistance of Jews to the gospel by making them jealous (Isa. 2:2–3; Micah 4:1–2).[71] The Jewish Christian church remained in Jerusalem, according to Georgi, as an "eschatological forepost, God's avant garde as the watchmen upon the battlements of that city" and from there would declare to the world that the "approach of the celestial monarch" was imminent.[72]

Fourth, whether intentionally or not, Paul preached the offering as a symbol of the unity of the church. The success of Paul's gentile mission that promised salvation outside the law strained the ties that held the gentile church and Jerusalem in a common bond. Paul's own argument in Galatians was that belonging to the people of God excluded entry through conversion to Judaism. The shouting match in Antioch between Peter and Paul would not have fostered harmony between the gentile mission and Jerusalem, and the Jewish Christian apostles who trailed Paul in Galatia, Philippi, and Corinth surely exacerbated tensions even though it is unlikely that they were from Jerusalem. The danger was real, therefore, that the church would break apart. As far back as 1938, W. M. Franklin argued that the gentile churches were in danger of losing a sense of their historical rootedness in Jerusalem and Israel and that Paul wrote to affirm that connection.[73] Such a thesis, if valid, would carry implications for our understanding of the self-designation of the Corinthians. The family network (8:1) and the community of saints (9:1, 12; 1:1) were expanded significantly by this act, and participation in the offering as an expression of love gave a focal instance of the ethos of the community. But the offering provided more than an expression of group solidarity; it provided a vehicle for announcing a set of eschatological convictions that involved believers in painful human struggles. By contrast, the super apostles preached a gospel that enriched themselves and, focused as it was on success and glory, disassociated its followers from earthly attachments and also from Christ who became poor (8:9). Paul argued for a reading of human experience through the Christ lens that allowed for an encounter with God in life's ambiguities. He claimed through Christ to find an aroma of life amid death's odors (2:14–17; 4:7–12), to see an "eternal weight of glory" in affliction (4:16–18), and to discover in his poverty a means of "making many rich" (6:10). In asking the Corinthians to respond to the poor among the saints in Jerusalem, Paul focuses not on a glitzy gospel of unambiguous success but on a way to find eschatological meaning in the suffering, weakness, mortality, and vulnerability of the poor among the saints in Jerusalem.

Participation in Christ

In his classic work, *The Mysticism of Paul the Apostle,* Schweitzer opened his discussion with a list of passages of Pauline mysticism, and prominent among them was 2 Cor. 5:17: "Therefore, if anyone is in Christ, there is a new creation; the old has passed away, behold the new has come" (NRSV modified).[74] Schweitzer, however, shows no interest in the context framing this passage. Although the worst of the storm of controversy with the super apostles is past, Paul continues to defend and explain his ministry. Expressing confidence before the imminent judgment of God (5:8–10), Paul claims to be giving his readers good reasons for boasting about himself and his co-workers to those who measure by outward appearances (5:12). Noting his commitment to his addressees, he says,

> the love of Christ urges us on, because we are convinced that one has died for all; therefore all have died. And he died for all, so that those who live might live no longer for themselves, but for him who died and was raised for them. (5:14–15)

There is little agreement about how to understand this passage. Did Paul mean that Christ's death was meant to be a sacrifice for all humanity, and, therefore, all share in the expiation for their sin? Or is he thinking, as E. P. Sanders suggests, not of redemption through the expiation of past sin but basically about participation in Christ, his death and life?[75] Perhaps this choice is too starkly drawn, for Paul later will use sacrificial language to speak of Christ's expiatory death (Rom. 3:25), and he will also speak of participation in Christ's death (Rom. 6:5). Even if one speaks of Christ's death as expiation, any attempt to link the metaphorical death of others to that death is at the very least mythic participation. That Paul's thought on the topic is inchoate may indicate that such a division never occurred to him. It does seem clear, however, that participation in Christ is the subject of Paul's remarks about the new creation (5:17). And one might also say that the participation in the offering that Paul promoted, in that it symbolized the union of Jew and Gentile in Christ and announced the imminent arrival of history's resolution, was also meant to suggest a participation in Christ.

Romans

Introduction

We have no idea who established the church in Rome or when it was founded. We only know that Paul had known of its existence "for many years" before writing Romans (15:23) and that the edict of Claudius from 49 CE confirms a "Christian" presence in 49 CE when Jews were expelled from Rome for "stirring up a tumult under the leadership of Chrestus."[76] It is thought that Aquila and Prisca (Acts 18:1–3, 18–19, 22, 26–27) and Jewish messianist co-workers of Paul in Corinth (1 Cor. 16:19) were exiled in 49 and returned to Rome after the ban was lifted by Nero in 54 (Rom. 16:3). This return inevitably strained relationships with gentile believers who had guided and supported the church for five years. Written to a church Paul had neither founded nor visited, Romans singles out no adversary to excoriate (2 Cor.), no rival preacher to anathematize (Gal.), no enthusiastic sectarians to condemn (1 Cor.), and no "dogs" to ridicule (Phil.). Nevertheless, Romans is a genuine letter written for a real situation. It has the form of a letter, the warmth and affection of a letter, and the concreteness of a letter. It deals with the relationship of the "weak" and the "strong," with charges against Paul and his gospel, and with support Paul sought for his mission to Spain. While we hear echoes of other letters in Romans, for example, Adam and Christ, charismatic gifts, law, Abraham, the church as Christ's body, and the love commandment, this letter is no calm summing up of the theological wisdom Paul had garnered throughout his life. Its lack of any reference to the cross, any mention of the trials that authenticate the integrity of his apostleship, or any discussion of the Eucharist disqualifies Romans as a simple compendium of Paul's theology. Moreover, even when Paul does recall earlier motifs he almost always changes their application.

Excursus on Galatians

While we have omitted Galatians from the chronological trajectory of 1 Thessalonians, 1 Corinthians, and Romans, it clearly forms a part of the backdrop of Romans. Although there is no agreement about the date of Galatians, scholars unanimously agree that Galatians was written before Romans.[77] Therefore, Galatians must be considered as a part of the broader context that informs Paul's thinking. Consequently, we shall include this short treatment of Paul's defense of his gentile gospel in Galatians and the impact it might have had on the authorship of Romans.

Sometime after the writing of 1 Thessalonians, Paul's practice of including Gentiles qua Gentiles was challenged, and he was forced to defend this inclusive gospel against "another gospel" with the usual markers of inclusion in God's elect community (Gal. 1:6). Had Paul earlier ignored the issues raised by including Gentiles because he simply assumed that Jews would recognize as legitimate the inclusion of Gentiles that Isaiah promised in the last days (2:2–3)? Had the baptismal tradition that in Christ "there is neither Jew nor Greek" (Gal. 3:28) persuaded Paul that the inclusion of Gentiles in the church without the benefit of the traditional marks of membership in the people of Israel was appropriate? Was he simply following practices he had already witnessed in some churches? Or, in the absence of any challenge to the practice, had he simply not thought through the implications of the inclusion of pagans in the family of God? While it is likely that he had simply not thought through the implications of his gentile gospel, by the time he wrote Galatians he was alarmed by the dimensions of the Judaizing threat. The believers who questioned his gospel and his right to be an apostle posed a formidable challenge. As if in a flash, he seemed to recognize the dimensions of this threat and called on all of his rhetorical skill to persuade his "children" of the truth of his gospel. The competitors posing this formidable challenge, Paul placed outside the pale. The religious conflict between Paul and the Judaizers was intramural; the argument pitted messianist against messianist, believer against believer, and possibly apostle against apostle. If these challengers had won the argument in the broader church, the course of history might have been very different.

Paul's response was savage. Flashing darts of contempt, he cursed his rivals (1:8–9); he shamed his converts (1:6); he defended his claim to be an apostle of Christ (1:1, 11–17); he recalled a shared baptismal liturgy and turned it on his adversaries (3:27–28); he took the Abrahamic tradition of circumcision used by his rivals for support of their gospel and spiritualized it in such a way as to make the uncircumcised heirs of the promise. And only here did he make the cross God's instrument for the inclusion of Gentiles in the people of God (3:13–14). For the first time, he outlined the process by which Gentiles were *adopted* into the family of God, thus becoming heirs, and in a bit of daring, he accorded these heirs a special intimacy, allowing them to approach the ineffable, crying out "Abba! Father!" (4:1–7). While Petersen sees the power of kinship metaphors, he little notes the claim and counter-claim of kin against kin and the role this dispute and its larger field of discourse played in the development of Paul's adoption metaphor.[78]

For the first time Paul introduces adoption language to describe the gentile believer's status. Prior to his appeal to the story of Abraham to support his gospel of righteousness by faith (3:6–29) for Gentiles qua Gentiles, he had made sparing use of inclusive language. He had addressed his Galatian converts as *adelphoi* only once (1:11). But, once Paul enters the Abrahamic world imaginatively, a veritable explosion of familial language accents the inclusion of Gentiles. Eight times in staccato fashion references to the *adelphoi* occur (3:15; 4:12, 28, 31; 5:11, 13; 6:1, 18). Not since the salutation (1:1, 3, 4) had Paul referred to God as father. But beginning with 3:26 family metaphors burst onto the horizon: For the first time those who recognized God as father were named by Paul as "children of God" (υἱοὶ θεοῦ, 3:26; 4:6, 7), "children of Abraham" (3:7), "children of the promise" (τέκνα ἐπαγγελίας, 4:28) and "children of freedom" (τέκνα ἐλευθέρας, 4:31). Moved by the story he was telling to move others Paul now radicalized the familial metaphors so deeply embedded in Jewish tradition to embrace gentile sinners. A status reserved for the elect of Israel was offered to pagans. Small wonder that some would see this as scandalous.[79]

Paul's appeal to the story of Abraham, a story that doubtless his critics and rivals had used against him, was ingenious to sympathizers but specious to critics. Abraham was a man of faith, they could agree; however, the Scriptures require circumcision as a seal of the promise (Gen. 17:5) and as a ratification of one's place among the elect (Gen. 17:10–11). In addition to Genesis, other Jewish traditions supported their claim (Sir. 44:19–21; Jub. 23:10; 24:11). Since Abraham kept all of the law before it was written, it was incumbent on them to keep the law as it was written.[80] Furthermore, since it was led by disciples of the Lord and even James his brother, the precedent of the Jerusalem church was weighty indeed—circumcision and law observance were a sine qua non for all males entering the messianic covenant community.

The challenge to Paul's gospel and his apostleship was so serious that the whole future of the gentile mission was threatened. Against this challenge, Paul offered a piece of inspired exegesis that had a revolutionary impact. He separated Abraham's belief (Gen. 15:6) and his Torah observance (Gen. 17:10–11). Arguing that God's promises were to Abraham's seed (*zera,* Gen. 12:7; 13:15; 17:7; 24:7), a singular that he read as referring to Christ (Gal. 3:16), Paul asserted that it is through the faithfulness of Christ, the seed, not Torah observance (e.g., circumcision) that Gentiles are made children of Abraham. We do not know what effect Paul's creative telling of the story had on this narrative circle, but from the explosion of metaphors emphasizing the right of Gentiles to belong to the people of God as Gentiles, the telling of the story clearly affected the teller. Wittingly or unwittingly, Paul's Galatian account had left the impression that the inclusion of Gentiles in the family of God required the treatment of nonmessianist Jews as the other, that is, the disowned. Like the Qumraners, Paul argued that his community in Christ was the true Israel of God (6:16).[81] Blessed with the gift of hindsight the church judged Paul to be correct in arguing for the inclusion of Gentiles, but in his own time such a conclusion was not self-evident, and there was no independent arbiter of truth that could be called on to verify the truth of Paul's position. The struggle, we might say, was political in that it dealt with control of the direction and destiny of the church. In the heat of this decisive battle, Paul overextended himself, leaving himself open to the charge of denying the validity of God's promises to the historical people of Israel. And thus he was forced in Romans to deal with the questions his liberal view of adoption raised for the classic view of election and God's promises.

Paul's argument in Galatians seems to imply the exclusion of Israel from the eschatological family of God. Concerned as he was in Galatians with his gentile audience, the issue of the reliability of God's promises to Israel either did not occur to him or went unmentioned because it was irrelevant. The care with which Paul dealt with this issue in Romans suggests that news of his Galatian defense may have spread and sparked sharp questioning from nonbelieving Jews or Jewish Christian challengers. By making gentile believers children of Abraham, was Paul suggesting that God had gone back on promises made to the biological descendants of Abraham? If God had reneged on those promises, can other promises, even to those in Christ, be trusted? Does the acceptance of one require the rejection of the other? Does Paul's strong emphasis on grace outside the law actually encourage immorality? Paul did not have these questions pressing in upon him in Galatians, but by the time he wrote Romans they had become so insistent that they demanded some response (Rom. 3:8).

Although Paul was satisfied that his readers were full of goodness and knowledge and able to instruct each other (15:14), he nevertheless could not be at all confident of a warm welcome in Rome. As he leaves Corinth for Jerusalem he writes poignantly of danger he faces from "unbelievers in Judea" (15:31). He openly worried that the offering he was delivering from the gentile churches in Asia, Macedonia, and Achaia would be spurned (15:31). A rejection of this token of God's final ingathering of the gentile sinners and symbol of the joining of Jew and Gentile in God's eschatological community would not just devastate Paul personally but would seriously and perhaps fatally cripple his mission and discredit his gospel. Moreover, surely some in Rome would know that Paul's mission in the east had been a turbulent one. Judaizers had undercut him in Galatia; he and Peter had engaged in an angry and ugly public exchange in Antioch (Gal. 2:14); he had been viciously attacked by Jewish Christian missionaries in Corinth (2 Cor. 10–13); the marks on his body bore witness to violent exchanges between him and members of Jewish synagogues: "Five times I received at the hands of the Jews forty lashes less one" (2 Cor. 11:24). Common sense suggests that the venomous charges against Paul were for preaching a gospel that while fundamentally Jewish appeared to devalue the core of the Hebrew religion—namely, the law. Underlying Paul's brutal experience surely lay the question: How can Paul's gospel of salvation outside the law to all those believing (3:22) not represent an attack on the law itself? Paul was right to fear that his notoriety in the east would prejudice his chance of getting a hearing in Rome and fatally compromise his Spanish mission.[82] Having endured searing conflicts with the Galatians and Corinthians, he was sensitive to the charge that he was a dangerous innovator and to the questions raised by Jewish messianists and nonbelieving Jews about his law-free gospel to Gentiles. And finally, he either had personal knowledge of gentile arrogance or intuited the risk of it. There is at least some evidence that the expulsion of Jewish Christians from Rome by Claudius in 49 had placed gentile believers in the ascendancy (14; 11:17–24). Given that position it would have been easy for them to forget the derivative nature of their faith. They owed everything to the religion of Israel now manifest in Christ, yet it would have been natural given their isolation from Jerusalem and their numerical strength for them to forget that the religion was the root that supported them, not viceversa (11:18). Paul's warnings against gentile boasting and pretentious wisdom (11:18, 25) make more sense as real warnings rather than as mere pro forma exhortations.

While the context evoking Romans differed markedly from that eliciting the earlier Galatians, some of the same ghosts haunted Paul. His profoundly negative view of the law (3:8), the libertine behavior his law-free gospel encouraged (6:1–7:5), his questionable statements about the purpose of the law, and his strong conviction that gentile entry into the eschatological people of God was direct and unconditional continued to raise hackles. Even though Paul did use Romans to correct the darkly critical though not totally negative view of law in Galatians, his central concern in Romans was not the law but the way God's righteousness manifested in the death and resurrection of Jesus Christ embraced the Gentiles without invalidating God's historic promises to Israel.[83]

Yahweh's promise to be Israel's God and Israel God's covenant people is a common theme of the Hebrew Bible (e.g., Gen. 15:5–20; 17:6–7; 18:19; 22:17–18; Hos. 2:21–23). In light of these traditions, Jews "in Christ" understandably might object to Paul's statement that Galatian believers were subjecting themselves to slavery if they observed law (4:9; 5:1), and believing males who had their foreskins "cut off" would be scandalized by Paul's ugly pun that they would be "cut off" from Christ (5:2–4). How could it be, some might ask, that those who observe God's very commands would be damned? And did not the bestowal of divine benefits on unrighteous Gentiles make a mockery of divine justice? Did not the adoption of Gentiles as heirs of God's promises while Jews were turned away raise serious questions about the trustworthiness of God's promises to Israel? How can one trust a God who arbitrarily chooses the rejected and rejects the chosen? Only in Rom. 9–11 does Paul attempt to think through this perplexing problem and to conceive of an election that embraces gentile sinners without vitiating God's promises.

Election

Rhetorical questions in 3:1, 8 prepare us for Paul's vigorous insistence that his law-free gospel to the Gentiles in no way suggests that God has reneged on the promises made to Israel. Paul already anticipates heated objections to his suggestion that true circumcision is not a physical marking but "a matter of the heart" (2:28–29) when he gives voice to his interlocutor: "Then what advantage has the Jew?" and "Let us do evil that good may come." Paul appears to blur the line historically drawn between the elect and the gentile sinners when he insists that in Jesus Christ God has offered equal access to the inner sanctum of God's holy people, Israel. In the process he appears to fatefully compromise not just the identity of Israel but the trustworthiness of God to fulfill promises made to Israel. Paul prepares his readers for the consideration of this unresolved issue in 8:33–34 with two rhetorical questions: "Who will bring any charge against God's elect? It is God who justifies [Jew and Gentile]. Who is to condemn?"

These questions as well as the entire discourse in 9–11 unfurl against the backdrop of Paul's summary of his gospel in 3:21–6. The summary articulates Paul's conviction that a radically new, even revolutionary change was under way that placed him and his readers at the climactic moment in history. God's final intervention was already in motion to reclaim the world and to make a place among the elect for the unrighteous. This righteousness of God outside the law, Paul wrote, was manifested in the faithfulness of Jesus Christ (3:22) for "*all* [even Gentiles] who believe" (3:22, emphasis added). Barriers to access are removed, placing all on an equal footing, because, as Paul notes, "all have sinned and fall short of the glory of God" (3:23). Through God's righteousness manifested in the redemption in Jesus Christ "they are now justified by his grace as a gift" (3:24). This Jesus Christ is the one "whom God put forward as a sacrifice of atonement by his blood effective through faith" (3:25). There are two issues here combined: (1) God's apocalyptic deed in Jesus and (2) God's divine impartiality that places all, Jew and non-Jew, on an equal footing as far as access to this eschatological salvation is concerned. It was this latter assertion that raised the question of God's trustworthiness, fairness, and constancy to which Paul turns in 9–11. In these chapters more than anywhere else in his letters, Paul struggles mightily with the implications of the inclusion of the irrational and despicable "other," that is, gentile sinners, among the elect. Aside from 1 Thess. 1:4, all of Paul's references to election (ἐκλογή) occur in these chapters (9:11; 11:5, 7, 28). Indeed, the main agenda of these three chapters is election.

The argument in these chapters is complex, complicated, and passionate, Paul's personal agony for his kin gives his opening remarks great pathos: "I have great sorrow and unceasing anguish in my heart. For I could wish that I myself were accursed and cut off from Christ for the sake of my own people" (9:2–3). He avoids any spiritualization of membership in the people of God that would ignore the history of Israel's special privileges (9:1–5). For to them belong the status as sons and daughters, glory, covenants, the giving of the law, worship and promises, and the Messiah "according to the flesh" (9:4). Instead of ignoring or diminishing that history, Paul praises God for it (9:5) and implicitly connects his gentile reader to it.

After this introductory paragraph, Paul turns to the story of election for an answer to the questions prompted by Paul's gentile gospel: "Has the word of God failed?" "Are the promises unreliable?" (9:6) Given the complexity of the thought that follows, an outline of Paul's argument might be useful. First, it is not, he suggests, that the word of God is untrustworthy. For Israel's rejection, even a final rejection, does not mean that God's word has failed (9:6–13). The argument pulls in contrary directions—affirming first God's freedom to include Gentiles qua Gentiles even if that means the exclusion of Israel and second, somewhat paradoxically God's firm commitment to Israel's salvation. Historically, God was free to choose Isaac's descendants over those of Ishmael and Jacob's over those of Esau. Thus, Paul suggests, the historical people of God (or the elect) was constituted by divine promise and not by fleshly descendancy (9:8). The second part of Paul's argument was that the divine election of the Gentiles, even if arbitrary, was not unjust (9:14–29). Embedded in the story of Israel is the theme of divine election and rejection. That God loved Jacob but hated Esau certainly would appear to raise the issue of fairness. Indeed, if God shows mercy on whomever is elected and likewise hardens the hearts of those rejected, God does seem to be arbitrary. If God acts whimsically, how can one be held accountable for choosing or rejecting the gospel? The third stage of his argument suggests, however, that God's election is not arbitrary and that all, whether Jew or Gentile, who turn to God will enjoy salvation (9:30–10:21). In his own words, "For there is no distinction between Jew and Greek; the same Lord is Lord of all and is generous to all who call on him. For, 'Everyone who calls on the name of the Lord will be saved'" (10:12–13). And fourth, Paul says, the rejection of the Jews is not final (11:1–32); a remnant will accept the gospel (11:1–6). Moreover, the rejection of the gospel of God by the Jews has led to the inclusion of the Gentiles (11:7–24), and the inclusion of Gentiles will so arouse the Jews to jealousy that they will be led to salvation. In the end, Paul says, "all Israel will be saved" (11:25–32). Fifth and finally, Paul concludes the argument with a doxological paean of praise to God (11:34–36).

While such an outline traces the contours of Paul's theologizing in 9–11 and takes us through rocky terrain, it uses metaphors that artfully explore complex issues. In fact, a metaphor Paul uses offers a valuable clue to the tensions in Paul's thinking and to the daring and innovative solution he improvises. The racing metaphor in 9:30–33; 11:11–12; 11:26–27 captures the progression and radicality of Paul's thought. The metaphor appears first in 9:30–33, where it rises from another—the metaphor of the potter. In 9:20–21 Paul comments on the creative freedom and right of the potter to shape each vessel for his or her own purposes (9:20–21). (Please note, Paul has no qualms about mixing metaphors if he can use one to illumine another.) The potter metaphor invites the reader to reflect on God's freedom to embrace "us" (9:24), that is, Gentiles (9:22–26) and also a remnant of the people of Israel (9:27–29).[84]

The first occurrence of the racing metaphor occurs in 9:30–33, a major section in which Paul argues that God's elective process is not arbitrary and that salvation is open to all, Jew and non-Jew. The picture Paul paints presents a ludicrous scene. First, gentile competitors who did not run after the righteousness goal nevertheless attain the prize, and second, Israel, while striving mightily to reach the goal, fails to reach the goal, stumbling over a rock that *God* placed in the path (9:30–33). What Paul intends the rock to mean— Christ, Torah, his gentile gospel—goes unsaid, but his aim to provoke thought about a process of inclusion that privileges Gentiles at the expense of Israel succeeds famously.[85]

The racing metaphor draws its evocative power from a venerable tradition of competitive sports in the Hellenistic culture. Each quadrennium thousands flocked to watch Olympic competition shrouded in legend since its inception in 776 BCE. Cities vied for the honor of staging major Greek games. Even Alexander the Great, so Arrian tells us, staged spectacular competitive events in sport and the arts when he rested his troops. Sports metaphors suffused the vernacular of philosophy, popular religion, and rhetoric. Cynics who roundly condemned the public obsession with sports as folly nevertheless appropriated sports imagery to illustrate the pursuit of virtue.[86] Stoics, likewise, translated sports imagery to deal with the control of desire and the athletic striving after virtue.[87]

Hellenized Jewish contemporaries of Paul such as Philo and Josephus reflect these same tendencies. Philo ridicules the great athlete Odysseus, condemning him for animal cruelty and savagery "counterfeiting the genuine coin of manly exercise, no wrestlers but wretches" (De Vita Cont., 41). If superior strength defined the true athlete, the animal would excel. Rather the pursuit of virtue makes an athlete. Abraham, Isaac, and Jacob, according to Philo, are like "athletes who are preparing for games which are really sacred, men who despise bodily training but foster robustness of soul in their desire for victory over their antagonists, the passions" (De Abr., 48). Though Hellenistic Jews, Cynics, and Stoics all scoffed at the popular obsession with sport, there is no evidence that they had any impact. The games continued without interruption for centuries to great popular acclaim. And it was widely believed that the gods frequented the games and often influenced if they did not actually fix the outcome.[88] Homer's *Iliad* (XXIII) offers an example of divine involvement in which Apollo and Athena intervened to influence the outcome of the games honoring the dead hero Patroclus, a victim of the Trojan war. Held outside the walls of Troy under siege, there was first a chariot race in which Apollo knocked the whip from Diomedes' hand to give Eumelus the lead, only to be frustrated by Athene's swift action bringing the prize to her favorite, Tydeus. Then came boxing, wrestling, and most importantly the footrace. Of the three contestants who toed the starting line, Aias, the swiftest of foot, was favored over the older but wily Odysseus and Antilochus. As expected Aias, surged out in front, but throughout the race Odysseus followed closely in his draft. Although he strove mightily, Odysseus still trailed Aias coming into the final stretch. In desperation he prayed to Athene, "Hear me, goddess, and come a goodly helper to my feet" (Loeb, XXIII, 770). Athene forthwith came to his aid either by tripping or pushing Aias, sending him sprawling in the gore and waste from the bulls sacrificed in honor of Patroclus. As Aias lay wallowing in the mess with his mouth and nostrils filled with filth, Odysseus darted ahead with a light footed burst to win. Even though Aias recovered in time to finish second, there was no honor in his prize. He protested that the goddess had cheated by tripping him, but the spectators greeted his complaint with hoots of laughter and ridicule. His consolation prize brought not honor but shame and disgrace.

Stories such as these stand in the background of Paul's metaphor, influencing both author and reader alike. Their basic premise was that winners required losers and that losing was not just disappointing but shameful. Winners were hailed and honored as heroes, and losers were shunned and shamed as failures. Against this backdrop Paul stages his metaphor. Israel stumbled, he says, not for lack of zeal (10:2) but rather from following the wrong strategy in the race and not seeing Christ as the goal of the law (10:4) and not realizing that God's righteousness is "for everyone who believes" (10:4). With this statement the racing metaphor drops out of sight until 11:11, when Paul almost as an afterthought asks, "have they stumbled so as to fall?" He answers emphatically, "Absolutely not!" Then he ends with a discussion of God's strategy for intervening in the race to cause Israel to stumble. The strategy is to make Israel jealous of the winning Gentiles (11:12–16) and lead to their "full inclusion" (11:12). By placing the Gentiles first in the race, making Jews jealous and reversing the order of entry (Jew first, then Gentile, 1:16), and then announcing nevertheless that "all Israel will be saved," Paul extends the logic of his sports metaphor to the breaking point (11:26). Incredibly, both Israel, which zealously ran the race toward righteousness, but tripped over the rock that *God* sneaked onto the track, and the Gentiles who were not even in the race both emerge as winners! Making a mash of the rules of the game and the popular understanding, Paul argued that the eschatological race is entirely different from traditional athletic events. Winners do not require losers. The gentile prize does not require that Israel endure its loss in shame, nor do Israel's laurels leave the Gentiles empty handed and wanting. Although in 11:23 Paul does make belief a precondition of Israel's participation in the eschatological community, E. P. Sanders is correct that in 11:26–32 Paul envisions the salvation of both Israel and the Gentiles in an eschatological future with no preconditions whatsoever.[89] And he states decisively of Israel, "As regards the gospel they are enemies of God for your [i.e., Gentiles] sake; for as regards election they are beloved, for the sake of their ancestors; for *the gifts and the calling of God are irrevocable*" (11:28–29, emphasis added). Even Paul does not seem to know how his preposterous game plan will be played out. The solution to his dilemma is "hidden in the mystery of the Godhead itself" (11:25).[90] In sheer wonderment Paul launches spontaneously into a marvelous benediction:

> O the depth of the riches, and wisdom and knowledge of God! How inscrutable are his judgments and untraceable his ways! "For who has known the mind of the Lord? Or who has been his counselor?" "Or who has given a gift to him, to receive a gift in return?" For out of him and through him and in him are all things. To him be the glory forever. Amen (11:33–36)

Paul's solution was even more radical in its native setting than it would be in our own. To make Gentiles into "honorary Jews," as Stendahl calls them, and to join Jews and Gentiles in God's common embrace as both elect was a proposal so radical that it did not long endure. By the second century Justin excluded Jewish Christians from salvation,[91] and Jerome later sharply criticized Jewish Christians who while "they wish to be both Jews and Christians, they are neither Jews nor Christians."[92] While difficult to construct, an identity that admits difference while eschewing otherness was even more difficult to maintain. To introduce a metaphor that does not simply mirror the world's construction of winners and losers offered a vision so lofty that it too lost favor within two generations. It is entirely possible that when Paul first began his composition of 9:1 he did not know that his theologizing would carry him to a soaring benediction of wonderment that left the resolution of his dilemma in God's hands. We have seen in this short discussion the enormous tensions in Paul's racing metaphor that extend his logic to the breaking point. Wrapped in a divine mystery the solution drew from both Hellenistic and Jewish traditions.

We see, therefore, how the racing metaphor contains tensions so great and suggests solutions so radical that they would bring both Jew and Greek into the presence of a new and dramatic reconfiguration of the familiar world. This reconfiguration was no abstract exercise but came through Paul's reevaluation of an election tradition in light of the shifting contexts of his churches and in light of the death, resurrection, and imminent return of the Messiah. The election was a constant, but for Paul its meaning was emergent. In 1 Thessalonians, we noted how the election tradition affirmed a solidarity that reached across the grave. In 1 Corinthians the emphasis on election affirmed a unity that deconstructed a divisive, individualistic, arrogant, condescending religious enthusiasm that put the body of Christ at risk. In Galatians the emphasis on God's adoption of gentile sinners as children and, therefore, heirs of the divine promises was aimed at reversing a gospel that made conversion to Judaism a precondition of acceptance in the elect community. Now in Romans, we have seen how election becomes the normative tradition that directs Paul's thinking about an exceedingly difficult problem—namely, how to affirm the reliability of God's promises to Israel while at the same time extending those same promises to gentile sinners.

Participation in Christ

Up to now we have argued that one must look at individual texts in context in order to see what Paul means by theological statements. In Romans more than elsewhere, Paul sets the believer's participation in Christ in a cosmic context. In 1:17 he articulates the theme of the epistle, namely, that in the gospel "the righteousness of God *is being revealed* through faith for faith" (emphasis added). Taking his cue from his Scriptures, Paul employs the phrase to refer not to a judgment of an unbiased, objective, remote judge but to the activity of one who intervenes on behalf of the accused, the marginalized, or the poor. We see, therefore, that righteousness in the biblical tradition is relational, that is, representing a God faithful to the covenant made with a people. "Righteous" refers neither to a purely personal nor an abstractly ethical concept.[93] For Paul, the divine intervention is on behalf of sinners, both Jewish and gentile. In the apostle's hands the phrase "the righteousness of God" carries an apocalyptic nuance with a cosmic dimension in which God triumphs over a world rebelling against its creator. God's active intervention in the death of Jesus to raise him up and establish him as Lord over the whole creation was believed to be a cosmic eschatological event. And in Christ, Paul believed, God was at war with demonic forces to reclaim a world rightfully belonging to its creator. In Rom. 8:19–22 we catch a glimpse of this cosmic struggle. The creation groans under the burden of futility, frustration, and grief. It yearns for fulfillment, awaiting its redemption when it will be "set free from its bondage to decay and will obtain the freedom of the glory of the children of God" (8:21). In 8:23, 26 Paul relates this cosmic redemption to the hopeful struggle of the saints, and finally in 8:30, 33 Paul links this cosmic activity to God's call, rightwising, and election. The word *rightwise* or *justify* of course is simply the verb form of the noun *righteousness* (vb. Δικαιόω, n. Δικαιοσύνη). This redemption of the creation and its creatures is an almost poetic expression of God's righteous work (8:29–30). And all of this glorious eschatological vision is bracketed by promises to those participating "in Christ" (8:1, 2, 39). Paul's vision is sketched first in negative colors—"There is therefore now no [eschatological] condemnation for those who are in Christ Jesus"—and then in positive hues—Absolutely nothing, he asserts, "will be able to separate us from the love of God in Christ Jesus our Lord." And Paul is careful to note that this circle of participants is inclusive: "For *all* who are led by the Spirit of God *are* children of God" (8:14, emphasis added).

Jewish objections to Paul's law-free, inclusive gospel can be heard not only in Rom. 3:8 but also in 6:1 and 6:15. His response to the charge of encouraging immorality is thoroughly participationist. Reminding his readers of their baptism "into his [i.e., Christ's] death" (6:3), Paul urges behavior consistent with this solidarity with Christ. Buried with Christ now they can look forward to being raised up *in the future* with Christ (6:5). By symbolically dying with Christ in baptism believers come to share in the destiny of Christ manifested in his death, and they may look forward to sharing the destiny of the resurrected Christ in the future. In the meantime, their identification with the risen Lord carried an ethical mandate: "just as Christ was raised from the dead by the glory of the Father, *so we too might walk in newness of life*" (6:4, emphasis added). Note that Paul does not say, "we too have been raised" in solidarity with Christ as the Corinthians had said shortly before! (Cor. 15:12). Avoiding such a realized eschatology, Paul focuses on this world, where the struggle continues, where dilemmas remain, where decisions have to be made. In the midst of these contrarieties, the believer walks in newness of life. Walking in newness of life does not remove the believer entirely from the influence of the cosmic power, sin, but it does remove one from the dominion of sin (6:12–14).

In 6:1–14 Paul forges a linkage between participation in Christ in death and participation in Christ in life as the path to integrity. In 6:15–23 Paul fights a rearguard action against a realized eschatology that he knew only too well from his experience in Corinth, an eschatology that made freedom into such an absolute that the question "why not sin?" completely eclipsed any sense of responsibility for the community. Paul here penetrates some of the subtle ambiguities of freedom that expose the tensions inherent in freedom. For the believer, freedom from slavery to sin is not to enjoy freedom from slavery to Christ (6:17, 18, 20), and for Paul a totally autonomous self free of any obligation or commitment is simply impossible. The question was rather the nature of one's commitment and the identity of one's master.

Paul's discussion continues through 7:6, but his point is clear. Through baptism the believer shares in a transfer from an old aeon dominated by the ruling powers of sin and death into a new aeon in which he or she participates in the life of Christ and looks forward to sharing in his resurrection. This eschatological transfer effected in baptism and the symbolic participation in Christ's death gave the believer new life. Implicit in this scenario was a question: How can a believer participating in the new age in Christ still behave as if he or she is in bondage to the old aeon? The implied answer is that one cannot. Thus Paul countered the charge raised against his gospel of an antinomianism that encouraged hedonistic excesses. Here again, Paul gives his participationist language a strong ethical nuance. While the ethical dimension is present in all of his letters, elsewhere Paul specifically employs participationist language to address other issues—for example, suffering (1 Thess. 1:5–8; 2:13–16) and corporate solidarity (1 Cor. 12). While Romans contains both motifs (8:17 on suffering and 12:3–13 on solidarity), Paul's most sustained use of participationist language deals with charges of antinomianism (Rom. 6) and life in the new age (Rom. 8).

The participationist dimension of Paul's thought, however, reaches beyond these present realities to embrace an eschatological future with Christ. 1 Thess. 4:13–18 anticipates such a future, when at the *parousia* of Christ dead and living believers will be reunited with each other to join Christ. And Rom. 6:8 notes Paul's conviction that believers who have shared in the death of Christ "*shall* live with him" in the future (emphasis added). But to abstract these statements from their specific applications robs them of some of their power.

When observing these various emphases one might note that they reflect a theological development rather than simple variations on a common theme. We noted, for example, that there is no evidence in 1 Thessalonians that Paul had thought through the implications of his gentile gospel. The challenges to his apostleship and gospel in Galatia, however, forced him to consider these implications. The way he self-consciously reinterprets texts central to the arguments of his adversaries suggests the approach here is entirely new. Yet Paul's response to the opposition in Galatia raised more insistent questions about the reliability of God's promises that he dealt with in Romans. Most would agree that in Rom. 9–11 Paul makes his most strenuous effort to hold together two items that were straining in opposite directions. At the end of chapter 11 one is aware that we have more than another variation on a theme; we have the extension of a process that clearly reveals Paul's theologizing. Troels Engberg-Pedersen aptly summarizes this point: "All this tends to emphasize the dynamic and open-ended character of Paul's theologizing. What we see in the letters is a symbolic universe *in the making*, not a fully worked out, static, and final one."[94] As P. W. Meyer has shown, such an understanding of Paul's theologizing has a practical effect on the reading experience itself: "Instead of assuming most of the time that Paul's 'theology' or 'convictions' are the *resource* or starting point *from* which he addresses the issues placed before him, may one rather, as a kind of 'experiment in thought,' think of them more consistently as the end-product and result, the *outcome to* which he arrives in the process of his argument, his "hermeneutic," or his 'theologizing.'"[95]

The root meaning of theology, thinking about God, aptly describes the nature of Paul's activity. New occasions not only teach new duties, they also require fresh thinking. Paul's theology, as we have seen, was a situational theology in the best sense of the term, and his conviction that in the last days God was including gentile sinners among the elect required all of his intellectual powers and energies to defend. In Galatians and Romans we see a theologizer at work, facing sharp challenges (Gal.) and then being pushed to the limit to deal with reactions to his response to those challenges (Rom.). While it is enormously difficult to know where or when the letters included in our 2 Corinthians were written, it is possible nevertheless to see an author there who strove mightily to forge links and maintain bonds between the gentile church and the symbolic center of the church in Jerusalem. The offering itself also carried a strong eschatological nuance that reinforced that association of Jew and Gentile and informed the Romans discussion at a deep level. Nowhere more than 1 Corinthians do we see Paul more upset with a form of religious hyperbole that almost shattered the corporate bond holding the church together. Paul here reflects less on the inherent difficulty of the new mode of election he was proposing than on the implications of that mode for the subversion of a charismatic hierarchy. Paul found gentile arrogance (Rom. 11:13–24) and pretentiousness repugnant, but he preached a gospel in which God in Christ embraced this lumpish lot. This investigation shows that the letters reflect not a smooth trajectory of the evolution of Paul's theologizing but rather a theologizing that was an interactive process. As we shall soon see, that process hardly ended with Paul's death.

CHAPTER FIVE

"The Model Ascetic"

It is for single ones (jihidaye) *that the contest calls,*
because they have turned their faces to what lies ahead,
and do not remember what lies behind.
                    Robert Murray

This mid–fourth century psalm from Aphrahat of the Syriac church celebrates the singleness that baptism initiates, a singleness that separates one from family, that marks one's devotion to God, and that unites one with the Single One. In spite of the fact that this doctrine of ascetic singleness was inspired by Paul, the model ascetic[1] who commended the single life, and in spite of Paul's public preference for celibacy as a divine gift (1 Cor. 7:7), scholars have paid surprisingly little attention to this historical datum of the apostle's life. This is where the trajectory of asceticism led, and it is the view here that the trajectory began long before the time of Paul and ran through him rather than around him as many scholars have argued.

Most ordinary folk tend to think of asceticism in starkly negative terms and in doing so they stand in a long tradition. The *Oxford English Dictionary* defines asceticism as the "principles or practices of the ascetics; *rigorous* self discipline, *severe* abstinence, *austerity*" (emphasis added). Others associate asceticism with pathological masochistic abuse of the Desert Fathers, and still others like George Bernard Shaw define asceticism as "thinking you are moral when you are uncomfortable." Others characterize asceticism as psychotic behavior.[2] Many New Testament scholars think of asceticism as morally perverse, defining it pejoratively as an "individualistic," self-absorbed form of behavior that is selfish, perverse, or an "end in itself." While Paul is widely praised as a theologian, apostle, missionary, and author, rarely is his asceticism acknowledged, and even then it is done so apologetically.[3]

The pejorative definition of asceticism may have obscured the potency and multifaceted character of this highly charged religious symbol and its ability to provide a coherent worldview and to effect religious renewal.

Faced with Paul's preference for singleness in 1 Cor. 7, Jeremias argued that Paul was a widower, therefore implying that Paul was no ascetic.[4] Walter Grundmann stated categorically that "the ascetic sense was 'for him an alien concept.'"[5] In a twenty-page treatment of "Askese in the New Testament and ancient church" in the *TRE*, Jean Gribomont gave Paul's celibacy only one paragraph,[6] and Kuhn concluded in his article on "Askese" in *Die Religion in Geschichte und Gegenwart* that Paul's celibacy was a simple pious act and not asceticism.[7] Michel saw nothing unusual about Paul's ascetic tendencies, noting that they were only the sublimation of sexual desires to religious, aesthetic, and political interests and that this behavior was not abnormal but normal and even necessary.[8] C. K. Barrett wrote that "it is impossible to describe his [Paul's] attitude as ascetic."[9] Gerhard Delling saw in Paul's sexual asceticism a "spätjüdische Frauenverachtung" (a late Jewish hatred of women) and a "hellenistische Ehemüdigkeit" (a Hellenistic marriage fatigue).[10] We see, therefore, that New Testament scholars almost unanimously undervalue the ascetic piety of Paul's time.

Many students of Judaica, likewise, find no evidence of asceticism either in Scriptures or in later Judaism. Hermann Strathmann asserts that Jewish piety is "thoroughly unascetic" (ist durchaus unasketisch)."[11] George Foot Moore similarly argued that Judaism contradicts at every point an ascetic piety that subjugates the evil flesh and its passions to achieve a mystical union with God.[12] "The goal of the true ascetic . . . is purely individualistic. . . . Now it can hardly fail to impress every one familiar with the sources that such a desperate concern of the individual about his own precious soul is conspicuously absent from Judaism; and that for reasons that lie deep in religious thinking."[13] Moore further noted that "Asceticism never occupied an important place in the Jewish religion."[14] Lietzmann acknowledged that there was a hyperasceticism among the Corinthians but observed that "This was an entirely un-Jewish point of view."[15]

In spite of this overwhelmingly negative view of asceticism, scholars have puzzled over Paul's celibacy in 1 Cor. 7, which Peter Brown notes was the one chapter "that was to determine all Christian thought on marriage and celibacy for well over a millennium."[16] Shortly after the turn of the century Johannes Weiss recognized Stoic and Cynic elements in Paul's argument but argued that his emphasis on holiness and eschatology informed his view of celibacy.[17] Weiss's instincts were correct but largely undeveloped. The last twenty years have witnessed a number of imaginative studies on this chapter. Kurt Niederwimmer suggested that Paul's repeated denunciations of *porneia*, immorality, inspired a pessimistic view of sexuality in Paul's churches, but there is no support for such a confusion in Corinth.[18] Richard Horsley has written that like the Therapeutae of Philo's "On the Contemplative Life" and the Wisdom of Solomon, the Corinthians rejected marriage for a "spiritual marriage" with Sophia, but we have no evidence for "spiritual marriages" in

Corinth, much less a marriage with Sophia or wisdom.[19] David Balch saw indications in 1 Cor. 7:32–35 that Paul was influenced by a *Theios Anēr* mythology like that of Philo's Moses, who descended the mountain aglow with effervescent glory never to engage in sex again, but the ties Balch tried to secure to that Philonic tradition through 2 Cor. 3 are very tenuous indeed.[20] Vincent Wimbush argues that in the discussion in 1 Cor. 7:29–31, 32–35 about anxiety and having as if not having we see how a single minded devotion to the Lord evident in singleness follows from an eschatological detachment that is panhellenic in nature (like Stoic ἀπάθεια).[21] Wimbush's thesis has merit, but it would be enriched by further development of the importance of this view for Paul's Christology. Quite recently, Will Deming makes a case for reading 1 Cor. 7 in light of a long-standing Stoic-Cynic argument about marriage with Cynics renouncing marriage, to pursue philosophy and Stoics supporting marriage as the institution in which one's responsibility for having children assures the future of the polis. An intermediate position is occupied by "mushy" Stoics, who in periods of poverty or war accept the Cynic recommendation against marriage.[22] Deming thinks the Stoic position was basic for Paul's understanding of celibacy and that he used the apocalyptic material to "define the 'circumstances' of his (Stoic) argument against marriage."[23] Deming boldly states that a "knowledge of Stoic and Cynic thinking on marriage is essential *to any proper understanding of Paul's statements on marriage and celibacy* in 1 Corinthians 7" (emphasis added).[24] While Deming is certainly correct that Stoic philosophy influenced Paul's thought in 1 Cor. 7, drawing on a rather thin base of texts he overstates their impact and undervalues the role Paul's Judaism played in his understanding of celibacy.[25] Conspicuously absent from the discussion is any mention of the significance of Qumran materials for this consideration or any treatment of the relationship of Paul's celibacy to his Christology. We see, therefore, that the picture of what inspired and informed Paul's asceticism as well as its substance is murky indeed.[26]

Our discussion here will assume a rather broad definition of asceticism. While the difficulty of framing a good working definition of asceticism is forbidding, in this work I have thought of asceticism as a symbolic act of self-denial, either physical or psychological, either individual or communal, either temporary or lifelong, both positive and negative that provides a coherent worldview and a guide to behavior.[27]

THE FOREGROUND OF PAUL'S ASCETICISM

Ascetic Traits in the Hebrew Bible

As we shall see subsequently, Judaism's recognition of the goodness of the creation would seem to argue against any ascetic tendencies. Nevertheless, within the oldest traditions of the Hebrew religion ascetic tendencies surfaced from time to time. Even if one grants Strathmann's point that there were no ascetics but only ascetic traits in the Hebrew Bible, those traits assumed importance, for they provided the language, myths, legends, and *topoi* that shaped later ascetic piety. Temporary periods of sexual restraint, for example, were common in Israel's experience. Priests, holy warriors, and Nazarites all practiced sexual abstinence for discrete periods when under vows or in the service of the altar (Lev. 15:18; 2 Sam. 11:11; Deut. 10:1–9). In some cases, however, Nazarites vowed lifelong chastity (Judg. 13:5, 7; 16:17), and Yahweh's command to Jeremiah—"You shall not take a wife, nor shall you have sons or daughters" (16:1–2)—made him a walking ascetic symbol of the horror to be visited on Judah by the invading Babylonian army. While these focal instances hardly argue for an ascetic movement, they do provide precedents and language to influence later Jewish and Christian ascetic expression.

Asceticism in Greek Philosophy and Hellenistic Traditions

By Paul's time the Greek and Hellenistic worlds had already emphasized the control of sensual passions for centuries.[28] Although abstention from sex had been commended by Plato (even though there was tension with his ethics organized around the right use of pleasure), the demise of the autonomy of the *polis* brought on by Alexander profoundly affected the social understanding of sex. A new emphasis on community in the family arose in the wake of the weakening of the *polis*.[29] With the emergence of an animus toward flesh in the Hellenistic world and the detailing of the hazards of sexual intercourse in medical texts went a continuing emphasis on the control or elimination of passion.[30] In the Hellenistic era *enkrateia,* that is, self- control or continence, which had once been a prerequisite for philosophical wisdom (Socrates in Xen. mem. 1, 5, 4) became a struggle of reason to exert its supremacy over passions and desires. With the emergence of a flesh-spirit dualism, the repression of passions and desires distinguished the philosopher from the common lot (Eth. Nic. VII, 1–11).[31] *Enkrateia* (ἐγκράτεια) became the trademark of the élite, the foundation of virtue, and with the decline of the *polis,* the impulse for public service or humanitarianism (Cic. off. 1, 23, 79). Increasingly, sexual abstinence became foundational for a single-minded commitment to philosophical ideals, and sexual passion was described as the enemy of the holy, the good, and the rational. Interestingly, anthropological dualism thrived in a period when confidence in civic institutions was on the wane and intellectuals were increasingly cynical about or skeptical of ancestral religious traditions.

In the late first century, the Stoic Epictetus rejected wine, house, city, servants, bed, and wife as distractions from philosophy.[32] A Cynic epistle to

Zeno recognizes that wife and children are an encumbrance that aggravates human weakness.[33] Orphics sought to kill the sexual appetite by abstaining from meat, and common people and philosophers alike took for granted that sexual chastity was a prerequisite for the divine encounter and revelation (Pausanius, II, 24, 1). Neo-Pythagoreans practiced a strict ascetic discipline to free the soul for contemplation of the divine. We would err by suggesting that this was the sole conviction of popular philosophy, for some Stoics encouraged childbearing to ensure the future of the *polis*. Our point here, however, is that a strong emphasis on ascetic piety was already in place in Hellenistic religion by the first century. That ascetic piety functioned in many different ways: as a precondition for entering sacred space, as an escape from a destitute world, as preparation for communion with the gods and for contemplation of the divine, and as the foundation of a life of virtue. Asceticism enabled one to transcend the physical limits so irrevocably imposed on all humanity and provided a means of escape from a sinister world and a bodily prison. Any literate Jew in touch with the major philosophical currents of the day would have been aware of and influenced by this rich body of ascetic tradition and practice.

Asceticism in Diaspora Judaism

Although many writings from the Jewish Diaspora reflect an ascetic piety characteristic of the Hellenistic world, it is Philo and Josephus who articulate it best.[34] In Philo especially we recognize the influence of this popular Hellenistic philosophy. Roughly contemporary to but not an acquaintance of Paul, Philo was an educated, cosmopolitan, Alexandrian Jew who was a prolific writer and commentator on Torah. Although he was profoundly influenced by Hellenistic philosophy, his center of gravity was in a Jewish tradition that he sought to keep open to Hellenistic culture.[35] He adopted the vocabulary and outlook of Stoic philosophy and appropriated its religious meaning. He, like his peers in Hellenistic philosophy, took asceticism (ἀσκήσεως) to refer to the fitness of the mind and soul as well as of the body. And he shared the pessimistic Hellenistic anthropology that took *askēsis* to refer primarily to the renunciation of base and irrational flesh in order to make absorption into the divine possible.[36] Like the popular Hellenistic philosphers, he subscribed to a flesh-spirit dualism that was highly elitist in its view that the mark of an educated "man" (Spec. Leg. I, 173, 6) was the control of fleshly desires that were inimical to the spirit. He also shared with popular philosophy a misogyny that doubtless influenced his views of asceticism.[37]

Even though Philo adopted much from Hellenism, he mastered its idiom and subordinated it to his Jewish tradition. His understanding of asceticism (ἀσκήσις), therefore, contrasts with that of the Cynics, who saw it as "training" for happiness. While Cynic asceticism aimed to break the fetters of the normative culture to secure autonomy, *askēsis* for Philo had strong traditional ties to his normative culture, the religion of Israel, and biblical figures whom he made to incorporate Jewish elements emphasizing corporate responsibility (De Abr., 42; 52–53). Philo was intensely loyal to the vibrant Jewish community in Alexandria, and though he spoke much of virtue in Hellenistic fashion, this virtue was never private but rather virtue informed by a civic obligation.

The most important term in Philo's vocabulary taken from Hellenistic philosophy was ἐγϰϱατεία (self-control), which he used over fifty times. Sanctioned by centuries of use, it was for Philo, as for the popular philosophers, the foundation of all other virtues and referred primarily to the bridling of desires and passions (Quis. Rer., 254; Spec. Leg., I, 149–50). The consummate incarnation of self-control was Moses. Since he is "a stranger to this world," his real home being heaven (De Conf. Ling., 78), he "loosens his ties to the world" (De Ebrie, 157) and cuts "off all passions everywhere" (Alleg. Int., III, 134). The quintessential expression of Moses' ἐγϰϱατεία was his control of his sexual urges to keep himself in readiness for divine revelation.

Relying on the Exodus account that prohibits sexual intercourse during the Sinai theophany (Exod. 19:15), Philo reports that after his prophetic call Moses never again "knew" his wife, Zipporah. In his own words, Moses "had disdained [sexual intercourse] for many a day, almost from the time when, possessed by the spirit, he entered on his work as a prophet, since he held it fitting to hold himself always in readiness to receive the oracular messages" (Vit. Mos., II, 68–69). Since this legend has a rabbinic parallel, it is altogether possible that the story had a dual ancestry.[38] Central to this story is Philo's recognition that celibacy is a sine qua non of spirit possession and prophecy. The rabbinic parallel may suggest that this was a popular tradition that may have influenced both Paul and his addressees in Corinth.

While Moses' celibacy was viewed as continuing lifelong, there were other instances of celibacy for an important interim. In Philo's comment on the flood story we have some interesting observations. There Noah's celibacy was motivated by quite a different set of conditions. Informed by both the holy war model of Israel and the humanitarianism and antipathy to passion in Hellenistic philosophy, Philo deftly merges these themes into his exegesis. One dictates the suspension of sexual contact in periods of crisis, another out of empathy with those enmeshed in catastrophe, and another out of a sense of the pathos of the sensual. In his comments on Gen 7:7 (LXX), which has Noah and his wife enter the ark separately, Noah with his sons, and his wife with her daughters-in-law, men with men and women with women, Philo takes the separation of men and women (7:7) to mean that they lived separate celibate lives in the ark. (Interestingly, the church fathers follow Philo, applying the same rule to the animals.) Being suspicious of sensuality and committed to humanitarian concern, he notes that during the calamity it would have been inappropriate to "sow seed in accordance with nature," for "to go to bed with your wives [while in the ark] is the part of those seeking and desiring sensual satisfaction. For these it was fitting to sympathize with wretched humanity, as kin to it."[39] As in holy war, after the emergency, when "they had been saved from evil," God instructed Noah's family through their order of leaving the ark "to hasten to procreate, by specifying not that men (should go out) with men nor women with women but females with males" (Quaes. Gen., 2:49). In this intriguing interpretation of the Flood story we see a complex blend of Jewish tradition and Hellenistic principles, a subtle integration of a holy war tradition with a humanitarian impulse and the use of temporary celibacy to sacralize sexual relationships after the Flood and give procreation a historical dimension.

Josephus, like Philo, was influenced by the popular philosophies of his day, and he shared Philo's misogyny as well as his negative anthropology.[40] In his positive and somewhat extensive treatment of the Essenes (*W* 2:120 and *Ant.* 17:1, 5) he noted that except for one rather unimportant branch of Essenes (*W* 2:160, 161), they all rejected marriage (*W* 2:121), and as a sign of their control of the passions they wrote ἐγκράτεια (self-control) on their flag. According to Josephus, they were to give proof of their *enkrateia* (or temperance as he has it) during the probationary period (*W* 2:138).[41] While few doubt the veracity of Josephus's report on Qumran celibacy, the importance he assigns *enkrateia* among them strains credulity. Surely, *enkrateia* as a Hellenistic virtue was not an important feature of Qumran piety, nor was it written on their flag. However, Josephus did think an idealized form of piety should include this important Hellenistic trait, and in this conviction he is at one with Philo. In both Josephus and Philo, therefore, we have a skillful integration of Hellenistic ascetic motifs with Israel's faith and traditions. In both cases while elevating the importance of *enkrateia* they bestowed on this continence a corporate significance that reinforced the identity of Israel as the people of God.

Asceticism at Qumran

Even though Paul was never a member of the Qumran community as Pinchas Lapide suggests,[42] the influence of Jewish apocalypticism on Paul makes a consideration of asceticism at Qumran valuable. Two items in the Qumran experience encouraged asceticism—a priestly character and an apocalyptic outlook.[43] The priestly character had two interlocking dimensions—the holy cult and the holy place—that strongly predisposed the community to live celibate lives. Both entry into the holy place and participation in the holy cult required celibacy. Just as the priest in a moment of sexual purity was an intermediary between the divine and human worlds, so also the ascetic priests of Qumran seemed to serve a bridging function.

Once the Qumran location became a symbol for Jerusalem, sexual intercourse was forbidden in the camp. Yadin first noted the relationship of the prohibition of sex in "the city of the Sanctuary" (CD 12:1–2)[44] and the extension of the period of ritual impurity from one to three days for the sexually active in other cities (1 QT XLV:11–12).[45] Either would have banned daily participation in the cult at Qumran, but taken together they were "tantamount to ordaining complete celibacy"[46] and provided "the most distinct halakhic core for the development of Essene celibacy."[47]

Yadin's position has found confirmation in the work on 4QMMT by Quimron and Strugnell that proves that the "camp of holiness" occupied by the community stood for Jerusalem.[48] (In an earlier study of 1QpHab 12:3–5, Qimron and Strugnell had shown that Qumran references to Lebanon signified the temple, a metaphor of the Qumran community.)[49] Since sexual intercourse was forbidden in Jerusalem, and since the community saw itself as the incarnation of Jerusalem,[50] Qimron and Yadin concluded that celibacy followed logically.[51] The presence of female skeletons in the Qumran burial site may require some qualification, but the celibacy of a majority of the priestly community seems irrefutable.

This emphasis on celibacy would have been reinforced by the expectation that during the final forty year eschatological battle between the Sons of Light and the Sons of Darkness the men would remain sequestered and neither women nor children would be allowed in the camp. Although the priestly, levitical tradition was central, clearly the holy war myth reinforced the Qumran commitment to celibacy.[52]

As in any priestly service, permission to enter the holy place and to share in the holy action required at least temporary celibacy. In her exploration of the connection between the sacred arena and the holy cult at Qumran, Carol Newsom offers independent confirmation of Yadin's thesis. In her study of Shabbath Shirot, Newsom sees a link between the purity of the temple ("There is n[o] unclean thing in their holy places" [4Q400 1i 14]) and priestly holiness ("He has established for Himself priests of the inner sanctum, the holiest of the holy ones [g]od[like], *èlim* priests of the lofty heavens who [draw] near [. . .]" [4Q400 1i 19–20]). In the praise of God in the heavenly temple, in the company of the angelic host, the Qumran priests experienced the divine world and in that encounter found an "experiential validation" of their own self understanding.[53] They joined the "Holy Ones" in the heavenly realm (1QH 3:21–23), and this priestly service as well as the asexuality of their angelic partners suggests that those sharing that ideal realm should be celibate.[54] Fervently devoted to a purity befitting a community joining the angels at the altar, they hoped through their celibacy to so eradicate impurity from their midst (CD 20:14) that they would achieve "a quite new and transformed mode of existence."[55] The apocalypticism of the community intensified and validated its preoccupation with purity.[56] Since the time was short, the need for diligence was urgent. Since the final cataclysmic suffering hovered on the horizon, perfectly normal, wholesome, and, some believe, commanded action to be sexually "fruitful" (Gen. 1:28) was suspended for the cosmic emergency.

Asceticism in the Pseudepigrapha

"*Endzeit* equals *Urzeit*" is a truism that well fits the speculation of some pseudepigraphical writings.[57] Celibacy in the pseudepigrapha was not only "a metaphor of the world-to-come," it also symbolized the recovery of a lost, primordial world.[58] Hidden in the regret over the passing of that world and the separation from Eden one sees a nostalgia for that land free of toil and pain, of frustration and fratricide, of guilt and alienation. While all of that is evident in the etiological legends of the Genesis narrative itself, the pseudepigrapha add an interest in continence and ascetic piety that is not present in the Genesis narrative. Although the Eden story inspired no coherent or consistent interpretation of sex in the garden, it was a fertile source of imagination and reflection for such interpretation.

According to *Jubilees,* for example, the initial sexual encounter between Adam and Eve occurred outside the garden when God "brought her to him and he knew her"(3:6).[59] Only after a lengthy period of purification were Adam and Eve allowed to enter the garden (forty days for Adam and eighty days for Eve). Once settled in the garden, "more holy than any land" (3:12), they were chaste until their expulsion seven years later (Jub. 3:34–35; 4:1). Not until the first Jubilee after their expulsion, however, did Adam and Eve have sexual intercourse and children (3:34), Cain being born when Adam was seventy and Abel seven years later (4:1). Anderson correctly notes that they remained chaste in the garden because they viewed Eden as a holy temple, but his belief that in spite of a seven year period of abstinence in the garden and a forty-eight year period of continence after the expulsion that *Jubilees* does not advocate celibacy is puzzling.[60] Certainly, the tradition does hold Eden in such reverential awe that sexual intercourse there was unthinkable. Had the sages thought that life in the garden cheats death and, therefore, obviates the need for procreation? In this case as in so many, we cannot be certain of the motivation for this Eden tradition of sexual purity.

In the late first or early second century, 2 *Baruch* also associates Eden with a period of sexual innocence. For example, 2 *Baruch* links sexual intercourse and childbearing with punishment for the transgression of Adam and Eve and their expulsion from the garden:

> For when he transgressed, untimely death came into being, mourning was mentioned, affliction was prepared, illness was created, labor accomplished, pride began to come into existence, the realm of death began to ask to be renewed with blood, *the conception of children came about, the passion of parents was produced*, the loftiness of humanity was humiliated, and goodness vanished. (2 *Baruch* 56:6, emphasis added)[61]

The catalog of tragedy ending with the somber "and goodness vanished" betrays a world-weariness that longs for a world of innocence and purity, a world without sexual passion and desire, a celibate world, lofty, good, and deathless. Though human entry to that world was barred, one could mythically reenter it through celibacy and catch a glimpse of what was to come. This vision of the future is apparently shared by at least one tradition of early Christianity.

Early Christian Asceticism

An early Christian asceticism inspired by a realized eschatology may have pre-dated Luke's gospel. In 20:34–36 Jesus responds to a hostile question from the Sadducees about the resurrection. If a woman, following levirate law, married seven brothers seriatim who all died in turn and then finally she herself died, to whom would she be married in her resurrected state?

> Jesus said to them, "Those who belong to this age marry and are given in marriage; but those who are considered worthy of a place in that age and in the resurrection from the dead neither marry nor are given in marriage. Indeed they cannot die anymore, because they *are like angels and are children of God*, being children of the resurrection." (emphasis added)

Aune thinks this unparalleled passage came from an early Christian[62] pre-Lucan tradition.[63] While most commentators read the expression "Those who are accounted worthy to receive that age" (20:35) as a reference to the future life, Aune takes the aorist participle (καταξιωθέντες) as a reference to the present. He notes "in Luke 20:34–36, the Evangelist views abstinence from marriage and sexual intercourse as characteristic of believers who, as 'sons of that age/world' refrain from the entanglements of marriage because of the nearness of the Parousia."[64] In this passage, two types of human beings—those who marry, that is, children of this age, and those who do not, that is, baptized Christians—are contrasted, and those who do not marry "*are* like angels and are children of God, being children of the resurrection" (Luke 20:36, emphasis added).[65] To be a Christian then was to be like an angel with no sexual life.[66] If Aune is correct, this pre-Lucan Christian tradition would be chronologically positioned to influence behavior in some of Paul's churches.[67]

Summary

The preceding survey shows that the Judaisms of Paul's day contained multiple traditions and practices of ascetic piety. The Hellenistic, Jewish, and early Christian expressions of this piety varied greatly. Holy war traditions, apocalypticism, popular lore, Diaspora Jewish speculation, and popular Hellenistic philosophy all played a role. Celibacy both temporary and permanent was thought to free one for the divine-human encounter. Celibacy allowed one mystically to share the company of angels, and fellowship with the communion of holy ones served to validate one's own status, offered a foretaste of the eschaton, and permitted one to reexperience the purity and innocence of a lost world. Through celibacy one could transcend the physical limits so uncompromisingly set for all humanity, and celibacy focused one's commitment on the divine Deliverer in times of crisis. Certainly, there was no single source of Paul's asceticism, as Deming holds, or of the asceticism of the early church. Instead, many strands combined to form the complex patterns we see in each. In the discussion that follows we shall examine two of those strands— one Jewish apocalyptic and the other Hellenistic—that shaped Paul's religious habits and views on celibacy.[68]

PAUL'S CELIBACY

1 Cor. 7 reveals the sharply different views of celibacy of Paul and the Corinthians, and embedded in Paul's remarks are the outlines of each. "It is well for a man not to touch a woman" was apparently a Corinthian ascetic slogan that he cites in 7:1.[69] In 7:3–5 he writes that some married Corinthian believers were remaining chaste; that chastity may have been a mark of religious status (7:3–5). In 7:7b Paul's claim of celibacy as a charism allowed Corinthians to make the same claim. Widows and virgins, Paul says, either chose or were under pressure to remain unmarried and chaste (7:8–9). Paul reports that believers were divorcing believing (7:10–11) and unbelieving spouses (7:12–16), perhaps to avoid being polluted by sexual intercourse and keep themselves in readiness for life in the new age.[70]

This Corinthian behavior contains features we have noted previously in both the church and popular piety. The ecstatic speech of the Corinthians appears to have mythically brought them into the company of angels (13:1), and the status of angels offered validation for asexual behavior (Luke 20:35–36). The symbol and its interpretation were circular. Possibly it was because of their angelic status that the ecstatics practiced celibacy.[71] Then in turn through celibacy the human world was mythically united with the realm of angels.[72] The tradition of Moses' continence to keep himself in perpetual readiness for divine revelation, if known, would have reinforced the need for celibacy for the charismatic prophets (13:2; 14:3). Participation in the cult or entry into the holy sanctum required at least temporary celibacy. Perpetual readiness to receive divine revelation demanded permanent celibacy. The report of Chloe's people suggested that identification with mystagogues (Paul, Apollos, Peter, Christ) in baptism had fractured the church (1:12–13). Since Paul's own ascetic behavior was doubtless viewed as paradigmatic by many in this messianist congregation, an identification with Paul could incline one to celibacy.[73] The underlying Jewish angel lore and Jewish apocalypticism, as well as the pervasive Hellenistic flesh-spirit dualism, would have reinforced any or all of these tendencies. It is important to realize that an ascetic piety was so widespread in the Mediterranean world that this Corinthian behavior would have hardly been novel and certainly would not have been considered pathological.[74]

Whatever its sources, the Corinthian practice posed a difficult problem for Paul. Paul had probably offered his own example as a paraenetic model (1 Thess. 1:6; 2:14; Phil. 3:17; 1 Cor. 4:16; 11:1), and so obvious a feature of his behavior invited imitation. Since he claimed his celibacy was a charismatic gift, how could he, a charismatic celibate, condemn other celibate believers also claiming a charismatic status? The delicacy of Paul's position is evident in his attempt to qualify their celibacy while commending his own.[75] Paul's response was informed by two contrasting worldviews, one apocalyptic and one Hellenistic.

First, the eschatological crisis provided an important rationale for Paul's celibacy. The imminent end of this world age required a single-minded focus on readiness. Like the Qumran community, Philo, and the ancient Israelites with their holy war ethos, Paul believed that in periods of eschatological crisis sexual relationships distract from one's devotion to the Lord and make one anxious about "worldly things" (τὰ τοῦ κόσμου) or about how to please one's spouse (7:32–34). Since he was convinced that the "appointed time has grown short" (7:29) and that already the "present form of this world is passing away" (7:31), the practical issue of this cosmic emergency was clear to him. Entanglements should be avoided. He wished "that all were as I myself am" (7:7). He warned that in light of the eschatological trauma that "those who marry will experience distress in the flesh" (7:28), and he wanted all "to be free from anxieties" (7:32) associated with sexual relationships. Although

Paul allowed those aflame with passion to marry, he thought this second best: The one "who refrains from marriage will do better" (7:38). Even though a widow is free to remarry "in my judgment she is more blessed if she remains as she is" (7:40). While Paul affirmed a mutually responsible sexual relationship between married partners, he believed it was inferior to the situation of the unmarried with no sex life at all. Thus, for Paul, marriage was an intermediate position between *enkrateia*, or self-control, and *porneia*, or immorality. Although he believed that the mutual obligations accepted in marriage compromise one's alertness, he nevertheless advised that, once accepted, those marital ties were to be responsibly honored. And though Paul discouraged sexual relationships as second best, it would be a mistake to assume that Paul's celibacy was individualistic or a search for private virtue. He was metaphorically both the father and the mother of this community; his apostleship was communally focused. His paraenesis in 1 Corinthians strongly emphasizes the corporate nature of the life in Christ, and it was this corporate focus that distinguished Paul's celibacy from that of the Corinthians. In other words, Paul was celibate at least in part for the good of the churches, while the Corinthians found in celibacy a means of increasing their own spiritual status.

Second, although the apocalyptic character of Paul's response is thoroughly Jewish and thus explains Paul's advice to remain unmarried because of the "crisis," one feature of that apocalyptic ethos was clearly Hellenistic,[76] namely the emphasis on self-control. Paul's use of ἐγκρατεία and ἐγκρατεύο-μαι or self-control (1 Cor. 7:9; 9:25; Gal. 5:23) is undeniably of a Hellenistic provenance and rooted in a dualistic Hellenistic anthropology. Under the influence of this anthropology, Paul viewed passions and desires as dangers to be curbed through the repression of the flesh. In 1 Cor. 7, for example, he links his discussion of three instances of sexual abstinence with the need for control. In 7:5 he advised married couples to forgo sexual activity only by mutual agreement and only for short periods, "so that Satan may not tempt you because of your lack of *self-control* (ἀκρασίαν, emphasis added)."[77] In 7:8 he urged the unmarried and widows to follow his example. "But if they are not *practicing self-control* (ἐγκρατεύονται), they should marry" (emphasis added). A synonym of *enkrateia* appears also in 7:37, where Paul suggested, "if someone stands firm in his resolve, being under no necessity but having his own desire *under control* (ἐξουσίαν), and has determined in his own mind to keep her as his virgin he will do well" (emphasis added). Whether the "virgin" is a daughter or fiancé is unclear; what is clear is that Paul, acutely conscious of the pathos of the sensual, views it as a distraction from a total commitment to God in the final apocalyptic crisis.

All three terms, ἐγκρατεία, ἀκρασίαν, and ἐξουσίαν, are part of the same language field. While ἐγκρατεία (or control) appears rarely in biblical texts, in other first century Jewish writings the word played a key role.[78] In earlier Jewish traditions, *enkrateia* was no mere human achievement, nor part of a system of autonomous ethics,[79] but was seen as a gift of God (Wisd. of Sol. 8:21; Ep. Arist. 327 and 248).[80]

In 1 Cor. 9:24–27 ἐγκράτεια refers to the control of the flesh or fleshly desires as part of an ascetic discipline. In 1 Cor. 9:24–27 especially, Paul used an athletic metaphor with rich ascetic associations. "Athletes exercise self-control (ἐγκρατεύεται) in all things; they do it to receive a perishable wreath." "Control in all things" for the athlete meant both renunciation and affirmation: renunciation of things that impair (sex, meat, and wine) and affirmation of things that improve performance (training, practice, and rest).[81] Paul ponders this metaphor seeking insight for his paranesis:

> So I do not run aimlessly, nor do I box as though beating the air; but I beat my body black and blue (ὑπωπιάζω) and enslave it, so that after proclaiming to others I myself should not be disqualified. (9:26–27)

Pfitzner holds that in these words "there is no trace of an ascetic mortification of the body, of self-castigation carried out for its own sake. Εγκράτεια does not assume the importance of an independent virtue, as in the Stoic diatribe. Nor does it serve a purely self-centered goal . . . but stands in the service of the apostolic commission."[82] Pfitzner would be correct if asceticism were necessarily "carried out for its own sake" or if *enkrateia* were by definition an independent virtue serving a self-centered goal, but he offers no evidence that was the case, nor can I find any in Jewish writers. On the contrary "training" and "self-control" in Hellenistic Jewish writings were hardly ends in themselves. Their supreme purpose was to serve some higher goal.

The context itself contradicts Pfitzner's point. This teaching by example—first positively [Paul's own] and then negatively [that of the Israelites at Sinai] (10:1–13)—shapes a context in which Paul warns against lack of control of primal urges: "We must not indulge in sexual immorality as some of them did, and twenty-three thousand fell in a single day" (10:8). While the absence of sexual immorality is hardly asceticism, the presence of self-control (ἐγκράτεια) linked to a sports metaphor that suggests temporary asceticism supports ascetic behavior. This usage associated with Paul's command to think not on the seen but the unseen (2 Cor. 4:18) introduces a conflict with the "flesh" that can readily serve as the foundation of an asceticism like that in 1 Corinthians.[83]

While our discussion of Paul's asceticism has drawn heavily on 1 Corinthians, those same inclinations appear elsewhere. In Rom. 14:6, for example, Paul is sympathetic in his treatment of the ascetic tendencies among the "weak" in Rome who abstain from meat "for the Lord." Although Paul nowhere refers to Jesus' singleness, the final referent for his celibacy as for so much else was Christ. The death of Christ in particular was Paul's paradigm. Obviously it stands behind the reference to the crucifixion of the flesh in Gal. 5:24[84] and is the grounding for his asceticism. It stands behind such self-referential statements as "I die daily" (1 Cor. 15:31), and it is succinctly summarized in Paul's own hand in his critique of the boasting of his competitors, who are proud of their trophies won by circumcision: "May I never boast of anything except the cross of our Lord Jesus Christ, through whom the world has been crucified to me, and I to the world" (Gal. 6:14). It also informed the famous early Christian hymn of Christ's self-denial, death, and exaltation in Phil. 2:5–8. As Paul amends the hymn to focus on the cross ("he humbled himself, becoming obedient unto death [*even death on a cross*]"), the nadir of his descent becomes the beginning of his exaltation. In contrast to this self-denial stands the self-indulgence of the "enemies of the cross of Christ" whose "god is their belly (κοιλία)" (Phil. 3:18–19). If Paul is here influenced by the Greek view of *koilia* as the seat of sensuality, then what he condemns is an "unbridled sensuality," either of gluttony or sexual license, that has directed their minds to "earthly things" (ἐπίγεια, 3:19).[85] The consequence is destruction. Christ's self-denial and crucifixion were, therefore, paradigmatic for Paul's asceticism that sought to crucify the flesh "with its passions and desires" (Gal. 5:24). Here "flesh" serves as the seat of sin but not its root; the root is its "passions and desires." The destruction of the flesh, therefore, deprives the passions and desires of their breeding ground. Ironically, both the rejection of and the preoccupation with flesh lead to a metaphorical death. One can either crucify the flesh and live or "set the mind on the flesh" and die (Rom. 8:6–7).

Summary

In the preceding discussion, we have seen that a multiform ascetic piety was present in both Jewish and Hellenistic religious expressions of the first century. And this ascetic piety enjoyed broad acceptance in popular, priestly, and philosophical circles. The asceticisms of Paul and the Corinthians reflect worldviews that are quite different: The genesis of the Corinthian celibacy was a realized eschatology that incorporated angel lore and popular religion. Paul's celibacy was rooted in Jewish and Hellenistic traditions, a christological focus on the cross and Jesus' self-denial, an apocalyptic mind-set, and an eschatological reserve emphasizing a continuing struggle. Both the self-denial of Christ and his crucifixion served as a model of Paul's asceticism, which he wanted his addressees to imitate (1 Cor. 11:1; cf. also Rom. 15:1–3). Moreover, an emphasis on grace, while surely present in Paul's theology, was not allowed to obscure a very strong emphasis also on human effort as expressed in self-control. Paul's view of his celibacy as a gift of the spirit, or as a powerful symbol of the new mode of existence, suggests that he believed that the energy driving continence (ἐγκρατεία) was also the Spirit. We have seen that Paul's pessimistic anthropology, his dark apocalyptic outlook in the near term, and his christology combine to shape his ascetic piety. Paul's anthropology, however, is not totally negative, for he can refer to Jesus in the flesh with no negative nuance, and he can use *sarx* (flesh) in a quite neutral sense.

There were also features of Paul's asceticism that sharply distinguished it from other ascetic expressions. His belief in God's final struggle against the "ruler of this world" (2 Cor. 4:4) brought an intensity to his theologizing that made his preference for celibacy understandable. Nevertheless, this eschatology was only inaugurated, not accomplished, thus ruling out a celibacy informed by a realized eschatology or an angel lore springing from a religious enthusiasm. His celibacy was not driven by the priestly considerations of Qumran, nor did it have the misogynist character of that of Philo and Josephus. While for Philo self-control or ἐγκρατεία was the mark of the educated in pursuit of virtue, for Paul ἐγκρατεία was spirit driven and egalitarian, and its aim was an undistracted devotion to the Lord in the crisis. Paul appeals to Jesus' crucifixion, not his celibacy, as his model of self-denial. So although Paul's celibacy was rooted in the philosophical and religious piety of the Hellenistic world and Jewish traditions, it also differed from them at points.

In the final chapter of this work we shall return to this discussion as we note how the second century church appropriated and expanded Paul's interest in celibacy. I hope this discussion has shown that Paul, though creative and original in his christological formulations, was also heavily indebted to both Jewish and Hellenistic traditions for his understanding of celibacy and that the trajectory of interpretation about celibacy ran through Paul rather than around him. In any consideration of Paul's celibacy the question often arises: Was Paul ever married? The argument can be made that the Jewish community expected young adults to marry and to raise families. The future of the community depended on the institution of marriage and the raising of at least five children in each family. The book of Genesis includes God's command to "be fruitful and multiply and fill the earth," (Gen. 1:22), and later rabbinic traditions with one voice condemn those who eschew marriage and childbearing. But there are arguments on the other side as well. We have seen strong cultural forces encouraging celibacy in both Hellenistic and Jewish circles. We have noted Paul's apocalypticism, and our study would suggest that his apocalypticism was rooted in his life as a Jew before his apostolic call. His religious zeal with its emphasis on keeping oneself in readiness for a divine revelation also would have encouraged celibacy. Then there is the comparison Paul at least implicitly draws between himself and Jeremiah as he reflects on his being "set apart from my mother's womb" for his apostolic task (Jer. 1:4; Gal. 1:15). Did Paul find God's command to Jeremiah not to marry and have children a guide for his own life? Did Paul associate the apocalyptic crisis he faced with the historical crisis Jeremiah experienced? We cannot know the answers to these questions, but these observations suggest that it is entirely conceivable that Paul never married.[86] We only know that during his service as an apostle of Christ he was celibate and counted that celibacy as a charismatic gift that was an appropriate response to the impending crisis.

CHAPTER SIX

The Mythic Apostle

In death as well as in life, Paul remained a controversial figure inviting both hate and awe. Only the grave was to grant Paul almost a generation of peace as an awkward silence hovered over him until Luke rescued him from obscurity by devoting over half of his Acts to Paul the missionary with wonder working powers. Although the author of 2 Peter smiled on Paul as "our beloved brother" (3:15), he frowned on "the ignorant and unstable" (3:16) who were twisting the Pauline letters. The stern warning in the letter of James that "faith by itself, if it has no works, is dead" (2:17) appears to criticize Paul's preaching of "justification by faith alone."[1] Even the invocation of Paul's name in the Deutero-Paulines, however, suggests conflicting interpretations that demanded a response (2 Thess., Col., Eph., 1 and 2 Tim., and Titus). Like the undisputed letters, these too face a void created by an absence imposed by Paul's death. Other writers invoked his name and authority for a new age, and the portrait they offer of Paul is heavily colored by their own interests. The story of Paul begets stories about Paul that create an awesome legendary figure. No longer is he an apostle but *the* apostle (Col. 1:24). No longer is his suffering a mere imitation of that of Christ, but rather it assumes vicarious significance (Col. 1:24). In what would have sounded grotesque to Paul, Ephesians gives him saintly status thirteen times and places him within the circle of "*holy* apostles" (3:5, emphasis added) who along with the Christian prophets form the very foundation of the church. When the Roman Jewish War and the first intense persecution of the church push the increasingly gentile church toward an ugly divorce of Jewish and gentile Christians, Paul pleads for unity (Eph. 2:11–22). In the struggle with Gnosticism evident in the pastoral epistles Paul is presented as the divine apostle who transmits his authority through the ordination of his successors, who are charged to refute false teaching with sound doctrine. 2 Thessalonians presents Paul as a laborer worthy of imitation (3:7–12). He prays for the suffering church (1:11–12; 2:17) and urges the letter recipients to hold onto the traditions (2:15). To be sure, these reconstructions sometimes flatly contradict the image of Paul we get from the undisputed epistles. The Paul who had female co-workers, who named women with authority as deacons, apostles, and prophets, now is made into a figure who reinforces a traditional subordination of women that took their voice from them (1 Tim. 2:9–15; Eph. 5:22–23). The apostle full of apocalyptic zeal is replaced by an apostle with little sense of apocalyptic urgency. The model ascetic is replaced by a Paul that urges both widows and the unmarried to marry.

Since the pseudepigraphic letter purports to be from the hand of the apostle, it does not readily lend itself to the development of legendary material about the assigned author. With the introduction of historical narrative, however, that situation changed dramatically. We cannot know with certainty why that should be so, but perhaps it was because the spotlight fell so directly on the apostolic figure himself. In the canonical and the apocryphal Acts, for example, Paul assumes dimensions only hinted at in the undisputed letters. We go awry if we think of these legendary materials as simply pure acts of fancy told for amusement, though amuse they did. They also labored to capture a truth about the apostle in story form that recaptured meaning in his history and provided inspiration for survival in times of crisis. More than moralistic clichés, they engaged the thought and imagination of the circle of hearers, and they offered a resolution to great human crises that nourished at very deep levels.

The Acts of the Apostles, most scholars believe, took shape in the second half of the second century, which was a fluid, tumultuous period of transition. If the second half of the first century was fluid and tumultuous, the second century, when the apocryphal Acts took shape, was even more so. A predominantly gentile church on the ascendancy was in danger of cutting itself loose from its moorings in the Hebrew religion. There was no agreement yet on what writings were scriptural. Great regional religious factions—for example, Jewish Christian Ebionites and Elkasites and Gnostic Valentinians—fought tenaciously for their versions of emerging Christianity. And there was profound disagreement about and ambivalence toward the apostle Paul. We are so conditioned to read Paul through Reformation lenses and to think of Paul as the great theologian of the early church that we may be quite shocked to learn that issues of primal importance in our reading of Paul played almost no role at all in the late first and entire second century.

Interestingly, almost none of the heated and abrasive exchanges of the second century reveal any interest in Paul the theologian. Schneemelcher has pointed out, for instance, that although Ignatius (ca. CE 107–17) revered Paul as a holy, praiseworthy apostle and martyr, he neither knew nor had ever read Paul's letters.[2] Polycarp, who died a martyr's death in 156, saw Paul as a valuable ally in his exhortations and unlike Ignatius spoke of multiple letters of Paul, yet there is no evidence that Paul's theology was important to him.[3]

The Greek apologists of the mid–second century—Justin, Tatian, Athenagoras, and Theophilus—nowhere mention the name of Paul.[4] In the mid second century, Hegisippus, who may have been a Jewish Christian, visited the West to learn the correct teaching of the church. In his later accounting of that visit, which is admittedly fragmentary, he found in the Lord's words and Hebrew Scriptures an authority for the church. What is remarkable about this summary is that nowhere is Paul mentioned though by the mid–second century a collection of his works would have been available in the West in both Rome and Corinth.[5]

From this we can hardly assume that Paul's letters were totally ignored, for they were not. Bitterly opposing views of Paul were offered, for example, by Marcion and the Gnostics on the one hand and the Jewish Christian church on the other. Scorned by his critics as a wealthy shipowner who sought to buy recognition in the church in Rome, Marcion was revered by his followers as one of the most interesting and most important interpreters of Paul in the second century. He so revered Paul as *the* apostle that he made the entire Pauline corpus (except for the Pastorals and Hebrews) purged of all Judaizing tendencies, the measure of truth and the core of his Bible. He may have been the first to oppose a "New Testament" to an "Old Testament," which he believed revealed an inferior demi-God of this world.[6] Although he did radically pit gospel against law and embraced the celibacy for all believers that he saw in 1 Cor. 7, he was certainly no systematic theologian, nor was he a deep and penetrating thinker. Yet, from the evidence available to us, one may legitimately call Marcion the first serious exegete of the Pauline letters and certainly the first to establish the letters as Holy Scripture. The attraction of his theology was due in part to its simplicity and its tightly drawn system of beliefs that was "narrow in focus and easy to defend."[7]

Between his break with the church in Rome ca. 144 CE and his death ca. 160 CE, Marcion founded a church that spread like wild fire. Some scholars believe the church of Marcion was nearly as large as the non-Marcionite church in the 170s, and even after it waned in the West, it remained a formidable force in the East for centuries. The Marcionite movement was dominant in Syria until the fifth century. The success of Marcion's version of Christianity is astonishing in view of its reservation of baptism for adults and its requirement of celibacy for baptized Christians. It was not until the fifth century that Marcionite Christianity was eclipsed and even then only under violent pressure from the eastern church. Marcionism suffered mightily when Bishop Rabbula (411–35 CE) presided over the destruction of its churches, transferred its property to the "Great Church," and "gently" urged Marcionite Christians to surrender their "error," accept the "truth," and be baptized.[8]

The other creative and imaginative pro-Pauline faction in the second century church was Valentinian Gnosticism.[9] Its devotees also greatly revered

Paul as their teacher of esoteric wisdom and also engaged in very creative exegesis of the Pauline letters, leading to a radical dualism between spirit and flesh. Admittedly, certain Pauline texts stripped of their contexts seem to carry Gnostic nuances. Paul's statement that "nothing good dwells . . . in my flesh" (Rom. 7:18), his plea for deliverance from "this body of death" (Rom. 7:24), his view that "flesh and blood cannot inherit the kingdom of God" (1 Cor. 15:50), and his yearning for "the redemption *of* our bodies" (easily read as "the redemption *from* our bodies") (Rom. 8:23) all could easily be made to serve Gnostic ends. The Valentinian and Naassene Gnostics claimed Paul's letters as the source of their theology and praised him as the wellspring of secret mysteries. They developed a powerful hermeneutical loop that found in Paul's letters the genesis of their antiworldly, dualistic religion and in their religion the hermeneutical key for understanding the letters. In response to this Gnostic Paul, Irenaeus, the Bishop of Lyon, 170–80, tried to construct an ecclesiastical Paul.[10] He aligned Paul with Peter and made the apostle Paul one of the guarantors of the truth of the church's teaching. He redefined Paul's understanding of faith to make it mean the acceptance of the church's teaching rather than the acceptance of God's deeds on behalf of a sinful humanity. But in spite of giving the entire Pauline corpus (including 1 and 2 Tim. and Titus) a close reading, Irenaeus did not set out to construct a Pauline theology.[11] Certainly the bold, imaginative exegesis of texts by the Gnostics contradicts Schneemelcher's flat assertion that "Irenaeus is the first known scriptural theologian of the Christian church."[12]

At the opposite end of the spectrum from the reverence for Paul seen in Marcion and the Gnostics was the vehement hatred of him by various Jewish Christian groups—for example, the Elkasites and the Ebionites. The Kerygmata Petrou of the Pseudo-Clementines describe Paul as a false prophet and impostor who preaches an untrue gospel (H II 17.4).[13] They portray him as "merely a helpmate of the feeble left hand [of God, i.e., the evil one]" (H II 15.5); and they view him as an "enemy" posing as a friend (H II 18.2). Compared to the revered Peter he was as darkness compared to light, as ignorance contrasted with knowledge, and as sickness juxtaposed against healing (Kerygmata Petrou, H II 17.3). Furthermore, they charged, Paul's claim to have received an apostolic commission directly from Christ through divine revelation (Gal. 1:12, 16–17) is a lie. A speech is placed on the lips of Peter to expose this claim as "preposterous" and "demonic":

We know . . . that many idolaters, adulterers and other sinners have seen visions and had true dreams, and also that some have had visions that were wrought by demons. For I maintain that the eyes of mortals cannot see the incorporeal being of the Father or the Son, because it is enwrapped in insufferable light. . . . But he who has a vision should recognize that this is the work of a wicked demon. But can any one be made competent to teach through a vision? And if your opinion is, "That is possible," why then did our teacher spend a whole year with us who were awake? How can we believe you even if he has appeared to you if you desire the opposite of what you have learned? But if you were visited by him for the space of an hour and were instructed by him and thereby have become an apostle, then proclaim his words, expound what he has taught, be a friend to his apostles and do not contend with me, who am his confidant; for you in hostility withstood me who am a firm rock, the foundation stone of the Church. (H XVII 19.1–4)

This vicious, anti-Pauline polemic, however, had little lasting impact on an increasingly gentile church, perhaps because it came from a shrinking minority that could be isolated and disregarded. Nevertheless, it represented an important current of opinion about Paul.

Given the opposition to Paul, and the reverence of the heretics for him, it is understandable why church leaders such as Papias, Justin, and Hegisippus were less than enthusiastic about Paul. Given his status as the darling of the heretics, it is astonishing that he was not tarred with the same brush that was used against them and that his letters were included in the New Testament at all. Schneemelcher thinks that the western church might have preferred to exclude them altogether from the canon, but by the time they might have been excluded, the late second century, "it was too late: he was already a chief apostle, and, next to Peter, the martyr of Rome, and despite the unfamiliarity of his theology, he already stood in high regard."[14] We could almost say that the person Paul became canonical before his writings did.

As we shall note in the subsequent discussion, this general indifference to Paul's theology permeated other streams of tradition as well. We think in particular of the apocryphal Acts and most especially of the Acts of Paul. Whether these apocryphal Acts were an anti-Gnostic polemic is unclear; what is clear is that in this later period apostolic legends multiplied portraying Paul not as the theologian but as the quintessential celibate, as a powerful miracle worker and martyr. In the remainder of this chapter we examine ways these legends expressed an interest not just in the words of the apostle but also in his life.

The perspective of the interpreters or the storytellers of the apocryphal materials offers valuable clues to the meaning of texts. The post Pauline letters differ in some important ways from the undisputed letters of the apostle himself, not just in matters of fact, though they do that, but more basically in their point of view. One important feature of Paul's point of view in the letters is his recognition of the primacy of the myth he inhabited. That myth was the sacred story of Israel's election now come to its culmination in the death and resurrection of Messiah Jesus. Although Paul passionately believed that he was playing an important role in that unfolding eschatological drama, he only reluctantly focused on himself to defend the authenticity of his apostleship and his gospel. He inhabited the myth, but he did not see himself as a mythic figure. That all changed dramatically in succeeding generations, when later believers increasingly saw Paul as a figure of mythic proportions whether he was viewed as demonic or divine. They saw and spoke often of Paul the celibate apostle, Paul the miracle working apostle, and Paul the apostolic martyr. In the following discussion we shall concentrate on these three important currents of tradition and legend in the postapostolic period.

PAUL AS CELIBATE

Paul's expressed preference for celibacy and his view that celibacy represented a superior charism (1 Cor. 7) determined "all Christian thought on marriage and celibacy for well over a millennium."[15] Whatever Paul's intentions, one thing is clear; in the centuries following, he was repeatedly invoked as the model ascetic.[16] Although he had argued that both marriage and singleness were valid expressions of life in Christ (1 Cor. 7:28), his unambiguous endorsement of celibacy (1 Cor. 7:7) was claimed by Marcion, Tertullian, Pseudo-Clement, and the authors of the apocryphal Acts as support for celibacy as a superior and sometimes sole expression of the Christian life.[17] Paul's view of asceticism developed in the face of the expected imminent *parousia* of Jesus and the divine denouement, and it remained as an important feature of the Christian life in apocalyptic movements like Montanism, but even when the feverish apocalyptic expectancy faded, the celibacy it inspired remained. Celibacy became a requirement for baptism in the early Syrian church. The unmarried were to remain so, and the married were to remain absolutely continent.[18]

Through this radical asceticism, the Marcionites sought to abolish all sexual distinctions and to create a community in which there was "no male or female." Women were permitted to hold office in the church.[19] Unlike other early interpreters, who judged Paul and his message in light of the gospels, Marcion did just the opposite. Paul became Marcion's measure of truth, Paul's gospel the measure of all gospels, and Paul's revelation the measure of all revelations. The God of Paul's Jesus, according to Marcion, was totally different from the God of the Old Testament, who was nothing more than a Demiurge or an inferior God. This categorical rejection of the "Old Testament"[20] as authoritative for believers in Paul's Christ made it easy for Marcion to set aside the injunction of Genesis to be fruitful and multiply as the command of an inferior deity. For him, celibacy was a sine qua non of the Christian life; if one were married when baptized then one must remain married as Paul had ordered (1 Cor. 7:12–16), but married believers must live celibate lives.

The Acts of Thomas, a Syriac document composed in the first half of the third century in Mesopotamia, offers some of the harshest language seen anywhere concerning marriage. A sexual relation in marriage was called a "deed of shame," a "deed of corruption," "dirty and polluted pleasures," and "filthy intercourse,"[21] and by contrast chastity was viewed as a source of countless blessings: "blessed are the bodies of the holy (chaste) ones, which are worthy to become clean temples in which the Messiah shall live [1 Cor. 6:19]."[22] And in all of this Paul was the archetypal celibate.

Arthur Vööbus, a noted scholar of Syriac Christianity, has done much to lift the veil hiding the physiogamy of the church in the east and one of its great fourth century writers, Aphrahat.[23] Drawing on the imagery of holy war, the seventh homily of Aphrahat urges those afraid, those concerned about their vineyards, those eager to take their betrothed as wives, and those worried lest they not live in the new house just built, all to retreat from the struggle because

> It is for Single ones (*ihidaye*) that the contest calls, because they have turned their faces to what lies ahead, and do not remember what lies behind; for their treasures are ahead and whatever booty they gain is for themselves, and they will gain great riches.[24]

While this great aspiration in its present form comes from the fourth century, Vööbus has shown that it is rooted in a baptismal liturgy from an earlier period.[25] The earlier era had required "singleness" as a condition for receiving the sacraments—"singleness [ihidayuta] from dear ones through separation by the 'sword' of Christ, singleness of mind (already in St. James [1:8; 4:8]!) through 'spiritual circumcision' by the same sword, and singleness by 'putting on' the Only-begotten and sole beloved, Christ."[26] The single ones, we are told, put on the Single One; they were given joy by the Single One who came from the Single God. This singleness became the quintessential expression of religious piety and life in Christ. Thus the Single One who came from the Single God stood for the curbing of sexual desire and baptism, and the life of discipleship had to do with leaving sex and clinging to the Single God.

One of the most interesting direct ties between Paul's celibacy and that of a later period may be seen in the Acts of Paul from the late second century. Since the Syrian and Armenian churches considered the rather imposing Acts of Paul canonical, we can be certain of its importance to a significant part of the eastern church.[27] That Paul's celibacy was seen as worthy of emulation and speculation we have independent witness in Pseudo-Clement, where his prowess in "treading down and subjugating the body" made him "a beautiful example" to believers.[28] The apostle's teaching in the Acts of Paul reenforces and enlivens that model as he, like Jesus, offers a set of beatitudes formally similar to those in Matt. 5 but substantially more akin to the Pauline letters:

> Blessed are they who have kept the flesh pure, for they shall become a temple of God [1 Cor. 3:16].
> Blessed are the continent, for to them will God speak . . . [1 Cor. 7:5].
> Blessed are they who have wives as if they had them not [1 Cor. 7:29], for they shall inherit God. . . .
> Blessed are the bodies of the virgins, for they shall be well pleasing to God, and shall not lose the reward of their purity [1 Cor. 7:38][29]

This preaching of the gospel of the beauty of the virgin life rose from a neighboring garden in Iconium, wafting through an open window above into the hearing of an eavesdropping "comely" Thecla betrothed to the respected, powerful Thamyris. This gospel of virginity and the resurrection and the sight of "many women and virgins going into Paul"[30] drew Thecla irresistibly into the apostle's company, and she left behind the cultural rewards of life with a rich, influential man. After Paul was arrested and imprisoned for proclaiming a gospel of virginity that was deemed antifamily, Thecla's poignant longing for Paul caused her to steal out of her own house by bribing the doorman and to gain access to Paul's cell by bribing the jailer (17–19). She spent the rest of the night with Paul in his cell receiving instruction, and she was so inspired by his serene confidence in God that she kissed his fetters. As her faith increased, she rolled on the spot where Paul had instructed her.[31] A frantic search located her in the prison with Paul, "bound with him in affection" (19). Though Paul was heard, scourged, and driven out of the city, Thecla was brought to trial before the governor. When in her sublime dignity she remained silent when the governor announced the charges against her, her own mother passed sentence: "burn the lawless one" (358). The Iconians gathered in the stadium to watch the execution of this follower of "the sorcerer [i.e., Paul]."[32] While bound to the stake atop a mountain of wood and straw with the flames licking at her feet, she saw the Lord "sitting in the form of Paul and [she] said: 'As if I were not able to endure, Paul has come to look after me.' And she looked steadily at him; but he departed into the heavens" (21). Miraculously she was saved by a rain- and hailstorm and released. Disguised in male attire she passionately searched for Paul like "a lamb in the wilderness" (20), until she found him in a tomb with Onesiphorus and his wife and children, fasting and praying for her release. As she entered the tomb she heard Paul praying, "Father of Christ, let not the fire touch Thecla, but be merciful to her, for she is thine!" (24). The reunion in the tomb, we are told, brought "much love" (25). Though Thecla vowed to cut her hair short and follow him wherever he went (25), Paul refused her wish: "The season is unfavorable, and thou art comely" (25). Thecla nevertheless accompanied Paul to Antioch, where she once again became the object of unwanted affections. Alexander, "one of the first of the Antiochenes" (26), fell madly in love with her and sought to take her physically for himself. He was slapped so hard by Thecla that the priestly crown of the imperial cult tumbled from his head. Condemned once more for desecrating "holy things" (28), Thecla was sentenced to die with the beasts. Again she was saved, once by a fierce lioness to which she was bound for the procession of the animals, which "licked her feet" (28) and once by a curtain of fire shielding her naked body from the beasts and the prurient gaze of spectators. Finally, she was to face a host of beasts in the coliseum. Facing the challenge, she turned to see a pit behind her, full to the brim with water. "Now is the time for me to wash" (34), she said and flung herself into the water filled with ferocious seals, which as soon as she entered the water were struck dead by a flash of lightning that left her unharmed. Since the baptized, whether married or not, were bound to live a celibate life, her baptism of herself symbolized her covenant with Christ that ruled out sexual intercourse forever.

The women of the city rushed to her aid. Some joined her in prayer. Some protested. The queen, Tryphaena, joined the protest of the women of the city, crying out, "May the city perish for this lawlessness! Slay us all, Proconsul! A bitter sight, an evil judgment!" (32). Again Thecla was delivered, and again her deliverance was succeeded by a desperate yearning to see Paul. After finding him, she recounted for him "everything" and announced "I have taken the bath [i.e., and the vow of lifelong celibacy], Paul; for he who worked with thee for the Gospel has also worked with me for my baptism" (40). Now Paul willingly offered her a commission: "Go and teach the word of God!" (41). This commission not only legitimized her apostleship but also saved her from the almost certain fate of marriage to either Thamyris or Alexander and service as a dutiful wife and servant.[33]

The Acts of Thecla have received increasing attention in recent years. Drawing on folklore studies, Virginia Burrus has argued that the Thecla stories, summarized here, were folk legends told by and for women actively engaged in the subversion of patriarchal marriage and in direct conflict with the social and political powers of the day. The Acts of Thecla, she argues, portray husbands and fiancés, rulers and governors as villains, and they depict Paul, the male, celibate apostle as a legitimator of female celibacy and an erotic substitute for the negative and oppressive male patriarchal figures.[34] The strong erotic motifs in the story, Burrus argues, reveal a tendency to project erotic fantasies onto the apostles as representatives of Christ who stand over against the restrictive and villainous male figures. In contrast to the lover or husband whose authority is limiting, "who does not understand, [and] . . . whose sexuality is threatening," the apostle Paul "is empowering and supportive, understanding, and sexually attractive."[35] Thus Paul supports Thecla as she transgresses the boundaries and restrictions of her social world, but is only an auxiliary to Thecla in the collection as a whole.

Burrus's treatment is imaginative and provocative. She correctly identifies the point of view of the Acts of Thecla as that of the female, but the narrative is not as one sided as she claims. Her diminution of the apostle's role in the Thecla sequence is misplaced. Paul's role as a model of celibacy and as an apostolic validator of Thecla's own vow to chastity and apostleship, and the psychological function that he serves in Burrus's own model, make him something more than an auxiliary figure in the story. On this point Kaestli's observation is sound: "For her, the apostles remain 'on the sidelines' in the struggle waged by the women and only stay with them temporarily. In reality, however, the apostle is a central figure in the chastity stories and not simply a 'donor.' He represents Christ, the beloved one for whose sake the heroines leave their husbands." Moreover, in the Acts of Paul, chastity is not exclusively a concern of women, but is also embraced and preached by the apostle and practiced even by the lion baptized by Paul, who intercedes on his behalf in the fight with the beasts at Ephesus.[36] Doubtless, Paul's own celibacy is the model for and model of Thecla's celibacy as well.[37] Moreover, if Caroline Bynum is correct that female saints and the Virgin Mary figured more centrally in the lives of males than females in the Middle Ages, Burrus's focus on this sequence as one of, about, by, and for women may be misplaced.

Paul, even in the Thecla sequence, is portrayed as the model of and teacher of the gospel of the virgin life. A most interesting presentation of celibacy may be seen in his relationship to a lion. As the narrator of the Acts of Paul tells the tale, the female hosts of an *agape* feast in Damascus accompanied Paul on an all night walk to Jericho (Jerusalem). During early morning prayers when Paul was separated from Lemma, the widow, and her daughter Ammia, a "great and terrible lion [came] out of the valley of the burying-ground."[38] The "great and terrible lion" patiently waited for Paul to complete his prayers and then prostrated himself at the apostle's feet and said, "I wish to be baptized."[39] Paul praised God, "who had given speech to the beast and salvation to his servant."[40] After a prayer of thanksgiving Paul "took the lion by his mane (and) in the name of Jesus Christ immersed him three times. But when he came up out of the water he shook out his mane and said to me: 'Grace be with thee!' And I said to him: 'And likewise with thee.'"[41] The tale has a remarkable conclusion: "[when t]he lion ran off to the country rejoicing.

. . . A lioness met him, and he did not yield himself to her but . . . ran off."[42] In other words, the pacified, baptized lion also took the vow to lead a celibate life from baptism onward.

And the remarkable story has a sequel. The pacified and celibate lion returned later to protect Paul when he was thrown to the beasts at Ephesus. Having heard of Paul's plight, the lion came to his rescue. Paul recognized the lion and again conversed with him: "Lion, was it thou whom I baptized?" The lion answered, "Yes!" Paul continued, "And how wast thou captured?" and the lion responded, "Even as thou, Paul." The presence of an animal helper in this story as is common in folk narrative assures not just Paul's survival but his triumph over his antagonists. Miraculously, a hailstorm intervenes, saving both Paul and the baptized lion, killing the attacking animals, and severing the ear of the governor, Hieronymous. Both Paul and the lion go free, and the ear of Hieronymous is restored.[43] A total success story is spread out before us with Paul as the hero.

We might be tempted to dismiss these stories as farcical tales with no lasting value, or as silly folklore told for its entertainment value, but the canonical status of these Acts of Paul in the Syrian and Armenian churches suggest they carried a deeper and sustained meaning. They all either implicitly or explicitly portray Paul as the model ascetic whose asceticism had lasting and salvific value not just for humanity but also for the animal kingdom. This asceticism enabled its adherents to reclaim a state of innocence, to reverse the Fall, and to be ushered into the company of angels and if successful made one even superior to angels, for humans must overcome the flesh to "master a nature which the angels do not possess."[44] This angelic state, once achieved, could free one from the body to forge an identity outside the shackles of gender specificity. Religious experience then could assume erotic dimensions safe from the liabilities of sex and the social restrictions of gender. The stories hold out the possibility of reentering a lost and unseen world and the ability to cross boundaries firmly fixed by society. The account of the talking lion, for example, as strange as it may sound to us, offered a mythic encounter with a possibility that the painful fracture that separates the human from the nonhuman world may be overcome. Many if not most of these tales offer an egalitarian world that elevated the status and importance of women. These stories inspired a resistance to a power of the world that faced alone was almost overwhelming. The strength and triumph of those like Thecla and Paul bearing up under the demands of a Hellenistic and Roman culture that was self-righteous and did not forgive transgressions brought the hearers into the presence of Christ. These stories reminded the listeners of who they really were and reaffirmed their status of being in but not of the world. Thus Thecla offered an example that both women and men could follow. As Peter Brown so aptly notes, the virgin life of Thecla "was a condensed image of the individual, always threatened with annihilation, poised from birth above the menacing pressures of the world."[45] These stories, though they may seem fanciful, were hardly disconnected from both the example and teaching of Paul as we saw in chapter five. This all suggests that the geneology of asceticism sketched here included preapostolic Jewish and Hellenistic parents and postapostolic Christian missionary descendants included Paul as well.

PAUL AS MIRACLE WORKER

The basic assumption of the modern world is that natural laws govern the natural order. In this context "miracle" is defined as a divine or supernatural "act (e.g., healing) exhibiting control over [or suspension of] the laws of nature."[46] This modern viewpoint differs markedly from the understanding of the first century Mediterranean world. In that setting, miracles were seen less as the suspension of laws governing the natural order than as signs of a divine presence and action in the human arena. Miracles, or more properly, "mighty works" appear in most traditions of this era. A rich legacy of miracle working suffuses the Jewish traditions. Moses was remembered as a miracle worker who beat the Egyptian magicians at their own game. Elijah stories recounted how the prophet had miraculously increased a supply of meal (1 Kings 17:8–16), brought the dead to life (1 Kings 17:17–24), and made brackish water drinkable (2 Kings 1:19–22). The Elisha cycle contained accounts of raising a dead child (2 Kings 4:25–37) and multiplying an oil supply (2 Kings 4:1–7). Writings from Qumran have Abraham perform an exorcism (Gen. Apoc. 20:16–19) and Daniel, a *Gāzer* or magician, heal an ulcer of King Nebuchadnezzar.[47] Philo's Moses was fully at home in the Hellenistic world among miracle workers like Apollonius of Tyana who raised the dead, exorcised demons, and healed a boy bitten by a "mad dog." Any figure believed to possess or be a vehicle of divine power would in that context be expected to perform miraculous deeds. So tales about Paul as a miracle worker would have placed him in an important popular religious tradition.

But did these traditions influence later portraits of Paul as a miracle worker? According to MacDonald it was the Gospels and not the Pauline epistles that most influenced the narrative of Paul and that transformed him into a type of Jesus or even a "deutero-Jesus."[48] When one reads the apocryphal material with attention to its fascination with Paul as a miracle worker that would certainly seem to be the case. We are given vivid descriptions of fabulosity wrought by Paul that reach beyond Paul's own accounting in the letters. And in MacDonald's view this presentation distorts the authentic Paul. This distortion, he attributes to the later use of the Acts genre that imitates the gospel genre.

Paul as Miracle Worker in the Undisputed Pauline Letters

But a closer look at the letters will show that the Acts of Paul may not be a distortion after all. While Paul's letters only sparingly refer to specific wondrous deeds of Paul, the apostle does speak rather frequently in them of powerful or miraculous deeds that he performed as a part of his mission. Defending himself against charges made by other apostles who made much of their miraculous deeds as proofs of their apostleship, Paul seems quite unwilling to cede the advantage to these super apostles: "the signs of an apostle were performed among you in all patience, signs and wonders and mighty works (2 Cor. 12:12)."[49] In 1 Cor. 2:4, he reminds his readers of his work among them: "My speech and my proclamation were not with plausible words of wisdom, but with a demonstration of the Spirit and of power." Likewise, in Rom. 15:18–19 in a distinctly defensive tone Paul notes with pride how his mission among the Gentiles was effected by "word and deed, in the power of signs and wonders, [and] in the power of the Spirit [of God], so that from Jerusalem and as far around as Illyricum, I have fully proclaimed the gospel of Christ." In 1 Thess. 1:5 he may be referring to miraculous deeds when he says "our gospel came to you not only in word, but also in power."

Paul makes two additional references to mighty deeds or miraculous works that manifest themselves in the community. In 1 Cor. 12:9, 28, 30, he lists the gift of healing among charismatic deeds, and Gal. 3:5 acknowledges miraculous deeds as fruits of the gospel: "Well then, does God supply you with the Spirit and work miracles among you by your doing works of the law, or by your believing what you have heard?" One might argue that in his failure to describe a concrete miracle that he performed, Paul is deliberately minimizing their importance, but if that were the case then his failure to qualify any of these several remarks is surprising. Or one might argue that Paul would have preferred not to mention his miraculous works at all, but his opponents forced him to do so.[50] But the summary of his apostolic deeds in Rom. 15:19 was hardly provoked by an adversary's attack. And while the Gospels offer examples of the type and nature of those mighty works, they do not exhaust or limit the imagination. It certainly is not as if the apocryphal and even canonical speculation about Paul's miracle working powers falsifies his own remarks. On the contrary, it provides amplification. Moreover, in the Acts of Paul, which MacDonald thinks follows the Gospels instead of the letters, there are many echoes of the Pauline letters. The travel itinerary at many points touches Paul's own journeys (e.g., Antioch, Derbe, Ephesus, Philippi,

Corinth, etc.), and the account of Paul's sermon in the Acts of Paul that takes the form of Matthean beatitudes also draws on Paul's letters repeatedly for content. (See especially the references to celibacy: those "who have wives as if they had them not," 1 Cor. 7:29.) In addition, a visit to the Hellenistic world reveals a fascination with *theioi androi,* or divine men, whose godly status is proven by their ability to do miraculous deeds. Apollonius of Tyana, for example, a neo-Pythagorean popular philosopher and miracle worker of the first century CE, is reported to have healed the sick, raised the dead, and performed exorcisms.[51]

This Hellenistic ethos influenced Jews as well. Philo of Alexandria, for example, presented Moses as a philosopher and friend of God who possessed the power to do mighty works, wonders, and incredible prodigies (*De Vita Moses*). And Paul himself faced Christian apostles who believed that the apostle should incorporate and demonstrate his powers as a divine man through the performance of miracles. If all of these influences coalesce in the apocryphal Acts, then no one foreground or influence accounts for the presentation of Paul as a miracle worker of legendary proportions; all played a role. Therefore, we would be more cautious than MacDonald, who thinks the presentation of Paul as a miracle worker in the apocryphal Acts distorts the "real" Paul. Factors not often noted are the importance of the miraculous element to Paul's mission and his profound belief that the spirit was active in him, making miraculous deeds a logical extension of that conviction.[52] Significantly, however, Paul nowhere describes in specific terms a miracle that he performed, which does set his statements off from those of the Gospels and the apocryphal Acts. And while he recognizes miracles as signs of his apostleship, he does not place as much weight on them to legitimate his apostleship as would later writers.

Paul as Miracle Worker in the Acts of the Apostles

Whatever the reason for Paul's reticence to talk concretely about specific miracles he performed, that gap was soon filled after his death. If Acts was written in the 80s or early 90s as most now believe, we have evidence that within a generation of Paul's death he was already on the way to becoming a wonder worker of epic proportions.

Acts abounds in detailed accounts of Paul's healing activity in his mission to the Gentiles. On Cyprus he strikes blind a Jewish false prophet for seeking to turn a Roman proconsul from the faith (13:4–12). In Iconium he and Barnabas perform "signs and wonders" (Acts 14:3). In Lystra he heals a man "crippled from birth," prompting the crowds to acclaim Paul and Barnabas as gods (14:8–18). "Barnabas they called Zeus, and Paul, because he was the chief speaker, they called Hermes. And the priest of Zeus, whose temple was in front of the city, brought oxen and garlands to the gates and wanted to offer sacrifice with the people" (14:11 RSV). In Jerusalem, Paul and Barnabas report on the "signs and wonders that God had done through them among the Gentiles" (15:12). In Philippi, Paul exorcises a spirit of divination possessing a slave girl whose ability to foretell the future was exploited for money (16:16–18). In Ephesus, "God did extraordinary miracles through Paul, so that when the handkerchiefs or aprons that had touched his skin were brought to the sick, their diseases left them, and the evil spirits came out of them" (19:11–12). In Troas, Paul brought the dead Eutychus back to life (20:7–12). On the island of Malta Paul was bitten by a viper but "suffered no harm," causing the natives to acclaim him as "a god" (28:3–6). Also on Malta he healed the father of Publius, "the leading man of the island," from dysentery by "praying and putting his hands on him" (28:7–8). As his fame as a healer spread, "the rest of the people on the island who had diseases also came and were cured" (28:9). In describing these exorcisms, healings, and raisings of the dead, Luke presents Paul's miraculous powers as an extension of those of Jesus and as proofs of divine activity if not divine status (Acts 14:8). While the correlations between these miracle traditions and those of popular Hellenistic religion are hardly exact, as Tiede has shown, they do share some features and appear here intended to authenticate Paul's charismatic status as a missionary to the Gentiles.[53] Unlike Paul's own references, however, they abound in vivid detail and specificity. Although they are offered as powerful authenticating signs of Paul's charismatic status, even in Acts they are hardly free of ambiguity. For believers, these miraculous events reveal the hand of the Lord; for hostile "Jews" and pagans they are evidence of a sinister presence. Inevitably in Acts, they cause a split among the observers (Acts 14:4, 18–20; 16:16–40; etc.).

The thematic parallels between Paul and Jesus as miracle workers have been pointed out by others.[54] Both perform exorcisms (e.g., Jesus: Luke 4:40–41; Paul: Acts 16:16–24); both heal a lame man (Jesus: Luke 5:17–26; Paul: Acts 14:8–18); both heal persons with a fever (Jesus: Luke 4:38–40; Paul: Acts 28:7–10); and both raise the dead, while noting that the person is not really dead (Jesus: Luke 8:40–42, 49–56; Paul: Acts 20:7–12). Such thematic parallels prompted Hans Windisch to view this Paul as "Jesus redivivus."[55] But that may be overstating the case, for while these thematic parallels do exist there are differences as well, as is evident in the curse Paul places on the Jewish antagonist, Bar-Jesus, (13:10–11), the magical power of handkerchiefs and aprons that he had touched (19:11–12), and the earthquake that miraculously springs open the doors of the prison, leading to the release of Paul and Silas (16:19–40). Even though there are thematic connections between the wonder working Paul in Acts and Jesus of Luke's gospel, Conzelmann is surely correct that the miracles of Jesus in the Gospels and those of the apostles in Acts function in quite different ways. Whereas the Gospels present the miracles of Jesus as signs of the inbreaking of God's rule, in the Acts of the Apostles the miracles legitimate the gospel the apostles preach, and the miraculous deeds typically lead to faith.[56]

And so Luke portrayed Paul as a powerful charismatic personality who validated his gospel with miraculous deeds. But, as Jervell noted, he failed completely to take account of Paul the weak and sickly personality, unskilled in speech and unimposing in appearance. Consequently, Acts reveals none of the gripping tension between power and weakness that we have in Paul's own self description (2 Cor. 11–12).[57] The "thorn in the flesh, the messenger of Satan" counterbalances the "abundance of revelations" (2 Cor. 12:7). The distress Paul felt was painful and unrelieved; even fervent prayer brought no respite. And then in his masterful summary of the dynamic tension between power and weakness Paul says, "For the sake of Christ, then, I am content with weaknesses, insults, hardships, persecutions, and calamities; for when I am weak then I am strong" (2 Cor. 12:10). The Lucan portrait of Paul in Acts, however, was not, as Jervell held, simply a "filling up of the pauline one,"[58] it was a concentration on the fabulosity of Paul's acts that was so strong that it elevated Paul above the *theioi andres,* or divine men, and validated his mission and gospel.

It would be a mistake to concentrate exclusively on the miraculous deeds of the apostle, for his mighty works were social actions. While it is true that there is no such thing as a miracle without a miracle worker, it is equally true that there is no such thing as a miracle without believers, witnesses, or even a community that sees in the mighty deed a divine presence or power manifesting itself. Especially in the apocryphal Acts of Paul we have evidence of the role the community played in the perpetuation, interpretation, and expansion of the legends about Paul. These stories did more than entertain, though they did do that; they also assisted in the construction and maintenance of a social world. In other words they survived because they served the church in a multitude of ways.

Paul as Miracle Worker in the Apocryphal Acts of Paul

The emphasis on the fabulous nature of the apostle's wonder working powers waxed ever stronger in later works such as the apocryphal Acts of Paul. Assembled already by 190 CE and containing stories with an oral tradition that was much earlier, the Acts of Paul remained popular well into the fifth century and were revered as Scripture by the Syrian and Armenian churches. This popular collection served as a model for other apocryphal writings such as the Acts of Peter and Paul, the Acts of Xanthippe and Polyxena, and the Acts of Titus.[59] Our present fragmentary document was once substantially longer than the canonical Acts;[60] nevertheless, it still contains a remarkable collection of legends that present Paul as a prodigious miracle worker whose powerful deeds prove that his gospel was true.[61]

The miracles Paul performed in the Acts of Paul cover a broad spectrum. He raised five persons from the dead; he healed the sick; he exorcised demons; he destroyed a pagan temple (of Apollo), and he evidently restored the ear of the governor who condemned him to die before the beasts when it was severed by a hailstone.[62] In Myra he healed a man of dropsy, and he struck blind a greedy son who was impatient to inherit his portion of his father's property and thus was incensed when Paul healed his father. The son's punishment and repentance led him to renounce worldly goods and his parents to distribute grain and money to widows.[63]

Of special interest in this collection is the attempt to fill out Paul's metaphorical remark that he had fought with the beasts at Ephesus (1 Cor. 15:32) in vivid, gripping detail. Arriving in Ephesus from Smyrna, Paul finds lodging with co-workers Aquila and Priscilla. His sermon that recounted the story of his conversion and his baptism of the "ferocious lion" lands him before the governor, invites Paul's defense filled with apologetic motifs, and leads to his condemnation when the governor bows to the demand of the people that Paul be thrown to the beasts. While Paul is awaiting his fight with the beasts, the governor's wife, Artemilla, hears of Paul, seeks him out in prison, is converted by Paul's short admonition to flee the world, is baptized, and receives the Eucharist of bread and water. The conversion of this prominent woman causes Paul more trouble, as it is reported that women are with Paul night and day receiving instruction in the Christian life. When a dignified and composed Paul finally faces the beasts, he is joined by the lion whom he had earlier baptized. When the lion befriends Paul, the governor orders other beasts to be released to destroy him and commands archers to kill the "friendly" lion. But in the nick of time a hailstorm pummels the beasts, the spectators, *and* the governor. Paul and the friendly lion escape unharmed; the lion returns to his mountain haunts, and the apostle goes down to the harbor to catch a ship for Macedonia. The terrified spectators flee the stadium, crying out as they leave, "Save us, O God, save us, O God of the man who fought with the beasts!"[65]

Other apocryphal books also glorify Paul as a miracle worker. In the Acts of Peter and Paul (fourth century CE) Paul's condemnation causes the city of Puteoli to sink into the sea, and in the Acts of Peter that predated the Acts of Paul, the apostle Paul pronounced judgment on an adulteress who came to take the Eucharist and she fell down immediately, "paralyzed on the left side from her head to her toe-nails. And she [Rufina] had no power to speak."(2) The story goes on to recount the assurance required for believers guilty of some unnamed sexual impropriety from the past who were terrified by the paralysis visited on Rufina.

Strikingly, the theology of Paul plays almost no role in these apocryphal Acts, for the focus is no longer on the theology of Paul but on Paul the man, a figure of epic proportions, a hero who does mighty works, who is executed, raised, and returns to reveal himself.

While Schneemelcher is correct that these stories were intended to edify and entertain, they did more. These tales like any collection of folk material, doubtless served a multitude of functions. Sometimes they reflect a point of view that was quite clearly from below. For example, Patroclus, Ceasar's cup-bearer, a convert, and martyr proclaims to Nero that *Christ* is the "King of the Ages" (Acts of Paul, 11:2). Such legends of the underdog have multiple purposes. With their emphasis on the success of an underling they offered encouragement to believers who come largely from an underclass, marginalized, and persecuted group. With their stress on power (δύναμις, forms the root for miracle) they embolden those in a weak position. With their focus on confession and proclamation they reinforce belief in the one God, belief in the divine judgment and the resurrection and reward of the just, belief in the importance of celibacy, belief in Paul as an incarnation of Christ, and belief in the importance of charity toward the poor and widows. Throughout the Acts it is clear that as much as Paul was praised as a heroic figure, there was nevertheless care taken to anchor this power in God. A good example of this piety is evident in Thecla's confession before the governor: "I am a handmaid of the living God. . . . For he alone is the God of salvation and the foundation of immortal life. To the stormtossed he is a refuge, to the oppressed relief, to the despairing shelter. . . . whoever does not believe in him shall not live, but die forever" (37). Such an affirmation, one will note, contains nothing that is novel but contains standard items of the early Christian confession. Finally, it is quite possible that the Thecla sequence encouraged and supported women transgressing social restrictions, but since such stories are polysemous it is risky to assign a single purpose to them. Just as fairy tales carry multiple possibilities so also this folklore offers a variety of meanings.

Miracle stories were part of the intellectual and emotional landscape of the Hellenistic world. And while miracles, most people believed, did present proof of the truth of the preaching of figures like Paul, they did more; they articulated core values and beliefs about the triumph of justice, they affirmed a faith in the presence of a power not of this world, and they most often gave that power a compassionate, human face. To those threatened by crisis miracles offered deliverance from the clutches of enormous physical and psychic challenges. They offered not just autonomy to the individual as Burrus suggests but also articulated a message of broad corporate inclusiveness. They provided a witness to integration and wholeness as a social reality, and they affirmed a future in which chaos, oppression, and dark moods were hardly the final realities of the day. They affirmed a faith that justice and mercy could and did invade a world governed by quite different concerns. And probably at some level they mediated the very power to which they witnessed. Thus we see that by the end of the second century Paul had emerged as a powerful figure, and he had done so without reference to justification by faith but rather through an emphasis on the oneness of God, the resurrection of Jesus as the Christ, and his own incarnation of miraculous powers linked to if not derived from his life as a celibate apostle.

PAUL AS MARTYR

Paul's letters name suffering and death as his constant companions. Although his mythic participation in the death of Jesus was often on his lips (Gal. 2:19; Phil. 3:10; etc.), 2 Cor. 4:7–12 best articulates the relationship of his suffering to the passion of Jesus. Responding to charismatic, wandering, Hellenistic Jewish Christian apostles who so focused on the glorified Jesus that the suffering Jesus was virtually eclipsed, Paul says:

> For we have this treasure in earthen vessels, to show that the transcendent power belongs to God and not to us. We are afflicted in every way, but not crushed; perplexed, but not driven to despair; persecuted, but not forsaken; struck down, but not destroyed; always carrying in the body the death of Jesus, so that the life of Jesus may be also be manifest in our bodies. For while we live we are always being given up to death for Jesus' sake, so that the life of Jesus may be manifested in our mortal flesh. So death is at work in us, but life in you. (RSV)

Paul revisited this catalog of sufferings time and again (2 Cor. 6:4–5; 11:23–29; 12:10; Rom. 8:35; 1 Cor. 4:9–13) to emphasize the way the apostolate mirrored the suffering and death of Jesus. The beatings, imprisonments, mob attacks, stoning, shipwreck, danger from bandits, danger from hostile Jews, danger from angry Gentiles, and painful betrayal by "false brothers and sisters" (2 Cor. 11:26) all presented physical associations with the passion of Jesus. The onerous toil, sleepless nights, inadequate clothing, cold, and real hunger he suffered, the sting of insults, and his discouragement and anxiety regarding the churches all, Paul believed, participated in the death of Jesus. Indeed, even the scars left on his body by physical blows Paul saw as marks of Jesus' crucifixion (Gal. 6:17).

Although he believed suffering was a sine qua non of the life of an apostle, it was more than a private experience, and more even than a bond with the suffering and dying Jesus; it forged a common bond between the apostle and his converts (1 Thess. 1:6). In the call to "be imitators of me as I am of Christ" Paul offered a model of the life of Christ dominated by the passion as a paradigm of the Christian life.

Succeeding generations found clues in these discussions for life in their own time. And while Luke's Acts offers no account of Paul's martyrdom, it does offer premonitions of martyrdom that are already known historical fact to Luke. Avoiding a bald and definite prediction of the hero's martyrdom, in his speech to the elders at Ephesus Luke's Paul nevertheless recognizes that "the Holy Spirit testifies to me in every city that imprisonment and afflictions await me" (Acts 20:23, RSV). Noting that he places no value on his life, Luke's Paul offers a somber and final valedictory to his audience—"you . . . will see my face no more" (20:25). Nevertheless, the Acts does not have Paul explicitly and definitely predict his martyrdom. And when Luke's Paul squarely faces the possibility of death, whether it will be in Jerusalem or Rome is left open.[66] While Luke does not have Paul prophesy his martyrdom, he does present Paul as an absolutely fearless, courageous messenger who displays a reckless disregard for his own safety. He refuses to heed Agabus's dire prophetic warning of danger that will stalk him in Jerusalem. He refuses to hearken to urgent and tearful pleas of believers that he not go up to Jerusalem (21:11–12): "I am ready not only to be imprisoned but even to die at Jerusalem for the name of the Lord Jesus," Paul says (Acts 21:13). He did go to Jerusalem, was betrayed by the Jews, was handed over to the Romans, and though innocent of any crime appealed and was taken to Rome for trial. The Acts narrative ends with Paul under house arrest in Rome, welcoming "all who came to him, preaching the kingdom of God and teaching about the Lord Jesus Christ quite openly and unhindered" (28:30–31).

Scholars have puzzled over why Luke thus ends his narrative with no accounting of the martyrdom about which he surely knew. I agree with MacDonald that Luke deliberately avoided any reference to the martyrdom of this innocent and heroic figure so as not to antagonize Roman authorities[67] Luke has Paul anticipate his martyrdom in the reference to the "death penalty" even though he was innocent (28:18), an echo of Jesus' death and the Roman centurion's lament, "Certainly this man was innocent!" (Luke 23:47).

I cannot go along with MacDonald's suggestion, however, that the death of Paul in the Acts of Paul requires the gospel model. Without question Paul did, as we noted previously, draw on the martyrological tradition (e.g., 4 Macc.) for understanding the saving significance of Jesus' death and the implications of that death for his own life and death. Carrying in one's body the death of Jesus (2 Cor. 4:10) is clearly a form of imitation of the death of Jesus that has significance in life and in death. Stowers's observation strikes me as correct: "If we look more narrowly for the generic relations of a complex pattern of thematic, stylistic, and rhetorical traits, then the gospels might be at best only one relative of the Pauline acts. . . . Certainly there are similarities between the gospels and the Acts of Paul, but are they the closest generic similarities we can find? And would they have been the most culturally pervasive similarities?"[68] Though the author of the Acts of Paul and the community that created and preserved its legends would have surely been aware of the martyrdom of Jesus, the author operated in a context with multiple traditions of heroic martyrdom.

Whereas Luke knew of but avoided reference to Paul's martyrdom at the hands of the Romans, later authors were under no such constraints, and the need to recognize that believers must "walk in the shadow of death" was more insistent. In the most graphic terms stories of the martyrs circulated, stories that embraced such notables as Polycarp bishop of Smyrna (d. 156) and such pious, common folk as the slave girl Blandina. It was Irenaeus presumably who told the gripping story of the martyrdom of Blandina. After being tortured "for a long time" she was tied to a stake to be devoured by wild animals. Hanging there "in the shape of a cross, and by her continuous prayer gave great zeal to the combatants, while they looked on during the contest, and with their outward eyes saw in the form of their sister him who was crucified for them, to persuade those who believe on him that all who suffer for the glory of Christ have for ever fellowship with the living God."[69] Although systematic persecutions by the Roman Empire were infrequent and episodic, martyrdom occurred often enough to elicit admiration and praise for "the struggles of the athletes of piety and their valor which braved so much, trophies won from demons, and victories against unseen adversaries, and the crowns at the end of all, that it will proclaim for everlasting remembrance."[70] Eusebius reports that twenty-four men and twenty-three women died as martyrs in Lyon in 171.[71] It is altogether understandable in such a context that the teachings and example of the martyr Paul should be a source of encouragement and comfort.

Tertullian, for example, displays a strong and explicit interest in Paul's martyrdom. He saw Paul as the ideal believer who was "reborn in Rome through martyrdom."[72] An altered context dictated Tertullian's emphasis on Paul's martyrdom, for by his time the church had repeatedly tasted the bitter fruit of persecution and martyrdom. This reality explains his emphasis on Paul's courageous and determined response to persecution, "making him a model for the Christian life and for Christian martyrdom."[73] His description of Paul in highly idealized terms fused the "historical Paul imaginatively remembered and . . . the portrait of the saint already become an icon."[74]

Tertullian's image of Paul the icon enjoys a certain kinship with the Paul of the apocryphal Acts. In the Acts of Peter, as Paul prepares to embark from Rome for Spain, believers gather round dolefully pleading with Paul to return in a year. While they beg him to return soon, a heavenly voice booms out: "Paul the servant of God is chosen for (this) service for the time of his life; but at the hands of Nero, that godless and wicked man, he shall be perfected before your eyes" (1).[75] In other words, Paul shall return, but to his martyrdom.

The legend of Paul's martyrdom in the Acts of Paul confirms this view of Paul as a confident, courageous, and even joyful saint on his way to his martyrdom. The legend places the hearer inside Nero's royal palace infiltrated and subverted by the gospel, for several members of Nero's staff turn out to be Christian. One such person was Nero's cupbearer, Patroclus. After slipping and falling to his death from his lofty perch in the rented barn where he sat listening to a sermon by Paul, Patroclus was revived by the apostle and returned to serve at Caesar's table. But the rumor of his death, racing ahead, reached the emperor before Patroclus could return and prompted a farcical exchange:

CAESAR: Patroclus, art thou alive?

PATROCLUS: I am alive, Caesar.

CAESAR: Who is he who made thee to live?

PATROCLUS: Christ Jesus, the king of the ages.

CAESAR: So he is to be king of the ages, and destroy all the kingdoms?

PATROCLUS: Yes, all the kingdoms under heaven he destroys, and he alone shall be for ever, and there shall be no kingdom which shall escape him.

CAESAR (*after slapping him*): Patroclus, dost thou also serve in that king's army?

PATROCLUS: Yes, lord Caesar, for indeed he raised me up when I was dead.

Then Barsabas Justus "of the flat feet" and Orion the Cappadocian and Festus the Galatian "Nero's chief men" chime in: "We also are in the army of the king of the ages." Nero orders them all imprisoned and issues the decree that "Christians and soldiers of Christ shall be put to death."[76] And Paul also is brought bound with a group for a hearing before Nero. Nero poses a question dripping with irony:

"Man of the great king, but (now) my prisoner, why did it seem good to thee to come secretly into the empire of the Romans and enlist soldiers from my province?" But Paul, filled with the Holy Spirit, said before them all: "Caesar, not only from thy province do we enlist soldiers, but from the whole world. . . . If thou also think it good, do him service! For neither riches nor splendor of this present life will save thee, but if thou submit and entreat him, then shalt thou be saved. For in one day he will destroy the world with fire." When Caesar heard this, he commanded all the prisoners to be burned with fire, but Paul to be beheaded according to the law of the Romans. But Paul did not keep silence concerning the word, but communicated it to the prefect Longus and the centurion Cestus.[77]

In this glorious legend, Paul predicts that he will rise after his decapitation and appear to Caesar as proof that he is not dead but alive "to my Lord Jesus Christ who is coming to judge the world."[78] When Longus and Cestus entreat him to cooperate and be released, Paul, like Socrates, refuses, answering, " 'I am no deserter from Christ, but a lawful soldier of the living God'. . . . Then Paul stood with his face to the east, and lifting up his hands to heaven prayed at length, and after communing in prayer in Hebrew with the fathers he stretched out his neck without speaking further. But when the executioner struck off his head, milk spurted upon the soldier's clothing. And when they saw it, the soldier and all who stood by were amazed, and glorified God who had given Paul such glory. And they went off and reported to Caesar what had happened. When he heard it, he marveled greatly and was at a loss."

But Paul was to have the last word. True to his prediction he appeared to Caesar, announcing triumphantly: "Caesar, here I am—Paul, God's soldier. I am not dead, but alive in my God. But for thee, unhappy man, there shall be many evils and great punishment, because thou didst unjustly shed the blood of the righteous, and that not many days hence!"[79] And Caesar was so flabbergasted that he set free the remaining imprisoned Christians. Now Longus and Cestus return to the grave site where Paul has promised to meet them, and sure enough they see Paul praying between Luke and Titus. Terrified of Longus, Luke and Titus flee but are reassured by Longus and Cestus, who come running after them, and they return to baptize these converts into the church (4, 7).

These fantastic stories, like the miracle stories, served multiple functions. First, they had meaning in a context in which a history of persecution was embedded. The question posed at one level by all of these stories is finally and ultimately who has power in a given society. The Mediterranean cultures were all hierarchical, and relationships were governed by certain assumptions in client-lord relationships. The higher one was in the hierarchical order, the more power one was assumed to have. That these stories either implicitly or explicitly subverted such assumptions is illustrated by Paul's appearance before the proconsul (in Ephesus) who has the ultimate power of life or death. Paul's response to the proconsul is defiant and heroic, courageous and confident: "For thou hast no power over me except over my body; but my soul thou canst not slay."[80] Similarly, when Paul stands before Nero, who is positioned at the apex of the social and political pyramid, Paul is presented as the person in control, the one whose king outranks the emperor Nero. Likewise, we see the same confident, composed, fearless, pious Paul in this final scene before his execution (3). So both at the beginning of the Acts of Paul and the end, the focus is on the character of this martyr that would serve to inspire the church in periods of repression and violent persecution.[81]

Second, the blood of the martyrs may be the seed of the church, but it is so not just because it emboldens one to face an execution serenely but also because it relates to daily life. Such an understanding of the relevance of the life of the martyrs is entirely consistent with Paul's own practice. Frequently Paul summons up the death of Jesus as a metaphor or model for life. In the apt summary of his position noted at the beginning of this section, Paul understood affliction, persecution, and being struck down on account of his gospel as tokens of "carrying in the body the death of Jesus" (2 Cor. 4:10). Even living under the threat of death from persecution could cause Paul to say, "I die daily" (1 Cor. 15:31; cf. Gal. 6:17).[82]

This participation in the death of Jesus as a metaphor for being in Christ is hardly limited to apostles only but applies to all believers.[83] Paul uses the death metaphor to speak of conduct befitting those who are in Christ in Rom. 6:3–8. Sensitive to the charge that his gospel of salvation outside the law for Gentiles encouraged immorality, the apostle calls on the baptismal experience that all of his readers would understand to make his point. "You know, don't you, that all of us who have been baptized into Christ Jesus have been baptized into his death?" (Rom. 6:3, my trans.). And then Paul draws the appropriate conclusion: "*Therefore* we have been buried with him by baptism into death, in order that as Christ was raised from the dead through the glory of the father, thus also *we might walk in newness of life*" (Rom. 6:4, emphasis added, my trans.). Obedience is the key to the translation of the death of the martyr Jesus into daily experience. Moreover, for Paul as for the later apocryphal writers, the terror of the death of Jesus and the martyrs was neutralized by the belief in the resurrection.

It is impossible not to notice rather striking differences between this mythic Paul and the author of the undisputed epistles. The heroic, courageous, dauntless, confident, powerful Paul we see in these stories is quite different from the autobiographical image that Paul sketches of himself. There we learn of a person tortured by his concern for the churches, who is capable of failure, who is physically weak and unimposing, unskilled in speech, and burdened by a "thorn in the flesh" from which he finds no relief. We see a person who knows inner turmoil. In the Acts of the Apostles and the Acts of Paul, this Paul is missing altogether. Necessarily then, the dynamic tension between strength and weakness, between the cross and the resurrection, between doubt and faith is also absent. In these legends we miss the humanity of Paul that connects him to his converts. We miss the Jewish Paul who survives to the end of Romans, and we miss the agony in the heart of this Jewish Paul for the salvation of Israel, even as he affirms without equivocation his gospel of salvation to Gentiles outside the law. We miss Paul the scriptural exegete, wrestling with Scripture, arguing with Scripture, calling on Scripture as a witness to the truth of his gospel. And, we miss the apocalyptic Paul. But, which is the real Paul—the Paul of the letters or the Paul of later tradition?

That is a very difficult question to answer for many reasons. In our discussion of Paul's theologizing we suggested that Paul himself changed over time as he faced new situations that forced him to think through his gospel and its application in new ways. We do well to remember that the letters were occasional documents written for specific, concrete situations. It is risky, therefore, to extract a body of teaching from these letters and to universalize it. If we cannot locate a single archimedean point from which to measure Paul himself in the letters, how shall we do the same with a later tradition? There are no doubt differences between the Pauline letters and later constructions or interpretations, but the times were different, the context was different, the demands were different. Given those variables it is more difficult to say if the later traditions reflect the real Paul.

Moreover, just as there are differences, as we have noted previously, there are also similarities. In one sense the Acts of Paul are a world apart from the apostle, but in another they offer an imaginative and perhaps a credible interpretation of emphases within the Pauline letters themselves—emphases on the death of Christ as model, on celibacy, and on miracle working. To be sure, some constructions are more credible than others, but the legends of Paul coming over a century later capture an important dimension of Paul that is worth pondering. Their omissions are also worth careful consideration. But, what the legends show most of all is that Paul's ability to provoke thought continued because he raised issues to which there were no easy answers.

CONCLUSION

The goal of this volume has been to capture something of Paul's humanity by providing biographical data about Paul the man—where he grew up, the language he spoke, the Bible he knew, the status of his parents, and his training at his father's side to work with leather. We have examined the passion and zeal not just of Paul as a Pharisee but also of Paul as a defender of what he thought was right, even if it meant repression of other Jews believed to be in error. In this setting came the Christophany that had radical implications for Paul. As we looked at the ensuing period, we tried to picture a figure writing, dictating, and sending and receiving letters. We tried to see a human side of an apostle worried sick over his churches, a man wrestling with tough questions antagonists posed for him; we saw a traveler at the mercy of the elements, almost constantly in danger from brigands, hostile Jews, and hostile Gentiles, attacked, maligned, beaten, stoned, jailed, and slandered. We saw the physically weak, even sickly Paul, the not especially eloquent Paul, Paul the exegete, and also Paul the intellectual, whose fertile mind could offer up sophisticated arguments, angry retorts, disappointment, or tenderness and encouragement.

Paul's humanity, however, can hardly be correctly understood outside of the sacred world that he inhabited. The great physical, personal struggle that he refers to, for example, belongs to a larger, even cosmic contest that he believed was under way and would soon be decided in favor of the righteousness of the God of Israel known in Jesus Christ. His celibacy, as physical as it surely was, was suffused with the consciousness of the dawning of a new world that reflected a lost world. To be properly understood, Paul's personal identity as a Jew, of the tribe of Benjamin and of Pharisaic persuasion requires an appreciation for Paul's ethnic and religious roots. The family metaphors that Paul used to describe the community of faith drew their energy and dynamism from a shared vision and conviction of life "in Christ."

We have become increasingly convinced in this exploration that Pauline anthropology and Pauline theology must be held in tension. Either without the other is a distortion. The theological Paul who is most often presented to us without the human dimension is docetic. And a human Paul without a theological dimension is a caricature. Paul's social and theological worlds intersect, and in their nexus we find a figure who has provoked controversy, aversion, and inspiration among all who have listened to him—friends and adversaries, Jews and Gentiles, men and women, past generations and succeeding generations as well.

Excursus on Pauline Chronology

Given the paucity of evidence it is exceedingly difficult to reconstruct a chronology of Paul's life that inspires confidence. Although we possess seven undisputed letters from Paul, none of them is dated and there are few clues that place them chronologically. Paul does refer to the ethnarch of Damascus, King Aretas (2 Cor. 11:32), presumably Aretas IV, whose approximate dates are known, and he refers to two visits to Jerusalem before his delivery of the offering, one "after three years" (Gal. 18) and another "after fourteen years" (Gal. 2:1). Sometime before Galatians was written, he tells us, a Jerusalem conference took place between him, Barnabas and Titus, and the Jerusalem apostles at which responsibilities for the mission were apportioned; Peter would go to the circumcised and Paul to the uncircumcised (Gal. 2:1–10). In Corinthians and Romans Paul refers to Aquila and Prisca (16:3; 16:19), whose names become important in the dating process. Some find in the letters internal evidence of the development of Paul's thought from an earlier stage (1 Thess.) to a later one (Rom.) with intermediate steps in between.

To these scraps of information from the letters scholars often try to coordinate chronological references in Acts. Acts 18:12–17 tells of Paul's arraignment before Gallio in Corinth, and Fitzmyer has shown that Gallio was proconsul of Achaia in 52–53; however, illness forced him to abandon his post before the winter of 52 when bad weather *ended* the sailing season.[1] The expulsion of Aquila and Priscilla (the same person as Paul's Prisca) from Rome (Acts 18:2) by the Roman emperor Claudius, some believe, was part of a larger expulsion of Jews because of Jewish unrest over "Chrestus" that was reported by the Roman historian Suetonius. Most scholars think this expulsion took place in 49 CE, but an increasing number tie it to another expulsion in 41 CE.

While it might appear that this is sufficient evidence to reconstruct a reliable chronology of Paul, there are difficulties with the data. Paul's references to "after three years" and "after fourteen years" are ambiguous. Does the number fourteen mark the time lapsed from the end of the three-year period or the beginning of the three-year period? Moreover, the date of the Jerusalem conference Paul mentions in Gal. 2:1–10 is exceedingly problematic, for it contradicts an Acts account which mentions *two* conferences instead of one. Furthermore, did the conference occur early in Paul's ministry or late? Even the Gallio reference is hardly free of difficulty, for we know from his own letters that Paul was in Corinth at least three times. On which visit was he haled before Gallio for a hearing? Was it on his first trip to Corinth, as I am inclined to believe, or on the third, as Lüdemann thinks?

One might be forgiven for wondering if all of this fuss over chronology is worth the bother. Yet surely it is the case that the chronology of the letters assumes a growing importance if one is convinced that Paul's theology developed over time rather than being rather fixed from the beginning. If that be the case then the placement of Galatians before Romans assumes great importance, for some time would be required for word of Paul's Galatian position to circulate, to generate a reaction, and then to require the response we see in Romans. Moreover, the placement of 1 Thessalonians plays a major role in deciding how much Paul's early, feverish apocalyptic expectation changed.

I have included below four chronologies of Paul's apostolic period, ranging from that of F. F. Bruce, which strongly relies on Acts, to that of G. Lüdemann, which relies almost entirely on evidence from the letters. Robert Jewett's reconstruction offers an intermediate solution, though he too gives Acts a rather prominent role in the shaping of his chronology. My own attempt is closer to that of Jewett but somewhat less dependent on Acts and less inclined to use Acts to round off the narrative of Paul's life. Even though they are useful, it is important to realize that these reconstructions are presented here only in summary form. An elaborate argument supports each of them that the constraints of space prohibit repeating here.

F. F. BRUCE'S RECONSTRUCTION[2]
(Adapted)

Paul's Conversion	33	
Paul's first post-conversion visit to Jerusalem	35	Acts 9:26
Paul in Syria and Cilicia	35–46	
Paul's second Jerusalem visit	46	Acts 11:27–30 famine visit
Paul and Barnabas in Cyprus and Galatia ("first missionary journey")	47–48	Acts 13:4–12
Letter to the Galatins	48?	

Council at Jerusalem. Paul's third Jerusalem visit	49	Acts 15 Edict of Claudius Expulsion of Jews Acts 18:2
Paul and Silas travel from Syrian Antioch through Asia Minor to Macedonia and Achaia (second missionary journey)	49–50	Acts 15:36–18:17
Letters to the Thessalonians	50	
Paul in Corinth	50–52	Gallio Inscription (51–52) Acts 18:12 Paul's hearing before Gallio
Jerusalem visit	52	Acts 18:22
Paul in Ephesus	52–55	Acts 19:1–20:38
Letters to the Corinthians	55–56	
Paul in Illyricum, Macedonia and Achaia (including Corinth)	55–57	Acts 19:21–22
Letter to the Romans	57	
Last visit to Jerusalem	57 (May)	Acts 21:17
Imprisonment at Caesarea	57–59	Acts 25:4
Paul's arrival at Rome	60	Acts 27:1–28:16
Paul under arrest in Rome	60–62	Acts 27:16
Paul writes the *Captivity Letters*	60–62?	
Paul visits Spain? *Pastoral Letters*	65?	
Paul dies	65?	

RECONSTRUCTION OF PAULINE CHRONOLOGY BY G. LUEDEMANN[3] (Adapted)

Paul's Conversion	30	Gal. 1:15, 16; 2 Cor. 12:2
Paul's first visit to Jerusalem	33	Gal. 1:18
Mission in Syria, Cilicia and Galatia	34	Gal. 1:21
Independent missionary activity in Europe including Philippi and Thessalonica	36	
Paul in Corinth. Wrote *1 Thessalonians*	41	Edict of Claudius Acts 18:2

Paul's second visit to Jerusalem Jerusalem Conference	47	Gal. 2:1; Acts 18:22 Heavily redacted version, Acts 15
Paul in Galatia to make collection for Jerusalem	48	1 Cor. 16:1
Paul in Ephesus	48–50	1 Cor. 15:32, 16:8
1 Corinthians	49	
Painful visit to Corinth tearful letter and dispatch of Titus	49 (summer)	2 Cor. 2:1–3 2 Cor. 2:4, 7:8
Paul travels to Macedonia to meet Titus with word of Corinth Writes *2* *Corinthians and Galatians*	50 50	2 Cor. 2:12–13, 7:5–7
Spends winter in Macedonia, completes the collection	50/51	2 Cor. 8–9
Journey to Corinth and winters there Paul writes *Romans*	51/52	Paul haled before Gallio Acts 18:12–17
Paul travels to Jerusalem to deliver the offering. We have no further information from Paul.	52	Rom. 15:25–33

RECONSTRUCTION OF PAULINE CHRONOLOGY BY ROBERT JEWETT[4]
(Adapted)

Paul's conversion	October (!) 34	
Paul's activities in Arabia	35–37	Gal. 1:17
Escape from Aretas IV in Damascus and first Jerusalem visit as an apostle	Late 37	2 Cor. 11:32–33 Acts 9:23–26
Paul's activities in Syria and Cilicia including "first missionary journey" (43–45) from Antioch to Cyprus, Pamphylia, and south Galatia	37–46	Gal. 1:21; Acts 15:41
"Second missionary journey" from Antioch to North Galatia, Troas, Philippi, Thessalonia, Beroea, Athens, Corinth; wrote *1 and 2* *Thessalonians*	46–51	Acts 15:36–18:17
Hearing before Gallio at Corinth	51	Acts 18:12–17 Gallio inscription
Second Jerusalem visit, apostolic conference	51	Acts 18:22; Gal. 2:1–10

Conflict with Peter in Antioch	52	Gal. 2:14–17
"Third missionary journey" through North Galatia Ephesus (52–54) *Galatians*	52–57	Acts 18:23; 19:1–20:38
Imprisoned in Ephesus (54–55) *Philippians*		2 Cor. 1:8–11
Released from prison (55) *Corinthian letters* (550 including painful visit and tearful letter		
Imprisoned in Asia winter (55/56) *Philemon* and *Colossians*		
Travel to Macedonia (56) last *Corinthian letter*		2 Cor. 2:12–13; 7:5–7 2 Cor. 8:18
Winter in Corinth (56/57) *Romans*		
Jerusalem to deliver the offering and arrest	57	
Imprisonment in Caesarea	58–59	
Imprisonment in Rome	60–61	
Execution	62	

MY OWN RECONSTRUCTION

Paul's apostolic call	34	
Activity in Arabia	34–36	
First visit to Jerusalem	36	
Activity in Syria and Cilicia	37–47	
Second visit to Jerusalem (**apostolic conference**)	47	
First mission in Asia Minor and Europe	47–52	
Edict of Claudis expelling Jews	49	
Ministry in Achaia, including Corinth *1 Thessalonians*	fall 50–summer 52	
Hearing before Ponconsul Gallio in Corinth	summer 52	
Ephesian ministry Visit to Galatia *Galatians*[5]	52–55 summer 52	Acts 18:18, 22f.
First Corinthian letter (lost)	53	1 Cor. 7:1

Corinthian letter to Paul and oral report	54	1 Cor. 1:11; 16:17
Second Corinthian letter (1 Corinthians)	54	
Timothy dispatched to Corinth	54	1 Cor. 4:17; 16:10
Timothy returns with report of failure	early spring 55	
Paul makes short "painful visit"	late spring 55	2 Cor. 2:1–2
Third Corinthian letter (2 Cor. 10–13) ("tearful letter" delivered by Titus)	late summer 55	2 Cor. 2:3–4, 9;7: 7:8–12
Paul imprisoned	late 55	
Philippians		
Philemon		
Paul's release from prison	spring 56	
Travels to Macedonia to meet Titus	spring 56	
Fourth Corinthian letter (2 Cor. 1–9) dispatched with Titus	summer 56	
Paul arrives in Corinth	fall 56	
Romans		
Paul departs from Jerusalem with offering	spring 57	

The letters offer no further information about Paul. Luke's Acts reports Paul was imprisoned, appealed, and eventually was sent to Rome for trial. Only later tradition reports that he was executed there (see later Acts of Paul). The Acts chronology would suggest Paul died between 62–64.

Notes

INTRODUCTION

1. Dennis R. MacDonald has pointed this out in "Apocryphal and Canonical Narratives about Paul," in *Paul and the Legacies of Paul,* ed. William S. Babcock (Dallas: SMU Press, 1990), 56–57. He refers especially to the Gnostic "Apocalypse of Paul."
2. Ludwig Wittgenstein, *Remarks on Frazer's Golden Bough,* ed. Rush Rhees, trans. A. C. Miles, rev. by Rush Rhees (Pockthorpe Cottage Denton, England: Brynmill Press, and Atlantic Highlands, NJ: Humanities Press International, 1979), 10e.

CHAPTER ONE: THE EARLY PAUL

1. From the "Acts of Paul and Thecla," in Edgar Hennecke, *New Testament Apocrypha,* ed. Wilhelm Schneemelcher, trans. R. McL. Wilson (Philadelphia: Westminster, 1963), vol. II, 354 (3:3).
2. "The Ascension of James," found in Epiphanius (bishop of Salamis, fourth century), *Panarion, haer.* 30:16.6–9. See Hennecke, *New Testament Apocrypha,* vol. II, 71.
3. In "Kerygmata Petrou," in Hennecke, *New Testament Apocrypha,* vol. II, 102–11.
4. See George Bernard Shaw, "The Monstrous Imposition upon Jesus," in *The Writings of St. Paul,* ed. Wayne A. Meeks (New York: W. W. Norton & Company, Inc., 1972), 301.
5. Hyam Maccoby, *The Mythmaker, Paul and the Invention of Christianity* (New York: Harper & Row, 1986).
6. Elizabeth A. Castelli, *Imitating Paul: A Discourse of Power* (Louisville: Westminster/John Knox Press, 1991).
7. This has suggested to some that a collection of Paul's letters had not yet been made when Luke wrote Acts. See John Knox, *Chapters in a Life of Paul* (Nashville: Abingdon Press, 1950), 23.

8. See 13:16–41; 13:46–47; 14:15–17; 17:22–31; 20:18b–35; 22:1–21; 24:10–21; 26:2–23; 28:17b–20.

9. Since the time of John Knox, *Chapters in a Life of Paul* (1950), Ernst Haenchen, *Die Apostelgeschichte* (Göttingen: Vandenhoeck & Ruprecht, 1963) Martin Dibelius, *Aufsätze zur Apostelgeschichte* (Göttingen: Vandenhoeck & Ruprecht, 1951) (English translation: *Studies in the Acts of the Apostles,* trans. Mary Ling and Paul Schubert [New York: Charles Scribner's Sons, 1956]), scholarly opinion has been very cautious in its use of Acts for a historical reconstruction of the Pauline context. Recently, however, Martin Hengel in his *The Pre-Christian Paul,* trans. John Bowden (London: SCM Press, and Philadelphia: Trinity Press International, 1991), has been more trusting of the historical veracity of Acts material.

10. Helmut Koester, *History, Culture, and Religion of the Hellenistic Age* (Philadelphia: Fortress Press, and Berlin: Walter de Gruyter, 1980), vol. II, 97–100 thinks Damascus was Paul's residence at the time of his call and possibly Paul's home. That view is also shared by Paula Fredriksen. Increasingly, archaeological records have accounted for abundant Hellenistic influence in Syria that would explain many of Paul's tendencies.

11. See W. C. van Unnik, *Tarsus or Jerusalem. The City of Paul's Youth,* trans. George Ogg (London: Epworth Press, 1962), 55.

12. Ibid., 55. Van Unnik's contrast of Tarsus, "a typically Hellenistic city . . . the intellectual centre of a flourishing Stoic School," and Jerusalem, where "syncretism secured no footing . . . and Hellenistic culture could force a way in only with difficulty and only very superficially" is historically untenable (3–4).

13. Adolf Deissmann, *Paul, A Study in Social and Religious History,* trans. William E. Wilson (New York: Harper & Brothers, 1957 [first English ed. 1912; German ed. 1911 from lectures given in Uppsala in 1909]), 99.

14. Hengel, *The Pre-Christian Paul,* 39.

15. Haenchen, *Apostelgeschichte,* 554, n. 1. In this Haenchen is obviously following Rudolf Bultmann, *Religion in Geschichte und Gegenwart,* 3d ed., rev. by F. von Campenhausen, Erich Dinkler, Gerhard Gloege, Knud E. Løgstrup; ed. Kurt Galling, 7 vols. (Tübingen: J. C. B. Mohr [Paul Siebeck], 1957–65), vol. IV, 1020–21.

16. On this point I agree with Hans Conzelmann, *History of Primitive Christianity,* trans. John E. Steely (Nashville: Abingdon Press, 1973), 79–80, and Knox, *Chapters in a Life of Paul,* 25–27.

17. See van Unnik, *Tarsus or Jerusalem,* 57.

18. Here I follow Haenchen, *Apostelgeschichte,* 554, who notes that in light of Gal. 1:22 the view that Paul studied under Gamaliel in Jerusalem "ist kaum richtig," and Kirsopp Lake and Henry J. Cadbury, *The Beginnings of Christianity* (Grand Rapids, MI: Baker Book House, 1965), part I, vol. IV, 279, who state that "the Pauline statement of the Jewish doctrine of the Law is so gross a caricature of anything which he could have learnt from Gamaliel. No Rabbis ever taught that salvation could only be obtained by the 'works of the Law.'" See also C. G. Montefiore, *Judaism and St. Paul* (London: Max Goschen, 1914), and Morton Scott Enslin, "Paul and Gamaliel," *JR* 7 (1927), 360–75.

19. See Martin Hengel, *Judaism and Hellenism. Studies in Their Encounter in Palestine during the Early Hellenistic Period,* trans. John Bowden (Philadelphia: Fortress Press, 1974), vol. I, 58–106.

20. An abundant secondary literature is available. Some of the more helpful works are the following: Hetty Goldman, ed., *Excavations at Gözlü, Tarsus, The Hellenistic and Roman Periods,* 5 vols. (Princeton: Princeton University Press, 1950–63), vol. I; A. H. M. Jones, *The Cities of the Eastern Roman Provinces* (Oxford: At the Clarendon Press, 1937), 192–216; W. M. Ramsay, *The Cities of St. Paul: Their Influence on His Life and Thought* (Grand Rapids, MI: Baker Book House, 1960), 95–244; C. Bradford Welles, "Hellenistic Tarsus," in *Mélanges de l'université Saint-Joseph* 38 (1962), 62–75; S. Carvilius Ruge, "Tarsos," in August Friedrich von Pauly-Georg Wissowa, *Real-Enzyklopädie der classischen Altertumswissenschaft,* ed. Wilhelm Kroll and Karl Mittelhaus (Stuttgart: H. Druckenmüller, 1932), vol. IV A.2, cols. 2413–39; Hans Böhlig, *Die Geisteskultur von Tarsos im augustischen Zeitalter mit Berücksichtigung der paulinischen Schriften* (Göttingen: Vandenhoeck & Ruprecht, 1913), 8–178.

21. See Goldman, *Excavations at Gözlü Kule,* vol. III, 21.

22. Goldman, *Excavations at Gözlü Kule,* vol. III, 110, 159.

23. See G. F. Hill, *British Museum. Catalogue of the Greek Coins of Lycaonia, Isauria and Cilicia* (London: The Trustees [of the British Museum], 1900); L. Robert, *Etudes de Numismatique Grecque,* (Paris: College de France, 1951); E. T. Newell, *The Coinage of the Western Seleucid Mints from Seleucus I to Antiochus III, Numismatic Studies,* No. 4 (Paris: College de France, 1941); D. H. Cox, in *Excavations at Gözlü Kule, Tarsus, The Hellenistic and Roman Periods,* ed. Hetty Goldman (Princeton: Princeton University Press, 1950). Information from literary sources may be seen in Strabo, *Geography,* trans. Horace Leonard Jones, LCL (Cambridge: Harvard University Press, 1917),14.5.9–15; Dio Chrysostom, "The Thirty-Third, or First Tarsic, Discourse," trans. by J. W. Cohoon and H. Lamar Crosby, LCL (Cambridge: Harvard University Press, 1961), 274–333; Cicero, *De Provinciis Consularibus,* trans. R. Gardner, LCL (Cambridge: Harvard University Press, 1965), 31; *Ad Familiares,* trans. W. Glynn Williams, LCL, 3 vols. (Cambridge: Harvard University Press, 1958–60), vol. I, bk. III, ch. VIII, para. 6; *Ad Atticum,* trans. E. O. Winstedt, LCL, 3 vols. (Cambridge: Harvard University Press, 1961), vol. 1, 1, 2, 6; vol. 2, 2, 6; vol. 3, 5, 21; Philostratus, *The Life of Apollonius of Tyana,* trans. F. C. Conybeare, LCL, 2 vols. (London: H. Heinemann and New York: Macmillan Co., 1912), 1, 7.

24. Because of the land built up by silt at the mouth of the river Cydnus it is difficult to know the exact distance Tarsus was from the Mediterranean Sea in the first century.

25. Dio Chrysostom, *Or.,* 33.1.

26. For sketch of the coin see Ramsay, *The Cities of St. Paul,* 127.

27. Ramsay argued that this change took place during the rule of Antiochus IV (Epiphanes), but that is largely speculation. See his *The Cities of St. Paul,* 159–65. See the rebuttal by Ruge, "Tarsos," 2420–22. Evidence exists that Theodotus knew Tarsus as Antioch on the Cydnus as early as 212 B.C.E. For numismatic

evidence for the name see the *British Museum Catalogue,* vol. LXXXV, 177, nos. 92, 93.

28. Strabo, *Geography,* 13.5.13.

29. *Geography,* 14.5.14–15.

30. See Welles, "Hellenistic Tarsus," 50.

31. Ibid.

32. Ibid., 58.

33. Strabo, *Geography,* 14.5.14, and Dio Chrysostom, "The Thirty-Third Discourse," in *Dio Chrysostom,* trans. J. H. Cohoon, H. Lamar Crosby, et al., LCL, (London: H. Heinemann and New York: G. P. Putnam's Sons, 1932–51), vol. IV, disc. 40, para. 11; disc. 47, para. 16–7.

34. In his commentary on Philemon, v. 23 ["Epaphras, my fellow prisoner in Christ Jesus"], Jerome suggests that Paul along with his parents and possibly Epaphras was captured by the Romans and relocated in Tarsus. Eduard Meyer's remark that this statement by Jerome is "Gänzlich ohne Wert . . . ganz absurde" is only a bit too extreme (*Ursprung und Anfänge des Christentums* 3 vols. [Stuttgart & Berlin: J. G. Cotta'sche Buchhandlung, 1923], vol. III, 312, n. 1). The text of Jerome reads: "*Aiunt, parentes apostoli Pauli de Byscalis regione fuisse Judaeae et eos, cum tota provincia Romana vastaretur manu et dispergerentur in orbem Judaei, in Tarsus urbem Ciliciae fuisse translatos; parentum condicionem adulescentulum Paulum esse secutum.* Does Jerome intend to say that Titus deported the family in 67 in response to the Jewish revolt? In *De viris illustribus* 5 Jerome offers a less objectionable report, claiming that Paul along with his parents had originated in Gischala and had relocated in Tarsus as a war prisoner. See *Selected Letters of St. Jerome,* LCL (Cambridge: Harvard University Press, 1954) and Jerome, *De viris illustribus,* trans. E. C. Richardson, in *The Nicene and Post-Nicene Fathers,* 2d ed., trans. E. C. Richardson (Grand Rapids, MI: Eerdmans, 1892), vol. III, 362. Presumably the grant of Roman citizenship came later and that would make a mash of Luke's claim in Acts that Paul was *born* a Roman citizen. The Latin text of Jerome reads: *Paulus apostolus, qui ante Saulus, extra numerum duodecim apostolorum de tribu Beniamin et oppido Judaeae Giscalis fuit, quo a Romanis capto cum parentibus suis Tarsus Ciliciae commigravit.* Hengel, *The Pre-Christian Paul,* 14, treats the Jerome tradition with more deference, arguing that uprisings under *Pompey* (63 B.C.E.) may have precipitated the enslavement of Paul's parents and the grant of freedom and citizenship by a Roman patron or provincial authority (14–15). A. N. Sherwin-White, *Roman Society and Roman Law in the New Testament* (Oxford: At the Clarendon Press, 1963), however, is quite skeptical about the granting of citizenship to slaves freed in the provinces.

35. The work of Dietrich-Alexander Koch, *Die Schrift als Zeuge des Evangeliums. Untersuchung zur Verwendung und zum Verständnis der Schrift bei Paulus* (Tübingen: J. C. B. Mohr [Paul Siebeck], 1986), leaves little doubt that the Septuagint was the Bible of Paul. Over a half century ago Adolf Deissmann, *Paulus,* 2d ed. (Tübingen: J. C. B. Mohr, 1925), 69, anticipated the work of Koch with his description of Paul as "a Septuagint Jew." Eng. trans. *Paul, A Study in Social*

and Religious History. Trans. William E. WIlson. 2d ed. (New York: Harper and Brothers, 1926).

36. Two things cause me to include Tarsus: (1) Paul's obvious dependence on the LXX and (2) the clear archaeological evidence that commercial and artistic exchanges took place between Alexandria and Tarsus. Given those exchanges it seems probable that some interaction also took place between the Jewish communities in the two cities.

37. For a fuller discussion see my *"Oikoumene* and the Limits of Pluralism in Alexandrian Judaism and Paul," in *Diaspora Jews and Judaism, Essays in Honor of, and in Dialogue with, A. Thomas Kraabel,* ed. J. Andrew Overman and Robert S. MacLennon (Atlanta: Scholars Press, 1992), 163–70.

38. A fuller argument for this point of view may be seen in my "The Grammar of Election in Four Pauline Letters," in *Pauline Theology,* vol. II: *1 and 2 Corinthians,* ed. David M. Hay (Minneapolis: Fortress Press, 1993), 211–33.

39. The pioneer in this discussion was Ludwig Wittgenstein. See especially his *Philosophical Investigations,* trans. G. E. M. Anscombe (New York: The Macmillan Company, 1968). Also note G. P. Baker and P. M. S. Hacker, *Wittgenstein: Rules, Grammar and Necessity* (Oxford: Basil Blackwell, 1985), esp. 34–80.

40. See George A. Lindbeck, *The Nature of Doctrine, Religion and Theology in a Postliberal Age* (Philadelphia: Westminster, 1984), one of the most stimulating theological treatises in two decades.

41. For example, thirty-three of fifty-four references in the Septuagint to *oikoumene* appear in Isaiah and the Psalms and only one anomalous reference in the Pentateuch.

42. See my *"Oikoumene* and the Limits of Pluralism," 166–67.

43. See I. L. Seeligmann, *The Septuagint Version of Isaiah. A Discussion of Its Problems* (Leiden: F. J. Brill, 1948), 106–7.

44. In *"Oikoumene* and the Limits of Pluralism," 179–82, I trace the agony in the Paul's heart over the question his gospel for the Gentiles raised about his reliance on God's promises to elect Israel.

45. See Nils Dahl, "The One God of Jews and Gentiles (Romans 3:29–30)," in his *Studies in Paul* (Minneapolis: Augsburg, 1977), 190.

46. Welles, "Hellenistic Tarsus," 61.

47. See also Sherwin-White, *Roman Society and Roman Law,* his *The Roman Citizenship,* 2d ed. (Oxford: At the Clarendon Press, 1973), and his "The Roman Citizenship, A Survey of Its Development into a World Franchise," in *ANRW,* ed. Hildegard Temporini (Berlin: Walter de Gruyter, 1972), vol. I.2, 40–58. An older but nevertheless valuable treatment is found in A. H. M. Jones, *Studies in Roman Government and Law* (Oxford: At the Clarendon Press, 1960), 67–68.

48. Sherwin-White, *Roman Society and Roman Law,* 181–85.

49. See Hengel, *The Pre-Christian Paul,* 11–12.

50. See Eduard Meyer, *Ursprung und Anfänge,* vol. III, 312, n. 1.

51. W. W. Tarn, *Hellenistic Civilization* (London: Edward Arnold, 1927), 176–77.

52. E. R. Goodenough, "The Perspective of Acts," in *Studies in Luke—Acts,* ed. Leander E. Keck and J. L. Martyn (New York: Abingdon Press, 1966), 55.

53. Victor A. Tcherikover, *Hellenistic Civilization and the Jews,* trans. S. Applebaum (Philadelphia: Jewish Publication Society, 1961), 328–29.
54. See Sherwin-White, *The Roman Citizenship,* 338.
55. Written in Alexandria, Egypt. 3 Maccabees knows of a certain Dositheus who "renounced the Law and abandoned his ancestral beliefs" (1:3) to become a servant of Ptolemy. We cannot say, however, that he was rewarded with citizenship.
56. See Josephus, *Antiquities,* trans. Louis H. Feldman, LCL (Cambridge: Harvard University Press, 1969), xx, 100.
57. See W. Stegeman, "War der Apostel Paulus römischer Bürger?" *ZNW* 78 (1987), 200–229; 225 here cited.
58. See ibid.
59. See John Ferguson, *Greek and Roman Religion* (Park Ridge, NJ: Noyes Press, 1980), 61–69, and Walter Burkert, *Greek Religion* (Oxford: Basil Blackwell, 1985); *Aelius Aristides,* trans. C. A. Behr, LCL, 4 vols. (Cambridge: Harvard University Press, 1973–), vol. I, 40–48.
60. Note the reservations of Stegemann, "War der Apostel Paulus römischer Bürger?" 200–229, about Luke's attribution of Roman citizenship to Paul.
61. See Hans Conzelmann, *Acts of the Apostles,* trans. James Limburg, A. Thomas Kraabel, and Donald Juel (Philadelphia: Fortress Press, 1987); Haenchen, *Die Apostelgeschichte;* Dibelius, *Studies in the Acts of the Apostles;* Stegeman, "War der Apostel Paulus römischer Bürger?" 200–229. Helmut Koester, *History and Literature of Early Christianity* (Philadelphia: Fortress Press, 1982), vol. II, 98–99, notes that "The claim that Paul had inherited Roman citizenship from his father (Acts 22:25–29) is scarcely credible because as a Roman citizen Paul would have had no difficulty in escaping from the various punishments that he received according to his own statements (2 Cor. 11:24–25)—and the Paul of Acts does so (Acts 22:25 and the following verse)."
62. See Stegeman's "War der Apostel Paulus römischer Bürger?," 200–229.
63. Tcherikover, *Hellenistic Civilization and the Jews,* 313–17; E. Schürer, *The History of the Jewish People in the Age of Jesus Christ,* rev. and ed. G. Vermes, F. Millar, and M. Black (Edinburgh: T. & T. Clark, 1973–87), vol. III, 76–79.
64. John Clayton Lentz, Jr., *Luke's Portrait of Paul* (Cambridge: Cambridge University Press, 1993), 40.
65. *Philonis Alexandrini Legatio ad Gaium,* ed. with an introduction, translation, and commentary by Mary Smallwood (Leiden: E. J. Brill, 1970), 6 and following pages.
66. See S. Applebaum, "The Legal Status of the Jewish Communities in the Diaspora," in *The Jewish People in the First Century: Historical Geography, Political History, Social, Cultural and Religious Life and Institutions,* ed. S. Safrai and M. Stern (Philadelphia: Fortress Press, 1974), vol. I, 453.
67. Note the report in Josephus, *Antiquities,* XIV, 213; 241–58; of Roman guarantees offered to Jews in Paros, Laodicea, Miletus, Halicarnassus, and Sardis.
68. Adolf Deissmann, *Paulus* (Tübingen: J. C. B. Mohr, 1911), 38.
69. W. M. Ramsay, *St. Paul the Traveller and Roman Citizen* (New York: G. P. Putnam's Sons, 1904).

70. Ronald F. Hock, *The Social Context of Paul's Ministry* (Philadelphia: Fortress Press, 1980), 35, says of the hostility heaped on manual laborers, "these experiences must have been doubly difficult for Paul, who, though he shared the life of artisans, was by birth a member of the *socially élite*, the very circles that maintained this social world" (emphasis added). This observation by Hock is puzzling, for he offers no support for this thesis, and indeed the bulk of his work goes against it.

71. Martin Dibelius, *Paul*, trans. Frank Clarke (Philadelphia: Westminster, 1953), 37.

72. The term *élite* is indeed quite slippery in this context, for Paul's literacy in and of itself distinguished him from the great masses of the period and in that sense it may be legitimately suggested that he was among the élite, but to place him among the socially or politically élite is something else altogether.

73. See Hock, *The Social Context*, 23–24. There is unresolved tension in Hock's view that Paul was trained by his artisan father and that he came from the elite. Hock's position would have been strengthened had he been more critical of the Lucan attribution of Roman citizenship to Paul. In this sense Deissmann may have been correct that Paul came from an artisan class. See his *Paul. A Study of Social and Religious History*, 2d ed. (London: Hodder & Stoughton, 1926), 6, 48–49, 74, 166, 224.

74. Jerome Murphy-O'Connor, *Paul, A Critical Life* (Oxford: Clarendon Press, 1996), 86.

75. Jacob Neusner is skeptical, "I don't know what to make of Pharisees born overseas which, by definition, is unclean." From a personal letter to Lentz cited in Lentz, *Luke's Portrait of Paul*, 54.

76. See Jacob Neusner, *The Rabbinic Traditions about the Pharisees before 70*, 3 vols. (Leiden: E. J. Brill, 1971), vol. III, 177, 244–47; Jacob Neusner, *From Politics to Piety: The Emergence of Pharisaic Judaism* (Englewood Cliffs, NJ: Prentice-Hall, 1973), 89; Jacob Neusner, "Two Pictures of the Pharisees: Philosophical Circle or Eating Club?" *ATR 64* (1982), 525–38; Ellis Rivkin, *A Hidden Revolution: The Pharisees' Search for the Kingdom Within* (Nashville: Abingdon Press, 1978), 72–75, 176, 242.

77. Neusner, *From Politics to Piety*, 89.

78. See Anthony J. Saldarini, "Pharisees," in *ABD*, ed. David Noel Freedman, Gary A. Herion, David F. Graf, John David Pleins, and Astrid B. Beck (New York: Doubleday, 1992), vol. V, 291.

79. Rivkin, *A Hidden Revolution*, 176.

80. Josephus, *The Jewish War*, trans. H. St. J. Thackeray, LCL, 9 vols. (Cambridge: Harvard University Press, 1976).

81. Anthony J. Saldarini, *Pharisees, Scribes and Sadducees in Palestinian Society. A Sociological Approach* (Wilmington: Michael Glazier, 1988), 128–33, esp. 133.

82. See ibid., 150.

83. Saldarini, *Pharisees, Scribes and Sadducees*, 150–51, however, underestimates the role theological issues played in the disputes between Jesus and his followers and the Pharisees. Even though he recognizes that it is difficult if not impossible to separate religious beliefs from politics, he nevertheless says, "Jesus and the

Pharisees did not argue over theological issues which were of interest to a limited number of Jews, but rather competed for control over the community."

84. On this point Rivkin is correct. See his *The Hidden Revolution,* 304.

85. See Rivkin, *The Hidden Revolution,* 72–75 and Neusner, *Rabbinic Traditions,* vol. III, 177.

86. The word *spiritualize* as used by Heikki Räisänen, *The Torah and Christ. Essays in German and English on the Problem of the Law in Early Christianity* (Helsinki: Finnish Exegetical Society, 1986), 288–95, is so burdened by a history of misuse that in the view of Klinzing it is better avoided. See Georg Klinzing, *Die Umdeutung des Kultus in der Qumrangemeinde und im NT* (Göttingen: Vandenhoeck & Ruprecht, 1971), 143–47. Yet Klinzing's preference for "Umdeutung," or "a new interpretation," is too cerebral and avoids entirely the powerful value of sacrifice as a symbolic act. A more sagacious use of the word *spiritualize* may be found in Daniel Boyarin, *A Radical Jew. Paul and the Politics of Identity* (Berkeley: University of California Press, 1994), 81–135.

87. See Hans Wenschkewitz, "Die stoische Philosophie, besonders die spätere Stoa," in *Die Spiritualisierung der Kultusbegriffe, Tempel, Priester und Opfer im Neuen Testament* (Leipzig: Verlag von Eduard Pfeiffer, 1932), 49–67.

88. S. K. Williams, "Jesus' Death as a Saving Event. The Background and Origin of a Concept," Harvard Dissertation in Religion, no. 2, 1975.

89. Those unable to read the Hebrew will find a fluent English translation edited by Florentino García Martínez, *The Dead Sea Scrolls Translated, The Qumran Texts in English,* trans. Wilfred G. E. Watson (Leiden: E. J. Brill, 1992).

90. See Klinzing, *Die Umdeutung,* 105–6.

91. Räisänen, Heikki. *The Torah and Christ,* 277–95.

92. In my view Räisänen's insistence on an Antiochene background for Paul's spiritualization of the cult is too simplistic. See his *The Torah and Christ,* 282–95.

93. I cannot agree with Robert Hammerton-Kelly, *Sacred Violence: Paul's Hermeneutic of the Cross* (Minneapolis: Fortress Press, 1992), that Paul repudiated the sacrificial cult as "sacred violence." On the contrary, the spiritualization of the cult recognizes the axiomatic nature of the sacrificial cult. By teaching us how sacrifice functioned in the ancient world at the psychological level, Marcel Mauss, *Sacrifice: Its Nature and Function,* trans. Henri Hubert (Chicago: University of Chicago Press, 1964), has done much to correct a Protestant bias against sacrifice. Ruled by an awareness of the gulf between the world we know and the world we know not, the sacrifice provided a nexus of these sundered worlds, a bridge across that void. Readied by careful and diligent acts of purification, the worshipper brought the ritually pure animal without blemish or the firstfruits of the harvest to the holy place. In an awesome moment, the victim's life was offered up to its maker. In that incandescent moment, the sacrificer joined ritually with the victim, catching a glimpse of the other side, moving silently into the very world of the Holy One. In the act of sacrifice, worshippers made atonement for sin, thanksgiving was offered, celebration of the covenant was "cut" with Yahweh once again in the company of the ancestors, and the gate was opened to the other world. Through offering what is precious one crossed the boundary

between the divine and human worlds. As a Pharisee, Paul would have taken this holy cult for granted and found in it a grammar for redemption and a metaphor of behavior.

94. Ernst Käsemann, *Commentary on Romans,* trans. Geoffrey W. Bromiley (Grand Rapids, MI: Eerdmans, 1980), 329.

95. Paul's use of "body" σῶμα as a synonym of the whole self resembles Philo's observation that worshippers who bring nothing but themselves "offer the best sacrifice, the full and perfect oblation θυσίαν of noble living, as they honour . . . their Benefactor and Saviour, God." See Philo, "On the Special Laws," 272. For the citations here see *Philo,* trans. F. H. Colson and G. H. Whitaker, LCL, 10 vols. (London, Cambridge: Harvard University Press, 1971). Klinzing, *Die Umdeutung,* 215, thinks the exhortation to present their bodies as a sacrifice offers a striking resemblance to the Qumran outlook against a Hellenistic spiritualization. Klinzing's view that Paul's use of "body" reflects not a Hellenistic but a Qumran provenance has no textual parallel to support it.

96. Hans Dieter Betz has suggested in his "Christianity as Religion: Paul's Attempt at Definition in Romans," *JR* 71 (1991), 315–44, that Paul here aims to define Christianity as a reasonable religion. This article has been reprinted in *Paulinische Studien, Gesammelte Aufsätze III* (Tübingen: J. C. B. Mohr [Paul Siebeck], 1994), 206–39.

97. I side with Käsemann against Cranfield, who thinks the reference here is to Levites. But in order for Cranfield's thesis to work, Christ must become the sacrificer. See C. E. B. Cranfield, "The International Critical Commentary," *A Critical and Exegetical Commentary on the Epistle to the Romans,* (Edinburgh: T. & T. Clark, 1985), vol. II, 755. We agree with Käsemann, *Commentary on Romans,* 393, who sees Paul's act here as a priestly function.

98. In "Sacrifice in Romans 12–15," *Word and World* VI (1986), 417, I argued that Paul here forges a link with 6:13–19, where Paul five times uses the imperatival form of παρίστημι, "to present," where it also carries cultic associations and a blending of the symbol of obedient slave with sacrificial victim. Undeniably, Paul's intent in Rom. 6 is to refute the charge that his gospel was antinomian.

99. One might mention Phil. 2:17, where the faith of the Philippians and Paul's own life appear as sacrificial images. Then there is 1 Cor. 3:16–17, where Paul speaks metaphorically of the church as the temple, an explicit spiritualization of the temple.

100. The lack of attention given to this prominent motif in Paul's letters is stunning. Except for theological dictionaries and encyclopedias the secondary literature is sparse. This is noted by Leander E. Keck, "The Quest for Paul's Pharisaism: Some Reflections," in *Justice and the Holy: Essays in Honor of Walter Harrelson,* ed. Douglas A. Knight and Peter J. Paris (Atlanta: Scholars Press, 1989), 163–75.

101. Robert Hodgson, Jr., "Holiness Tradition and Social Description: Intertestamental Judaism and Early Christianity," in *Reaching Beyond: Chapters in the History of Perfectionism,* ed. Stanley M. Burgess (Peabody, MA: Hendrickson Publishers, 1986), 65–91, corrects the tendency to view holiness as an inward

quality of the divine or human that has little to do with the social construction of reality.

102. Mary Douglas, *Purity and Danger, An Analysis of Concepts of Pollution and Taboo* (New York: Frederick A. Praeger, Publishers, 1966).

103. W. Zimmerli, " 'Heiligkeit' nach dem sogenannten Heiligkeitsgesetz," *VT* XXX (1980), 493–517.

104. In my *"Oikoumene* and the Limits of Pluralism," 163–82, this tension is more fully treated.

105. See "Heiligkeit," 511–12.

106. Keck, "The Quest for Paul's Pharisaism," 163–75.

107. Of course, Paul was quite capable of giving the temple metaphor an individualistic application as well. To new converts who were accustomed to visits with prostitutes Paul poses the rhetorical question: "You know, don't you, that your body is a temple of the holy Spirit in you which you have from God, and that you are not your own? For you were bought with a price; therefore, glorify God in your body" (adapted from NRSV of 1 Cor. 6:19–20). Even in this context, however, Paul associates individual conduct with the welfare of the community (1 Cor. 6:15). Interestingly, Philo offers an individualistic application of the soul as the "house of God, a holy temple, a most beauteous abiding-place," which perchance God, the Master of the whole world, will "keep thee under His care as His special house, to preserve thee evermore strongly guarded and unharmed" (De somn., I, 149).

108. While the expression *kletoi hagioi* resembles the formula *mikra qodesh* of the priestly code (Exod. 12:16; Lev. 23:2, 3, 4, 7, 8, 21, 24, 27, 35, 36, 37), I cannot agree with Ragnar Asting, "Forschungen zur Religion und Literatur des Alten und Neuen Testaments," in *Die Heiligkeit im Urchristentum,* bd. 46 (Göttingen: Vandenhoeck & Ruprecht, 1930), 142, that "holy convocation" and "called holy ones" are functional equivalents.

109. Asting, *Heiligkeit,* 194–95, has noted the synonymity at times between Christ and the spirit in Paul. In 2 Cor. 3:17, for example, Paul says explicitly, "the Lord is the Spirit," evidently meaning *Holy* Spirit, and makes no distinction between being "in the Spirit" (Rom. 8:9) and simultaneously "in Christ" (Rom. 8:10; 2 Cor. 13:5; Gal. 2:20, etc.). And the reverse is also true for Paul, with the spirit being in the believer (Rom. 8:9; 1 Cor. 3:16; 6:19) as is also Christ (Rom. 8:10; 2 Cor. 13:5; Gal. 2:20).

110. The NRSV reads "that each of you know how to control your own body in holiness and honor, not with lustful passion, like the Gentiles who do not know God," and as an alternate reading has "that each of you know how to take a wife for himself," etc. While either reading is possible, good reasons exist for the reading we have offered here.

111. Asting, *Heiligkeit,* 226, where he calls holiness for Christians "ein Ziel und eine Aufgabe" (a goal and a task).

112. Following Gedalyahu Alon, "The Levitical Uncleanness of Gentiles," in *Judaism and the Classical World* (Jerusalem: Magnes Press, 1977), 146–89. Peter J. Tomson, *Paul and the Jewish Law. Halakha in the Letters of the Apostle to the*

Gentiles (Assen/Maastricht, Minneapolis: Van Gorcum, Fortress Press, 1990), 222–81, argues that there were few restrictions on Jews eating with Gentiles, or on inviting Gentiles to their homes for meals, but both of these works are so flawed methodologically that they are virtually useless. Continuing to use Mishnaic and Talmudic texts as primary evidence for pre-70 Jewish practice with no attention given to the historical critical exercise necessary to date traditions is hardly responsible. I was disappointed to see that Neil Elliott's *Liberating Paul, The Justice of God and the Politics of the Apostle* (Maryknoll, NY: Orbis Books, 1994), 146–51 uncritically accepts the conclusions of Tomson and Alon, thus marring an otherwise stimulating work.

113. Here I am at odds with Jürgen Becker, *Paul: Apostle to the Gentiles,* trans. O. C. Dean, Jr. (Louisville: Westminster/John Knox Press, 1993), 33, who says, "the Christian Paul has almost entirely disposed of the Jewish period of his life. He experienced his calling as such a profound reorientation and identity crisis that the previous part of his life becomes almost totally inessential and the time after his calling comprises his real life. Therefore in Paul's letters the Jewish portion of his life is not presented at all for its own sake. It only serves here and there, sporadically and typified by a few narrowly limited statements, as a dark background and as harshly drawn contrast to the beginning of his second, real life."

114. As Rudolf Bultmann claimed. See his "Paul," in *Existence and Faith,* trans. Schubert Ogden (New York: Meridian, 1960), 114. His students essentially agreed with this position. See Hans Conzelmann, *An Outline of the Theology of the New Testament,* trans. John Bowden (New York: Harper & Row, 1969), 163–64, and Günther Bornkamm, *Paul,* trans. D. M. G. Stalker (New York: Harper & Row, 1971), 14–16. Others who share this view are Ernst Haenchen, "The Book of Acts as Source Material for the History of Early Christianity," in *Studies in Luke—Acts,* 263–64, and Walter Schmithals, *Paul and James,* trans. Dorthea M. Barton, Studies in Biblical Theology, 1/46 (London: SCM Press, 1965), 28.

115. As Arland Hultgren claims. See his "Paul's Pre-Christian Persecutions of the Church: Their Purpose, Locale, and Nature," *JBL* 95 (1976), 97–111; 103 here cited. This goes against those who argue that contra Acts, the persecution could not have been in Judaea because Paul himself says that he "was unknown by sight to the churches of Judea" (Gal. 1:22). See, for example, Knox, *Chapters in a Life of Paul,* 35–36, Bultmann, "Paul," 113 and Bornkamm, *Paul,* 15. Hultgren responds by saying that Paul "simply did not 'show his face' in the churches in Judea *as an apostle,*" but that places more weight on Paul's statement than it will bear.

116. As Hengel argues. See his *The Pre-Christian Paul,* 84; see also 72–86.

117. This point was made some time ago by Douglas R. A. Hare, *The Theme of Jewish Persecution of Christians in the Gospel according to St. Matthew* (Cambridge: Cambridge University Press, 1967), 2–3.

118. Jack T. Sanders, *Schismatics, Sectarians, Dissidents, Deviants. The First One Hundred Years of Jewish-Christian Relations* (Valley Forge, PA: Trinity Press International, 1993) 262, n. 17, argues that there was a vicious response from the Jewish majority which leads him to challenge Mack's thesis that the response

was less brutal. Sanders correctly notes of Burton Mack's thesis: "Rejection is not persecution." See Burton L. Mack, *A Myth of Innocence: Mark and Christian Origins* (Minneapolis: Fortress Press, 1988), 262, n. 17.

119. Paula Fredriksen, "Judaism, the Circumcision of Gentiles, and Apocalyptic Hope: Another Look at Galatians 1 and 2," *JTS* 42 (1991), 556.

120. Jack T. Sanders, *Schismatics, Sectarians, Dissidents, Deviants,* 95–99, and esp. 150.

121. Correctly, Sherwin-White, *Roman Society and Roman Law,* 1–47.

122. Hultgren, "Paul's Pre-Christian Persecutions of the Church,"108.

123. See Hultgren's "Paul's Pre-Christian Persecutions of the Church," 109. Fredriksen's view that the phrase *kath' hyperbolen* refers to the maximum number of lashes allowable appears to be something of a stretch. See her "Judaism, the Circumcision of Gentiles, and Apocalyptic Hope," 549.

124. Craig C. Hill, *Hellenists and Hebrews. Reappraising Division within the Earliest Church* (Minneapolis: Fortress Press, 1992).

125. See Hultgren's "Paul's Pre-Christian Persecutions," 98, which follows Jacob Jervell, "The Law in Luke—Acts," *Luke and the People of God: A New Look at Luke—Acts* (Minneapolis: Augsburg, 1972), 138, who says of the charge that Stephen has abandoned Torah, "for Luke these accusations are patently false, which among other things the speech of Stephen is intended to prove."

126. Fredriksen, "Judaism, the Circumcision of Gentiles, and Apocalyptic Hope," 553–56.

127. Ibid., 554.

128. See Jack T. Sanders, *Schismatics, Sectarians, Dissidents, Deviants,* 95–99.

129. Hultgren, "Paul's Pre-Christian Persecutions of the Church," 100, 103.

130. Ibid., 103.

131. Peter Richardson, *Israel in the Apostolic Church* (London: Cambridge University Press, 1969), 46, notes that from the point of view of the persecutors "any punishment might be viewed as necessary internal correction."

CHAPTER TWO: THE APOSTLE TO THE GENTILES

1. See Johannes Munck, *Paul and the Salvation of Mankind,* trans. Frank Clarke (Richmond: John Knox Press, 1959), 26.

2. On this point I agree with Krister Stendahl, *Paul among Jews and Gentiles and Other Essays* (Philadelphia: Fortress Press, 1976), 7–23.

3. Accepted and restated by Wilhelm Schneemelcher, "Apostle and Apostolic," in Hennecke, *New Testament Apocrypha,* vol II, 1.

4. Walter Schmithals, *The Office of Apostle in the Early Church,* trans. John E. Steely (Nashville: Abingdon Press, 1969), 12.

5. Gerhard Kittel, ed., and Geoffrey W. Bromiley, trans., *TDNT* (Grand Rapids, MI: Eerdmans, 1964–74), vol. I, 407–47.

6. Ibid., 407.

7. Ibid., 409.

8. Schneemelcher, "Apostle and Apostolic," 29.

9. Schmithals, *The Office of Apostle*, 114–230.

10. Hans Dieter Betz, *Galatians* (Philadelphia: Fortress Press, 1979), 75. Interestingly, Betz's later article "Apostle" allows for the possibility of influence from a Socratic tradition "in which Socrates was seen as a messenger sent by the deity." In *ABD*, vol. I, 310–11.

11. Betz, "Apostle," 310.

12. On this point Schmithals's dependence on Harnack is essentially correct. Schmithals, *The Office of Apostle*, 92, n. 153.

13. In my *The Letters of Paul, Conversations in Context*, 3d ed. (Louisville: Westminster/John Knox Press, 1991), 100–102, I outline three options and prefer the Northern Galatian theory.

14. Here I go with Walter Schmithals, *Paul and the Gnostics*, trans. John E. Steely (Nashville: Abingdon Press, 1972), 19–30. See also Ragnar Bring, *Commentary on Galatians*, trans. Eric Wahlstrom (Philadelphia: Muhlenberg, 1961), 37–38, as compared with Betz, *Galatians*, 65.

15. I am here obviously at odds with Schmithals, *The Office of Apostle*, 27, who says "it is all the more noteworthy that the decisive thing in the call visions in the Old Testament (and in the Synoptics)—the command of sending one forth—is completely lacking in Paul."

16. In taking this repetition as an emphasis directed against a challenge I agree with Schmithals, *Paul and the Gnostics*, 19–29, instead of Betz, *Galatians*, 65.

17. Hennecke, *New Testament Apocrypha*, 122.

18. Ibid., 123.

19. Albrecht Oepke, *Der Brief des Paulus an die Galater* (Berlin: Evangelische Verlagsanstalt, 1973), 141.

20. Heinrich Schlier, *Der Brief an die Galater* (Göttingen: Vandenhoeck & Ruprecht, 1971), 208.

21. See Oepke, *Der Brief des Paulus an die Galater,* 141, and Franz Mussner, *Der Galaterbrief* (Freiburg: Herder, 1974), 304–5. More compelling is Betz's position, *Galatians,* 220–21.

22. Beverly Roberts Gaventa, "The Maternity of Paul: An Exegetical Study of Galatians 4:19," in *The Conversation Continues. Studies in Paul & John in Honor of J. Louis Martyn*, ed. Robert T. Fortna and Beverly Roberts Gaventa (Nashville: Abingdon Press, 1990), 189–201, was the first to take seriously the maternal imagery in Galatians and 1 Thessalonians, and a study of her work is a helpful starting place for a discussion of Paul's maternal imagery. See also her "Apostles as Babes and Nurses in 1 Thessalonians 2:7," in *Faith and History. Essays in Honor of Paul W. Meyer,* ed. John T. Carroll, Charles H. Cosgrove, and E. Elizabeth Johnson (Atlanta: Scholars Press, 1990), 193–207.

23. Caroline Walker Bynum, *Jesus as Mother: Studies in the Spirituality of the High Middle Ages* (Berkeley: University of California Press, 1982).

24. In *The Office of Apostle,* 22, Schmithals says, "The special commission and the special authority which the apostles receive are functions of the congregation. . . . No charisma . . . essentially elevates its bearer out of the community." While

at one level Schmithals is correct—Paul's focus is clearly on the congregation—yet at the same time Paul's apostolic authority, as he understands it, comes directly from Christ and is not mediated or dispensed by the congregation whether in Antioch or Jerusalem.

25. See ibid., 40–42.

26. The manuscript support for reading "babes" rather than "gentle" is, as Gaventa shows, compelling. See her "Apostles as Babes and Nurses," 204.

27. An old but still valuable treatment is available in Mary Rosaria Gorman, "The Nurse in Greek Life," a Catholic University dissertation from 1917.

28. See Gaventa, "Apostles as Babes and Nurses," 206.

29. See Schmithals, *The Office of Apostle,* 48.

30. There is considerable difference of opinion about the identity of the opponents. Walter Schmithals agrees with Bultmann that they were Gnostics. C. K. Barrett and Käsemann think they were missionaries of the Palestinian church sent out to correct Paul's defective gospel. Hans Dieter Betz sees them as missionaries heavily influenced by Sophist propaganda and Cynic philosophy. Here I side with Dieter Georgi, who argues that they were Hellenistic Jewish Christian apostles who modeled their missionary work after the "god man" (*theos anēr*) of Hellenistic popular religion. Since we have no evidence of a fully developed Gnosticism in the first century, the position of Schmithals and Bultmann is untenable. The absence of any discussion of law in 2 Corinthians argues against the argument that these super apostles were from the Jerusalem church. Betz's attempt to root the gospel of the opposition in Cynic philosophy and Sophist positions understates the Jewishness of Paul's competitors. And given the questions raised by David Tiede and Carl Holladay about Georgi's *theos anēr* construction, it is unlikely that that theory can survive unaltered. In light of the dependence of the opposition on the Abraham traditions—a tendency abundantly evident in Philo—Georgi probably is correct that the apostles were Hellenistic Jewish missionaries.

31. Hans Windisch, *Der zweite Korintherbrief,* reprint of 9th ed. [1924] (Göttingen: Vandenhoeck & Ruprecht, 1970), 302–3; C. K. Barrett, *The Second Epistle to the Corinthians* (New York: Harper & Row, 1973), 257.

32. Here I agree with Ernst Käsemann, "Die Legitimität des Apostels. Eine Untersuchung zu II Korinther 10–13," *ZNW* 41 (1942), 33–71, esp. 36–37.

33. Although few follow Dieter Georgi's thesis that these missionaries were "God men" θεῖοι ἄνδρες, his discussion of Paul's opponents in 2 Corinthians is quite valuable. *See The Opponents of Paul in Second Corinthians* (Philadelphia: Fortress Press, 1986), esp. 230–64.

34. See Martin Dibelius, *An die Thessalonicher 1, 2. An die Philipper,* 3d ed. (Tübingen: J. C. B. Mohr, 1937), in his discussion of 1 Thess. 2:7. See also Georgi, *The Opponents of Paul,* 238–42.

35. Georgi, *The Opponents of Paul,* 282.

36. See my "'As Dying, and Behold We Live,' Death and Resurrection in Paul's Theology," in *INT* XLVI (1992), 5–18, in which I consider how the discussion of this important set of opposites was related to the argument between Paul and the visiting apostles.

37. George Lyons, *Pauline Autobiography: Toward a New Understanding* (Atlanta: Scholars Press, 1985), 107–12, argues that the antithetical statements in 1 Thessalonians and Galatians are simply rhetorical statements emphasizing the second statement, not denying the first, but the polemic is so harsh in 2 Corinthians that I cannot convince myself that the harsh antitheses have no opponent in mind.

38. Schmithals's view that the statement that they preach "another Jesus" suggests a Gnostic provenance is almost universally rejected. But it appears likely that their theology of glory virtually eclipsed the early emphasis on the suffering and dying Savior.

39. Windisch, *Der zweite Korintherbrief,* esp. 345, but also 315–98.

40. See especially the work of Hans Dieter Betz, *Der Apostel Paulus und die sokratische Tradition. Eine exegetische Untersuchung zu seiner Apologie 2 Korinther 10–13* (Tübingen: J. C. B. Mohr [Paul Siebeck], 1972), 74–89.

41. I do not use the term propaganda here in a pejorative sense but rather as it was widely recognized as an attempt to advance a position with the skillful use of rhetoric.

42. Windisch, *Der zweite Korintherbrief,* 316, where the author says, "That Paul himself saw the mime and that he learned from him does not seem impossible to me. He differentiated himself from the true mime only in the way he bears his role in bitter seriousness and that it is true. He plays the role of Paul himself."

43. In calling this a parody, I concur with E. A. Judge, "St. Paul and Classical Society," *Jahrbuch für Antike und Christentum* 15 (1972), 19–36, and Hans Dieter Betz, "Eine Christus-Aretologie bei Paulus (2 Cor 12. 7–10)," *ZTK* 66 (1969), 288–305.

44. While most agree that 2 Corinthians contains fragments of at least two letters and possibly more, the textual history of the letter is so complex that scholars have been unable to agree on the number of letters that may be included in this collection. We cannot here explore them all here, but the thanksgiving does telegraph Paul's concern in at least one part of the collection, and it may report a concern of an earlier epistle.

45. Victor Paul Furnish, *II Corinthians* (Garden City, NY: Doubleday & Co., 1984), 187.

46. See Georgi, *The Opponents of Paul,* 25, n. 95.

47. See the claim of Windisch, *Der zweite Korintherbrief,* 396.

48. See Windisch, *Der zweite Korintherbrief,* 396–97 who also connects these passages.

49. Betz, *Der Apostel Paulus und die sokratische Tradition,* 139.

50. Furnish, *II Corinthians,* 556.

51. Hans Joachim Schoeps, *Paul: The Theology of the Apostle in the Light of Jewish Religious History,* trans. Harold Knight (Philadelphia: Westminster, 1961), 102.

52. See my "*Oikoumene* and the Limits of Pluralism," 163–82.

53. See Dahl, "The One God of Jews and Gentiles," 190.

54. I am here drawing on the seminal work of Victor Turner, *The Ritual Process, Structure and Anti-Structure* (Ithaca, NY: Cornell University Press, 1969). This tendency, however, is not limited to ritual, as he acknowledges in his "Myth and

Symbol," in *The International Encyclopedia of Social Sciences,* ed. David L. Sills (New York: Macmillan & the Free Press, 1968), vol. 10, 576–79.

55. See Paul's use of εὐαγγελίζω in 1 Cor. 1:17; 9:16, 18; 15:1, 2; 2 Cor. 10:16; 11:7; Gal. 1:8, 9, 11, 16, 23; 4:13; Rom. 1:15; 10:15; 15:20, and κηρύσσω in 1 Cor. 1:23; 9:27; 15:11, 12; 2 Cor. 1:19; 4:5; 11:4; Gal. 2:2; 5:11; Phil. 1:15; 1 Thess. 2:9. The noun κήρυγμα, preaching or proclamation, appears in 1 Cor. 1:21; 2:4; 15:14; Rom. 16:25.

56. See Dibelius, *Studies in the Acts of the Apostles,* 57.

57. Haenchen, *Die Apostelgeschichte,* 467 calls it "eine lukanische Schöpfung."

58. See Charles Harold Dodd, *The Apostolic Preaching and Its Developments* (New York: Harper & Brothers, 1960).

59. See my "The Grammar of Election in Four Pauline Letters," 211–33.

60. *Natural History,* trans. Harris Rackham, LCL (Cambridge: Harvard University Press, 1938), II, v, 22.

61. E. P. Sanders, *Paul and Palestinian Judaism* (Philadelphia: Fortress Press, 1977), 442–46. Paul's treatment of sin in Rom. 1:18–3:20, however, could, and some critics argue should, be read in just the opposite way—as a description of a desperate plight requiring and receiving a divine solution in Christ.

62. See H. Richard Hays, *The Faith of Jesus Christ* (Chico, CA: Scholars Press, 1983), 64–67.

63. See Gregory Nagy, *Pindar's Homer: The Lyric Possession of an Epic Past* (Baltimore: Johns Hopkins University Press, 1990), 52–81.

64. On this point I trust I am in partial agreement with E. P. Sanders, *Paul and Palestinian Judaism,* 502–7 who emphasizes the participatory character of Paul's religion, but I would not, as Sanders does, juxtapose this against the juridical or apocalyptic character of Paul's outlook.

CHAPTER THREE: THE LETTER WRITER

1. According to Pseudo-Demetrius that is exactly what letters should do. See *On Style,* trans. W. Rhys Roberts, LCL (Cambridge: Harvard University Press, 1926), 227.

2. See the discussion that follows.

3. James B. Pritchard, ed., *Ancient Near Eastern Texts Relating to the Old Testament* ed. James B. Pritchard (Princeton, NJ: Princeton University Press, 1955), 486 (EA, No. 270).

4. See *Ancient Near Eastern Texts,* 321–22, for a translation of the most important letters. Written from an "inferior" ostraca, number IV speaks of no longer being able to see the smoke signals from Azekah, ten miles north of Lachish mentioned in Jer. 34:6–7, which probably means that that fortress has already fallen. See "Lachish Letters," by Robert A. Di Vito in *ABD,* vol. IV, 126–28.

5. See Suetonius (b. ca. 68 CE), 49, who reports that Augustus "first stationed young men along the military roads and afterwards post-chaises. The latter has seemed the more convenient arrangement, since the same men who bring the

dispatches from any place can, if occasion demands, be questioned as well." "Augustus" in *Lives of the Caesars,* trans. J. C. Rolfe, LCL (Cambridge: Harvard University Press, 1979).

6. As John L. White has pointed out, our word post has its genesis in the Latin *positus* that means " 'fixed' or 'placed' and refers to the fixed posts or stations in the relay system." *Light from Ancient Letters* (Philadelphia: Fortress Press, 1986), 214.

7. White notes that government officials did use the system for their own private correspondence, but that practice was widely condemned. See his *Light from Ancient Letters,* 215.

8. Ibid., 215.

9. See William G. Doty, *Letters in Primitive Christianity,* (Philadelphia: Fortress Press, 1973), 1.

10. See Stanley K. Stowers, "Greek and Latin Letters," in *ABD,* vol. IV, 293.

11. Adolf Deissmann, *Light from the Ancient East. The New Testament Illustrated by Recently Discovered Texts of the Graeco-Roman World,* trans. Lionel R. M. Strachan (New York: George H. Doran Co., 1927), 230.

12. Ibid., 234. Ironically, Deissmann obviously experienced great aesthetic pleasure from reading the "real letters" of Paul. Of Philemon, he says that it "is one of the most valuable self-revelations that the great apostle has left us: brotherly feeling, quiet beauty, tact as of a man of the world—all these are discoverable in the letter" (234).

13. See the groundbreaking work of Betz, *Galatians.*

14. In these points, but not in others, I agree with the critique of Deissmann offered by Stanley K. Stowers, *Letter Writing in Greco-Roman Antiquity* (Philadelphia: Westminster, 1986), 18–21. Stowers discounts the importance of the papyrus letters for our study of Paul in obvious preference for the philosophical traditions. I am a bit less certain of the value of this dichotomy. Stowers has argued, for example that the papyrus letters coming from small, remote provincial Egyptian towns were quite unlike those one might unearth in a "trash heap or private archive from Ephesus or Corinth" (19). So Stowers is less impressed by the form, content, and function of the papyrus letters from Egypt than he is by the letters from the great Hellenistic urban areas that were centers of high culture. The philosophical emphasis in those centers on the ideals of friendship, client-patron relationships, and familial ethos and language is, he thinks, a more fitting context for the consideration of the Pauline letters. I, however, am less certain than he that those emphases, even in their subtle and nuanced forms, would not have penetrated provincial towns throughout the delta. Moreover, the letter form of the papyrus letters is highly instructive for our study of the Pauline letters, as we shall see subsequently.

15. See Klaus Berger, "Hellenistische Gattungen im Neuen Testament," in *ANRW,* vol. II, 25.2, 1326–63.

16. See ibid., 1336, 1339.

17. Also important for this consideration are the works of Abraham J. Malherbe, *The Cynic Epistles, A Study Edition* (Missoula: Scholars Press, 1977), and Harold W.

Attridge, *First- Century Cynicism in the Epistles of Heraclitus: Introduction, Greek Text and Translation* (Missoula: Scholars Press, 1976).

18. Malherbe, *The Cynic Epistles,* 38–39.
19. Ibid., 64–65.
20. Ibid., 178–79.
21. Ibid., 76–77.
22. In his "Hellenistische Gattungen im Neuen Testament," 1338, Klaus Berger says, "What is decisive here is the meaning of what is communicated [in the letters] for the relationship between the sender and the receiver. In this [relationship], the writer, as the sole spoken voice in the letter, has a genre-specific advantage of authority. It is often this authority that first determines the worthiness of any particular content being communicated."
23. See Malherbe, *The Cynic Epistles,* 38–39, 64–65, 76–77, 178–79. For example: "Εὐμόλπῳ" (to Eumolpus), "Τοῖς νέοις" (to the youths), "Τοῖς ἑταίροις" (to the students), "Ἀντιπάτρῳ" (to Antipater), "Κράτητι" (to Crates), and so on.
24. Stowers, *Letter Writing in Greco-Roman Antiquity,* 25.
25. See Dennis Pardee, "Hebrew Letters," *ABD,* vol. IV, 282–85, and Paul E. Dion, "Aramaic Letters," *ABD,* vol. IV, 285–90.
26. From Ostracon III, *Ancient Near Eastern Texts,* 322.
27. See Pardee, "Hebrew Letters," 283.
28. Paul E. Dion, "Aramaic Letters," 287, 289. See, for example, the Egyptian family letter: "Greetings, House of Banit in Assuan! To my lord Psami, your servant Makkibanit. I bless you by Ptah, that he may allow me to see your face in well-being [or peace]."
29. White, *Light from Ancient Letters,* 201.
30. John L. White, "New Testament Epistolary Literature in the Framework of Ancient Epistolography," *ANRW,* II, 25.2, 1739.
31. See, for example, Nils A. Dahl, "Letters," in *IDB,* ed. Keith Crim, supplementary vol. (Nashville: Abingdon Press, 1976), 539—"The purpose of letters is in general (*a*) to maintain contacts." Also Stowers, "Greek and Latin Letters," 290: "Three important characteristics of the letter are its occasionality, its *fiction of personal presence*" (emphasis added), or Klaus Berger, "Hellenistische Gattungen im Neuen Testament," 1329, "Letters are a substitute for presence." These points of view are not so different from those of Artemon (as Pseudo-Demetrius states), the collector and editor of the letters of Aristotle, who recognized that "the letter should be a worthy substitute for one's conversation, [and] the theorists advise that one speak to the absent party as though he were actually present" (*On Style,* sec. 227). See also the very provocative work of Heikki Koskenniemi, *Studien zur Idee und Phraseologie des griechischen Briefes bis 400 n. Chr.* (Helsinki: Akateeminen Kirjakauppa, 1956), 88: "It is the nature of the letter that it provides not only a means [for conveying] information, or a vehicle for all that which one wants to execute, but at the same time [provides] a connecting link, a form of intercourse between persons who are physically separated from one another."
32. Pseudo-Demetrius, *On Style.*

33. See Robert W. Funk, "The Apostolic Parousia: Form and Significance," in *Christian History and Interpretation: Studies Presented to John Knox*, ed. W. R. Farmer, C. F. D. Moule, and R. R. Niebuhr (Cambridge: At the University Press, 1967), 249, 266.

34. "The Apostolic Parousia," 249.

35. On this point I hope I am in agreement with Hays, *The Faith of Jesus Christ*, 265–66.

36. See Stowers, *Letter Writing in Greco-Roman Antiquity*, 51–173.

37. Ibid., 114.

38. Ibid., 77–152.

39. Ibid., 142.

40. The context of this reference argues against Stowers's view that Paul like other writers "eased the sting of death by calling it sleep." Ibid., 145.

41. G. A. Kennedy, *The Art of Persuasion in Greece* (London: Longman, 1963); G. A. Kennedy, *The Art of Rhetoric in the Roman World* (Princeton: Princeton University Press, 1972); G. A. Kennedy, *New Testament Interpretation through Rhetorical Criticism* (Chapel Hill: University of North Carolina Press, 1984).

42. David E. Aune, *The New Testament in Its Literary Environment* (Philadelphia: Westminster, 1977), 160–61.

43. See Betz, *Paulinische Studien: Gesammelte Aufsätze III*, essay number IV.

44. For example, see Robert A. Jewett, *The Thessalonian Correspondence. Pauline Rhetoric and Millenarian Piety* (Philadelphia: Fortress Press, 1986); Margaret M. Mitchell, *Paul and the Rhetoric of Reconciliation. An Exegetical Investigation of the Language and Composition of 1 Corinthians* (Tübingen: J. C. B. Mohr [Paul Siebeck], 1991; Louisville: Westminster/John Knox Press, 1992); Rudolf Pesch, *Paulus ringt um die Lebensform der Kirche. Vier Briefe an die Gemeinde Gottes in Korinth* (Freiburg: Herder, 1986); W. H. Wuellner, "Paul's Rhetoric of Argumentation in Romans: An Alternative to the Donfried-Karris Debate over Romans," *CBQ* 36 (1976), 330–51; W. H. Wuellner, "Greek Rhetoric and Pauline Argumentation," in *Early Christian Literature and the Classical Tradition*, ed. W. R. Schoedel and R. L. Wilken (Paris: Editions Beauchesne, 1979), 177–88; W. H. Wuellner, "Paul as Pastor. The Function of Rhetorical Questions in First Corinthians," in *L'apôtre Paul. Personnalité, style et conception du ministère*, ed. A. Vanhoye (Leuven: Peeters, 1986), 49–77; M. Bachmann, *Sünder oder Übertreter. Studien zur Argumentation in Gal 2, 15ff.* (Tübingen: J. C. B. Mohr [Paul Siebeck], 1991), are a sample from a broader offering in this area.

45. See David E. Aune's review of Betz's commentary on Galatians in the *RSR* 7 (1981), 323–28.

46. See Aune's review of Betz's commentary on Galatians in the *RSR* 7 (1981), 326.

47. See Jewett, *The Thessalonian Correspondence*, 72–76, 221, and Kennedy, *New Testament Interpretation*, 142–44.

48. See Pesch, *Paulus ringt um die Lebensform der Kirche*.

49. See W. H. Wuellner, "Where Is Rhetorical Criticism Taking Us?" *CBQ* 49 (1987), 460, and Kennedy, *New Testament Interpretation*, 87, 93.

50. See Jerome Murphy-O'Connor, *Paul the Letter-Writer: His World, His Options, His Skills* (Collegeville: The Liturgical Press, 1995), 80–85.

51. Stowers, *Letter Writing in Greco-Roman Antiquity,* 52.
52. See Aune, *The New Testament in Its Literary Environment,* 158.
53. See John L. White, *Light from Ancient Letters,* 53, from the first century B.C.E.
54. For the entire letter see my *The Letters of Paul. Conversations in Context,* 60.
55. Of course, it would be misleading to think of Paul's letters as private correspondence. In four of the seven undisputed letters Paul is joined in the salutation by others. Timothy appears with him in 2 Cor. 1:1; Phil. 1:1; and Philem. 1:1; and Silvanus and Timothy in 1 Thess. 1:1.
56. Murphy-O'Connor, *Paul the Letter-Writer,* 47.
57. In this Paul is certainly not unique. From the first century b.c.e we hear a person who identifies himself by name and profession address a group of mummy dressers in Egypt: "Athenagoras, *the chief physician,* to the *priests of the stolistai* at the Labyrinth" (emphasis added). See White, *Light from Ancient Letters,* 101.
58. See Murphy-O'Connor, *Paul the Letter-Writer,* 50.
59. See ibid., 51.
60. See Paul Schubert, *The Form and Function of the Pauline Thanksgivings* (Berlin: Alred Töpelmann, 1939).
61. Of course, Schubert was the first to notice the form and function of the Pauline thanksgiving, and while his thesis has been refined it has never been refuted. See his *The Form and Function of the Pauline Thanksgivings.*
62. See White, *Light from Ancient Letters;* White, "New Testament Epistolary Literature," 1730–56; Stowers, *Letter Writing in Greco-Roman Antiquity* ; Stowers, "Greek and Latin Letters"; Dahl, "Letters," 538–41; William G. Doty, *Letters in Primitive Christianity;* Robert W. Funk, "The Letter: Form and Style," in *Language, Hermeneutic, and the Word of God* (New York: Harper & Row, 1966), 250–74; Funk, "The Apostolic Parousia," 249–68.
63. Joseph A. Fitzmyer, *Romans. A New Translation with Introduction and Commentary* (New York: Doubleday, 1993), 243.
64. James D. G. Dunn, *Romans 1–8* (Dallas: Word Books, 1988), 27.
65. This last proposal has the advantage of including 1:16–17 with 1:15 their clear antecedent. Moreover, if 1:16–17 is a thematic statement for the entire letter and the purpose of the thanksgiving is to signal the topics to be discussed, it would not be too much of a stretch to include these verses in the thanksgiving.
66. Schubert, *The Form and Function of the Pauline Thanksgivings,* 5–6.
67. See ibid., 89, where he notes that every one of the thanksgivings has a parenetic function.
68. See also 1 Thess. 2:1, "For you yourselves know (οἴδατε), brothers and sisters," 2 Cor. 1:8, "For we do not want you to be ignorant, brothers and sisters," and Philem. 8–9, "For this reason, though I am bold enough in Christ to command you to do your duty, yet I would rather appeal to you (παρακαλῶ) on the basis of love" (NRSV).
69. Carl J. Bjerkelund, *Parakalô. Form, Funktion und Sinn der parakalô-Sätze in den paulinischen Briefen* (Oslo: Universitetsforlaget, 1967), offers a comprehensive treatment of the *Parakalô* form used throughout the Pauline letters.
70. For example, see Lyons, *Pauline Autobiography,* 177–218.

71. Ibid., 123–76.
72. Victor Paul Furnish, *Theology and Ethics in Paul* (Nashville: Abingdon Press, 1968), 68–111, made this oft recognized point.
73. See my *The Letters of Paul*, 67.
74. Abraham J. Malherbe, "Exhortation in 1 Thessalonians," *NT* 25 (1983), 238–56, classes 1 Thessalonians as a parenetic letter.
75. This view is now common knowledge since the displacement of Martin Dibelius's older view that Paul's paraenesis was "not formulated for special churches and concrete cases, but for the general requirements of earliest Christendom." See his *From Tradition to Gospel*, trans. Bertram Lee Woolf (New York: Charles Scribner's Sons, 1935), 38.
76. Funk, "The Apostolic Parousia," 249–268.
77. See ibid., 249.
78. See ibid., 266.
79. David G. Bradley, "The Topos as a Form in the Pauline Paraenesis," *JBL* 72 (1953), 246.
80. As the perfect passive imperative of ῥώννυμι, which by Paul's day had fallen into disuse, ἔρρωσο was a standard feature of the papyrus letter. See F. X. J. Exler, *The Form of the Ancient Greek Letter. A Study of Greek Epistolography* (Washington: Catholic University of America, 1923).
81. See my *Judgement in the Community. A Study of the Relationship between Eschatalogy and Ecclesiology in Paul* (Leiden: E. J. Brill, 1972), 145–47, 161. Also, Murphy-O'Connor, *Paul the Letter-Writer*, 108, who quite appropriately takes issue with the view that the "holy kiss" liturgically signaled the beginning of the Eucharist after the public reading of the letter.

CHAPTER FOUR: THE THEOLOGIZER

1. James D. G. Dunn is perhaps the most eloquent defender of this view, but certainly he is not alone. See his "In Quest of Paul's Theology: Retrospect and Prospect," in *Society of Biblical Literature 1995 Seminar Papers*, ed. Eugene H. Lovering, Jr. (Atlanta: Scholars Press, 1995), 713, in which he says "the most obvious place to locate oneself within the dialogue of Paul's theology is in Romans itself."
2. I use the word *composed* to cover both the physical writing and the dictation of letters. Also, in its root sense of course theo-logia θεο-λογια refers to thinking about, pondering, or reflecting on god or the gods.
3. Repeatedly I resort to the use of words like *evolve* and *develop* to refer to the process taking place when Paul theologized. There is some risk in thinking of this development as naturally evolutionary as if it were automatic once set in motion. Such a conclusion would do a disservice to Paul; it would undervalue the struggle required of Paul to understand the new life of the elect in Christ that was set in motion by his apocalyptic gospel. And it would falsely presume that the outcome is already determined by the beginning point. Although Paul was

absolutely convinced that God was doing something radically new and that God was in control of the outcome of history, his own place in that great cosmic drama was in the process of being improvised in the light of each new set of realities, and Paul could not presume the outcome that we now see with some clarity. Rather I use the word to refer to the way Paul's confrontation with challengers and competitors and the internal disputes of churches stimulated the development of his thinking, fostered fresh combinations, and sparked new theological formulations. To us they may appear as "higher," for they prevailed, but to his opposition they may have had quite a different appearance.

4. Steven J. Kraftchick, "Seeking a More Fluid Model: A Response to Jouette M. Bassler," *Pauline Theology,* vol. II: *1 and 2 Corinthians,* ed. David M. Hay (Minneapolis: Fortress Press, 1993), 24. Often it is in the process of writing that we learn what we think.

5. *The Faith of Jesus Christ,* 264–66.

6. I especially note the temptation to take Romans as the most mature, developed, and comprehensive statement of Paul's theology as the theological template for synthesizing Paul's theological activity in all of his other letters.

7. Readers will recognize an echo here of a statement from Michel Foucault, *The Archeology of Knowledge,* trans. A. M. Sheridan Smith (New York: Pantheon Books, 1972), 25, as he there says, "all these syntheses that are accepted without question, must remain in suspense. They must not be rejected definitively of course, but the tranquility with which they are accepted must be disturbed."

8. I am mostly in agreement with Victor Paul Furnish, *Jesus according to Paul* (Cambridge: Cambridge University Press, 1993).

9. On this basic point see my *The Letters of Paul. Conversations in Context,* chap. 4.

10. Roetzel, "The Grammar of Election in Four Pauline Letters," 215.

11. In order to be able to track the emergence of Paul's theology we recognize the need for a credible chronology of Paul's letters. While absolute certainty about the order of some of the letters is impossible to ascertain, we can operate within certain parameters. A scholarly consensus recognizes 1 Thessalonians as Paul's first letter, and most think Romans was the last. We shall argue for a relatively early placement of Philippians and a location of Galatians within a year of the writing of 1 Corinthians. At least some of the Corinthian correspondence would then fall between Galatians and Romans.

12. The exact chronology of these events is uncertain. Betz, *Galatians,* 83–84, correctly notes the ambiguity of Paul's statement after his first Jerusalem visit that "*then* after fourteen years again I went up to Jerusalem with Barnabas" (emphasis added). It is impossible to say with certainty whether the adverb *then* refers to his first visit to Jerusalem or his call to be an apostle.

13. The Acts 17 report that Paul spent three weeks disputing in the synagogue and a bit longer in the city at large before the "Jews" stirred up "the rabble" who created such an uproar that Paul and his co-workers were forced to leave the city is a stereotypical scenario that finds no support in Paul's letters. For an account of differing positions on Paul's stay in Thessalonica see Gerd Lüdemann, *Paulus*

der Heidenapostel, vol. I (Göttingen: Vandenhoeck & Ruprecht, 1980), 203–4. In any case, Paul's stay in Thessalonica was probably a short one, that is, weeks long.

14. Space limitations prohibit a full discussion of Paul's theological activity in each and every letter. We have chosen to deal with Paul's concern with issues of identity that are broad enough for us to gain some appreciation of the range of Paul's theological activity and narrow enough to allow some treatment in depth. Even more narrowly we shall focus on issues related to gentile participation in the people of God. To the critic who argues that this choice is arbitrary and offers no improvement over the synthetic treatment of Paul's theology, I would emphatically disagree. As the Apostle to the Gentiles, Paul faced challenges from without and within. Inevitably, issues of self-definition and self-understanding surfaced in his letters to gentile Christians, and vigorous challenges from Jewish Christian apostles to Paul's apostleship and his gospel required fresh thinking. As a substitute for his presence Paul's letters attempt to correct misunderstandings, to encourage the despondent, to silence critics, to deal with questions, to reconcile factions, and to offer ethical instruction. All of these functions in one way or another address issues of the identity, destiny, and ethos of the people of God.

15. See John L. White, "God's Paternity as Root Metaphor in Paul's Conception of Community," *Forum* 8 (1992), 271–95.

16. Norman R. Petersen, *Rediscovering Paul, Philemon and the Sociology of Paul's Narrative World* (Philadelphia: Fortress Press, 1985), 237.

17. See White, "God's Paternity as Root Metaphor," 282.

18. See Deissmann, *Paul: A Study in Social and Religious History,* 135. Although his views so forcefully articulated brought public ridicule and fierce challenges, he was hardly the first to make this point. Richard Reitzenstein, *Die Hellenistischen Mysterienreligionen nach ihren Grundgedanken und Wirkungen,* 3d ed. (Leipzig: B. G. Teubner, 1927; 1st ed. 1909), and Johannes Weiss, "Paulinische Probleme, 2. Die Formel ἐν χριστῷ Ἰησοῦ," in *TSK* (1896) and Wilhelm Bousset, *Kurios Christos: A History of the Belief in Christ from the Beginnings of Christianity to Irenaeus,* trans. John E. Steely (Nashville: Abingdon Press, 1979; first published in German in 1913) were all moving in the same direction.

19. See Deissmann, *Paul,* 143.

20. See ibid., 150.

21. See preceding discussion on Jesus.

22. Largely in reaction to Deissmann, and later Schweitzer, scholars emphasized either the juridical or mystical aspects of Paul's thought but rarely both. The view taken here is that there were important linkages between both concepts and choosing the one does not require the rejection of the other.

23. See Albert Schweitzer, *The Mysticism of Paul the Apostle,* trans. William Montgomery (London: Adam & Charles Black, 1967 [first Eng. ed. 1931]), viii.

24. Ibid., 138.

25. Ibid., 125.

26. E. P. Sanders, *Paul and Palestinian Judaism,* 462–63.

27. Peter Berger, *The Sacred Canopy, Elements of a Sociological Theory of Religion* (Garden City, NY: Doubleday, 1969), 40, where he notes that one of the functions of ritual, and we would add teaching, is to remind people of what they are prone to forget. As he notes, "They must . . . be reminded over and over again."

28. I am persuaded on this point made by Schweitzer, *Mysticism,* 122–23.

29. See John C. Hurd, Jr., *The Origin of 1 Corinthians* (New York: Seabury Press, 1965), 284, and Martin Dibelius, *An die Thessalonicher I, II, An die Philipper,* 2d ed. (Tübingen: J. C. B. Mohr [Paul Siebeck], 1923), 23–28.

30. Lüdemann, *Paul, Apostle to the Gentiles,* 212. Lüdemann follows Günter Klein, "Apokalyptische Naherwartung bei Paulus," in *Neues Testament und christliche Existenz: Festschrift für Herbert Braun zum 70. Geburtstag,* ed. Hans Dieter Betz and L. Schottroff (Tübingen: J. C. B. Mohr [Paul Siebeck], 1973), 245, n. 22.

31. Lüdemann, *Paul, Apostle to the Gentiles,* 225–31.

32. See 2 Baruch 13:3; 76:2 and Ethiopic Enoch 70–17 for references to the apocalyptic rescue of the righteous remnant. The cloud motif is well known from Dan. 7:13 as well as the idea of the resurrection of the just (Dan. 12:1–3). See also 4 Ezra 13.

33. Paul does not, as Koester suggests, totally demythologize the apocalyptic symbolism with his emphasis on faith, love and hope "as the presence of eternity." See Helmut Koester, "I Thessalonians—Experiment in Christian Writing," in *Continuity and Discontinuity in Church History: Essays Presented to George H. Williams* (Leiden: E. J. Brill, 1979), 44.

34. Here, I agree completely with Gerd Lüdemann, *Paul, Apostle to the Gentiles,* 213.

35. Twenty-three times in this short letter Paul refers to Jesus as *kurios.* The idiomatic nature of the term *lord* in the Hellenistic world and its popularity in Hellenistic Jewish circles certainly illumine Paul's use of the term, but they do not fully explain its meaning. In Hellenistic popular religion the term designated powerful divine figures such as Isis, Asclepius, and Chronos and rulers such as Augustus, Herod, and Agrippa. (See "κύριος," in *TDNT,* vol. III, 1039–95), and it also was used as a title of respect to a superior meaning something like "sir." The LXX followed this tendency by using the term both as a translation of Yahweh and a form of honorific address. Paul's usage, however, was distinctive in the way it was used as an apocalyptic title of Jesus (3:13; 4:6, 15:16, 17; 5:2, 23) and as the one who suffered and died (1:6).

36. In *"Theodidaktoi* [the God taught] and Handwork in Philo and 1 Thessalonians," in *L'apôtre Paul, personnalité, style et conception du ministère,* ed. A. Vanhoye (Leuven: Leuven University Press, 1986), 330, I argued that the waiting that Paul admonishes is active. One should maintain the respect of outsiders, be sober and alert as one keeps oneself in readiness for the end, work with one's hands, and seek to be dependent on no one (4:12; 5:6).

37. For a nice summary see Jonathan Z. Smith, "Differential Equations: On Constructing the 'Other' " a lecture printed and distributed by the Arizona State University Department of Religious Studies.

38. See Smith, "Differential Equations," 3.
39. While θλῖψις in its root sense refers to pressure and can mean tribulation or affliction, the context here suggests that it connotes persecution. See Heinrich Schlier, "θλίβω, θλῖψις," *TDNT,* vol. III, 147.
40. On the importance of the imperial cult in Thessalonica, I find Holland Hendrix's work convincing: "Thessalonians Honor Romans" (Harvard Th.D. Thesis, 1984).
41. I agree with Dieter Lührmann, "The Beginnings of the Church at Thessalonica," in *Greeks, Romans, and Christians. Essays in Honor of Abraham J. Malherbe,* ed. David L. Balch, Everett Ferguson, and Wayne A. Meeks (Minneapolis: Fortress Press, 1990), 243, who thinks the reference to "compatriots" (συμφυλετῶν, 2:14) refers to Gentiles, not Jews as Acts suggests (17:5–10).
42. See Karl Donfried, "The Cults of Thessalonica and the Thessalonian Correspondence," *NTS* 31 (1985), 336–56, and "The Theology of 1 Thessalonians as a Reflection of its Purpose," a paper prepared for the "Pauline Theology Consultation" (S83, 1986). Donfried's conclusions are similar to those of John S. Pobee, *Persecution and Martyrdom in the Theology of Paul* (Sheffield: JSOT Press, 1985), and F. F. Bruce, *The Acts of the Apostles* (Grand Rapids, MI: Eerdmans, 1951), 327–28.
43. See Donfried, "The Cults of Thessalonica."
44. Note that the NRSV translators offer quite a different translation of this passage to have Paul address both women and men: "For this is the will of God, your sanctification: that *each one of you know how to control your own body in holiness and honor, not with lustful passion, like the Gentiles who do not know God*" (4:3–5, emphasis added) While I personally would prefer this gender-neutral application, the Greek does not allow for it. The more literal rendering has instead: "let each one of you know how to take a vessel (σκεῦος) [RSV wife] for himself."
45. See my "No 'Race of Israel' in Paul," in *Putting Body & Soul Together. Essays in Honor of Robin Scroggs,* ed. Virginia Wiles, Alexandra Brown, and Graydon F. Snyder (Valley Forge: Trinity International Press, 1997), 230–44.
46. In this case I find Acts 18:11 credible. The ministry in the city and the countryside would take a more extended period than he spent in Thessalonica.
47. I find Joseph A. Fitzmyer's argument persuasive that the dates of Gallio's proconsulship were 52–53 rather than 51–52. Moreover, his evidence is compelling that Gallio did not serve the whole year in 52–53 but left in the fall because of illness before the shipping season closed. See his "The Pauline Letters," in *According to Paul: Studies in the Theology of the Apostle* (New York: Paulist Press, 1993), 46.
48. They would be Galatians, the four Corinthian letters, Philemon, and three letters to the Philippians. That Philippians contains fragments of three letters is, however, disputed.
49. See "Excursus on Pauline Chronology" (pp. 178–83 above) for a more complete accounting.
50. See, for example, Victor Paul Furnish, "Theology in 1 Corinthians," in *Pauline Theology,* vol. II: *1 and 2 Corinthians,* ed. David M. Hay (Minneapolis: Fortress Press, 1993), 59–89.

51. Note the twenty-one references to ecstatic speech in chapters 12–14.

52. A voluminous secondary literature exists on this topic, and most agree the wisdom being claimed is salvific in some sense.

53. See S. Scott Bartchy, *MAΛΛON XPHΣAI: First-Century Slavery and the Interpretation of 1 Corinthians 7:21* (Missoula: Scholars Press, 1973).

54. Note also 1 Cor. 8:1–3, where Paul also emphasizes the upbuilding character of love and relates it both to loving God and being "known by him." Likewise, a sin or loveless act toward "a member of your family" (8:12; NRSV), Paul writes, is a sin against Christ. Furnish argues that Paul anchors human love in the love of God mediated through Christ, and, therefore, the love Paul commends to the Corinthians "is nothing else than God's love as disclosed in Christ." However, as correct as this sounds theologically, it finds no explicit articulation in 1 Corinthians. God's ownership is explicit in 3:23—"you are Christ's and Christ is God's"—and to be in Christ is to be in the body of Christ characterized by love, but the suggestion that genuine human love comes from God mediated through Christ is at best only implied in 1 Corinthians. See Furnish, "Theology in 1 Corinthians," 88.

55. Ernst Käsemann, "The Pauline Doctrine of the Lord's Supper," in *Essays on New Testament Themes,* trans. W. J. Montague (Philadelphia: Fortress Press, 1964), 118–19.

56. Günther Bornkamm, *Die Vorgeschichte des sogenannten zweiten Korintherbriefes* (Heidelberg: Winter 1961); also appearing in his *Geschichte und Glaube II, Gesammelte Aufsätze* IV (Munich: Kaiser, 1971), 162–94. A somewhat more accessible treatment for English readers offers a shorter synopsis: Günther Borntamm, "The History of the Origin of the So-Called Second Letter to the Corinthians," *NTS* 8 (1962), 258–63. Arranged in order they are: (1) 2:14–6:13; 7:2–4, an apology; (2) 10:1–13:10, the "tearful letter"; (3) 1:1–2:13; 7:5–16; 13:11–13; and possibly chap. 8, a "letter of reconciliation"; (4) chap. 9, a letter to churches in Achaia, and (5) 6:14–7:1, a non-Pauline interpolation. Chapter 8, Bornkamm allows, may have been a separate letter.

57. Walter Schmithals, "Die Korintherbriefe als Briefsammlung," *ZNW* 64 (1973), 275–88. Arranged sequentially they are: (1) 6:14–7:1; (2) 2:14–6:2; (3) 6:3–13; 7:2–4; (4) 10–13; (5) chap. 9; (6) 1:1–2:13; 7:5–8:24.

58. Hans Dieter Betz, "Corinthians, Second Epistle to the," in *ABD,* vol. I, 1149–50. Betz offers a masterful summary of partition theories in his *2 Corinthians 8 and 9. A Commentary on Two Administrative Letters of the Apostle Paul* (Philadelphia: Fortress Press, 1985), 3–36. Betz follows Bornkamm's partition of the letter almost exactly.

59. Anton Halmel, *Der Zweite Korintherbrief des Apostels Paulus. Geschichte und literarkritische Untersuchungen* (Halle: Niemeyer, 1904), found evidence of three letters in 2 Corinthians: (1) 1:1–2; 1:8–2:13; 7:5–8:24; 13:13; (2) 10:1–13:10; (3) 1:3–7; 1:14–7:4; 9:1–15; 13:11–12. Note that he omitted 3:12–18; 4:3–4, 6; 6:14–7:1 as non-Pauline interpolations. Johannes Weiss, *Earliest Christianity,* trans. F. C. Grant (New York: Harper, 1959), 323–57, suggested the following partition: (1) 2:14–6:13 and 7:2–4 plus chapters 10–13, "the tear-

ful letter"; (2) 6:14–7:1 and parts of 1 Corinthians make up the missing letter mentioned in 1 Cor. 5:9, (3) chapter 8 and early letter sent with Titus on his first solo visit commissioned by Paul, and (4) chapter 9 and 1:1–2:13 plus 7:4–16 was Paul's final letter to Corinth also sent by Titus.

60. See Adolf Hausrath, *Der Vier-Capitel-Brief des Paulus an die Korinther* (Heidelberg: Bassermann, 1870).

61. Adolf Hausrath, *Neutestamentliche Zeitgeschichte. 3: Die Zeit der Apostel II*, 2d ed. (Heidelberg: Bassermann, 1875), 302–14.

62. Furnish, *II Corinthians*, 35–48.

63. See Betz, "Corinthians, Second Epistle to the," 1150.

64. Georgi, *The Opponents of Paul in Second Corinthians.*

65. Please note that of fifty-five references to boasting in the undisputed Pauline letters, twenty-nine appear in 2 Corinthians.

66. See my "'As Dying, and Behold We Live,'" 5–18.

67. Nils A. Dahl, "Paul and Possessions," in *Studies in Paul. Theology for the Early Christian Mission* (Minneapolis: Augsburg, 1977), 37–38.

68. Ibid., 37–38.

69. I am indebted to Victor Furnish for this phraseology. See his *II Corinthians*, 401, for example.

70. Bengt Holmberg, *Paul and Power: The Structure of Authority in the Primitive Church as Reflected in the Pauline Epistles* (Philadelphia: Fortress Press, 1978).

71. Munck, *Paul and the Salvation of Mankind*, 303.

72. Dieter Georgi, *Remembering the Poor. The History of Paul's Collection for Jerusalem* (Nashville: Abingdon Press, 1965), 37.

73. W. M. Franklin, *Die Kollekte des Paulus* (Scottsdale, PA: Mennonite Publishing House, 1938).

74. Schweitzer, *Mysticism*, 3–4.

75. E. P. Sanders, *Paul and Palestinian Judaism*, 466.

76. Suetonius, "Claudius," 25 in *The Lives of the Twelve Caesars.*

77. Note, for example, that Robert A. Jewett, *A Chronology of Paul's Life* (Philadelphia: Fortress Press, 1979), in his graph of dates, places Galatians in either 53 or less probably 54 before all of the letters save those to Thessalonica. Appealing to Gal. 1:6 and Paul's expression of astonishment "that you are *so quickly* deserting the one who called you in the grace of Christ" (emphasis added) suggests to many an early date, like that of Jewett, for Galatians, but Betz, *Galatians*, 47–48, is more cautious, noting that the reference to "so quickly" "should not be used too quickly to date the letter. The words would make little sense, to be sure, if a considerable length of time had passed since the founding of the churches, but that is about all one can say." Others, however, noting the development of thought that has taken place from Galatians to Romans and not between Galatians and any of the other letters, would date the letter relatively late. Furnish, *II Corinthians*, 55, places the letter as late as 56 as Paul was on his way to Corinth for the last time and, therefore, shortly before the writing of Romans. The difficulty with this date, however, is that it allows insufficient time for the opposition to Paul's position taken in Galatians to congeal, to raise questions, and to force the

response from Paul that we see in Romans. In short, there is absolutely no way to know with certainty when the letter was written. The best we can do is to say it was written between 53 and 56.

78. Petersen, *Rediscovering Paul,* 206–70. More recently John L. White has offered a highly suggestive look at Paul's kinship metaphors, but again it is weakened by a synoptic view that mushes together metaphors from different letters without taking note of their differing valences from letter to letter. See his "God's Paternity as Root Metaphor," 271–95.

79. Betz, *Galatians,* 186.

80. See ibid., 158.

81. I side here with Betz, *Galatians,* 323, who says that there is no doubt that Paul makes a distinction here between the "true" and the "false" Israel.

82. Some of these same points I have made elsewhere in "Sacrifice in Romans 12–15," 413.

83. Scholars have noted that Paul's view of law in Galatians is almost totally negative, and at first glance that would appear to be so. There is no reference in Galatians to "the law of God" (Rom. 7:25; 8:7), to the holiness or goodness of the law (Rom. 7:12, 16), to the holiness and goodness of the commandment (Rom. 7:12), to the spirituality of the law (Rom. 7:14), to the knowledge and truth coming from the law (Rom. 2:20), to the righteousness of the law (Rom. 2:26), or to the witness of the Law and the Prophets (Rom. 3:21). At one level Paul's angry polemic aiming to confute the Judaizers paints the law as negatively as possible. Yet, on the other hand, there *are* positive sides of the law as well in Galatians. He finds in the law the example of Abraham, who authorizes his "law-free" gospel to the Gentiles. He cites the love commandment of Lev. 19:18 (LXX) as a summary of the whole law that receives expression in the fruits of the spirit (5:22–26). He views law as an important interim disciplinary measure until Israel has reached its majority (3:19–20). He emphatically states that the law is not opposed to the promises of God (3:21). If the law has a positive side, then why does Paul scold the Galatians for law observance? Paul attacks the imposition of law observance as a supplement that subverted the sufficiency of his gospel and as a condition for gentile participation in the people of God.

84. There is no support whatsoever in the Greek text for the negative reading "*only* a remnant" of the NRSV. The reference might just as easily be read in a positive sense "a remnant of them *will* be saved."

85. P. W. Meyer, "Romans," in *Harper's Bible Commentary,* ed. James L. Mays, Joseph Blekinsopp, Jon D. Levenson, Wayne A. Meeks, Carol A. Newsom, David L. Petersen (San Francisco: Harpers, 1988), 1157 thinks that "it" refers to Torah. John G. Gager, *The Origins of Anti-Semitism: Attitudes toward Judaism in Pagan and Christian Antiquity* (New York: Oxford University Press, 1983), 252 thinks that Israel stumbled over Paul's gentile gospel. Fitzmyer, *Romans,* 580, shares the traditional view that the stumbling block was Christ in spite of the fact that there is no reference to Christ in the context.

86. Diogenes Laertius, *Lives of the Eminent Philosophers,* trans. R. D. Hicks, LCL, 2 vols. (Cambridge: Harvard University Press, and London: Heinemann, 1965),

VI 70; Dio Chrysostom, trans. J. H. Cohoon and H. L. Crosby, LCL, 2 vols. (Cambridge: Harvard University Press, and London: Heinemann, 1932–1951), *Or.*, XXVIII 535.

87. Note the example of Hercules used to reinforce this effort: Epictetus, *The Discourses as Reported by Arrian,* trans. H. A. Oldfather, LCL, 2 vols. (Cambridge: Harvard University Press, and London: Heinemann, 1925–28), III, 22:57; 26:31; and IV 10:10.

88. Stanley K. Stowers, *A Rereading of Romans. Justice, Jews, and Gentiles* (New Haven: Yale University Press, 1994), 314–16.

89. Sanders, *Paul,* 125 notes how Paul shifts the grounds for the discussion in 11:25–27 and expands the circle of salvation to include all people in 11:32: "For God has imprisoned all in disobedience so that he may be merciful to all."

90. See my "*Oikoumene* and the Limits of Pluralism," 181.

91. Justin Martyr, *Dialogue with Trypho, The Apologies of Justin Martyr* (New York: Harper and Brothers, 1877), 47.

92. *Selected Letters of St. Jerome,* trans. F. A. Wright. LCL (Cambridge: Harvard University Press, 1963), 112.13.

93. For this understanding of the righteousness of God I acknowledge my debt to Ernst Käsemann, "God's Righteousness in Paul," in *The Bultmann School of Biblical Interpretation: New Directions?* ed. James M. Robinson (New York: Harper & Row, and Tübingen: J. C. B. Mohr [Paul Siebeck], 1965), 100–110. In the German the essay appeared as "Gottesgerechtigkeit bei Paulus," *ZThK* 58 (1961), 367–78.

94. See Troels Engberg-Pedersen, "Proclaiming the Lord's Death: 1 Corinthians 11:17–34 and the Forms of Paul's Theological Argument," *Pauline Theology,* vol. II, 106.

95. P. W. Meyer, "Pauline Theology: Some Thoughts for a Pause in Its Pursuit," in *Society of Biblical Literature 1995 Seminar Papers,* ed. Eugene H. Lovering, Jr. (Atlanta: Scholars Press, 1995), 697.

CHAPTER FIVE: "THE MODEL ASCETIC"

1. This apt title was fixed on Paul by Wayne A. Meeks, *The Writings of St. Paul,* 193.

2. J. Moussaieff Masson, "The Psychology of the Ascetic," *JAS* 35 (1976), 611–25.

3. There are notable exceptions to this view, for example, Hurd, *The Origin of First Corinthians,* 154–69.

4. Joachim Jeremias, "War Paulus Witwer?" *ZNW* 25 (1926), 310–12, argued that Paul followed rabbinic tradition, marrying between eighteen and twenty, but since he nowhere mentions her in his letters, his wife probably died before his "conversion." Jeremias's position was disputed by E. Fascher, "Zur Witwerschaft des Paulus und der Auslegung von 1 Cor. 7," *ZNW* 28 (1929), 62–69, who felt Jeremias's use of late rabbinic materials to interpret Paul's singleness was anachronistic, and who argued that 1 Cor. 7:1 ("It is well for a man not to touch

a woman") could not have come from Paul's rabbinic phase and that Paul's commendation of celibacy to virgins would have had no force whatever if Paul had been married. Jeremias responded in 1931, but the public discussion ended there.

5. Kittel and Bromiley, *TDNT,* vol. II, 342.

6. See Jean Gribomont, "Askese: Neues Testament und Alte Kirche," in *Theologische Realenzyklopädie,* ed. Gerhard Krause and Gerhard Müller. (Berlin: Walter de Gruyter, 1979), vol. IV, 206.

7. K. G. Kuhn, "Askese im Judentum," in *Die Religion in Geschichte und Gegenwart,* 3d ed. (Tübingen: J. C. B. Mohr [Paul Siebeck], 1957–62), vol. 1, cols. 639–47, esp.col. 641, where he says, "Still all of that is not asceticism in a real sense, but simply a pious exercise."

8. Otto Michel, "Wie Spricht Paulus über Frau and Ehe? Ein Blick auf G. Delling's Untersuchung," *TSK* 105 (1933), 217: "The conquest of the sensual desires through spiritual interests of a religious, aesthetic, or even a political type is not something abnormal, but thoroughly normal and to a certain degree generally necessary."

9. See C. K. Barrett, *The First Epistle to the Corinthians,* Harper's New Testament Commentaries (New York: Harper & Row, 1968), 155.

10. Gerhard Delling, *Paulus' Stellung zu Frau und Ehe* (Stuttgart: W. Kohlhammer, 1931), and the response by Michel, "Wie Spricht Paulus über Frau und Ehe?" 215–25, esp. 217. Michel correctly sees Corinthian enthusiasts behind Paul's response, but he does not deal with the home ground of Paul's own thinking on the question. For Michel's view that Diaspora Judaism played no role in Paul's thinking about celibacy see 148.

11. See Hermann Strathmann, *Geschichte der frühchristlichen Askese* (Leipzig: A. Deichertsche Verlagsbuchhandlung Werner Scholl, 1914), 34. Note also his statement that "In the time of Jesus the main features of the piety of Palestinian Judaism were not ascetic," 41.

12. See George Foot Moore, *Judaism in the First Centuries of the Christian Era. The Age of the Tannaim,* 3 vols. (Cambridge: Harvard University Press, 1954), vol. II, 262–66.

13. Ibid., vol. II, 264.

14. See George Foot Moore, "Asceticism," in *Encyclopaedia Judaica* (Jerusalem: Encyclopaedia Judaica, 1971), vol. I, 678–83, esp. 678.

15. Hans Lietzmann, *The Beginnings of the Christian Church,* trans. B. L. Woolf, 3d ed. rev. (London: Lutterworth Press, 1953), 135.

16. Peter Brown, *The Body and Society: Men, Women and Sexual Renunciation in Early Christianity* (New York: Columbia University Press, 1988), 54.

17. Johannes Weiss, *Der erste Korintherbrief* (Göttingen: Vandenhoeck & Ruprecht, 1925), 169–210.

18. Kurt Niederwimmer, *Askese und Mysterium: Über Ehe, Ehescheidung und Eheverzicht in den Anfängen des christlichen Glaubens* (Göttingen: Vandenhoeck & Ruprecht, 1975), 67–74.

19. See especially Richard A. Horsley, "Pneumatikos vs. Psychikos: Distinction of Spiritual Status among the Corinthians," *HTR* 69 (1976), 269–88.

20. David L. Balch, "Backgrounds of I Cor. VII: Sayings of the Lord in Q; Moses as an Ascetic ΘΕΙΟΣ ΑΝΗΡ in II Cor. iii," *NTS* 18 (1971/72), 351–64.

21. Vincent L. Wimbush, *Paul the Worldly Ascetic: Response to the World and Self-Understanding according to 1 Corinthians 7* (Macon, GA: Mercer University Press, 1987).

22. See Will Deming, *Paul on Marriage and Celibacy. The Hellenistic Background of 1 Corinthians 7* (Cambridge: Cambridge University Press, 1995). This important work will doubtless influence the discussion for some time to come.

23. Ibid., 196.

24. Ibid., 108.

25. Even if one allows Deming's pairing of the Cynic renunciation of marriage/sex versus the Stoic dutiful practice of marriage/sex to stand, there are still difficulties. One notices, for example, the Cynic exception to this rule in Antisthenes, who indulges his sexual passions rather freely (Xenophon, "Banquet," *Symposium and Apology,* trans. O. J. Todd, LCL [Cambridge: Harvard University Press, and London: Heinemann, 1968], vol. IV, 34–44). See also his positive description of marriage in Diogenes Laertius VI, 11.

26. See Steven D. Fraade, "Ascetical Aspects of Ancient Judaism," in *Jewish Spirituality from the Bible through the Middle Ages,* ed. Arthur Green (London: Routledge & Kegan Paul, 1986), 253–88. Earlier Yitzhak Baer held that from the time of Alexander to the Hasmoneans Greek ideals and prophetic traditions combined to shape a Hasidic piety emphasizing ascetic, martyrological, and spiritual themes. This Hasidism stands behind the Essenism (and asceticism) of Qumran. A synopsis of his *Yisrael ba Ammim,* 20–57, is offered by E. E. Urbach, *The Sages. Their Concepts and Beliefs,* trans. Israel Abrahams (Jerusalem: At the Magness Press, Hebrew University, 1975), 12. Urbach's attack of Baer's thesis that Hellenistic Judaism under the influence of Greek philosophy had no impact on rabbinic thinking will not stand investigation.

27. Guiding my thinking on this question have been the works of Fraade, "Ascetical Aspects of Ancient Judaism," 257, and Arthur Vööbus, "Asceticism," in *The New Encyclopaedia Britannica,* 15th ed., (Chicago: Encyclopaedia Britannica, 1995), vol. 1, 615–17: "Asceticism, in religion, is the practice of the denial of physical or psychological desires in order to attain a spiritual ideal or goal."

28. For a useful discussion see Henry E. Chadwick, "Enkrateia" in *Reallexikon für Antike und Christentum* (Stuttgart: Anton Hiersemann, 1962), vol. 5, col. 343 and the following columns, and for a collection of texts see Vincent L. Wimbush, ed., *Ascetic Behavior in Greco-Roman Antiquity. A Source Book* (Minneapolis: Fortress Press, 1990).

29. See Michel Foucault, *The History of Sexuality* vol. III: *The Care of Self,* trans. Robert Hurley (New York: Pantheon Books, 1986), 634–36. See review by Elizabeth A. Clark, "Foucault, the Fathers, and Sex," *JAAR* 56 (1988), 619–41.

30. See Foucault, *The History of Sexuality,* vol. III, 109–11, 112–17.

31. See note 25 for complete citation.

32. See Epictetus's quite negative observation: "To make a long story short, he must get a kettle to heat water for the baby, for washing it in a bathtub; wool for his

wife when she has had a child, oil, a cot, a cup (the vessels get more and more numerous); not to speak of the rest of his business, and his destruction. . . . Where, pray, is this king, whose duty it is to oversee the rest of men . . . making the rounds like a physician, and feeling pulses?" (*Discourses,* trans. H. A. Old-father [Cambridge: Harvard University Press, and London: Heinemann, 1928]), vol. II, book III, 69, 70–72.

33. See Wimbush, *Ascetic Behavior in Greco-Roman Antiquity,* 127.

34. Among others emphasizing the importance of *enkrateia,* note, for example, the "Letter of Aristeas" in *The Old Testament Pseudepigrapha,* ed. James H. Charlesworth (Garden City, NY: Doubleday,1985), vol. 2, vss. 222, 237–38, 277–79.

35. Among others emphasizing the importance of "self-control," for example, is "Letter of Aristeas," 222, 237f, 277–9.

36. See Walter D. Kaelber, "Asceticism," *Encyclopedia of Religion,* ed. Mircea Eli-ade, *et al* (New York: Macmillan, 1987), vol. I, 441.

37. See "Hypothetica," in *Philo,* trans. F. H. Colson, LCL, 10 vols. (Cambridge: Harvard University Press, and London: Heinemann, 1967), vol. IX, 11.14–17: "For no Essene takes a wife, because a wife is a selfish creature, excessively jealous and an adept at beguiling the morals of her husband and seducing him by her continued impostures. For by the fawning talk which she practises and the other ways in which she plays her part like an actress on the stage she first ensnares the sight and hearing, and when these subjects as it were have been duped she cajoles the sovereign mind. And if children come, filled with the spirit of arrogance and bold speaking she gives utterance with more audacious hardi-hood to things which before she hinted covertly and under disguise, and casting off all shame she compels him to commit actions which are all hostile to the life of fellowship. For he who is either fast bound in the love lures of his wife or under the stress of nature makes his children his first care ceases to be the same to others and unconsciously has become a different man and has passed from freedom into slavery."

38. The report in b. Shab. and Sifre on Num. is somewhat fuller: "He reasoned that if the Israelites, to whom the Lord spoke only once and briefly, were ordered to abstain from women temporarily, he, being in continual dialogue with Heaven, should remain chaste permanently." (See *Shabbath,* trans. Jacob Neusner, "Brown Judaic Studies," no. 270 [Atlanta: Scholars Press, 1992–95], 87a.) An interesting legend features Zipporah's reaction to this unilateral action by Moses to become celibate. Miriam, Moses' sister, noting Zipporah's unkempt appear-ance, queried her. Zipporah's response was, "Your brother does not care about the thing" (Sifre on Num. 12:1 [99]). As the legend continues, her bitterness is reported by R. Nathan: "Miriam was standing by Zipporah, when the young man came running to Moses and told him that Eldad and Medad were prophesying in the camp" (Sifre on Num. 11:27). Zipporah is reported to have responded, "Woe to the wives of these men!" (Sifre on Num. 12:1) Although the story is highly embroidered in rabbinic materials, the Talmudic version shares with Philo's ac-count the belief that holy, prophetic figures suspend sexual relations to remain in

a constant state of purity and readiness for interaction with God. See *Midrash Sifre on Numbers,* trans. P. P. Levertoff (London: S.P.C.K., and New York: Macmillan, 1926). A more modern translation is available in *Sifr. To Numbers: An American Translation and Explanation,* trans. Jacob Neusner (Atlanta: Scholars Press, 1986).

39. Quaes. Gen. 2:49 in *Philo,* supplementary vol. 1. Note how in the conclusion Philo invokes holy war imagery: "When the soul is about to wash off and cleanse its sins, man should join with man. . . . For it is a time of war, in which one must separate one's ranks and watch out lest they be mixed up and bring about defeat instead of victory."

40. See Josephus's comments in the *War,* 120–21: "The Essenes have a reputation for cultivating peculiar sanctity. . . . They shun pleasures as a vice and regard temperance and the control of passions as a special virtue. Marriage they disdain. . . . They do not, indeed, on principle, condemn wedlock and the propagation thereby of the race, but they wish to protect themselves against women's wantonness and are convinced that none of them is faithful to one man."

41. Josephus also praises Mariamme for her *enkrateia,* and in this case the word appears to mean "nobility" rather than celibacy, although one can hardly be certain that Josephus made such a separation: "Thus died Mariamme, a woman unexcelled in continence (ἐγκράτεια) and in greatness of soul" (*War* 15, 237).

42. Pinchas Lapide, *Paulus zwischen Damaskus und Qumran* (Gütersloh: Gütersloher Verlagshaus Gerd Mohn, 1993), thinks that it was Qumran, not Damascus, where Paul may have spent as many as three years.

43. John J. Collins, "Was the Dead Sea Sect an Apocalyptic Movement?" in *The Madrid Qumran Congress, Proceedings of the International Congress on the Dead Sea Scrolls. Madrid, 18–21 March 1991,* ed. Julio Trebolle Barrera and Luis Vegas Montaner (Leiden: E. J. Brill, 1992), 25–51, responds to Harmut Stegemann's comment that the Qumran community was "keine apokalyptische Bewegung" by noting that Qumran originated in the "same general milieu as the apocalyptic movements" and notes both the dualism and the eschatology of the community were compatible with apocalyptic formulations (46 and 51, n. 74).

44. Whereas formerly only pilgrims were forbidden to have sexual intercourse in the city of Jerusalem, the prohibition was stricter at Qumran: "No man shall lie with a woman in the city of the Sanctuary, to defile the city of the Sanctuary with their uncleanness." CD is the standard abbreviation for the *Damascus Document* from Qumran.

45. "And if a man lies with his wife and has an emission of semen, he shall not come into any part of the city of the temple, where I will settle my name, for three days." QT is the standard abbreviation for the Aramaic fragment of the Testament of Levi found in cave 1.

46. Yigael Yadin, ed. *The Temple Scroll* (Jerusalem: The Israel Exploration Society, 1983), vol. I, 288.

47. Ibid., 289.

48. Elisha Qimron and John Strugnel, "*Miqsat Ma'ase Ha-Torah,*" in *Discoveries in the Judaean Desert,* vol. X (Oxford: Clarendon Press, 1994). See especially 58–

62a: "And one must not let dogs enter the holy camp, since they may eat some of the flesh of the bones of the sanctuary while the flesh is (still) on them. *For Jerusalem is the camp of holiness,* and is the place which He has chosen from all the tribes of Israel. For Jerusalem is the capital of the camps of Israel." (emphasis added) 4QMMT is the standard abbreviation for a so-called Halakhic letter from cave 4.

49. See Elisha Qimron, "Celibacy in the Dead Sea Scrolls and the Two Kinds of Sectarians," in *The Madrid Qumran Congress, Proceedings of the International Congress on the Dead Sea Scrolls. Madrid 18–21 March 1991,* ed. Julio Trebolle Barrera and Luis Vegas Montaner (Leiden: E. J. Brill, 1992), 287–94.

50. 4 QMMT, sec. B, lines 29–30, 59–62, "For the camp of holiness is Jerusalem" seems to be a reference to Qumran.

51. Elisha Qimron, "Celibacy in the Dead Sea Scrolls," 287–94.

52. On this point I agree with Matthew Black, "The Tradition of the Hasidaean-Essene Asceticism: Its Origins and Influence," in *Aspects du Judéo-Christianisme,* ed. Université de Strasbourg. Centre de recherches d'histoire des religions (Paris: Presses Universitaires de France, 1965), 19–33.

53. Carol A. Newsom, " 'He Has Established for Himself Priests': Human and Angelic Priesthood in the Qumran Sabbath *Shirot,*" in *Archeology and History in the Dead Sea Scrolls. The New York University Conference in Memory of Yigael Yadin,* ed. Lawrence H. Schiffman (Sheffield: Sheffield Academic Press, 1990), 101–20, esp. 115. 4Q400 is the standard reference to 4QshirShabb, referring to the songs of the Sabbath sacrifice found in cave 4.

54. See P. Suso Frank, *Angelikos Bios. Begriffsanalytische und begriffsgeschichtliche Untersuchung zum 'Engelgleichen Leben' im Frühen Mönchtum* (Münster: Aschendorfsche Verlagsbuchhandlung, 1964). 1QH is the standard reference to the Hymn Scroll.

55. Barbara Thiering, "The Biblical Source of Qumran Asceticism," *JBL* 93 (1974), 429–44, esp. 433. Thiering thinks the provenance of Paul's asceticism is to be found in Hebrew prophecy. While prophecy may have played a role, it hardly serves as the single genesis of Qumran asceticism.

56. See Collins, "Was the Dead Sea Sect an Apocalyptic Movement?" 45. Collins notes how its dualism, messianism, feverish expectation of the final eschatological battle, anticipation of the destruction of Jerusalem and the dispersion of Israel as punishment for sin, its periodization of history, and its belief in a final traumatic period of wrath when Belial would be let loose on Israel (CD 4:13), as well as its belief in the the restoration of Israel under the leadership of the two Messiahs, amply demonstrate the apocalyptic character of the community. Also see Hengel, *Judaism and Hellenism,* vol. I, 175–80.

57. See especially Louis Ginsberg, *Legends of the Jews,* 7 vols. (Philadelphia: Jewish Publication Society, 1908–38), vol. 5, 134, n. 4.

58. Gary Anderson, "Celibacy or Consummation in the Garden? Reflections on Early Jewish and Christian Interpretations of the Garden of Eden," *HTR* 82 (1989), 121.

59. See ibid., 121–48, esp. 129.

60. See ibid., 121–48, esp. 148.
61. Translation of 2 *Baruch* by A. F. J. Klijn in *The Old Testament Pseudepigrapha,* vol. I, 641.
62. Attridge believes the tradition is even pre-Christian. See Harold W. Attridge, "On Becoming an Angel: Rival Baptismal Theologies at Colossae," in *Religious Propaganda and Missionary Competition in the New Testament World. Essays Honoring Dieter Georgi,* ed. Lukas Bormann, Kelly del Tredici, and Angela Standhartinger (Leiden, New York, Köln: E. J. Brill, 1994), 481–497. Attridge finds in 1 Enoch 71:1–17, 2 Enoch 22:4–7, and 3 Enoch 7 evidence that legendary seers were believed to be transformed into an angelic state, and at least in some instances that angelic state assumed an ascetic character. See also Carol A. Newsom, "Angels," in *ABD,* vol. I, 248–53.
63. David Edward Aune, *The Cultic Setting of Realized Eschatology in Early Christianity* (Leiden: E. J. Brill, 1972), 20–3.
64. Ibid., 205.
65. Interestingly Luke 18:29 alone commands/mentions leaving one's wife (cf. Matt. 19:29; Mark 10:29–30).
66. Aune, *The Cultic Setting,* 210.
67. In this Aune agrees in part with Erik Peterson, "Einige Beobachtungen zu den Anfängen des christlichen Askese," in his *Frühkirche, Judentum und Gnosis. Studien und Untersuchungen* (Rome: Herder, 1959), 209–20 who believes Christian asceticism was closely associated with a belief in the imminent arrival of the kingdom of God (219). Aune, however, is somewhat more judicious than Peterson, who holds that neither Greek philosophy nor a metaphysical dualism played any role in the emergence of this phenomenon.
68. See the excellent article by Georg Kretschmar, "Ein Beitrag zur Frage nach dem Ursprung frühchristlicher Askese," *ZThK* 70 (1964), 27–67, that captures very nicely the complexity of the relationships of these ascetic traditions.
69. Still valuable is Hurd, *The Origin of 1 Corinthians.*
70. In 7:5 Paul seems to grant that abstinence was appropriate or required for approaching God in prayer.
71. As early as 1901 scholars began treating Corinthian asceticism. John Massie in JTS II (1901), 537, 539, argued that the Corinthians believed they were obligated to be celibate. Also Lietzmann, *Beginnings,* 135; Kirsopp Lake, *The Earlier Epistles of St. Paul: Their Motive and Origin,* 2d ed. (London: Rivingtons, 1914), 180, notes "Some of the Corinthians were opposed altogether to marriage (cf. 1 Cor. vii, 1,2); and some were anxious to deprive it of any sexual significance." Also, Archibald Robertson and Alfred Plummer, *A Critical and Exegetical Commentary on the First Epistle of St. Paul to the Corinthians,* 2d ed. (Edinburgh: T. & T. Clark, 1914); Theodor Zahn, *Introduction to the New Testament,* 2d ed., 3 vols., trans. J. M. Trout, William Arnot Mather, Louis Hodous, Edward Strong Worcester, William Hoyt Morrell, Rowland Backus, et al., ed. M. W. Jacobus (New York: Charles Scribner's Sons, 1917); James Moffatt, *An Introduction to the Literature of the New Testament,* 3d ed. rev. (Edinburgh: T. & T. Clark, 1918).
72. Here I agree with Averil Cameron, "Early Christianity and the Discourse of Female Desire," in *Women in Ancient Societies, "An Illusion by Night,"* ed. Le'onie

J. Archer, Susan Fischler, and Maria Hyke (New York: Routledge, 1994), 152–68.

73. See Carl R. Holladay, "I Corinthians 13, Paul as Apostolic Paradigm," in *Greeks, Romans, and Christians. Essays in Honor of Abraham J. Malherbe,* ed. David L. Balch, Everett Ferguson, and Wayne A. Meeks (Minneapolis: Fortress Press, 1990), 80–98.

74. As Masson, "The Psychology of the Ascetic," holds.

75. Paul's statement in Gal. 1:15 that he was "set aside from his mother's womb" is widely recognized as an appeal to the prophet Jeremiah. How important was Jeremiah as a model for Paul? If we knew the answer to that question we might be able to answer the intriguing question of whether Paul believed that he, like Jeremiah, had been forbidden to marry for life (Jer. 16:1–4).

76. I find Delling's position unacceptable that Paul's celibacy is rooted in a Jewish hatred of women and a Hellenistic marriage weariness. See his *Paulus' Stellung zu Frau und Ehe,* 147. Although there are certainly misogynist texts in Jewish and Hellenistic writings, his generalization goes too far.

77. *Akrasian* is used here as an antonym of *enkrateia.*

78. They do appear in Sir. 18:15, 30 and 4 Macc. 5:34 (LXX) but they are there because of Hellenistic influence on these books.

79. Walther Grundmann, "ἐγκράτεια," *TDNT,* vol. II, 342. Grundman's wrongly held that "the biblical man regarded life as determined and directed by the command of God. There was thus no place for the self-mastery which had a place in autonomous ethics."

80. Here I share the view of Adolf Büchler, *Types of Jewish-Palestinian Piety from 70 B.C.E. to 70 C.E.* (London: Gregg International Publishers Limited, 1969). See especially "The Ancient Pious Man," 42–65.

81. See Fraade, "Ascetical Aspects," 256, and Robin Lane Fox, *Pagans and Christians* (New York: Viking, 1986), 349.

82. Victor C. Pfitzner, *Paul and the Agon Motif* (Leiden: E. J. Brill, 1967), 93–94.

83. Kretschmar, "Ein Beitrag zur Frage nach dem Ursprung frühchristlicher Askese," 29, 60–67.

84. Note Paul's violent metaphor: "But those of Christ have crucified the flesh with its passions (παθήμασιν) and desires (ἐπιθυμίαις). See also Rom. 7:18; 8:12–13. This metaphor would appear to be sui generis, but a similar expression appears in Philo, "De Somn.," II, 213: "But thanks be to the victorious God who, however perfect in workmanship are the aims and efforts of the passion-lover, makes them to be of none effect by sending invisibly against them winged beings to undo and destroy them. Thus the mind stripped of the creations of its art will be found as it were a headless corpse, with severed neck *nailed like the crucified to the tree of helpless and poverty-stricken indiscipline*" (my emphasis).

85. I am indebted to Carl Holladay for pointing out this association to me. But also see Johannes Behm, "κοιλία," *TDNT,* III, 786–789, esp. 788.

86. Here I cannot agree with Murphy-O'Connor, *Paul, A Critical Life,* 64, who says, "It is most probable . . . that Paul had a wife."

CHAPTER SIX: THE MYTHIC APOSTLE

1. Others argue that this passage from James is less a critique of Paul himself than of those misinterpreting his letters: Andreas Lindemann, *Paulus im ältesten Christentum* (Tübingen: J. C. B. Mohr [Paul Siebeck], 1979), 240–51; Gerd Lüdemann, *Paulus, der Heidenapostel, Antipaulinismus im frühen Christentum* (Göttingen: Vandenhoeck & Ruprecht, 1985), 194–205; Ernst Dassmann, *Der Stachel im Fleisch. Paulus in der frühchristlichen Literatur bis Irenäus* (Münster: Aschendorf, 1979), 108–18. R. Joseph Hoffmann, *Marcion: On the Restitution of Christianity. An Essay on the Development of Radical Paulinist Theology in the Second Century* (Chico, CA: Scholars Press, 1984), 101, would read the evidence as we have. He also may be correct that such passages as Rev. 2:2, 9, 14–15, 20–24; 3:9; 21:14 may point to an eclipse of Paul already within the first century, but this is more problematic if one thinks the use of the letter form in Rev. 2–3 reveals the influence of Paul as a letter writer.

2. H. Schneemelcher, "Paulus im der griechischen Kirche des zweiten Jahrhunderts," *ZKG* 75 (1964), 6.

3. Ibid., 7.

4. Ibid., 8.

5. Ibid., 9.

6. See Wolfram Kinzig, "Καινὴ διαθήκη." The Title of the New Testament in the Second and Third Centuries," *JTS,* new series, 45 (1994), 519–44, who argues that Marcion coined the term Old Testament for the Hebrew Scriptures. This hypothesis, if correct, has profound implications for New Testament scholarship and the church.

7. See John J. Clabeaux, "Marcion," in *ABD,* vol. IV, 515.

8. "Life of Rabbula" as cited in Walter Bauer, *Orthodoxy and Heresy in Earliest Christianity,* ed. Robert A. Kraft and Gerhard Krodel, 2d ed. (Philadelphia: Fortress Press, 1971), 26–27.

9. The Valentinians were proud descendants of Valentinus, who left Alexandria in 138 to migrate to Rome, where he remained for almost thirty years. At the time the word *gnostic* hardly carried the pejorative associations that would later be laid on it but instead referred to those who possessed or were possessed by knowledge of salvation. This information went beyond the conceptual realm to speak compellingly of a knowledge with esoteric, secret, and relational aspects. So skillful and adept was Valentinus as a Christian thinker that Tertullian reports that he was a viable candidate for the bishopric (Adversus Valentinianos 4.1).

10. Note how Irenaeus links Paul with Peter as one of the "two most glorious apostles" who "founded and organized the [the church] at Rome" ("Against Heresies," III, III, 2. See also his "Against Heresies," I, VII, 4; I, X, 1; II, IX, 2; esp. III, XIII–XV. A fuller accounting of the use of Paul by the Gnostics may be seen in Elaine H. Pagels, *The Gnostic Paul, Gnostic Exegesis of the Pauline Letters* (Philadelphia: Fortress Press, 1975). See Alexander Roberts and W. H. Rambaut,

"Ante-Nicene Christian Library," in *The Writings of Irenaeus* (Edinburgh: T. & T. Clark, 1868–69), vols. V and IX.

11. See Schneemelcher, "Paulus im der griechischen Kirche," 19.

12. Ibid., 19. For example, in Hippolytus, Ref. 5.6.4, there is evidence that the Naassene Gnostic system claimed to go *beyond* Paul. See M. J. Edwards, "Neglected Texts in the Study of Gnosticism," *JTS,* new series, 41 (1990), 41, n. 24.

13. See Hennecke, *New Testament Apocrypha,* vol. II.

14. See Schneemelcher, "Paulus im der griechischen Kirche," 11.

15. Brown, *The Body and Society,* 54. For a somewhat more nuanced view of the early church's use, especially that of Jerome, of Paul on celibacy and related issues, see John Oppel, "Saint Jerome and the History of Sex," *Viator* 24 (1993), 1–22. Note especially Jovinian, an unorthodox monk, who was condemned by the synod at Milan in 393. Jovinian's view was that celibacy was a higher state than marriage or that it would be more highly rewarded in the life to come. Jerome, however, argued in his *Against Jovinian* that through celibacy women could compensate for the sin of Eve in causing Adam's, ergo man's, downfall. Jovinian took with utmost seriousness the "first" commandment given by God to humankind: "Be fruitful and multiply, and fill the earth" (Gen. 1:28). Jerome believed the command referred not to the realization of a blessed and holy state but to a "grim duty." The Jovinian "attempt to equate marriage and celibacy, [and] his teaching that there is no external distinction of merit among baptized Christians, is like the hissing of a serpent" (Oppel, 8). Jovinian, the heretic, would appear to have been closer to Paul's view than was Jerome. Please see chapter five for a discussion of the foreground and nature of Paul's asceticism.

16. Arthur Vööbus, *History of Asceticism in the Syrian Orient. A Contribution to the History of Culture in the Near East:* vol. I, *The Origin of Asceticism: Early Monasticism in Persia* (Louvain: Secretariat du Corpus, 1958), 15–30, argues quite compellingly that the church in Syria had its genesis in an Aramaean Jewish Christianity that displayed ascetic tendencies.

17. Meeks, "The Model Ascetic," 193–207, esp. 196.

18. A. Vööbus, *Celibacy, a Requirement for Admission to Baptism in the Early Syrian Church* (Stockholm: The Estonian Theological Society in Exile, 1951). Also see his *History of Asceticism.*

19. See ibid., 15–16.

20. See note 6.

21. Vööbus, *History of Asceticism,* vol. I, 70.

22. See ibid.

23. The writings of Aphrahat from around 340 make clear that all of the "single ones are given joy by the 'Single One' from the bosom of his Father" (see Aphrahat's "Seventh Demonstration," VI, 269. 3–4).

24. Robert Murray, "The Exhortation to Candidates for Ascetical Vows at Baptism in the Ancient Syriac Church," *NTS* 21 (1975), 61.

25. See Vööbus, *Celibacy,* 56.

26. See Murray, "The Exhortation to Candidates for Ascetical Vows," 79.

27. Hans von Campenhausen, *The Formation of the Christian Bible,* trans. J. A. Baker (Philadelphia: Fortress Press, 1972), 212, n. 15.

28. Pseudo-Clement, "The First Epistle Concerning Virginity," in *The Ante-Nicene Fathers,* ed. Alexander Roberts, James Donaldson (Grand Rapids, MI: Eerdmans, 1951), vol. VIII, 58.

29. Meeks, *The Writings of St. Paul,* 199–200.

30. "Acts of Paul and Thecla," in Hennecke, *New Testament Apocrypha,* 7.

31. Ibid., 20.

32. The life expectancy at birth of only twenty-five years and the rarity of survival beyond fifty made it a duty to marry and beget children. This heavy threat of mortality placed enormous political pressure on the young to marry as early as fourteen and to procreate. In order to maintain a steady state population in that setting every woman would have had to give birth to five children on average. Given these conditions the charge against Thecla is understandable even if it is deplorable. For a further discussion see Bruce W. Frier, "Roman Life Expectancy: Ulpian's Evidence," *Harvard Studies in Classical Philology* 86 (1982), 213–51, esp. 248. Virginia Burrus, "Chastity as Autonomy: Women in the Stories of the Apocryphal Acts," in *Semeia,* 38 (1986), 110, quite correctly notes that "this social order is above all the order of marriage and household, in which the woman's position is well-defined and well-bounded." Naturally, when "this social order is threatened, the prominent citizens call upon the Roman governor to protect it."

33. In this I agree with Brown, *The Body and Society,* 14.

34. Burrus, "Women in the Apocryphal Acts," 111, 116.

35. Ibid., 116.

36. Schneemelcher, in Hennecke, *New Testament Apocrypha,* vol. II, 222, offers a rather caustic criticism of Burrus's feminist construction of the Acts of Paul: "On a sober treatment of the evidence, hypotheses of such a kind appear to be largely no more than the products of modern fancy, without any basis in the sources." Given his remark we wonder how Schneemelcher would explain Paul's almost constant associations with women in the Acts of Paul, and the liberation Thecla enjoys from the limits of marriage.

37. Readers will recognize my debt here to Clifford Geertz, "Religion as a Cultural System," in *Interpretation of Cultures, Selected Essays* (New York: Basic Books, 1973), 93–94.

38. This is from an appendix to the Acts of Paul entitled "The Beginning of the Stay in Ephesus," Hennecke, *New Testament Apocrypha,* vol. II, 388.

39. Ibid., 389.

40. Ibid.

41. Ibid.

42. Ibid.

43. See ibid., 253–54, 372–73.

44. Novatian, "On Purity," 7 from around 340 CE.

45. Brown, *The Body and Society,* 159.

46. See "Miracle" in the *Oxford English Dictionary,* prepared by J. A. Simpson and E. S. C. Weiner (Oxford: Clarendon Press, 1989), vol. IX, 836.

47. See Geza Vermes, "The Prayer of Nabonidus," in *Essene Writings from Qumran,* trans. Geza Vermes (Cleveland: World Publishing Co., 1962), 322–23.

48. William S. Babcock, ed. *Paul and the Legacies of Paul* (Dallas: SMU Press, 1990), xvii.
49. Here I am obviously following the work of Dieter Georgi, *The Opponents of Paul in Second Corinthians,* which is now something of a classic.
50. Karl Heinrich Rengstorf, "σημεῖον," *TDNT,* VII, 258, n. 388.
51. The late account of his life by Philostratus, *The Life of Apollonius of Tyana,* trans. F.C. Conybeare, LCL, 2 vols. (Cambridge: Harvard University Press, 1960), it is now generally agreed incorporates early traditions of the popular philosopher. See Holger Thesleff, *An Introduction to the Pythagorean Writings of the Hellenistic Period* (Abo: Abo Akademi, 1961).
52. On this point I agree with Stanley K. Stowers, "Comment: What Does Unpauline Mean?" in Babcock, *Paul and the Legacies of Paul,* 70–77. See also the powerful argument of Stefan Schreiber, *Paulus als Wundertäter, Redaktionsgeschichtliche Untersuchungen zur Apostelgeschichte und den authentischen Paulusbriefen* (Berlin: Walter de Gruyter, 1996), 161–284. The inattention to this aspect of Paul may reflect a bias that comes with living in a scientific age. Note, for example, that the report on Pauline scholarship by Otto Merk, "Paulus-Forschung 1936–1985," *TR* 53 (1988), 1–81, contains no mention of Paul's miraculous deeds. The same goes for the survey by Hans Hübner, "Paulusforschung seit 1945. Ein kritischer Literaturbericht," in *ANRW,* II, 25.4, 2649–2840. Bornkamm, *Paul,* offers an explanation that sounds strangely modern, that is, that for Paul the true "signs of an apostle" were not miracles but the awakening of the community through the proclamation of the gospel. The same viewpoint is expressed by F. F. Bruce, *Paul: Apostle of the Free Spirit* (Exeter: Paternoster Press, 1977). J. Christiaan Beker, *Paul the Apostle. The Triumph of God in Life and Thought* (Philadelphia: Fortress Press, 1980), 151, 286, does mention the signs and wonders as works of the spirit but offers no discussion of Paul as the miracle worker. Betz, *Der Apostel Paulus,* 71, notes that "clear evidence that Paul performed miracles does not exist. It is only clear that he rejected the understanding of miracles of his opponents." To those who are silent on Paul as miracle worker one could add the names of Heinrich Schlier, *Grundzüge einer paulinischen Theologie* (Freiburg: Herder, 1978), and Joseph A. Fitzmyer, *Pauline Theology, A Brief Sketch* (Englewood Cliffs, NJ: Prentice-Hall, 1968), who makes only a very brief comment in his Romans commentary. Walther Schmithals, *Das kirchliche Amt. Eine historische Untersuchung* (Göttingen: Vandenhoeck & Ruprecht, 1961), avoids the question of miracles altogether. (The English translation of this Schmithals work is *The Office of Apostle in the Early Church,* trans. John E. Steely [Nashville: Abingdon Press, 1969]. And John Knox can specifically deal with Romans 15:19 and leave the question of miracles untouched: "Romans 15:14–33 and Paul's Conception of His Apostolic Mission," *JBL* 83 (1964), 1–11. Commentaries seem somewhat more circumspect on this question: Note, for example, that, Fitzmyer, *Romans,* 713, commenting on 15:19, only says, "Paul thus admits that some miracles have been wrought through him. . . . Paul uses traditional language, *sêmeia kai terata,* for miraculous deeds." Furnish, *II Corinthians,* 555, notes that apostolic signs were performed in Corinth but that

Paul refused to get into a bragging contest with his rivals. There are scholars, however, who do take note of the wonder-working powers of Paul. See, for instance, Ernst Käsemann, "Die Legitimität des Apostels," 33–71; Jacob Jervell, "Die Zeichen des Apostels. Die Wunder beim lukanischen und paulinischen Paulus," *Studien zum Neuen Testament und Seiner Umwelt* 4 (1979), 54–75, and "Der schwache Charismatiker," in *Rechtfertigung: Festschrift für Ernst Käsemann zum 70. Geburtstag,* ed. J. Friedrich, W. Pöhlmann, and P. Stuhlmacher (Tübingen: J. C. B. Mohr [Paul Siebeck], and Göttingen: Vandenhoeck & Ruprecht, 1976), 185–198, argues that Paul did indeed see miraculous deeds as a validation of his apostleship, but the difference between him and his opponents was that though he performed miracles, he himself was sickly, thus raising doubt about the integrity of his apostleship. A healer who could not heal himself was suspect, according to Jervell. More than two generations ago, Windisch, *Der zweite Korintherbrief,* 397, noted "that Paul performed miracles, need not be doubted, and that they offered proof of his apostolate, is in no way astonishing." Also see Gerhard Lohfink, *Wie hat Jesus Gemeinde gewollt? Zur gesellschaftlichen Dimension des christlichen Glaubens* (Freiburg: Herder, 1982), 234–41.

53. See David L. Tiede, *The Charismatic Figure as Miracle Worker,* (Missoula: Scholars Press, 1970), 241–92.

54. Perhaps the definitive work in this linkage of the Pauline and Jesus miracle stories was that of Bruno Bauer, *Die Apostelgeschichte. Eine Ausgleichung des Paulinismus und des Judentums innerhalb der christlichen Kirche* (Berlin: G. Hampel, 1850), 9–12.

    More recently see the work by A. J. Mattill, Jr., "The Jesus-Paul Parallels and the Purpose of Luke—Acts: H. H. Evans Reconsidered," *NT* 17 (1975), 15–46.

    Of value also is Susan Marie Praeder, "Miracle Worker and Missionary: Paul in the Acts of the Apostles," in *SBL 1983 Seminar Papers,* ed. Kent Harold Richards (Chico, CA: Scholars Press, 1983), 107–29.

    Also see Franz Neirynck, "The Miracle Stories in the Acts of the Apostles: An Introduction," in *Les Actes des Apôtres. Traditions, rédaction, théologie,* ed. J. Kremer (Leuven: Leuven University Press, 1979), 169–213.

55. Hans Windisch, "Paulus and Jesus," *TSK* 106 (1934–35), 465.

56. Hans Conzelmann, *The Theology of St. Luke,* trans. Geoffrey Buswell (New York: Harper & Row, 1960), 181–83, and his *Acts of the Apostles,* 37, 76, 77, 223.

57. Jacob Jervell, "Paul in the Acts of the Apostles," in *Les Actes des Apôtres. Traditions, Redaction, Théologie,* ed. J. Kremer (Leuven: Leuven University Press, 1979), 305.

58. See ibid., 300.

59. MacDonald, "Apocryphal and Canonical Narratives about Paul," 57, and Hennecke, *New Testament Apocrypha,* vol. II, 219.

60. Schneemelcher, "Introduction to the Acts of Paul," in Hennecke, *New Testament Apocrypha,* vol. II, 231, notes that according to the Stichometry of Nicephorus the Acts of Paul was 3,600 lines long compared to the 2,800 lines of the canonical Acts.

61. See Schneemelcher, "Introduction to the Acts of Paul," in *New Testament Apocrypha,* vol. II, 221.

62. Hennecke, *New Testament Apocrypha,* 256–57.
63. Acts 27:5–6 speaks of Paul changing ships in Myra, but no activity is mentioned. These legends evidently grow up to fill the gap in the narrative.
64. See Hennecke, *New Testament Apocrypha,* 253.
65. Ibid., 253–54.
66. MacDonald, "Apocryphal and Canonical Narratives about Paul," 64, goes beyond the text when he says categorically that Luke "has Paul forecast his imprisonment *and death* to the elders of Ephesus at Miletus" (emphasis added).
67. See MacDonald, "Apocryphal and Canonical Narratives about Paul," 66.
68. Stowers, "Comment: What Does Unpauline Mean?" 74.
69. Eusebius, *Ecclesiastical History,* V. I. 41.
70. See ibid., V. 4.
71. Ibid., V. I. 3–53.
72. As cited in Robert D. Sider, "Literary Artifice and the Figure of Paul in the Writings of Tertullian," in *Paul and the Legacies of Paul,* 106.
73. Ibid., 107.
74. Ibid., 109.
75. Hennecke, *New Testament Apocrypha,* vol. II, 288.
76. Hennecke, ibid., 261.
77. Hennecke, ibid., 261–62.
78. Hennecke, ibid., 262.
79. Hennecke, ibid., 263.
80. See ibid., 251.
81. Bruce J. Malina and Jerome H. Neyrey, *Portraits of Paul. An Archaeology of Ancient Personality* (Louisville: Westminster/John Knox Press, 1996), 100–152, give an interesting reading of the physical description of Paul offered at the beginning of the Acts of Paul, entitled, "Physiognomics and Personality: Looking at Paul in *The Acts of Paul.*" While one would take exception to certain points in the narrative—for instance, the rather confident assumption that the reference to Paul's baldness suggests he has taken a religious vow—nevertheless, the basic point of the treatment strikes me as correct, namely, that the physical description of Paul is a positive one. Such an interpretation of this physical description is certainly consistent with everything we see in the remainder of the Acts of Paul.
82. If one follows Henry Chadwick one might add a third function. By occurring in a mythically significant location, Rome, these stories of martyrdom served to legitimate Rome as the new center of the church for western Christians. See Henry E. Chadwick, "St. Peter and St. Paul in Rome: The Problem of the Memoria Apostolorum ad Catacumbas," in *History and Thought of the Early Church* (London: Variorum Reprints, 1982), 31–52, and "Pope Damascus and the Peculiar Claim of Rome to St. Peter and St. Paul," in *History and Thought of the Early Church* (London: Variorum Reprints, 1982), 313–18.
83. In this regard one recalls the Deutero-Pauline text, Col. 1:24, which is fascinating in this regard.

EXCURSUS ON PAULINE CHRONOLOGY

1. See Fitzmyer, *Romans*, 87.
2. From *Paul: Apostle of the Free Spirit.* Copyright by F. F. Bruce 1977. Published by Paternoster Press, Carlisle, UK. Permission granted for use here.
3. Gerd Lüdemann, *Paul, Apostle to the Gentiles: Studies in Chronology,* trans. F. Stanley Jones (Philadelphia: Fortress Press, 1984), 262–63. Note that Lüdemann's chronology is based on two possible dates for the crucifixion of Jesus, 27 and 30. We shall follow his earlier date here. By adding the number 3 to each date one arrives at its alternative. In some cases, that poses difficulty especially in synchronizing Paul's visits to Corinth with the Gallio proconsulship. Used with permission.
4. Jewett, *A Chronology of Paul's Life.* See Jewett's foldout graph of dates and time spans. Used with permission from Fortran Press.
5. The dating of Galatians is notoriously difficult. In favor of this early date is the remark by Paul in the letter: "I am astonished that you are so soon deserting him who called you in the grace of Christ" (1:6). The argument is that Paul could not have expressed shock that church members were so quickly deserting Christ had he written the letter at a later date. Moreover, Romans seems to be reacting to criticisms of positions taken in Galatians, and more time would be needed for Jewish Christian criticisms to surface. However, scholars may be making too much of Paul's scolding the Galatians for falling away "so soon." One is surprised by the fact that Galatians exerts little if any influence on the Corinthian correspondence or on Philippians and Philemon, and that this is surprising, given the passion Paul expresses there. A later date for Galatians would make more sense and would explain its influence on Romans only. Furnish and Räisänen, for example, would date Galatians shortly before Paul leaves Macedonia for Corinth, where he probably wrote Romans. These contrary positions, both of which are plausible, suggest that any dating of Galatians must be extremely tentative. (See, for example, Furnish, *II Corinthians,* 55.)

Bibliography

ABD. Anchor Bible Dictionary. ed. David Noel Freedman, Gary A. Herion, David F. Graf, John David Pleins, Astrid B. Beck. 6 vols. New York: Doubleday, 1992.

Alon, Gedalyahu. "The Levitical Uncleanness of Gentiles." In his *Judaism and the Classical World.* Jerusalem: Magnes Press, 1977.

Anderson, Gary. "Celibacy or Consummation in the Garden? Reflections on Early Jewish and Christian Interpretations of the Garden of Eden." *HTR* 82 (1989), 121–48.

Applebaum, S. "The Legal Status of the Jewish Communities in the Diaspora." In *The Jewish People in the First Century: Historical Geography, Political History, Social, Cultural and Religious Life and Institutions,* ed. S. Safrai and M. Stern. Philadelphia: Fortress Press, 1974. Vol. 1.

Asting, Ragnar. *Die Heiligkeit im Urchristentum.* Göttingen: Vandenhoeck & Ruprecht, 1930.

Attridge, Harold W. *First-Century Cynicism in the Epistles of Heraclitus: Introduction, Greek Text and Translation* (Missoula: Scholars Press, 1976).

———. "On Becoming an Angel: Rival Baptismal Theologies at Colossae." In *Religious Propaganda and Missionary Competition in the New Testament World. Essays Honoring Dieter Georgi,* ed. Lukas Bormann, Kelly del Tredici, and Angela Standhartinger. Leiden: E. J. Brill, 1994. 481–97.

Aune, David E. *The Cultic Setting of Realized Eschatology in Early Christianity.* Leiden: E. J. Brill, 1972.

———. *The New Testament in Its Literary Environment.* Philadelphia: Westminster, 1977.

Babcock, William S. *Paul and the Legacies of Paul.* Dallas: SMU Press, 1990.

Bachmann, M. *Sünder oder Übertreter. Studien zur Argumentation in Gal 2,15ff.* Tübingen: J. C. B. Mohr (Paul Siebeck), 1991.

Baker, G. P., and P. M. S. Hacker. *Wittgenstein: Rules, Grammar and Necessity.* Oxford: Basil Blackwell, 1985.

Balch, David L. "Backgrounds of I Cor. VII: Sayings of the Lord in Q; Moses as an Ascetic ΘΕΙΟΣ ANHP in II Cor. iii." *NTS* 18 (1971/72), 351–64.

Barrett, C. K. *The First Epistle to the Corinthians.* Harper's New Testament Commentaries. New York: Harper & Row, 1968.

———. *The Second Epistle to the Corinthians.* Harper's New Testament Commentaries. New York: Harper & Row, 1973.

Bartchy, S. Scott. *MAΛΛON XPHΣAI: First-Century Slavery and the Interpretation of I Corinthians 7:21*. Missoula: Scholars Press, 1973.

Bauer, Bruno. *Die Apostelgeschichte. Eine Ausgleichung des Paulinismus und des Judentums innerhalb der christlichen Kirche*. Berlin: G. Hampel, 1850.

Bauer, Walter. *Orthodoxy and Heresy in Earliest Christianity*, ed. Robert A. Kraft and Gerhard Krodel. Eng. trans. from a team from the Philadelphia Seminar on Christian Origins. 2d ed. Philadelphia: Fortress Press, 1971.

Becker, Jürgen. *Paul: Apostle to the Gentiles*. Eng. trans. O. C. Dean, Jr. Louisville: Westminster/John Knox Press, 1993.

Behm, Johannes. "κοιλία." *TDNT*, ed. Gerhard Kittel. Eng. trans. Geoffrey W. Bromiley. Grand Rapids, MI: Eerdmans, 1964–74. Vol. III, 786–89.

Beker, J. Christiaan. *Paul the Apostle. The Triumph of God in Life and Thought*. Philadelphia: Fortress Press, 1980.

Berger, Klaus. "Hellenistische Gattungen im Neuen Testament." In *ANRW*, ed. Hildegard Temporini. Berlin: Walter de Gruyter, 1972. Vol. 25.2, 1326–63.

Berger, Peter. *The Sacred Canopy. Elements of a Sociological Theory of Religion*. Garden City, New York: Doubleday, 1969.

Betz, Hans Dieter. "Eine Christus-Aretologie bei Paulus (2 Cor 12. 7–10)." *ZThK*, 66 (1969), 288–305.

———. *Der Apostel Paulus und die sokratische Tradition. Eine exegetische Untersuchung zu seiner Apologie 2 Korinther 10–13*. Tübingen: J. C. B. Mohr (Paul Siebeck), 1972.

———. *2 Corinthians 8 and 9. A Commentary on Two Administrative Letters of the Apostle Paul*. Philadelphia: Fortress Press, 1985.

———. "Christianity as Religion: Paul's Attempt at Definition in Romans." *JR* 71 (1991), 315–44. (Also in his *Paulinische Studien. Gesammelte Aufsätze III*. Tübingen: J. C. B. Mohr [Paul Siebeck], 1994. 206–39.)

———. "Corinthians, Second Epistle to the." In *ABD*, Vol. I, 1148–54.

———. "Galatians." In *ABD*, Vol. II, 872–79.

———. *Galatians*. Philadelphia: Fortress Press, 1979.

Bjerkelund, Carl J. *Parakalô. Form, Funktion und Sinn der parakalô-Sätze in den paulinischen Briefen*. Oslo: Universitetsforlaget, 1967.

Black, Matthew. "The Tradition of the Hadidaean-Essene Asceticism: Its Origins and Influence." In *Aspects du Judéo-Christianisme*, ed. Université de Strasbourg. Paris: Presses Universitaires de France, 1965. 19–33.

Böhlig, Hans. *Die Geisteskultur von Tarsos im augusteischen Zeitalter mit Berücksichtigung der paulinischen Schriften*. Göttingen: Vandenhoeck & Ruprecht, 1913.

Bornkamm, Günther. "The History of the Origin of the So-Called Second Letter to the Corinthians." *NTS* 8 (1962), 258–63.

———. *Paul*. Eng. trans. D. M. G. Stalker. New York: Harper & Row, 1971.

———. *Die Vorgeschichte des sogenannten zweiten Korintherbriefes*. Heidelberg: Winter, 1961. Also in his *Geschichte und Glaube II. Gesammelte Aufsätze IV*. Munich: Kaiser, 1971.

Bousset, Wilhelm. *Kurios Christos: A History of the Belief in Christ from the Beginnings of Christianity to Irenaeus*. Eng. trans. John E. Steely. Nashville: Abingdon Press, 1970 (first published in German in 1913).

Boyarin, Daniel. *A Radical Jew. Paul and the Politics of Identity.* Berkeley: University of California Press, 1994.

Bradley, David G. "The Topos as Form in the Pauline Paraenesis." *JBL* 72 (1953), 283–96.

Bring, Ragnar. *Commentary on Galatians.* Eng. trans. Eric Wahlstrom. Philadelphia: Muhlenberg, 1961.

Brown, Peter. *The Body and Society: Men, Women and Sexual Renunciation in Early Christianity.* New York: Columbia University Press, 1988.

Bruce, F. F. *The Acts of the Apostles.* Grand Rapids, MI: Eerdmans, 1951.

———. *Paul: Apostle of the Free Spirit.* Exeter: Paternoster Press, 1977.

———. *Paul: Apostle of the Heart Set Free.* Grand Rapids, MI: Eerdmans, 1978.

Büchler, Adolf. *Types of Jewish-Palestinian Piety from 70 B.C.E. to 70 C.E.* London: Gregg International Publishers Limited, 1969.

Bultmann, Rudolf. "Paul." In his *Existence and Faith. Shorter Writings of Rudolf Bultmann.* Eng. trans. Schubert Ogden. New York: Meridian, 1960.

Burkert, Walter. *Greek Religion.* Oxford: Basil Blackwell, 1985.

Burrus, Virginia. "Chastity as Autonomy: Women in the Stories of the Apocryphal Acts." *Semeia* 38 (1986), 101–17. Response by J.-D. Kaestli, 118–31.

Bynum, Caroline Walker. *Jesus as Mother: Studies in the Spirituality of the High Middle Ages.* Berkeley: University of California Press, 1982.

Cameron, Averil. "Early Christianity and the Discourse of Female Desire." In *Women in Ancient Societies. "An Illusion by Night,"* ed. L'eonie J. Archer, Susan Fischler, and Maria Hyke. New York: Routledge, 1994. 152–68.

Campenhausen, Hans von. *The Formation of the Christian Bible.* Eng. trans. J. A. Baker. Philadelphia: Fortress Press, 1972.

Casteli, Elizabeth A. *Imitating Paul: A Discourse of Power.* Louisville: Westminster/ John Knox Press, 1991.

Chadwick, Henry E. "Enkrateia." In *Reallexikon für Antike und Christentum.* Stuttgart: Anton Hiersemann, 1962. Vol. 5, col. 343 and following columns.

———. "Pope Damascus and the Peculiar Claim of Rome to St. Peter and St. Paul." In *History and Thought of the Early Church.* London: Variorum Reprints, 1982.

———. "St. Peter and St. Paul in Rome: The Problem of the Memoria Apostolorum ad Catacumbas." In *History and Thought of the Early Church.* London: Variorum Reprints, 1982.

Charlesworth, James H., ed. *The Old Testament Pseudepigrapha.* 2 vols. New York: Doubleday, 1983.

Clabeaux, John J. "Marcion." In *ABD.* Vol. IV, 514–21.

Clark, Elizabeth A. "Foucault, the Fathers, and Sex." *JAAR* 56 (1988). 619–41.

Collins, John J. *Between Athens and Jerusalem. Jewish Identity in the Hellenistic Diaspora.* New York: Crossroad, 1983.

———. "Was the Dead Sea Sect an Apocalyptic Movement?" In *The Madrid Qumran Congress. Proceedings of the International Congress on the Dead Sea Scrolls. Madrid, 18–21 March 1991,* ed. Julio Trebolle Barrera and Luis Vegas Montaner. Leiden: E. J. Brill, 1992. 25–51.

Conzelmann, Hans. *The Theology of St. Luke.* Eng. trans. Geoffrey Buswell. New York: Harper & Row, 1960.

————. *An Outline of the Theology of the New Testament.* Eng. trans. John Bowden. New York: Harper & Row, 1969.

————. *History of Primitive Christianity.* Eng. trans. John E. Steely. Nashville: Abingdon Press, 1973.

————. *Acts of the Apostles.* Eng. trans. James Limburg, A. Thomas Kraabel, and Donald Juel. Philadelphia: Fortress Press, 1987.

Cranfield, C. E. B. *A Critical and Exegetical Commentary on the Epistle to the Romans.* 2 vols. Edinburgh: T. & T. Clark, 1985.

Dahl, Nils A. "Letters." In *IDB,* supplementary vol., ed. Keith Crim. Nashville: Abingdon Press, 1976.

————. "The One God of Jews and Gentiles, (Romans 3:29–30)." In his *Studies in Paul.* Minneapolis: Augsburg, 1977.

————. "Paul and Possessions." In *Studies in Paul. Theology for the Early Christian Mission.* Minneapolis: Augsburg, 1977.

Dassmann, Ernst. *Der Stachel im Fleish. Paulus in der frühchristlichen Literatur bis Irenäus.* Münster: Aschendorf, 1979.

Deissmann, Adolf. *Light from the Ancient East. The New Testament Illustrated by Recently Discovered Texts of the Graeco-Roman World.* Eng. trans. Lionel R. M. Strachan. New York: George H. Doran Co., 1927.

————. *Paulus.* Tübingen: J. C. B. Mohr, 1925. *Paul, A Study in Social and Religious History.* Eng. trans. William E. Wilson. 2d ed. New York: Harper & Brothers, 1926.

Delling, Gerhard. *Paulus' Stellung zu Frau und Ehe.* Stuttgart: W. Kohlhammer, 1931.

Deming, Will. *Paul on Marriage and Celibacy. The Hellenistic Background of 1 Corinthians 7.* Cambridge: Cambridge University Press, 1995.

Dibelius, Martin. *From Tradition to Gospel.* Eng. trans. Bertram Lee Woolf. New York: Charles Scribner's Sons, 1935.

————. *An die Thessalonicher 1, 2. An die Philipper.* 3d ed. Tübingen: J. C. B. Mohr, 1937.

————. *Paul.* Eng. trans. Frank Clarke. Philadelphia: Westminster, 1953.

————. *Aufsätze zur Apostelgeschichte.* Göttingen: Vandenhoeck & Ruprecht, 1951. (*Studies in the Acts of the Apostles.* Eng. trans. Mary Ling and Paul Schubert. New York: Charles Scribner's Sons, 1956.)

Dion, Paul E. "Aramaic Letters." In *ABD,* Vol. IV, 285–90.

Di Vito, Robert A. "Lachish Letters." In *ABD,* Vol. IV, 126–28.

Dodd, Charles Harold. *The Apostolic Preaching and Its Developments.* New York: Harper & Brothers, 1960.

Donfried, Karl. "The Cults of Thessalonica and the Thessalonian Correspondence." *NTS* 31 (1985), 336–56.

Doty, William G. *Letters in Primitive Christianity.* Philadelphia: Fortress Press, 1973.

Douglas, Mary. *Purity and Danger. An Analysis of Concepts of Pollution and Taboo.* New York: Frederick A. Praeger, Publishers, 1966.

Dunn, James D. G. *Romans 1–8.* Dallas: Word Books, 1988.

————. "In Quest of Paul's Theology: Retrospect and Prospect." In *Society of Biblical Literature 1995 Seminar Papers,* ed. Eugene H. Lovering, Jr. Atlanta: Scholars Press, 1995.

Dupont-Sommer, A. *The Essene Writings from Qumran.* Eng. trans. Geza Vermes. Cleveland: World Publishing Co., 1961.

Edwards, M. J. "Neglected Texts in the Study of Gnosticism." *JTS,* new series, 41 (1990), 26–50.

Elliott, Neil. *Liberating Paul. The Justice of God and the Politics of the Apostle.* Maryknoll, NY: Orbis Books, 1994.

Engberg-Pedersen, Troels. "Proclaiming the Lord's Death: 1 Corinthians 11:17–34 and the Forms of Paul's Theological Argument." In *Pauline Theology,* Vol. II: *1 & 2 Corinthians,* ed. David M. Hay. Minneapolis: Fortress Press, 1993.

Enslin, Morton Scott. "Paul and Gamaliel." *JR* 7 (1927), 360–75.

Exler, F. X. J. *The Form of the Ancient Greek Letter. A Study of Greek Epistolography.* Washington: Catholic University of America, 1923.

Fascher, E. "Zur Witwerschaft des Paulus und der Auslegung von 1 Cor. 7." *ZNW* (1929), 62–69.

Ferguson, John. *Greek and Roman Religion.* Park Ridge, NJ: Noyes Press, 1980.

Fitzgerald, J. T. *Cracks in an Earthen Vessel: An Examination of the Catalogue of Hardships in the Corinthian Correspondence.* Atlanta: Scholars Press, 1988.

Fitzmyer, Joseph A. *Pauline Theology, A Brief Sketch* (Englewood Cliffs, NJ: Prentice-Hall, 1968).

————. "The Pauline Letters." In his *According to Paul: Studies in the Theology of the Apostle.* New York and Mahwah, N.J.: Paulist Press, 1993.

————. *Romans. A New Translation with Introduction and Commentary.* New York: Doubleday, 1993.

Foucault, Michel. *The Archeology of Knowledge.* Eng. trans. A. M. Sheridan Smith. New York: Pantheon Books, 1972.

————. *The History of Sexuality.* Eng. trans. Robert Hurley. New York: Pantheon Books, 1986. Vol. 3: *The Care of Self.* 634–36.

Fox, Robin Lane. *Pagans and Christians.* New York: Viking, 1986.

Fraade, Steven D. "Ascetical Aspects of Ancient Judaism." In *Jewish Spirituality from the Bible through the Middle Ages,* ed. Arthur Green. London: Routledge & Kegan Paul, 1986. 253–88.

Frank, P. Suso. *Angelikos Bios. Begriffsanalytische und begriffsgeschichtliche Untersuchung zum 'Engelgleichen Leben' im Frühen Mönchtum.* Münster: Aschendorfsche Verlagsbuchhandlung, 1964.

Franklin, W. M. *Die Kollekte des Paulus.* Scottsdale, PA: Mennonite Publishing House, 1938.

Fredriksen, Paula. "Judaism, the Circumcision of Gentiles, and Apocalyptic Hope: Another Look at Galatians 1 and 2," *JTS* 42 (1991), 532–64.

Frier, Bruce W. "Roman Life Expectancy: Ulpian's Evidence." *Harvard Studies in Classical Philology* 86 (1982), 213–51.

Funk, Robert W. "The Letter: Form and Style." In his *Language, Hermeneutic, and the Word of God.* New York: Harper & Row, 1966.

————. "The Apostolic Parousia: Form and Significance." In *Christian History and Interpretation: Studies Presented to John Knox,* ed. W. R. Farmer, C.F.D. Moule, and R. R. Niebuhr. Cambridge: Cambridge University Press, 1967.

Furnish, Victor Paul. *Theology and Ethics in Paul.* Nashville: Abingdon Press, 1968.
———. *II Corinthians.* Garden City, NY: Doubleday & Co., 1984.
———. *Jesus according to Paul.* Cambridge: Cambridge University Press, 1993.
———. "Theology in 1 Corinthians." In *Pauline Theology,* ed. David M. Hay. Minneapolis: Fortress Press, 1993. Vol. II: *1 & 2 Corinthians.*
Gager, John G. *The Origins of Anti-Semitism: Attitudes toward Judaism in Pagan and Christian Antiquity.* New York: Oxford University Press, 1983.
Gaventa, Beverly Roberts. "Apostles as Babes and Nurses in 1 Thessalonians 2:7." In *Faith and History. Essays in Honor of Paul W. Meyer,* ed. John T. Carroll, Charles H. Cosgrove, and E. Elizabeth Johnson. Atlanta: Scholars Press, 1990.
———. "The Maternity of Paul: An Exegetical Study of Galatians 4:19." In *The Conversation Continues. Studies in Paul & John in Honor of J. Louis Martyn,* ed. Robert T. Fortna and Beverly R. Gaventa. Nashville: Abingdon Press, 1990.
Geertz, Clifford. "Religion as a Cultural System." In his *The Interpretation of Cultures, Selected Essays.* New York: Basic Books, 1973.
Ginsberg, Louis. *Legends of the Jews.* Philadelphia: Jewish Publication Society, 1908–38. Vol. 5.
Georgi, Dieter. *Remembering the Poor. The History of Paul's Collection for Jerusalem.* Nashville: Abingdon Press, 1965.
———. *The Opponents of Paul in Second Corinthians.* Eng. trans. Philadelphia: Fortress Press, 1986.
Goldman, Hetty, ed. *Excavations at Gözlü Kule, Tarsus, The Hellenistic and Roman Periods.* Princeton: Princeton University Press, 1950.
Goodenough, E. R. "The Perspective of Acts." In *Studies in Luke—Acts,* ed. Leander E. Keck and J. L. Martyn. New York: Abingdon Press, 1966.
Gorman, Mary Rosaria. "The Nurse in Greek Life." In her Catholic University dissertation from 1917.
Grundmann, Walter. "ἐγκράτεια." In *TDNT,* ed. Gerhard Kittel. Eng. trans. Geoffrey W. Bromiley. Grand Rapids, MI: Eerdmans, 1964–74. Vol. II, 339–42.
Haenchen, D. Ernst. *Die Apostelgeschichte.* Göttingen: Vandenhoeck & Ruprecht, 1963.
———. "The Book of Acts as Source Material for the History of Early Christianity." In *Studies in Luke—Acts,* ed. Leander E. Keck and J. L. Martyn. Nashville: Abingdon Press, 1966.
Halmel, Anton. *Der Zweite Korintherbrief des Apostels Paulus. Geschichte und literarkritische Untersuchungen.* Halle: Niemeyer, 1904.
Hammerton-Kelly, Robert. *Sacred Violence: Paul's Hermeneutic of the Cross.* Minneapolis: Fortress Press, 1992.
Hare, Douglas R. A. *The Theme of Jewish Persecution of Christians in the Gospel according to St. Matthew.* Cambridge: Cambridge University Press, 1967.
Hausrath, Adolf. *Der Vier-Capitel-Brief des Paulus an die Korinther.* Heidelberg: Bassermann, 1870.
———. *Neutestamentliche Zeitgeschichte.* 2d ed. Heidelberg: Bassermann, 1875. Vol. 3: *Die Zeit der Apostel II.*
Hays, H. Richard. *The Faith of Jesus Christ.* Chico, CA: Scholars Press, 1983.

Hendrix, Holland. "Thessalonians Honor Romans." Harvard Th.D. thesis, 1984.

Hengel, Martin. *Judaism and Hellenism. Studies in Their Encounter in Palestine during the Early Hellenistic Period.* 2 vols. Eng. trans. John Bowden. Philadelphia: Fortress Press, 1974.

———. *The Pre-Christian Paul.* Eng. trans. John Bowden. London: SCM Press, and Philadelphia: Trinity Press International, 1991.

Hennecke, Edgar. *New Testament Apocrypha,* rev. ed., ed. Wilhelm Schneemelcher. Eng. trans. R. McL. Wilson. 2 vols. Philadelphia: Westminster, 1963.

Hill, Craig C. *Hellenists and Hebrews. Reappraising Division within the Earliest Church.* Minneapolis: Fortress Press, 1992.

Hill, G. F. *British Museum. Catalogue of the Greek Coins of Lycaonia, Isauria and Cilicia.* London: The Trustees (of the British Museum), 1900.

Hock, Ronald F. *The Social Context of Paul's Ministry.* Philadelphia: Fortress Press, 1980.

Hodgson, Robert, Jr. "Holiness Tradition and Social Description: Intertestamental Judaism and Early Christianity." In *Reaching beyond: Chapters in the History of Perfectionism,* ed. Stanley M. Burgess. Peabody, MA: Hendrickson Publishers, 1986.

Hoffmann, R. Joseph. *Marcion: On the Restitution of Christianity. An Essay on the Development of Radical Paulinist Theology in the Second Century.* Chico, CA: Scholars Press, 1984.

Holladay, Carl R. "I Corinthians 13, Paul as Apostolic Paradigm." In *Greeks, Romans, and Christians. Essays in Honor of Abraham J. Malherbe,* ed. David L. Balch, Everett Ferguson, and Wayne A. Meeks. Minneapolis: Fortress Press, 1990.

Holmberg, Bengt. *Paul and Power: The Structure of Authority in the Primitive Church as Reflected in the Pauline Epistles.* Philadelphia: Fortress Press, 1978.

Horsley, Richard A. "Pneumatikos vs. Psychikos: Distinction of Spiritual Status among the Corinthians." *HTR* 69 (1976), 269–88.

Hübner, Hans. "Paulusforschung seit 1945. Ein kritischer Literaturbericht." In *ANRW,* ed. Hildegard Temporini. Berlin : Walter de Gruyter. Vol II, 25.4, 2649–2840.

Hultgren, Arland J. "Paul's Pre-Christian Persecutions of the Church: Their Purpose, Locale, and Nature." *JBL* 95 (1976), 97–111.

Hurd, John C., Jr. *The Origin of 1 Corinthians.* New York: Seabury Press, 1965.

Jeremias, Joachim. "War Paulus Witwer?" *ZNW* 25 (1926), 310–12.

———. "Nochmals: War Paulus Witwer?," *ZNW* 31 (1929), 321–22.

Jervell, Jacob. "The Law in Luke—Acts." In *Luke and the People of God: A New Look at Luke—Acts.* Minneapolis: Augsburg, 1972.

———. "Der schwache Charismatiker." In *Rechtfertigung: Festschrift für Ernst Käsemann zum 70. Geburtstag,* ed. J. Friedrich, W. Pöhlmann, and P. Stuhlmacher. Tübingen, Göttingen: J. C. B. Mohr (Paul Siebeck), Vandenhoeck & Ruprecht, 1976.

———. "Paul in the Acts of the Apostles." In *Les Actes des Apôtres. Traditions, rédaction, théologie,* ed. J. Kremer. Leuven: Leuven University Press, 1979.

———. "Die Zeichen des Apostels. Die Wunder beim lukanischen und paulinischen Paulus." *Studien zum Neuen Testament und Seiner Umwelt* 4 (1979), 54–75.

Jewett, Robert A. *A Chronology of Paul's Life.* Philadelphia: Fortress Press, 1979.

————. *The Thessalonian Correspondence. Pauline Rhetoric and Millenarian Piety.* Philadelphia: Fortress Press, 1986.

Jones, A. H. M. *The Cities of the Eastern Roman Provinces.* Oxford: At the Clarendon Press, 1937.

————. *Studies in Roman Government and Law.* Oxford: At the Clarendon Press, 1960.

Judge, E. A. "St. Paul and Classical Society." *JAC* 15 (1972), 19–36.

Kaelber, Walter D. "Asceticism." In *Encyclopedia of Religion,* ed. Mircea Eliade, et al. New York: Macmillan, 1987. Vol. I, 441.

Käsemann, Ernst. "Die Legitimität des Apostels. Eine Untersuchung zu II Korinther 10–13." *ZNW* 41 (1942), 33–71.

————. "The Pauline Doctrine of the Lord's Supper." In his *Essays on New Testament Themes.* Eng. trans. W. J. Montague. Philadelphia: Fortress Press, 1964.

————. "God's Righteousness in Paul." In *The Bultmann School of Biblical Interpretation: New Directions?* ed. James M. Robinson. New York: Harper & Row, and Tübingen: J. C. B. Mohr (Paul Siebeck), 1965. German in "Gottesgerechtigkeit bei Paulus." *ZThK* 58 (1961), 367–78.

————. *Commentary on Romans.* Eng. trans. Geoffrey W. Bromiley. Grand Rapids, MI: Eerdmans, 1980.

Kaestli, Jean-Daniel. Response to V. Burrus, "Chastity as Autonomy: Women in the Stories of the Apocryphal Acts." *Semeia* 38 (1986), 118–31.

Keck, Leander E. "The Quest for Paul's Pharisaism: Some Reflections." In *Justice and the Holy: Essays in Honor of Walter Harrelson,* ed. Douglas A. Knight and Peter J. Paris. Atlanta: Scholars Press, 1989.

Kennedy, G. A. *The Art of Persuasion in Greece.* London: Longman, 1963.

————. *The Art of Rhetoric in the Roman World.* Princeton: Princeton University Press, 1972.

————. *New Testament Interpretation through Rhetorical Criticism.* Chapel Hill: University of North Carolina Press, 1984.

Kinzig, Wolfram. "Καινὴ διαθήκη: The Title of the New Testament in the Second and Third Centuries." *JTS,* new series, 45 (1994), 519–44.

Klein, Günter. "Apokalyptische Naherwartung bei Paulus." In *Neues Testament und christliche Existenz: Festschrift für Herbert Braun zum 70. Geburtstag,* ed. Hans Dieter Betz and L. Schottroff. Tübingen: J. C. B. Mohr (Paul Siebeck), 1973.

Klinzing, Georg. *Die Umdeutung des Kultus in der Qumrangemeinde und im NT.* Göttingen: Vandenhoeck & Ruprecht, 1971.

Knox, John. *Chapters in a Life of Paul.* Nashville: Abingdon Press, 1950.

————. "Romans 15:14–33 and Paul's Conception of His Apostolic Mission." *JBL* 83 (1964), 1–11.

Koch, Dietrich-Alexander. *Die Schrift als Zeuge des Evangeliums: Untersuchung zur Verwendung und zum Verständnis der Schrift bei Paulus.* Tübingen: J. C. B. Mohr (Paul Siebeck), 1986.

Koester, Helmut. "I Thessalonians—Experiment in Christian Writing." In *Continuity and Discontinuity in Church History: Essays Presented to George H. Williams.* Leiden: E. J. Brill, 1979.

————. *History, Culture, and Religion of the Hellenistic Age.* Vol. I. Philadelphia: Fortress Press, and Berlin: Walter de Gruyter, 1980.

————. *History and Literature of Early Christianity.* Philadelphia: Fortress Press, 1982. Vol. II.

Koskenniemi, Heikki. *Studien zur Idee und Phraseologie des griechischen Briefes bis 400 n. Chr.* Helsinki: Akateeminen Kirjakauppa, 1956.

Kraftchick, Steven J. "Seeking a More Fluid Model: A Response to Jouette M. Bassler." In *Pauline Theology II, 1 and 2 Corinthians,* ed. David M. Hay. Minneapolis: Fortress Press, 1989.

Kretschmar, Georg. "Ein Beitrag zur Frage nach dem Ursprung frühchristlicher Askese." *ZThK* 70 (1964), 27–67.

Kuhn, K. G. "Askese im Judentum." In *Die Religion in Geschichte und Gegenwart.* 3d ed. Tübingen: J. C. B. Mohr (Paul Siebeck), 1957–62. Vol. 1, cols. 639–47.

Lake, Kirsopp, *The Earlier Epistles of St. Paul: Their Motive and Origin.* 2d ed. London: Rivingtons, 1914.

Lake, Kirsopp, and Henry J. Cadbury. *The Beginnings of Christianity.* Grand Rapids, MI: Baker Book House, 1965. Part I, Vol. IV.

Lapide, Pinchas. *Paulus zwischen Damaskus und Qumran.* Gütersloh: Gütersloher Verlagshaus Gerd Mohn, 1993.

Lentz, John Clayton, Jr. *Luke's Portrait of Paul.* Cambridge: Cambridge University Press, 1993.

Lietzmann, Hans. *The Beginnings of the Christian Church.* Eng. trans. B. L. Woolf. 3d ed. rev. London: Lutterworth Press, 1953.

Lindbeck, George A. *The Nature of Doctrine, Religion and Theology in a Postliberal Age.* Philadelphia: Westminster, 1984.

Lindemann, Andreas. *Paulus im ältesten Christentum.* Tübingen: J. C. B. Mohr (Paul Siebeck), 1979. 240–51.

Lohfink, Gerhard. *Wie hat Jesus Gemeinde gewollt? Zur gesellschaftlichen Dimension des christlichen Glaubens.* Freiburg: Herder, 1982.

Lüdemann, Gerd. *Paulus der Heidenapostel.* Göttingen: Vandenhoeck & Ruprecht, 1980. Vol. I. Same as *Paul, Apostle to the Gentiles: Studies in Chronology.* Eng. trans. F. Stanley Jones. Philadelphia: Fortress Press, 1984.

————. *Paulus, der Heidenapostel. Antipaulinismus im frühen Christentum.* Göttingen: Vandenhoeck & Ruprecht, 1985.

Lührmann, Dieter. "The Beginnings of the Church at Thessalonica." In *Greeks, Romans, and Christians. Essays in Honor of Abraham J. Malherbe,* ed. David L. Balch, Everett Ferguson, and Wayne A. Meeks. Minneapolis: Fortress Press, 1990.

Lyons, George. *Pauline Autobiography: Toward a New Understanding.* Atlanta: Scholars Press, 1985.

Maccoby, Hyam. *The Mythmaker: Paul and the Invention of Christianity.* New York: Harper & Row, 1986.

MacDonald, Dennis R. "Apocryphal and Canonical Narratives about Paul." In *Paul and the Legacies of Paul,* ed. William S. Babcock. Dallas: SMU Press, 1990.

Maier, Johann, et al. "Askese." In *Theologische Realenzyklopädie,* ed. Horst Robert Balz, Stuart G. Hall, et al. Berlin: Walter de Gruyter, 1979. Vol. IV, cols. 195–259.

Malherbe, Abraham J. *The Cynic Epistles. A Study Edition.* Missoula: Scholars Press, 1977.

———. "Exhortation in 1 Thessalonians." *NT* 25 (1983), 238–56.

Malina, Bruce J., and Jerome H. Neyrey. *Portraits of Paul. An Archeology of Ancient Personality.* Louisville: Westminster/John Knox Press, 1996.

Marguerat, D. "2 Corinthiens 10–13, Paul et l'expérience de Dieu." *ETR* 63 (1988), 407– 519.

Masson, J. Moussaieff. "The Psychology of the Ascetic." *JAS* 35 (1976), 611–25.

Mattill, A. J., Jr. "The Jesus-Paul Parallels and the Purpose of Luke—Acts: H. H. Evans Reconsidered." *NT* 17 (1975), 15–46.

Mauss, Marcel. *Sacrifice: Its Nature and Function.* Eng. trans. Henri Hubert. Chicago: University of Chicago Press, 1964.

Meeks, Wayne A., ed. *The Writings of St. Paul.* New York: W. W. Norton & Company, 1972.

Merk, Otto. "Paulus-Forschung 1936–1985." *TR* 53 (1988), 1–81.

Meyer, Eduard. *Ursprung und Anfänge des Christentums.* 3 vols. Stuttgart & Berlin: J. G. Gotta'sche Buchhandlung, 1923.

Meyer, P. W. "Romans." In the *Harper's Bible Commentary,* ed. James L. Mays, Joseph Blenkinsopp, Jon D. Levinson, Wayne A. Meeks, Carol A. Newsom, David L. Peterson. San Francisco: Harpers, 1988.

———. "Pauline Theology: Some Thoughts for a Pause in Its Pursuit." In *Society of Biblical Literature 1995 Seminar Papers,* ed. Eugene H. Lovering, Jr. Atlanta: Scholars Press, 1995. 688–703.

Michel, Otto. "Wie Spricht Paulus über Frau und Ehe? Ein Blick auf G. Delling's Untersuchung." *TSK* 105 (1933), 215–25.

Mitchell, Margaret M. *Paul and the Rhetoric of Reconciliation. An Exegetical Investigation of the Language and Composition of 1 Corinthians.* Tübingen: J. C. B. Mohr (Paul Siebeck), 1991; Louisville: Westminster/John Knox, 1992.

Moffatt, James. *An Introduction to the Literature of the New Testament.* 3d ed. rev. Edinburgh: T. & T. Clark, 1918.

Montefiore, C. G. *Judaism and St. Paul.* London: Max Goschen, 1914.

Moore, George Foot. *Judaism in the First Centuries of the Christian Era. The Age of the Tannaim,* 3 vols. Cambridge: Harvard University Press, 1954. Vol. II, 262–66.

———. "Asceticism." In *Encyclopaedia Judaica.* Jerusalem: Encyclopedia Judaica, 1976. Vol. I, 678–83.

Munck, Johannes. *Paul and the Salvation of Mankind.* Eng. trans. Frank Clarke. Richmond: John Knox Press, 1959.

Murphy-O'Connor, Jerome. *Paul the Letter-Writer: His World, His Options, His Skills.* Collegeville: The Liturgical Press, 1995.

———. *Paul. A Critical Life.* Oxford: Clarendon Press, 1996.

Murray, Robert. "The Exhortation to Candidates for Ascetical Vows at Baptism in the Ancient Syriac Church." *NTS* 21 (1975), 59–80.

Mussner, Franz. *Der Galaterbrief.* Freiburg: Herder, 1974.

Nagy, Gregory. *Pindar's Homer: The Lyric Possession of an Epic Past.* Baltimore: Johns Hopkins University Press, 1990.

Neirynck, Franz. "The Miracle Stories in the Acts of the Apostles: An Introduction." In *Les Actes des Apôtres. Traditions, rédaction, théologie,* ed. J. Kremer. Leuven: Leuven University Press, 1979.

Neusner, Jacob. *The Rabbinic Traditions about the Pharisees before 70.* 3 vols. Leiden: E. J. Brill, 1971.

————. *From Politics to Piety: The Emergence of Pharisaic Judaism.* Englewood Cliffs, N.J.: Prentice-Hall, 1973.

————. "Two Pictures of the Pharisees: Philosophical Circle or Eating Club?" *ATR* 64 (1982), 525–38.

Newell, E. T. *The Coinage of the Western Seleucid Mints from Seleucus I to Antiochus III, Numismatic Studies,* No. 4. Paris: College de France, 1941. Repr. New York: American Numismatic Society, 1977.

Newsom, Carol A. " 'He Has Established for Himself Priests': Human and Angelic Priesthood in the Qumran Shabbath *Shirot.* " In *Archeology and History in the Dead Sea Scrolls. The New York University Conference in Memory of Yigael Yadin,* ed. Lawrence H. Schiffman. Sheffield: Sheffield Academic Press, 1990. 101–20.

————. "Angels." *ABD,* I, 248–53.

Niederwimmer, Kurt. *Askese und Mysterium: Über Ehe, Ehescheidung und Eheverzicht in den Anfängen des christlichen Glaubens.* Göttingen: Vandenhoeck & Ruprecht, 1975.

Oepke, Albrecht. *Der Brief des Paulus an die Galater.* Berlin: Evangelische Verlagsanstalt, 1973.

Oppel, John. "Saint Jerome and the History of Sex," *Viator* 24 (1993), 1–22.

Pagels, Elaine H. *The Gnostic Paul. Gnostic Exegesis of the Pauline Letters.* Philadelphia: Fortress Press, 1975.

Pardee, Dennis. "Hebrew Letters." In *ABD,* vol. IV, 282–85.

Pesch, Rudolf. *Paulus ringt um die Lebensform der Kirche. Vier Briefe an die Gemeinde Gottes in Korinth.* Freiburg: Herder, 1986.

Petersen, Norman R. *Rediscovering Paul. Philemon and the Sociology of Paul's Narrative World.* Philadelphia: Fortress Press, 1985.

Peterson, Erik. "Einige Beobachtungen zu den Anfängen des christlichen Askese." In his *Frühkirche, Judentum und Gnosis. Studien und Untersuchungen.* Rome: Herder, 1959.

Pfitzner, Victor C. *Paul and the Agon Motif.* Leiden: E. J. Brill, 1967.

Pobee, John S. *Persecution and Martyrdom in the Theology of Paul.* Sheffield: JSOT Press, 1985.

Praeder, Susan Marie. "Miracle Worker and Missionary: Paul in the Acts of the Apostles." In *SBL 1983 Seminar Papers,* ed. Kent Harold Richards. Chico, CA: Scholars Press, 1983. Pp. 107–29.

Pritchard, James B., ed. *Ancient Near Eastern Texts Relating to the Old Testament.* 2d ed. Princeton, NJ: Princeton University Press, 1955.

Qimron, Elisha. "Celibacy in the Dead Sea Scrolls and the Two Kinds of Sectarians." In *The Madrid Qumran Congress. Proceedings of the International Congress on the Dead Sea Scrolls. Madrid 18–21 March 1991,* ed. Julio Trebolle Barrera and Luis Vegas Montaner. Leiden: E. J. Brill, 1992. 287–94.

Qimron, Elisha and John Strugnel. *"Miqsat Ma'ase Ha-Torah."* In *Discoveries in the Judaean Desert,* Oxford: Clarendon Press, 1994. Vol. X.

Räisänen, Heikki. *The Torah and Christ. Essays in German and English on the Problem of Law in Early Christianity.* Helsinki: Finish Exegetical Society, 1986.

Ramsay, W. M. *St. Paul the Traveller and the Roman Citizen.* New York: G. P. Putnam's Sons, 1896.

———. *The Cities of St. Paul: Their Influence on His Life and Thought.* Grand Rapids, MI: Baker Book House, 1960.

Reitzenstein, Richard. *Hellenistic Mystery-Religions: Their Basic Ideas and Significance.* Eng. trans. John E. Steeley. Pittsburgh, PA: Pickwick Press, 1978. German ed. *Die Hellenistischen Mysterienreligionen nach ihren Grundgedanken und Wirkungen.* 3d ed. Leipzig: B. G. Teubner, 1927. 1st ed. 1909.

Rengstorf, Karl Heinrich. "σημεῖον." In *Theological Dictionary of the New Testament,* ed. Gerhard Friedrich. Eng. trans. Geoffrey W. Bromiley. Grand Rapids, MI: Eerdmans, 1971.

Richardson, Peter. *Israel in the Apostolic Church.* London: Cambridge University Press, 1969.

Rivkin, Ellis. *A Hidden Revolution: The Pharisees' Search for the Kingdom Within.* Nashville: Abingdon Press, 1978.

Robert, L. *Etudes de Numismatique Grecque.* Paris: College de France, 1951.

Robertson, Archibald, and Alfred Plummer. *A Critical and Exegetical Commentary on the First Epistle of St. Paul to the Corinthians.* 2d ed. Edinburgh: T. & T. Clark, 1914.

Roetzel, Calvin J. *Judgement in the Community. A Study of the Relationship Between Eschatology and Ecclesiology in Paul.* Leiden: E. J. Brill, 1972.

———. "Sacrifice in Romans 12–15." *WW* VI (1986), 410–19.

———. *"Theodidaktoi* and Handwork in Philo and 1 Thessalonians." In *L'apôtre Paul, personnalité, style et conception du ministère,* ed. A. Vanhoye. Leuven: Leuven University Press, 1986.

———. *The Letters of Paul. Conversations in Context.* 3d ed. Louisville: Westminster/ John Knox Press, 1991.

———. " 'As Dying, and Behold We Live,' Death and Resurrection in Paul's Theology." In *INT* XLVI (1992), 5–18.

———. *"Oikoumene* and the Limits of Pluralism in Alexandrian Judaism and Paul." In *Diaspora Jews and Judaism, Essays in Honor of, and in Dialogue with A. Thomas Kraabel,* ed. J. Andrew Overman and Robert S. MacLennon. Atlanta: Scholars Press, 1992.

———. "The Grammar of Election in Four Pauline Letters." In *Pauline Theology,* ed. David M. Hay. Minneapolis: Fortress Press, 1993. Vol. II: *1 & 2 Corinthians.*

———. "No 'Race of Israel' in Paul," in *Putting Body & Soul Together: Essays in Honor of Robin Scroggs,* ed. Virginia Wiles, Alexandra Brown, Graydon F. Snyder (Valley Forge: Trinity International Press, 1997).

Ruge, S. Carvilius. "Tarsos." In August Friedrick von Pauly-Georg Wissowa, *Real-Enzyklopädie der classischen Altertumswissenschaft,* ed. Wilhelm Kroll and Karl Mittelhaus. Stuttgart: H. Druckenmüller, 1932. Vol. IV A.2.

Saldarini, Anthony J. *Pharisees, Scribes and Sadducees in Palestinian Society. A Sociological Approach.* Wilmington: Michael Glazier, 1988.

———. "Pharisees." *ABD*, Vol. V, 289–303.

Sanders, E. P. *Paul and Palestinian Judaism.* Philadelphia: Fortress Press, 1977.

———. *Paul.* Oxford: Oxford University Press, 1991.

Sanders, Jack T. *Schismatics, Sectarians, Dissidents, Deviants. The First One Hundred Years of Jewish-Christian Relations.* Valley Forge, PA: Trinity Press International, 1993.

Schlier, Heinrich. *Der Brief an die Galater.* Göttingen: Vandenhoeck & Ruprecht, 1971.

———. *Grundzüge einer paulinischen Theologie.* Freiburg: Herder, 1978.

Schmithals, Walter. *Paul and James.* Eng. trans. Dorthea M. Barton. Studies in Biblical Theology 1/46. London: SCM Press, 1965.

———. *The Office of Apostle in the Early Church.* Eng. trans. John E. Steely. Nashville: Abingdon Press, 1969.

———. *Paul and the Gnostics.* Eng. trans. John E. Steeley. Nashville: Abingdon Press, 1972.

———. "Die Korintherbriefe als Briefsammlung." *ZNW* 64 (1973), 275–88.

Schneemelcher, Wilhelm. "Paulus in der griechischen Kirche des zweiten Jahrhunderts." *ZKG* 75 (1964), 3–21.

———. "Apostle and Apostolic." In *New Testament Apocrypha,* ed. Edgar Hennecke. Eng. trans. R. McL. Wilson. Philadelphia: Westminster, 1965.

Schoeps, Hans Joachim. *Paul: The Theology of the Apostle in the Light of Jewish Religious History.* Eng. trans. Harold Knight. Philadelphia: Westminster, 1961.

Schreiber, Stefan. *Paulus als Wundertäter. Redaktionsgeschichtliche Untersuchungen zur Apostelgeschichte und den authentischen Paulusbriefen.* Berlin: Walter de Gruyter, 1996.

Schubert, Paul. *The Form and Function of the Pauline Thanksgivings.* Berlin: Alfred Töpelmann, 1939.

Schürer, E. *The History of the Jewish People in the Age of Jesus Christ.* Rev. and ed. G. Vermes, F. Millar, and M. Black. Edinburgh: T. & T. Clark, 1973–87.

Schweitzer, Albert. *The Mysticism of Paul the Apostle.* Eng. trans. William Montgomery. London: Adam & Charles Black, 1967. First Eng. ed. 1931.

Seeligmann, I. L. *The Septuagint Version of Isaiah. A Discussion of Its Problems.* Leiden: E. J. Brill, 1948.

Shaw, George Bernard. "The Monstrous Imposition upon Jesus." In *The Writings of St. Paul,* ed. Wayne A. Meeks. New York: W. W. Norton & Company, Inc., 1972.

Sherwin-White, A. N. *Roman Society and Roman Law in the New Testament.* Oxford: At the Clarendon Press, 1963.

———. The Roman Citizenship, A Survey of Its Development into a World Franchise," in *ANRW,* ed. Hildegard Temporini. Berlin: Walter de Gruyter, 1972. Vol. I.2.

———. *The Roman Citizenship.* 2d ed. Oxford: At the Clarendon Press, 1973."

Sider, Robert D. "Literary Artifice and the Figure of Paul in the Writings of Tertullian." In *Paul and the Legacies of Paul,* ed. William S. Babcock. Dallas: SMU Press, 1990.

Smallwood, Mary. *Philonis Alexandrini Legatio ad Gaium*. Leiden: E. J. Brill, 1961.

Smith, Jonathan Z. "Differential Equations: On Constructing the 'Other,'" lecture printed and distributed by the Arizona State University Department of Religious Studies.

Spencer, A. B. "The Wise Fool (and the Foolish Wise): A Study of Irony in Paul." *NT* 23 (1981), 349–60.

Stegeman, W. "War der Apostel Paulus römischer Bürger?" *ZNW* 78 (1987), 220–29.

Stendahl, Krister. *Paul among Jews and Gentiles and Other Essays*. Philadelphia: Fortress Press, 1976.

Stowers, Stanley K. *Letter Writing in Greco-Roman Antiquity*. Philadelphia: Westminster, 1986.

———. "Comment: What Does Unpauline Mean?" In *Paul and the Legacies of Paul*, ed. William S. Babcock. Dallas: SMUP, 1990.

———. "Greek and Latin Letters." In *ABD*, Vol. IV, 290–93.

———. *A Rereading of Romans. Justice, Jews, and the Gentiles*. New Haven: Yale University Press, 1994.

Strathmann, Hermann. *Geschichte der frühchristlichen Askese*. Leipzig: A. Deichertsche Verlagsbuchhandlung Werner Scholl, 1914.

Tarn, W. W. *Hellenistic Civilization*. London: Edward Arnold, 1927.

Tcherikover, Victor A. *Hellenistic Civilization and the Jews*. Eng. trans. S. Applebaum. Philadelphia: Jewish Publication Society, 1961.

Thesleff, Holger. *An Introduction to the Pythagorean Writings of the Hellenistic Period*. Abo: Abo Akademi, 1961.

Thiering, Barbara. "The Biblical Source of Qumran Asceticism." *JBL* 93 (1974), 429–44.

Tiede, David L. *The Charismatic Figure as Miracle Worker*. Missoula: Scholars Press, 1970.

Tomson, Peter J. *Paul and the Jewish Law. Halakha in the Letters of the Apostle to the Gentiles*. Assen/Maastricht: Van Gorcum, and Minneapolis: Fortress Press, 1990.

Turner, Victor. "Myth and Symbol." In *The International Encyclopedia of Social Sciences*, ed. David L. Sills. New York: Macmillan & the Free Press, 1968.

———. *The Ritual Process, Structure and Anti-Structure*. Ithaca, NY: Cornell University Press, 1969.

Urbach, E. E. *The Sages. Their Concepts and Beliefs*. Eng. trans. Israel Abrahams. Jerusalem: At the Magness Press, Hebrew University, 1975.

Van Unnik, W. C. *Tarsus or Jerusalem. The City of Paul's Youth*. Eng. trans. George Ogg. London: Epworth Press, 1962.

Vööbus, Arthur. *Celibacy, a Requirement for Admission to Baptism in the Early Syrian Church*. Stockholm: The Estonian Theological Society in Exile, 1951.

———. *History of Asceticism in the Syrian Orient. A Contribution to the History of Culture in the Near East*. Louvain: Secretariat du Corpus, 1958. Vol. I: *The Origin of Asceticism: Early Monasticism in Persia*.

———. "Asceticism." In *The New Encyclopaedia Britannica*. 15th ed. Chicago: Encyclopaedia Britannica, 1995. Vol. 1, 615–17.

Weiss, Johannes. *Der erste Korintherbrief*. Göttingen: Vandenhoeck & Ruprecht, 1925.

————. *Earliest Christianity.* Eng. trans. F. C. Grant. New York: Harper, 1959.

Welles, C. Bradford. "Hellenistic Tarsus." In *Mélanges de l'université Saint-Joseph* 38 (1962), 62–75.

Wenschkewitz, Hans. *Die Spiritualisierung der Kultusbegriffe, Tempel, Priester und Opfer im neuen Testament.* Lepizig: Verlag von Eduard Pfeiffer, 1932.

White, John L. "New Testament Epistolary Literature in the Framework of Ancient Epistolagraphy." In *ANRW,* ed. Hildegard Temporini. Berlin: Walter de Gruyter. II, 25.2, 1730–156.

————. *Light from Ancient Letters.* Philadelphia: Fortress Press, 1986.

————. "God's Paternity as Root Metaphor in Paul's Conception of Community." In *Forum* 8 (1992), 271–95.

Williams, S. K. "Jesus' Death as a Saving Event. The Background and Origin of a Concept." Harvard Dissertation in Religion, no. 2, 1975.

Wimbush, Vincent L., ed. *Paul the Worldly Ascetic: Response to the World and Self-Understanding according to 1 Corinthians 7.* Macon, GA: Mercer University Press, 1987.

————. *Ascetic Behavior in Greco-Roman Antiquity. A Source Book.* Minneapolis: Fortress Press, 1990.

Windisch, Hans. "Paulus und Jesus." *TSK* 106 (1934–35), 432–68.

————. *Der zweite Korintherbrief.* Reprint of 9th ed. [1924]. Göttingen: Vandenhoeck & Ruprecht, 1970.

Wittgenstein, Ludwig. *Philosophical Investigations.* Eng. trans. G. E. M. Anscombe. New York: The Macmillan Company, 1968.

————. *Remarks on Frazer's Golden Bough.* Ed. Rush Rhees. Trans. A. C. Miles. Rev. Rush Rhees. Pockthorpe Cottage Denton, England: Brynmill Press, and Atlantic Highlands, NJ: Humanities Press International, 1979.

Wuellner, W. H. "Paul's Rhetoric of Argumentation in Romans: An Alternative to the Donfried-Karris Debate over Romans." *CBQ* 36 (1976), 330–51.

————. "Greek Rhetoric and Pauline Argumentation." In *Early Christian Literature and the Classical Tradition,* ed. W. R. Schoedel and R. L. Wilken. Paris: Editions Beauchesne, 1979. 177–88.

————. "Paul as Pastor. The Function of Rhetorical Questions in First Corinthians." In *L'apôtre Paul. Personnalité, style et conception du ministère,* ed. A. Vanhoye. Leuven: Peeters, 1986. 49–77

————. "Where Is Rhetorical Criticism Taking Us?" *CBQ* 49 (1987), 448–63.

Yadin, Yigael, ed. *The Temple Scroll.* Jerusalem: The Israel Exploration Society, 1983.

Zahn, Theodor. *Introduction to the New Testament,* ed. M. W. Jacobus. Eng. trans. J. M. Trout, William Arnot Mather, Louis Hodous, Edward Strong, et al. 2d ed. 3 vols. New York: Charles Scribner's Sons, 1917.

Zimmerli, Walter. " 'Heiligkeit' nach dem sogenannten Heiligkeitsgesetz." *VT* XXX (1980), 493–517.

Zmijewski, J. *Der Stil der paulinischen Narrenrede.* Köln: Hanstein, 1978.

Index of Passages

Old Testament Apocrypha

Index of Subjects